Palgrave Studies in Comparative Global History

Series Editors
Manuel Perez Garcia
Shanghai Jiao Tong University
Shanghai, China

Lucio De Sousa
Tokyo University of Foreign Studies
Tokyo, Japan

This series proposes a new geography of Global History research using Asian and Western sources, welcoming quality research and engaging outstanding scholarship from China, Europe and the Americas. Promoting academic excellence and critical intellectual analysis, it offers a rich source of global history research in sub-continental areas of Europe, Asia (notably China, Japan and the Philippines) and the Americas and aims to help understand the divergences and convergences between East and West.

More information about this series at
http://www.springer.com/series/15711

Manuel Perez Garcia · Lucio De Sousa
Editors

Global History and New Polycentric Approaches

Europe, Asia and the Americas in a World Network System

Editors
Manuel Perez Garcia
Shanghai Jiao Tong University
Shanghai, China
Pablo de Olavide University
Seville, Spain

Lucio De Sousa
Tokyo University of Foreign Studies
Fuchu, Tokyo, Japan

Palgrave Studies in Comparative Global History
ISBN 978-981-10-4052-8   ISBN 978-981-10-4053-5   (eBook)
https://doi.org/10.1007/978-981-10-4053-5

Library of Congress Control Number: 2017937489

© The Editor(s) (if applicable) and The Author(s) 2018, corrected publication 2018. This book is an open access publication.
Open Access This book is licensed under the terms of the Creative Commons Attribution 4.0 International License (http://creativecommons.org/licenses/by/4.0/), which permits use, sharing, adaptation, distribution and reproduction in any medium or format, as long as you give appropriate credit to the original author(s) and the source, provide a link to the Creative Commons license and indicate if changes were made.
The images or other third party material in this book are included in the book's Creative Commons license, unless indicated otherwise in a credit line to the material. If material is not included in the book's Creative Commons license and your intended use is not permitted by statutory regulation or exceeds the permitted use, you will need to obtain permission directly from the copyright holder.
The use of general descriptive names, registered names, trademarks, service marks, etc. in this publication does not imply, even in the absence of a specific statement, that such names are exempt from the relevant protective laws and regulations and therefore free for general use.
The publisher, the authors and the editors are safe to assume that the advice and information in this book are believed to be true and accurate at the date of publication. Neither the publisher nor the authors or the editors give a warranty, express or implied, with respect to the material contained herein or for any errors or omissions that may have been made. The publisher remains neutral with regard to jurisdictional claims in published maps and institutional affiliations.

Cover credit: © Science History Images/Alamy Stock Photo

Printed on acid-free paper

This Palgrave Macmillan imprint is published by Springer Nature
The registered company is Springer Nature Singapore Pte Ltd.
The registered company address is: 152 Beach Road, #21-01/04 Gateway East, Singapore 189721, Singapore

"The development of a global economy has generated a movement for a truly global history. There is still a long way to go, but this volume of essays by Western and Asian historians constitutes a brave attempt to bridge the great divide."
—Sir John Elliott, *Regius Professor of Modern History, University of Oxford, UK*

"The multiple perspectives offered by this volume's chapters together make an important contribution to the goal of transforming global history from an aspiration to a reality."
—Jan de Vries, *Ehrman Professor Emeritus, University of California at Berkeley, USA*

"These scholars delve deeply into Asian data and global interpretation, showing the centrality of East Asia in the trade networks of the early modern world. They successfully set Atlantic developments in the context of the Asia-Pacific region."
—Patrick Manning, *Andrew W. Mellon Professor of World History, Emeritus, University of Pittsburgh, USA*

"This is a stimulating attempt to present Global History, focusing on comparison of Maritime History between the Asia-Pacific and the Atlantic. Readers may clearly understand a rich historiography in East Asia on Global/World History studies."
—Shigeru Akita, *Chairman, Asian Association of World Historians, South Korea and Professor of British Imperial History and Global History, Osaka University, Japan*

"Manuel Perez Garcia and Lucio de Sousa have edited a thought-provoking volume, addressing the question of global history as conceived by European, Chinese and Japanese scholars, and revitalizing this field of studies in East Asian historiography. No doubt that this volume, linking maritime history and global history, will open new paths of research free of any "centrisms" as has often been the case so far. The various chapters that make up this volume combine different scales of analysis (local, regional, transnational and global) to implement a truly interdisciplinary analysis of a world network system that has shaped international trade from the the XVIth through the XIXth centuries."
—Francois Gipouloux, *Emeritus Research Director, National Centre for Scientific Research, France*

"A thoroughly, well-organised and outstanding book for a deeper understanding of the real impact of global history on East Asian historiographies and fresh insights on intercontinental comparisons."
—Liu Beicheng, *Professor, Tsinghua University, China*

"This book demonstrates superbly the important contribution of GECEM project and the Global History Network (GHN) in bringing together diverse Asian, European and American historiographical approaches based on different methods, sources, and theories. The cases presented urge a careful reconceptualization of our received streams of thought, a process that will open exciting new routes for grasping history and expanding our cognitive capabilities, as the challenges of our rapidly globalizing world demand."
—J. B. Owens, *Research Professor, Idaho State University, USA*

"Global history releases itself from the straightjacket of national boundaries and supersedes the East-West divide that still characterises much scholarship: in this book, the early modern world is analysed by a new type of global polycentric history."
—Giorgio Riello, *Professor, University of Warwick, UK*

"Global History and New Polycentric Approaches features a group of scholarly essays from western and eastern historians that clearly show how to assess the great questions posed by a truly global history. The book is a must – read for academics and students that want to deepen their understanding of modern world history."
—Antonio Ibarra Romero, *Professor, Universidad Nacional Autonoma de Mexico, Mexico*

"Manuel Perez Garcia and Lucio de Sousa have magisterially collected fresh research works by outstanding scholars in Global History and East Asian studies. Certainly, it gives a new 'polycentric' turn going beyond Eurocentric and Sinocentric perspectives in Global history."
—Bernd Hausberger, *Professor, Colegio de Mexico, Mexico*

This research has been sponsored and financially supported by GECEM ('Global Encounters between China and Europe: Trade Networks, Consumption and Cultural Exchanges in Macau and Marseille, 1680–1840') project hosted by the Pablo de Olavide University, UPO (Seville, Spain). The GECEM project is funded by the ERC (European Research Council)-Starting Grant, under the European Union's Horizon 2020 Research and Innovation Programme, ref. 679371, www.gecem.eu. The P.I. (Principal Investigator) is Professor Manuel Perez Garcia (Distinguished Researcher at UPO).

We would like to dedicate this book to Liu Beicheng (Tsinghua University) and Naotoshi Kurosawa (Tokyo University of Foreign Studies), respectively our mentors in China and Japan.

Foreword

History is marked by alternating movements across an imaginary line, separating East from West in Eurasia.[1]

As an evangelical advocate for the inclusion of courses in global history for systems of higher education throughout the world, I strongly applaud the endeavours of two young Iberians, with posts at major universities in China and Japan, to persuade their East Asian colleagues to make real space in their curricula for an engagement with history that is 'truly global'.

'Truly global' means that teaching and research in faculties of history should represent something much more profound, heuristic and modern than extensions to the histories of East Asian or European societies that includes hard-won knowledge of other countries and cultures. The editors and their distinguished colleagues conceive of global history as a challenge to obsolete, patriotic and centric histories of all kinds.

Located as both editors are as foreign academics in cultures with ancient and strong national identities, their laudable mission has met with a different kind and quality of resistance to both the now-moribund antipathies of post-modern critics in the West to grand narratives, as well as the more conventional and explicable obsessions of professional historians everywhere with erudition, detail and archival research. How could this contemporaneously significant, politically necessary and morally imperative style of history meet the standards of rigour long established for the social sciences and for national and international histories are not questions that are easy to evade or to answer. Could the respect for evidence, the comprehension of contexts, aspirations for imaginative insights and elegant clarification demanded by modern micro-history be satisfied?

Japanese history with deep roots in Rankean scholarship continues to be meticulous in its attention to detail, while China's ancient tradition in writing encyclopaedic histories of imperial dynasties could only strengthen a preference for world, rather than the more refined and complex approach to global history that the editors have in mind. Furthermore, objections to the whole notion for global history (particularly if it is explicitly comparative) as a moral malign agenda for Western triumphalism and cultural domination continue to be made by European as well as Chinese radicals, who have suffered from both.

Nevertheless, there has been a revival of grand narratives and most historians now recognize that further and prolonged engagement with philosophers for history, linguistic turns and literary theory are producing diminishing returns and bore their students.

For millennia, historians from all civilizations (Chinese, Japanese, Islamic and European) have been involved with the problem of how best to reconcile religious beliefs, cultural norms and packages of "modernities" from outside their communities, polities and empires with the indigenous traditions and traditional values they wish to preserve.

How these interactions between the local and the global played out historically in the port cities of East Asia and the Spanish Empire in the context of maritime commerce is cogently analysed with respect for facts and imaginatively conveyed by the chapters in a book that sets out to expose the role and connections rather than the divisions or ranks in a global history of civilizations.

This collection of scholarly essays exposes and illustrates an early modern history of the East in the West. They represent the most persuasive way of persuading a conservative profession to welcome a style of history that has escaped from national narratives, avoids centrisms and evades invidious comparisons. This volume should allay the fears or anxieties of Chinese, Japanese and European and Latin American historians who have been explicably sceptical if not antipathetic to the global turn. Indeed, as the editors hoped, they are 'polycentric' and represent an innovative, ideologically neutral and enlightened approach to a global history for these times of inescapable and intensified globalization.

These chapters represent history that is politically, economically and culturally significant for the great debates of our times, not because the subject could recover truth and hard evidence about the past, but because an understanding of the economic, social and political processes that are intrinsic to maritime commerce can be acute and useful. The opportunity should be seized because history without purpose or agendas is just another form of literature. Yes, ironic detachment and careful attention to evidence are universal virtues to be nurtured. But so too are the construction and reconfiguration of meta-narratives, which will educate societies, appeal to the young and serve the needs of dangerous times for a sense of global citizenship. Anything less would be folly and, as Bolingbroke anticipated, folly can be remedied 'by historical study which should purge the mind of national partialities and prejudices. For a wise man looks upon himself as a citizen of the world'.[2]

Patrick O'Brien
Emeritus Professor University of London and
Fellow of St. Antonys College
University of Oxford

NOTES

1. Quoted by A.G. Frank, *ReOrient: Global Economy in the Asian Age* (Berkeley, University of California Press, 1998), p. ix.
2. B. Southgate, *Why Bother with History?* (London, Longman, 2000), p. 163.

Acknowledgements

This book is the result of the 1st GECEM ('Global Encounters between China and Europe: Trade Networks, Consumption and Cultural Exchanges in Macau and Marseille, 1680–1840') workshop, *Quantitative Economic History and Open Science in China and Europe* (host by the University of Chicago-Center in Beijing, China, November 21, 2016), and the 2nd GECEM workshop, *New Technologies, and Databases to Analyse Modern Economic Growth in China and Europe* (host by the Pablo de Olavide University, Seville, Spain February 8, 2017). The long-lasting academic cooperation between Lucio de Sousa and I through the organization of several academic meetings and talks in Beijing, Macau and Tokyo, helped us to come up with the idea of founding an academic network on global history in 2011, *Global History Network* (GHN), invigorating the field in China and Japan. Joining synergies with outstanding experts from Asia, Europe, and the Americas, we might gain a complete picture on the implementation and new directions of global history. The obtaining of my European Research Council (ERC) Starting-Grant in the Fall of 2015, *Global Encounters between China and Europe* (GECEM project) has made possible the current cooperation with Palgrave Macmillan. This book is the first in the series on *Palgrave Studies in Comparative Global History*. The GECEM project, in constant cooperation with the GHN, has contributed to this book. Liu Beicheng, Naotoshi Kurosawa, Patrick O'Brien, Joe McDermott, François Gipouloux, Patt Manning, Shigeru Akita, Antonio Ibarra, Jack Owens, Richard Von Glahn, Bartolome Yun, Anne McCants, Gakusho Nakajima, Mihoko Oka, Carlos Marichal and Colin Mackerras have been constantly offering us the support, courage and confidence to undertake this work and continue to develop the field of global history in China and Japan respectively. The GECEM team, Sergio Serrano as research fellow of GECEM, Marisol Vidales Bernal as project manager of GECEM, Lei Jin and Guimel Hernandez as GECEM PhD researchers, and professor Bartolome Yun Casalilla as senior staff, have correspondingly contributed to arrange the final format, style and edition, as well as the preparation with Palgrave Macmillan to have the book in Open Access.

The task for Lucio and myself, in China and Japan respectively, to implement global history proved to be a daunting yet rewarding journey. Recognized Sinologists and experts in Japanese studies might know what we are referring to. In our case, as Western scholars and faculty staff in China and Japan, the marginal internationalization and very recent 'academic openness' in both countries to engage a global academic agenda in higher education systems constitutes the final frontier and obstacle that we both must confront on an everyday basis. For this reason, we sincerely express our gratitude to scholars and friends, as well as our families, who generously give us support in Beijing, Shanghai and Tokyo. This mission requires patience, but mostly personal sacrifices that we have already undertaken. Without the constant support of our parents in Spain and Portugal, this mission might have been fruitless. A big word of thanks to my father, Manuel Perez, who gave me the courage to come to China in 2011, and of course to my wife Marisol, as we have both gone through many odds in our Chinese venture and have of course shed tears of joy. My gratitude to all my family members and friends for their constant inspiration and support. Special thanks to my deceased friend Pedro Lança. You died very young , but your life will always live on in my spirit.

We are undoubtedly grateful to Sara Crowley Vigneau, Senior Editor in Humanities and Social Sciences at Palgrave Macmillan in the China and Asia Pacific region, as well as her team, for their continuous support for this book and the new Palgrave series in *Comparative Global History*. We are greatly grateful to the sponsor institution of the *GECEM project-679371, ERC-Starting Grant under the European Union's Horizon 2020 Research and Innovation Programme*, being the University Pablo de Olavide (UPO) in Seville the European host institution of GECEM. This project has made possible the Open Access publication of this book. Such achievement constitutes a breakthrough for GECEM and therefore, as the ultimate result has made the scientific work open to the world for both academic and non-academic audiences.

In this way, the support of the ERC stands out as being of great importance. Likewise, the assistance of the Delegation of the European Union to China and Mongolia and Euraxess China has been crucial in order to carry out outreach activities and scientific networking in China. I have no words to express my thanks for the constant and generous support of Laurent Bochereau (Minister Counsellor, Head of Science, Technology and Environment Section of the Delegation of the European Union to China and Mongolia) and Andrea Strelçova (former Chief Representative of Euraxess China), their work being of the utmost importance for European and non-European researchers based in China.

Mistakes could have been made, but we can learn from them and improve. Risks must be taken to achieve our goals and objectives, as in life one must bet high: *high risk, high gain*.

Beijing, Fall 2016

Contents

Introduction: Current Challenges of Global History in East
Asian Historiographies   1
Manuel Perez Garcia

Part I   Escaping from National Narratives: The New Global History in China and Japan

Global History, the Role of Scientific Discovery
and the 'Needham Question': Europe and China
in the Sixteenth to Nineteenth Centuries   21
Colin Mackerras

RETRACTED CHAPTER: Encounter and Coexistence:
Portugal and Ming China 1511–1610: Rethinking the
Dynamics of a Century of Global–Local Relations   37
Harriet Zurndorfer

Challenging National Narratives: On the Origins
of Sweet Potato in China as Global Commodity
During the Early Modern Period   53
Manuel Perez Garcia

Economic Depression and the Silver Question
in Nineteenth-Century China   81
Richard von Glahn

Kaiiki-Shi and World/Global History: A Japanese Perspective   119
Hideaki Suzuki

Part II Trade Networks and Maritime Expansion
         in East Asian Studies

The Structure and Transformation of the Ming
Tribute Trade System   137
Gakusho Nakajima

The *Nanban* and *Shuinsen* Trade in Sixteenth
and Seventeenth-Century Japan   163
Mihoko Oka

The Jewish Presence in China and Japan in the Early Modern
Period: A Social Representation   183
Lucio de Sousa

Quantifying Ocean Currents as Story Models: Global Oceanic
Currents and Their Introduction to Global Navigation   219
Agnes Kneitz

Part III Circulation of Technology and Commodities
          in the Atlantic and Pacific

Global History and the History of Consumption:
Congruence and Divergence   241
Anne E.C. McCants

Mexican Cochineal, Local Technologies and the Rise
of Global Trade from the Sixteenth to the Nineteenth
Centuries   255
Carlos Marichal Salinas

Social Networks and the Circulation of Technology and Knowledge in the Global Spanish Empire   275
Bartolomé Yun-Casalilla

Global Commodities in Early Modern Spain   293
Nadia Fernández-de-Pinedo

Big History as a Commodity at Chinese Universities: A Study in Circulation   321
David Pickus

Index   341

Editors and Contributors

About the Editors

Manuel Perez Garcia is Associate Professor at the Department of History, School of Humanities, Shanghai Jiao Tong University (China). He obtained his PhD at the European University Institute (Italy). He has been awarded with an ERC-StG 679371, under the framework of Horizon 2020 European Union Funding for Research & Innovation, to conduct the GECEM project (Global Encounters between China and Europe), www.gecem.eu. He is also Distinguished Researcher at the Pablo de Olavide University (Seville, Spain), European host institution of GECEM. He is founder and director of the Global History Network (GHN) in China, www.globalhistorynetwork.com. He was Associate Professor at the School of International Studies, Renmin University of China from 2013 until 2017. Prof. Perez was postdoctoral fellow and Assistant Chair at the Department of History at Tsinghua University (Beijing, China) from 2011 to 2013. He was research fellow at UC Berkeley, International Institute for Asian Studies (Leiden University) as Marie Curie fellow and visiting professor at UNAM (Mexico), University of Tokyo (Japan) and University of Macerata (Italy).

Among his publications stands out the book *Vicarious Consumers: Transnational Meetings between the West and East (1730–1808)*, published by Routledge (2013), and several articles in SSCI journals.

Lucio de Sousa is Associate Professor at Tokyo University of Foreign Studies (Japan). He obtained his PhD in Asian Studies at University of Oporto (Portugal). He is a member of the Steering Committee of Global History Network and Chair of the Board of advisors of GECEM project. He was a postdoctoral fellow at European University Institute (Italy). He was a book winner of the Macao Foundation, the Social Science in China Press and the Guangdong Social Sciences Association (2013). His primary field of research is the slave trade and Jewish diaspora in Asia in the Early Modern Period.

Contributors

Nadia Fernández-de-Pinedo is Senior Lecturer at the Universidad Autónoma of Madrid, Spain. Her work covers a wide range consumption and distribution networks, including eighteenth- and nineteenth-century Spanish and Atlantic history. She participates in various cross-disciplinary projects where she has embarked on research for examining technology transfer processes, institutions, fabric distribution and material culture.

Agnes Kneitz is Assistant Professor of World Environmental History at Renmin University of China, Beijing. She finished a PhD dissertation on representations of environmental justice in the nineteenth century social novels in 2013 and since then has been on working on interdisciplinary environmental historical topics with an increasingly global focus.

Colin Mackerras has published very widely in Chinese history and contemporary China, including Western images of China, China's ethnic minorities and its musical theatre. He has visited and taught in China many times, the first time being from 1964 to 1966, and is based at Griffith University, Australia.

Anne E.C. McCants is Professor of History at MIT and the Vice-President of the International Economic History Association. She is the author of *Civic Charity in a Golden Age: Orphan Care in Early Modern Amsterdam*, and numerous articles on welfare in the Dutch Republic, European historical demography, and technological change, material culture and global consumption.

Gakusho Nakajima is Doctor of Literature at Waseda University, Japan. Currently he is Associate Professor at the Faculty of Humanities, Kyushu University, Japan. His fields of research are Chinese social history and East Asian maritime history.

Mihoko Oka is Associate Professor at the Historiographical Institute, University of Tokyo, with which she has been affiliated since 2003. Her chief research interests are maritime history surrounding Japan in the sixteenth and seventeenth centuries, Christian history in Japan and Christian merchants in Nagasaki.

David Pickus is Associate Professor in the Global Engagement Program, School of International Studies at Zhejiang University (Hangzhou, China). He received his PhD from the University of Chicago in 1995, specializing in German intellectual history. His current research covers the topics of refugee intellectuals, the history of globalization and improving higher education in East Asia.

Carlos Marichal Salinas is Professor of Latin American history at El Colegio de Mexico, a leading research and postgraduate institute. He is author or editor of some 20 books in English and Spanish on Mexican and Latin American economic history. He was also the founder and former president (2000–2004) of the Mexican Association of Economic History.

Hideaki Suzuki is Associate Professor at the School of Global Humanities and Social Sciences, Nagasaki University, Japan. His research interests cover Indian Ocean history, world/global history, slavery and the slave trade, the Indian merchant network and medieval Arab geography. He is the editor of *Abolitions as a Global Experience* (Singapore: NUS Press, 2016).

Richard von Glahn is Professor of History at the University of California, Los Angeles and the author of *The Economic History of China from Antiquity to the Nineteenth Century* (Cambridge, 2016), *Fountain of Fortune: Money and Monetary Policy in China* (California, 1996) and other books.

Bartolomé Yun-Casalilla is Full Professor at the Pablo de Olavide University in Seville, Spain. He specializes in the study of political economies, the Spanish Empire, the history of consumption and the history of the aristocracy. An expert on global, transnational and comparative history, from 2003 to 2013 he taught at the European University Institute of Florence, where he directed the Department of History and Civilization from 2009 to 2012.

List of Figures

Challenging National Narratives: On the Origins of Sweet Potato in China as Global Commodity During the Early Modern Period

Fig. 1	The trend of academic articles on the research of the introduction of sweet potato (1958–2015)	57
Fig. 2	Two kinds of potato: Dioscorea Esculenta and Ipomoea Batatas	63
Fig. 3	Population growth in China from 1000 to 1820	72

Economic Depression and the Silver Question in Nineteenth-Century China

Fig. 1	Population density and rates of growth, 1776–1820	92
Fig. 2	Grain prices in South China, 1660–1850	92
Fig. 3	Rice prices in five major markets, 1826–1852	93
Fig. 4	Prices of agricultural and manufactured goods in Ningjin (Hebei), 1800–1850	94
Fig. 5	Prices and wages (Silver equivalents) in Ningjin (Hebei), 1800–1850	95
Fig. 6	Daily wages of unskilled labourers in Beijing, 1807–1838. Wages in coin: *wen*/day (based on Buck). Wages in silver equivalent: *li*/day (based on exchange ratios in Tongtaisheng ledgers). Wages in grain equivalent: *shao*/day (based on Jiangnan rice prices)	96
Fig. 7	Growth of the money supply, 1726–1833 (annual averages)	97
Fig. 8	Silver: Bronze coin exchange ratios and bronze coin output, 1691–1800. 1721–1730 = 100	98

Fig. 9	Tea and silk exports, 1756–1833. (annual averages; tea exports in thousands of piculs; silk exports in hundreds of piculs): Silk data is incomplete and no silk data is available for 1756–1762 and 1814–1820	101
Fig. 10	Silver: Bronze coin exchange ratios, 1790–1860	102
Fig. 11	Silver–Bronze coin exchange ratios, 1870–1906	104
Fig. 12	Silver: Coin exchange ratios in Vietnam, 1807–1860	105

Kaiiki-Shi and World/Global History: A Japanese Perspective

Fig. 1	The number of accepted KAKEN-HI projects under the title including "Kaiiki"	126

Global History and the History of Consumption: Congruence and Divergence

Fig. 1	World History' as a subject in 20th c. English language books	245
Fig. 2	The rise of 'Global History' since 1940	246
Fig. 3	World history as a subject in 20th c. French language books	246
Fig. 4	World history as a subject in 20th c. German language books	247

Mexican Cochineal, Local Technologies and the Rise of Global Trade from the Sixteenth to the Nineteenth Centuries

Fig. 1	The cochineal trade: Mercantile networks in Mexico	263
Fig. 2	The Commodity Chain of Cochineal from Oaxaca and Veracruz to Europe, circa 1780	268
Fig. 3	Annual Production and Prices of Cochinilla Registered at the Oficina del Registro y la Administración Principal de Rentas, Oaxaca, 1758–1854	269

Global Commodities in Early Modern Spain

Fig. 1	Classification by record registered and social status	297

Big History as a Commodity at Chinese Universities: A Study in Circulation

Fig. 1	Student responses to the question: 'What qualities do nations need to engage successfully in international trade?'	331
Fig. 2	Student responses to the question: 'Do you know the history of any individual commodities? How did you learn about it?'	331
Fig. 3	Student responses to the question: 'How important is it to know world economic history and why?'	331
Fig. 4	Students' responses to the question 'Do you have specific knowledge of the history of any commodity?'	332

List of Tables

Challenging National Narratives: On the Origins of Sweet Potato in China as Global Commodity During the Early Modern Period

Table 1	Period and areas of introduction of sweet potato in China during the Ming Dynasty	66
Table 2	The field area statement in Central China and Southwestern China in the Qing Dynasty (units: 1000 *Mu*)	71
Table 3	The yield and increment of corn and sweet potato in the Qing Dynasty	71

Economic Depression and the Silver Question in Nineteenth-Century China

Table 1	Estimates of Chinese GDP	87
Table 2	Population of Qing China	91
Table 3	Lin Man-houng's estimates of net silver flows in and out of Qing China. Unit: millions of silver pesos	99
Table 4	Net flow of silver from China, 1818–1854 (all figures in millions of pesos)	100
Table 5	Customs revenues, 1725–1831. (thousands of silver taels)	106

The Structure and Transformation of the Ming Tribute Trade System

Table 1	Tributaries of the Ming listed in *Ta-Ming huitian* 大明會典 (1587 edn)	139
Table 2	The number of tributes by main tributary states in the Ming (1368–1566)	141
Table 3	The structure of the 1570 system in the late sixteenth century	153

Global Commodities in Early Modern Spain

Table 1	Per Capita/Per Year purchases by social groups in pounds (weight)	299
Table 2	Items from China introduced in Madrid for personal consumption, 1741–1743	304

Introduction: Current Challenges of Global History in East Asian Historiographies

Manuel Perez Garcia

The Global History Network (GHN) was recently founded by a group of scholars working on global history at prestigious universities and institutions in China, Japan, Mexico and Europe. This ambitious project began in 2011 when Professor Lucio de Sousa and I, working respectively in China and Japan, jointly identified the historiographical need to render the expanding field of global history that might be defined as truly relevant for the new

---

This research has been sponsored and financially supported by the GECEM ('Global Encounters between China and Europe: Trade Networks, Consumption and Cultural Exchanges in Macau and Marseille, 1680–1840') project hosted by the Pablo de Olavide University, UPO (Seville, Spain). The GECEM project is funded by the ERC (European Research Council)-Starting Grant, under the European Union's Horizon 2020 Research and Innovation Programme, ref. 679371, http://www.gecem.eu. The P.I. (Principal Investigator) is Professor Manuel Perez Garcia (Distinguished Researcher at UPO). I am grateful to comments and suggestions on the earliest version of this chapter by Professor Joe McDermott (University of Cambridge)and François Gipouloux (National Center for Scientific Research, France), who are outstanding specialists in the field of East Asian and Chinese Studies. Any mistakes and errors in this chapter are under author's responsibility.

M. Perez Garcia (✉)
Shanghai Jiao Tong University, Shanghai, China

© The Author(s) 2018
M. Perez Garcia and L. de Sousa (eds.), *Global History and New Polycentric Approaches*, Palgrave Studies in Comparative Global History, https://doi.org/10.1007/978-981-10-4053-5_1

century. Our current institutions, Shanghai Jiao Tong University and the Tokyo University of Foreign Studies, serve as academic platforms to expand our network and research in China and Japan. Undertaking such endeavours in both countries represents an opportunity to expand global history in environments with diverse academic traditions. Regardless of current efforts to internationalize Chinese and Japanese universities and research institutions, nobody can ignore the fact that today they remain very far from embracing a truly international and global academic agenda. Such a challenge should be filled with the use of new empirical data and cross-referencing sources from European, Asian and American archives and texts. This enables us to refresh the field of global history via concrete case studies, especially when we confront meta narratives that aim to answer big-questions such as why the West (or, more specifically, Great Britain and the Netherlands) flourished economically before China during the first Industrial Revolution. As a result, our project crystalized with the award of the ERC-Starting Grant, *Global Encounters between China and Europe* (GECEM), by which this book is sponsored, as well as ongoing related projects.

We believe that by joining forces and harmonizing diverse theories, sources and methods of different academic traditions like those from China and Japan, the field of global history receives a new impulse through diverse case studies. The constant participation of specialists in this field is crucial, as they share their experiences and new ideas on how re-addressing new approaches and questions. The main partner institutions that take part of this network are the University Pablo de Olavide (Spain), Tokyo University of Foreign Studies, Shanghai Jiao Tong University, followed by Tsinghua University, Renmin University of China, Guangdong Academy of Social Sciences, the University of Tokyo, the Universidad Nacional Autónoma de México (UNAM) and the École de Hautes Études en Sciences Sociales (France).

Global history is in some instances a very sensitive field, challenging both traditional and sometimes obsolete national narratives. It is crucial for this project, through concrete case studies, to rethink the ways in which global history is envisioned and conceptualized in China and Japan, as well as European and American countries. When a historian constructs a meta narratives, this will always contain a subjective element borne out of ideological and national constraints. Therefore, we should formulate the following pertinent question: how do global events connect to our local and national communities, and, by extension, to our academic environment? Global history is not a practice by which we can arbitrarily combine all type of histories, be it local, national, continental or transcontinental. It is rather an approach through which the historian seeks connections across space, chronologies and boundaries, combining local and global perspectives.[1] Challenging and going beyond obsolete patriotic narratives should be the ultimate goal of a global historian.

National narratives are still very present in Western historiographies. Though global history is very popular in Anglo-Saxon historiographies, it has been mainly focused on the history of Great Britain and its colonies due to primary attention to study the core economic areas of Europe, mainly Great Britain, that took off during the first Industrial Revolution. In the case of southern European historiographies—Spain, France, Italy or Portugal—the long-standing influence of Marxist ideology in the area of social sciences and humanities, the political and ideological conquests of May 1968 and the Annales School have for a long time held sway in the form and method of making history. This was also followed by the dependency theorists of Latin America that came about as a reaction to Anglo-American modernization theories. In such historiographies, it is no coincidence that, when debating the meaning and significance of global history, prejudices arise in the belief that it is a mindset inherited from Anglo-Saxon historiography. This has served as a justification not to give enough emphasis to global history. In southern European historiographies until the present day, only the magnum opus by Braudel, *Civilization and Capitalism*, or Immanuel Wallerstein's *The Modern World System* are the classic works that such traditional scholarship uniquely identifies with global history. Yet, when mentioning the debate of the great divergence, the 'Needham question', the essential works by Pomeranz or the California School, among others, there is little understanding and knowledge of such vital debates and works. The lack of translation into Spanish or Portuguese of such works exacerbates a problem founded on an absence of sharing academic and analytical perspectives.

This is the case for the presence or, to put it better, marginal existence of global history in European historiographies. The chapter by Anne McCants in this volume truly illustrates the marginal position of global history in Europe, not only in the countries mentioned above, but also in Germany and France. In the former, world history has had a greater presence than global history, and for the latter, when we find global history books, such works are more closely related to the history of commerce and consumption somehow following the Braudelian tradition of the *longue durée* and markets in the Mediterranean area. As McCants mentions, the Word History Association (WHA), as well as the three major refereed academic journals in global history—the *Journal of*

World History (begun in 1990), the *Journal of Global History* (begun in 2006) and the *New Global Studies Journal* (begun in 2007)—has exerted a notable role in expanding the field, mainly in the last 10 years.

When turning to Chinese historiography, we should notice that global history has been recently introduced. Until the present day, the main contribution of Chinese scholars in this field has been translations of main western works such as *The Great Divergence* (K. Pomeranz 2000) into Chinese by Shǐ Jiànyún 史建云 in 2003 and when the World History Association (WHA) organized its 20th annual meeting at Capital Normal University (Beijing, China) in 2011. From that moment, Capital Normal University (Shǒudū Shīfàn Dàxué 首都师范大学), Nankai University (Nánkāi Dàxué 南开大学) and latter in 2014 Beijing Foreign Studies University (Běijīng Wàiguóyǔ Dàxué 北京外国语大学) respectively started to embrace global history by founding research centres, as well as journals related to this field. The first publishes the *Global History Review*, the *Translation of Global History Series* and the *Global History Reader*. Nevertheless, the missions and goals of such centres and journals have an orientation of China's history that is separate from the rest of the world. Any research centre in China must be within the parameters of the Chinese government, by following the 一带一路 yīdài yīlù ('One Belt, One Road') policy whose goal is to present a new national history of China. Therefore, the focus is utterly Sinocentric observing global history or, to put it better, world history as the history of nations and territories outside China, i.e. the history of Japan, Russia or Germany, among others. The objective and result is to build a very patriotic narrative.

The use and meaning of concepts to understand global history and distinguish it from world history appears to be of great importance. Although they might have similar labels and terms, they are used differently according to academic traditions and principles which are regularly jumbled together. There is a lack of a clear distinction between global history (quánqiú shǐ 全球史) or world history (shìjiè lìshǐ 世界历史), both of which have different meanings and connotations relating to the political context that dominates the academic environment in China. This is not only a problem of the current moment. A long-standing trope for conceptualizing world history in China is through the concept of cóngshū (丛书), which specifically refers to big encyclopaedic volumes that categorize and compile history in separate geographical units. This form and narrative was profoundly rooted in Song and Ming Dynasty historiographies, and spread through the then-new networks of knowledge and the literati in China. However, this practice remains present in Chinese historiography until today, existing alongside contemporary attitudes towards history writing. The search for interconnections, use of new approaches considering both local and macro scales, is practically absent in Chinese narratives. An explanation or clue for such a lack might be that global history in the last few decades in China has merely been linked with a decided subfield of international history. Likewise, another reason for such a vacuum is related to the concept of collecting and transcribing national narratives by doing encyclopaedic series on the history of Russia, Japan or other neighbouring nations that had important political links with China during the Cold War period. Furthermore, it is also important to consider that international history, mainly after the foundation of People's Republic of China (PRC), had as its main goal the study of how Marxism was interpreted in other nations, with history itself playing a secondary role.

The same case and use of concepts can be found in Japanese historiography, as presented in the chapter by Suzuki Hideaki on kaiiki-shi 海域史 (according to the Japanese translation, it means maritime history) and world/global history, or the Japanized pronunciation of global history (global history = グローバル・ヒストリー) 'gurobaru hisutori'[2] (Haneda 2015). Both Chinese and Japanese scholars find themselves at a crossroads in an attempt to accommodate the current fashion of global history with their national peculiarities and academic traditions. In the case of Japan, as Haneda (2015) refers to 'new world history', the Japanese translation is 'atarashii sekaishi' (新しい世界史).[3] Regarding the case of China, Liang Zhan-Jun (2006) makes an effort to distinguish the terms global history (quánqiú shǐ 全球史) and world history (shìjiè lìshǐ 世界历史) mentioned above. Nevertheless, the main academic trend in China is to embrace global history with 'Chinese characteristics' (zhōngguó tèsè 中国特色) (Qian C. 2001; Yu P. 2006). In other words, we could observe a neo-nationalization of historical narratives with the 'global' fashionable label.

The same problem in Japanese historiography might be found in the case of Chinese historiography in relation to the confusion of world and global history, which tends to be a universal one, as it also appears in Western historiographies. Likewise, global history is regarded in Japan as a Western, more clearly Anglo-Saxon form and narrative, and therefore as a non-indigenous one. Thus, historians and new practitioners of global history feel more comfortable using the form of world history, which separates nation-states as geographical units for the historical analysis using national narratives and jointly embracing sub-disciplines such as maritime history in the case of Japanese historiography. The sea in China and Japan has historically been conceptualized as the main space through which foreigners or invaders arrived. As such, the concept of 'sea' in

Chinese, hǎi (海), is closely linked to the concept of foreigner, hǎiwài rén (海外人). Similarly, we find the same in Japanese, gaikokujin (外国人) or gaijin (外人), which denotes people who entered the country from overseas.

It appears natural that world and global history are interconnected with maritime history. The same is the case in other East Asian historical traditions. Likewise, the case of maritime history, in East Asian historiographies, the aforementioned Chinese and Japanese historical traditions, as well as those from South Korea, the Philippines, Singapore, Taiwan, Hong Kong and Macau, have a clear tendency, due to their geographical nature, to develop maritime studies. Consequently, global history in these areas is quite concentrated on the study of trans-Pacific trade, maritime networks and inner local economic development, such as the area of the lower Yangzi Delta in China (Li Qingxin 2010; Antony 2014; Kee-long So 2011; Li Bozhong 2000; Hamashita 1997).

In this sense, global history, even though it is a substantially new and fashionable field in Chinese historiography, has not sympathized with traditional scholars. This issue also appears in some European areas. Here the traditional school is essentially defined as the Marxist school. Scholars belonging to this tradition reject global history and argue that it "is not a compact, uniform normative narrative". Global history might be a form of a "neo-colonialist strategy" that can potentially contaminate the meaning, concept and narrative of Chinese history and civilization (Wu Xiaoqun 2005; Li Qiang 2011; Wang Lincong 2002; Wang Yunlong 2002; Qian Chengdan 2001; Yu Pei 2006). Therefore, it is envisaged as a Western form and product of the conquest of capitalism used to diminish China's national history and its cultural uniqueness.

In order to accommodate global history within the peculiar political and social features of the academic system and environment in China, the discipline has even been embraced by the group of critics in the form of using global history with national imperatives and the neo-Confucian policies applied to academic life. Such policies seek the internationalization of the academic community, while maintaining the national essence. Therefore, we might find a new distorted form of global history in China masked as scientific internationalization and diversity, but with a profoundly nationalist spirit. This could be defined as global history with 'Chinese characteristics' (zhōngguó tèsè 中国特色). However, several groups of scholars in China embrace the discipline of global history and capture the real meaning of it. This is the so-called group of 'neo-colonialists'—in terms of the Marxist school—as they have been influenced by Western historiographies (Liang Zhan-Jun 2006; Liu Xincheng 2012; Li Longqing 2000; Liu Beicheng 2000). A paramount example is the translation of the book *Re-Orient* (Gunder Frank) by Liu Beicheng, the Chinese title being Báiyín Zīběn 白银资本 (*Silver Capital*). From the moment that *Re-Orient* and *The Great Divergence* were translated into Chinese, global history, the California School and the great divergence debate progressively spread in Chinese scholarship (Liu Beicheng 2000).

To be sure, recent openings in China have created new ground for other related fields, such as international relations (IR) and international political economy (IPE), whose aim is to analyse the political system in the era of globalisation and the impact of political factors of the world economy respectively. This clearly shows the interdisciplinary scope of global history and the dialogue with other disciplines and sub-disciplines. Still, misuses and misunderstandings remain in the practice and concept of global history. The field did not make its debut in Chinese historiography until the translation of *Re-Orient* (Frank, A.G. 1998), and, as mentioned above, *The Great Divergence* (Pomeranz, K. 2000) into Chinese at the beginning of the twenty-first century. The works of such scholars just started to make an influence approximately seven years ago in Chinese academic circles. This beginning of the discipline coincided with the rapid development of the Chinese economy and the rise of its gross domestic product (GDP) (Deng and O'Brien 2016). And, of course, finding the roots of the uniqueness of the Chinese economy in its long-lasting civilization was very tempting for Chinese scholars, some of whom had strong ideological and political motivations to legitimate the current uniqueness of the history and the economy of the nation. Therefore, in the case of Chinese historiography, global history is often confusingly interwoven with the modern use of globalization and new foreign policies for business, trade and the import-export market. Global history in Japanese historiography also faces similar obstacles to Chinese historiography. National issues, political implications and the resistance in Japanese academia to embracing other historiographical traditions can equally explain such a vacuum. In addition, one of the major contributions in the field, *The Great Divergence*, has not been translated into Japanese. When making global history in Japan, as was mentioned above, maritime history and the role of port cities such as Nagasaki are crucial in understanding the process of modernization in Japan and how its economy was integrated into the Pacific region. The galleons that travelled westwards from Acapulco (New Spain) to Manila (the Philippines), connecting south-east Asian, south Chinese and Japanese ports stands out as a key factor in terms of analysing such global market integration in the Pacific.

Thus, the case of the Americas and their historical and geostrategic position needs to be given greater emphasis. In this particular case, the classic analysis by A. Gunder Frank's *Latin America: Underdevelopment or Revolution* (1969) and Wallerstein's (1974) world-system theories that identify core and peripheral economic areas, i.e., those that supply raw materials and those that provide manufactures, should be refreshed with new empirical work and case studies. This could be made by applying social networks analysis and spatial analysis using a Geographic Information System (GIS), identifying social actors and commodities, and observing through the movement of people, goods and technologies how markets were progressively integrated. Such integration is and was prompted not only by the economic stimulus of modern institutions on local economies, but also by a dynamic transcultural interaction (Gipouloux 2011) of merchants and consumers through economic exchanges and trade routes. A very good instance of such a process of transculturation can be found in the Manila–Acapulco route, also called the Nao of China. This trans-Pacific route is an excellent 'laboratory' for a global historian. Traditionally, it has been studied as a round-trade route connecting Manila (the Philippines) and Acapulco (New Spain). In other words, it has been commonly defined, though inaccurately, as an exclusive market of the Spanish Empire. Such a misinterpretation could be also linked to national narratives which ignore that such a route corresponded with global networks of trade and people that integrated Western and Eastern markets. Manila and Acapulco were just one more link in the Pacific area that connected China with the West.

Across continental units, somehow global history has been 'haunted' by national narratives. The practice of global history requires making cross-geographical sections going beyond European, American and Asian nations, as well as disciplines. There is a tendency to observe and/or identify global history with economic history, whereas it is a very interdisciplinary field which requires a constant dialogue with other areas of history and social sciences. This view historiographically opens up a wider perspective for connections on historical phenomena across boundaries, spatialities and temporalities for the understanding of a more complex historical process. Global history is not simply a field or subject—it should also be defined as an approach that complements and challenges other forms of historical analysis. Historical comparisons are undoubtedly attached to the methodological package of global historians to analyse the economic development in the long term and how regions were interconnected. The analysis of the global movement of people, technology and goods is a must in the agenda of the global historian, intertwining socio-economic, political and cultural features. The process of the circulation of human, material and technological capital, which could be defined as 'strange', 'exotic' or 'foreign' and might confront or challenge local traditions and cultures, has been of great importance in the analysis of global historians.

Humanity's history has been one of constant movement, from the nomad tribes of the Near and Middle East to the early modern explorers and expeditioners of the Americas and Asia. For this reason, I argue against the use of unidirectional applications of global history as a concept. Scholars normally identify the first globalization with the overseas ventures of the Vereenigde Oost-Indische Compagnie (V.O.C.), East India Company (E.I.C.), or the Western settlement in China after the Opium Wars. Globalization is a very modern concept which emerged after the Second World War and developed increasingly during the Cold War. The aim of the developed world during this era was to spread new technologies to 'globalize' the farthest corners of the world. These processes began long before the post-modern form of globalization of the twentieth century. This search of prosperity is what Vere Gordon Childe called "the drama of hunger", which set humankind in constant movement:

> the inadequacy of the soil to maintain its occupants, partly owing to their ignorance of the art of renewing the exhausted energies of the earth by the agency of manure, and partly to the constant increase in population. This much truth certainly lay in the assertion, which used to be accepted without demur, that these waves moved westward from some region beyond the banks of the Euphrates and Tigris. The vast tract of territory which extends along the breadth of Asia, running between the 40th and 50th degrees of latitude, as far as the Rhine, and even the Bay of Biscay, has been from immemorial the highway of roving barbarians in search of home. (Childe 1950: 28)

The naïve epitome that global history is a consequence of the modern process of globalization is challenged in this book. Thus, our aim is to contribute to the revitalization of the field of global history in East Asian historiographies, mainly in China and Japan, which has remained 'haunted' by national narratives, as well as its connections moving westwards via the Pacific and Atlantic regions. On the European side, global history has mainly focused on the study of the main economic powers of Europe (core areas) and its colonies, without taking into consideration comparisons among European, American and/or Asian parts, either Chinese or Japanese, which were importantly positioned in larger and continental units fostering the economic links of cores to their hinterlands. Hence, the goal of this project is to escape from locating 'centres', either in European, American or Asian areas. On the contrary, it will observe the world economy as a polycentric system with no dominant place through well-defined case studies using both Asian and Western sources.

The parts and sections of this book are drawn in such polycentric scheme analyzing the importance of the continental and sub-continental units without emphasizing in one dominant area. The big questions and narratives of global history in the chapters of this book not only present the commonly theoretical debates on global history and models of economic growth between East and West, but also present a thorough analysis with historical evidence of concrete regions, whether Asian, European or American, to compare on a global scale the role of peripheral areas in East Asia and Europe in the process of modernization. Why the West (in particular Great Britain and the Netherlands) took off in the eighteenth century and China's economy stagnated or why modern science and capitalism did not emerge in China could be tackled in a more profound fashion. Such big questions and theories on global history are supported and complemented in this book with empirical evidence and new archival findings.

The case studies presented by Richard Von Glahn, Harriet Zurndorfer, Manuel Perez Garcia, Colin Mackerras and Suzuki Hideaki draw attention to the impact of global history in China and Japan. Richard Von Glahn, through the 'silver question', makes a thorough analysis with empirical data (i.e., population, prices, wages and income, standards of living, silver flows and money supply for the first half of the nineteenth century). Harriet Zurdorfer explores Sino–Portuguese relations during the Ming period beyond the general binary analysis

(West and East or China and Europe), paying more attention to how European settlers fitted in and dealt with local communities. Manuel Perez Garcia gives some insights into how global history is penetrating in Chinese academic circles, analysing the case of the introduction of crops of American origin, such as the sweet potato, in China during the Ming period. The chapters by Colin Mackerras and Suzuki Hideaki present a detailed picture on global history in Chinese and Japanese historiographies. Mackerras' rethinking and refreshing of the 'Needham question' explores global history through the development of scientific discoveries in China, making a final reflection as to whether such question is worth asking. Suzuki Hideaki presents the evolution of global history in Japan, which has been linked to maritime studies, in Japanese (as mentioned above) Kaiiki-shi (海域史). In a similar manner to that in Chinese academia, in Japanese scholarship, global history confronts, as a main obstacle, new national narratives.

Suzuki Hideaki's chapter links with section two, focusing on networks and maritime expansion in the region of East Asia in which the works on Japan and China give a full picture from the local to the macro-scale of the big nodes and network systems that connected and integrated China and Japan with South-East Asia, as well as the Pacific and Atlantic regions through the Manila-Acapulco galleon. It is paramount to analyse such trade networks and the role of port cities that fostered such market integration. Gakusho Nakajima, Mihoko Oka and Lucio de Sousa explore in an in-depth manner such big nodes, also paying attention to social and economic agents. Gakusho Nakajima analyses the tributary trade system of the Ming period and proposes that we should talk of a 'tribute and trade system' rather than a 'mutual trade system', hushi (互市), to observe the interactions between private Chinese and foreign merchants. Mihoko Oka explores the maritime trade networks between Japan and South China (mainly Macau) through the role of merchants as main mediators. Oka mentions an important concept in understanding trade relations in Japan with foreigners (mainly Portuguese): (1) *nanban* (南蛮) trade, which means trade with uncivilized peoples of the South of China; and (2) shuinsen (朱印船), which means 'red seal ships' or officially approved ships. With an analysis of socioeconomic agents and networks, Lucio de Sousa examines the role and presence of the Jews in China and Japan and their participation in trade networks that connected Nagasaki with Macau. The role of the *judeo-conversos* in the Atlantic trade accounts is supported by an abundance of material from Spanish and

Portuguese scholarship, but in the case of China and Japan, we still need more studies combining both Western and Eastern sources. This is what Lucio de Sousa provides in his chapter. This part concludes with Agnes Kneitz's chapter, embracing the accounts in previous chapters through Rennell's theories, models of maritime worlds and networks, as well as practices of collecting data and measuring the world navigation system.

Finally, in Part III we move from the Pacific to the Atlantic region, in which the main European powers (chiefly Great Britain and the Netherlands) from the moment of the discovery of the Americas established colonies for the extraction of raw materials and energy resources as one of the main factors of the first Industrial Revolution. The well-known theories on dependency as well as the world-systems theory applied by Wallerstein contributed to set core and peripheral economic areas, in which scholars made a strong division between developed and underdeveloped countries, fostering the idea and focus on Eurocentric approaches. Following this idea, Part III begins with a very illustrative chapter by Anne McCants in which she shows in different academic traditions—the Anglo-Saxon, French and German historiographies—the evolution of global history during the twentieth century, which is linked to research on global trade and consumption. Thus, the development of sub-fields such as the history of consumption, maritime history or material culture shows the robustness of global history over the last 30 years. In this case, we might observe such evolution in European historiographies as French historiography developing the sub-fields of *Société de consommation*, *histoire mondiale* and *histoire du monde*; in the case of German historiography, *Alltagsgeschichte* and *Weltgeschichte*; and in the case of Anglo-Saxon historiography, *global trade*, *global history* and the *consumer revolution*. Likewise, adding the above-mentioned cases of 'Kaiiki-shi' (maritime history) in Japan or agricultural and economic history (the introduction of crops of American origin) in China, we can truly observe and corroborate McCants' suggestions that the development of global history has in recent decades hinged on such sub-fields.

In order to explore the circulation of new commodities, changes in consumer behaviour and the transfer of new technologies, the chapters by Carlos Marichal, Bartolome Yun and Nadia Fernandez stand out as good case studies for a better understanding of the role of the Spanish Empire in the Atlantic and Pacific regions. Carlos Marichal in his chapter analyses both Mexican cochineal, as an essential dye that transformed the textile sector in the early modern period, and local technologies as crucial elements that fostered the rise of global trade. He suggests the importance of further studies on silk commodity chains from China with cochineal commodity chains, originally from colonial Mexico, which over centuries connected Asian with European markets through the Indian Ocean, but also through crossing the Pacific and reaching the Atlantic via the Manila-Acapulco galleons.

It is very important to conceptualize such circulation of goods and technologies according to the geographical delimitation and space. Bartolome Yun outlines the importance of the role of the Spanish Empire in the circulation of technology and technological knowledge during the early modern period, as well as the importance of informal institutions and social networks that regulated the political power and control of knowledge. Such networks and the circulation of books, imprints, engravings and maps were crucial in the circulation of knowledge. Therefore, the institutional framework that regulated such circulation and the political and intellectual elites, which controlled the main institutions, were crucial in efficiently applying such knowledge in order to develop new technologies and foster local economies.

Reducing the scale from the global framework of the Spanish Empire presented by Bartolome Yun to a local perspective—the case of the city of Madrid—we find the contribution of Nadia Fernandez analysing consumer behaviour in this urban area. The tastes and desires for goods that came from afar and colonial trade, involving such items as sugar, Chinese porcelain or other luxury goods, changed over time consumer behaviour in the city of Madrid, one of the largest cities of southern Europe. The transnational dimension of such commodities and the way and form they were accepted and consumed either by a noble from Madrid or a landowner from La Havana was not the same and clearly shows the different connotations of these commodities in the diverse territories of the Spanish Empire.

Part III concludes in a similar fashion to Part II, having as a corollary the chapter by David Pickus, who presents the acceptance, knowledge and degree of implementation of European research and global history in Chinese academia as a sort of new 'commodity' for the new generation of scholars in Chinese universities.

This book seeks to develop the awareness of new approaches in East Asian and Western historiographies by reviewing concepts which commonly have predominated in Western historiography. Such concepts are the different revolutions (industrial, intellectual, social or political revolutions), colonial system, enlightenment or post-modernism, which are quite divergent if we apply them to analyse the process of modernization in the East. However, a 'common global historical project' could be defined through the application of a methodology that compares cross-cultural areas (either Western or Eastern), using a synchronic or diachronic time series, as well as employing and ultimately comparing empirical data.

Applying our energy to this common project among research institutions is a genuine historiographical need—to mediate between the long-lasting confrontation between the hegemonic powers of the West and East. We do not naïvely expect to arrive at a single scholarly consensus or establish a common worldwide model on how to approach global history. But it is more pertinent to promote a debate to open new venues in which important features for implementing and institutionalizing global history, such as scholarly mobility, diversity and internationalization, are firmly rooted, putting aside national characteristics.

Therefore, this volume aims to create a new forum of discussion on how global history has penetrated in Western and Eastern historiographies, provoking an intensive debate among scholars on how to theorize and write history. In addition, it mainly deals with new approaches on the use of empirical data by framing the proper questions and hypotheses, ones that connect both Western and Eastern sources, while building up global narratives within particular case studies. Recent scholarship is reviewing how the field of global history is taking new positions by escaping controversial 'isms', whether Eurocentrism or Sinocentrism, when analysing the diverse models of economic growth of the West and the East. Such a historiographical review also considers that global history is a domain that is not solely related to economic history, as it is an interdisciplinary field, which is related to other historical fields such as social or cultural history, international relations, sociology or economics.

The series of conferences on global history organized by the GHN in China, the first of which was held in Beijing in 2012 at Tsinghua University, followed by another hosted in Beijing at Beihang University and the latest organized at Tokyo University of Foreign Studies in April and June 2015 respectively, is proof of the new historiographical effort to renew the field of global history. The aim is to move the pivotal axis of analysis from national perspectives to a polycentric perspective. Such joint effort in bringing together researchers from different countries has been the milestone of departure to establish and open new venues of global history. The use of Western and Eastern sources in new case studies within a comparative approach enables us to better observe divergences and/or convergences between the East and the West.

Notes

1. The latest works on global history explore and analyse such interconnectivities and the range of comparisons. See Manning 2003; McNeill and McNeill 2004; Northrop 2012; Berg 2013; O'Brien 2013; Perez Garcia 2014; Olstein 2015; Belich et al. 2016; Conrad 2016.
2. The term itself expresses the foreign form, as it does not exist in the Japanese historical tradition. Therefore, instead of using the traditional writing with kanji for global history, the katakana is used to adapt and translate words and terminology, such as global history, from other countries.
3. For this term, we find the same case as for 'gurobaru hisutori' (global history). 'Atarashii sekaishi' (new world history) is a mixed word with kanji (世界史, world history) and hiragana (in Japanese *atarashii* means new).

References

Antony, R. 2014. Maritime Violence and State Formation in Vietnam: Piracy and the Tay Son Rebellion, 1771–1802. In *Persistent Piracy: Maritime Violence and State-Formation in Global Historical Perspective*, eds. S. Amirell and L. Muller, 113–130. Palgrave-Macmillan US.

Belich, J., Darwin, J., Frenz, M., and Wickham, Ch. (eds.). 2016. *The Prospect of Global History*. Oxford: Oxford University Press.

Berg, M. (ed.). 2013. *Writing the History of the Global Challenges for the Twenty-First Century*. Oxford: Oxford University Press.

Childe, Vere Gordon. 1950. *The Dawn of European Civilization*. UK: Routledge & Kegan Paul.

Conrad, S. 2016. *What Is Global History?*. Princeton: Princeton University Press.

Deng, K. and O'Brien, P. 2016. China's GDP Per Capita from the Han Dynasty to Communist Times. *World Econmics*, vol. 17, n. 2, April-June: 79–123.

Frank, A.G. 1969. *Latin America: Underdevelopment or Revolution. Essays on the Development of Underdevelopment and the Immediate Enemy*. New York: Monthly Review Press.

Frank, A.G. 1998. *Re-Orient. Global Economy in the Asian Age*. Berkeley: University of California Press.

Gipouloux, F. 2011. *The Asian Mediterranean: Port Cities and Trading Networks in China, Japan and Southeast Asia, 13th–21st century*. Cheltenham: Edward Elgar Publishing.

Hamashita, T. 1997. The Intra-Regional System in East Asia in Modern Times. In: *Network Power, Japan and Asia*, ed. P.J. Katzenstein. Ithaca and London: Cornell University Press: 113–135.

Haneda, M. 2015. Japanese Perspectives on "Global History". *Asian Review of World Histories* 3:2 (July): 219–234.

Kee-long So, B., and R.H. Myers. 2011. *The Treaty-port Economy in Modern China: Empirical Studies of Institutional Change and Economic Performance*. Berkeley: Institution of East Asian Studies, University of California at Berkeley.

Li, Bozhong. 2000. *Jiāngnán de zǎoqí gōngyèhuà, 1550–1850* [*Early Industrialization in the Yangzi Delta, 1550–1850*]. Beijing: Zhongguo shehui kexue wenxian chubanshe, (first edition).

Li, Longqing. 2000. Embracing a New Framework for Reconstructing World History. *Journal of Central China Normal University* (Humanities and Social Sciences edition) 39, no. 4: 118–122.

Li, Qiang. 2011. Global History: A Representative of Those Reflecting on Occident-Centrism. *China Social Sciences Today*, 9 June.

Li, Qingxin. 2010. *Nanhai I and The Maritime Silk Road*. Beijing: China Intercontinental Press.

Liang, Zhan-jung. 2006. Comparing World History and Global History: A Chinese Scholar's View. *Journal of Capital Normal University* (3): 1–5.

Liu, Beicheng. 2000a. *Báiyín zīběn [Silver Capital]*. Beijing: Central compilation & translation press.

Liu, Beicheng. 2000. The Challenges of Reconstructing World History. *Shixuelilunyanjiu* [Historiography Quarterly] 4: 67–69.

Liu, Xincheng. 2012. The Global View of History in China. *Journal of World History*, Volume 23, Number 3, September, pp. 491–511.

Manning, P. 2003. *Navigating World History: Historians Create a Global Past*. Palgrave Macmillan: US.

McNeill, W.H., and J.R. McNeill. 2004. *The Human Web. A Bird's-Eye View of World History*. New York: Norton.

Northrop, D. 2012. Introduction: the challenge of World History. In *A Companion to World History*, ed. D. Northrop, 1–13. Oxford: Wiley-Blackwell.

O'Brien, P. 2013. Historical Foundations for a Global Perspective on the Emergence of a Western European Regime for the Discovery, Development, and Diffusion of Useful and Reliable Knowledge. *Journal of Global History* 8: 1–24.

Olstein, D. 2015. *Thinking History Globally*. Palgrave Macmillan UK.

Perez Garcia, M. 2014. From Eurocentrism to Sinocentrism: The New Challenges in Global History. *European Journal of Scientific Research* 119 (3): 337–352.

Pomeranz, K. 2000. *The Great Divergence*: China, Europe, and the Making of the Modern World Economy. Princeton: Princeton University Press.

Pomeranz, K. trans. Jiànyún Shi 史建云. 2003. 大分流: 欧洲, 中国及现代世界经济的发展 [Dà fēnliú: Ōuzhōu, zhōngguó jí xiàndài shìjiè jīngjì de fā zhǎn]. 南京: 江苏人民出版社 [Nánjīng: Jiāngsū rénmín chūbǎn shè].

Qian, Chengdan. 2001. Probing into the Idea of 'Global History': An Impression of the 19th Congress of the International Historical Sciences. *Shixue Yuekan* [History Monthly] 2: 145–150.

Wallerstein, I. 1974. *The Modern World-System, vol. I: Capitalist Agriculture and the Origins of the European World-Economy in the Sixteenth Century*. New York: Academic Press.

Wang, Lincong. 2002. A Brief Comment on the "Global View of History". *Shixuelilunyanjiu* [Historiography Quarterly] 3: 100–109.

Wang, Yunlong. 2002. From Modernization to Globalization. *Xuexiyu Tansuo* [Study and Exploration] 3: 121–125.

Wu, Xiaoqun. 2005. Do We Really Need a 'Global View of History'? *Xueshu Yanjiu* [Academic Research] 1: 22–27.

Yu, Pei. 2006. Global History and National Historical Memory. *Shixuelilunyanjiu* [Historiography Quarterly] 1: 18–30.

Open Access This chapter is licensed under the terms of the Creative Commons Attribution 4.0 International License (http://creativecommons.org/licenses/by/4.0/), which permits use, sharing, adaptation, distribution and reproduction in any medium or format, as long as you give appropriate credit to the original author(s) and the source, provide a link to the Creative Commons license and indicate if changes were made.

The images or other third party material in this chapter are included in the chapter's Creative Commons license, unless indicated otherwise in a credit line to the material. If material is not included in the chapter's Creative Commons license and your intended use is not permitted by statutory regulation or exceeds the permitted use, you will need to obtain permission directly from the copyright holder.

PART I

Escaping from National Narratives: The New Global History in China and Japan

This part aims to integrate the big questions with an accurate methodology and historical evidence. Such well-known questions are why modern science and capitalism did not emerge in China or why North-Western Europe (Great Britain and the Netherlands) took off and China got left behind. They were formulated by global historians in order to shed light on the different paths of modern economic growth between China and Europe. Our aim is to refresh such questions with a satisfactory theoretical and methodological framework, presenting empirical evidence through specific case studies.

An issue that deserves further explanation is how such practice of global history is penetrating Chinese academia, which is currently undergoing a new adjustment of its national narrative that ultimately serves to present the uniqueness of the long-lasting Chinese civilization. This is of course due to the current national echoes of the Chinese government policies based on the concept of 'soft power' closely linked with the revision of Chinese culture and history. This can be observed through the presentation in this part of the big questions that can be used to understand the development of modern science and economic growth in China. The main issues to be analysed in this part are: (1) the depression of the Chinese economy, whether or not provoked as cause-effect of the foreign intervention in China in the late eighteenth and early nineteenth centuries; (2) changes in the Chinese economy due to the introduction of overseas commodities; (3) the joint action of foreign merchants with private Chinese traders mainly in the port of Macau and the provinces of Guangdong and Fujian; and (4) how global history challenges national narratives in China and Japan.

Global History, the Role of Scientific Discovery and the 'Needham Question': Europe and China in the Sixteenth to Nineteenth Centuries

Colin Mackerras

1 Introduction

One of the most important and intriguing facts in global history is the dominance that the West established over the rest of the world in terms of scientific discovery and innovation from the sixteenth century onwards. It is not too much to say that this scientific spirit was one of the key factors behind the Industrial Revolution and the growth of the technology that enabled Europe to colonize so much of the world and to assume a position of some degree of domination more or less everywhere. This scientific spirit remains a key feature of the contemporary world, with access to advanced technology among the most important of all levers of power.

C. Mackerras (✉)
Renmin University of China, Beijing, China

C. Mackerras
Griffith University, Brisbane and Gold Coast, Australia

Yet the fact is that civilizations other than the West have developed significant bodies of scientific discovery and thought. In particular, China had developed a body of scientific knowledge before the time of the Mongol invasion of the thirteenth century that placed it well ahead of Europe. The most famous, and probably the most important, scholar to research and disclose the pre-eminence of Chinese science before that time was the British biochemist and Sinologist Joseph Needham (1900–1995), who masterminded and contributed extensively to a multi-volume and multi-authored work entitled *Science and Civilisation in China*.

This chapter aims to explore global scientific history through the prism of what has become known as 'the Needham question'. This can be formulated as follows: why, having been so far ahead of Europe in the Middle Ages, did China fail to produce the scientific revolution that occurred in Europe and in effect was crucial in creating the modern world. Why did 'universally verifiable' science 'commanding universal rational assent' develop 'round the shores of the Mediterranean and the Atlantic, and not in China or any other part of Asia'? (Needham and Wang 1954: 19).

There can be no definitive answer to such a big question, as Needham himself acknowledged in the foreword he wrote for a book that came out five years after he died (Zilsel 2000). Yet it remains an important question and the present chapter argues in favour of regarding scientific development as a major site of global history. It argues in support of Needham's appeal to social and cultural history for an explanation to this major driver of human history. This author stands in awe of a scholar willing and able to probe Chinese science in such detail as a counterpart to that of the West.

It should be added that the centrality of this 'Needham question' is by no means the only way of approaching the development of Chinese science from the sixteenth to the nineteenth centuries. One major study is specifically 'agnostic' about any claims that try 'to explain why China or the Islamic world failed to develop the rigorous mental mind-set of modern science' (Elman 2005: xxv–xxvi). Elman gives a great deal of credit to the European missionaries and others for scientific development in China over those centuries, but also emphasises the maintenance of a specifically Chinese science. In another balanced view, he attacks the pretensions of those who see modern science in China only as the result of Western influence and intervention, but also presents Chinese science as no more than a 'qualified success story' and eschews any 'nationalistic claim' about 'the march of science in contemporary China' (Elman 2005: xxxviii).

2   Joseph Needham and His *Science and Civilisation in China*

There is already an extensive literature on Joseph Needham and his many works (Sivin 2015). A major biochemist and Sinologist, his *Science and Civilisation in China* can claim to be the largest-scale English-language Sinological work since the Second World War that was basically the product of a single guiding mind. He has been honoured as a scientist both by China and his own country, Britain.

As a person, Needham was unconventional. He was a Christian socialist, a nudist and a folk dancer, as well as a scientist. He had a long-term wife, Dorothy Moyle (1896–1987), and a long-term lover, Lu Gwei-djen 鲁桂珍 (1904–1991), as well as other relationships. Both women and Needham lived to advanced ages, and he did not marry Lu Gwei-djen until 1989, that is, after his wife Dorothy had died. All three were distinguished scientists in their own right and his first wife did not oppose his affair with Lu Gwei-djen.

Needham was not only very pro-China, he was also very sympathetic to the Chinese Communist Party. He got involved in the International Science Commission set up by China and North Korea to investigate the charge that the USA was using germ warfare in the Korean War. He believed the evidence produced in favour of this accusation, which later turned out to be false. His reputation suffered seriously as a result. He was blacklisted by the US Department of State and even after this was revoked in the 1970s, he found it difficult to obtain a US visa.[1]

Despite his anti-Americanism, Needham obviously had a very firm foot not only in China but also in the West. Another major point about him is that he straddled both the disciplines of the natural sciences and the humanistic sciences. He was a major historian and Sinologist, as well as an extremely important scientist. This needs to be said because there are scientists who tend to look down on 'those whose careers are not primarily in the sciences', but still want to research the history of science. One scholar who strongly advocates the value of the humanities says that: 'While training in science is a marvellous benefit for the historian of science, it is not a substitute for historical precision' (Elman 2005: xxx). It is not possible to direct any such criticism against Needham.

Needham's great work was first proposed to Cambridge University Press in 1948, and the first volume came out in 1954. The original plan was for seven volumes, but although this schema survived, all except the first three were expanded into multiple parts. As of 2016, twenty-five volumes have been published, the most recent being in 2015,[2] with two volumes still in progress. These two incomplete items will belong among the thirteen planned parts of Volume 5:

> Most of the earlier volumes were written in their entirety by Needham himself, but as time went by he gathered an international team of collaborators, to whom the completion of the project is now entrusted. As the project has broadened, so has the range of questions under investigation. It is now clear that no simple answer to Needham's original question will be possible. The question has opened out into an investigation of the ways in which scientific and technical activity have been linked with the development of Chinese society over the last four millennia.[3]

This gigantic project aimed to reveal the scope and originality of Chinese scientific thinking. 'There can be no doubt', Needham writes, 'that China was, among the ancient civilisations of the Old World, the one which was most isolated from the others. The originality of its characteristic cultural patterns was therefore greater' (Needham and Wang 1954: 156).

3 THE DEVELOPMENT OF SCIENCE AND 'THE NEEDHAM QUESTION'

Although it has received some criticism for being too positive about China, Needham's *Science and Civilisation in China* has been widely admired and praised for opening up new thinking about Chinese science. The well-known Dutch science historian Hendrik Floris Cohen comments that 'for all his idiosyncrasies,' Needham 'was an intellectual giant' (Cohen 2010: 30). Even a scholar prepared to criticize Needham quite severely for putting too great a stress on the 'benevolent, pacific aspects of Chinese culture' (Keightley 1972: 370) concedes that *Science and Civilisation in China* was 'one of the major scholarly enterprises of the [twentieth] century' (Keightley 1972: 367).

Possibly Needham's most important contribution was to suggest that China has a rich history of science. As Cohen has put it (2001: 23): 'Needham had very little time for explaining the absence of a Chinese Scientific Revolution out of some alleged inability of the Chinese to think scientifically.' The whole point of his magnum opus was to prove precisely the reverse.

Yet, the Chinese ability to think scientifically was a point that needed demonstration. The eminent Chinese philosophy historian Fung Yu-lan (Feng Youlan 馮友蘭, 1895–1990) had argued in essence that China did not develop science because China's values standards rendered it redundant. From the time of the Han dynasty (206 BCE–220 CE) onwards, Chinese were more concerned with looking after and influencing humankind than exploring the natural world. Chinese thinkers 'had no need of scientific certainty, because it was themselves that they wished to know; so in the same way they had no need of the power of science, because it was themselves that they wished to conquer' (Fung 1922: 261). Philosophies like Daoism and Buddhism were more concerned with admiring and following nature than controlling or even influencing it. For Fung Yu-lan to say that there was no science in pre-modern China is not to condemn that civilization, but to praise it; it was not that Chinese were incapable of thinking scientifically, it was simply that they did not do so because China had no need for science.

The fact that Needham knew he had found no final answers did not prevent him from speculating and making some pretty definitive statements. In particular, he rejected any suggestion that historical accident was involved. Moreover, he appealed more to economic, environmental, social and cultural factors than to scientific factors (Mackerras 1989: 130).

So, in this chapter we can divide Needham's reasons as to why China failed to produce the scientific revolution, including the factors that may have inhibited the development of Chinese science, into several categories. These include the material factors, such as the physical environment and economic matters, as well as the non-material or spiritual, such as the philosophical and the politico-cultural. Because it is global history we are dealing with and because Needham himself had plenty to say not only about China but also about the West, we shall be exploring some factors that compare and contrast China and Europe.

3.1 *Material Factors: Physical Environment and Economics*

We might begin with an interesting passage comparing Europe and China in one of Needham's main works outside *Science and Civilisation in China*. In it he places heavy emphasis on territory and economy, as well as raising some other issues. He explains Europe's 'built-in quality of instability' by referring to:

> the perennial tradition of independent city-states based on maritime commerce and jostling military aristocrats ruling small areas of land, the exceptional poverty of Europe in the precious metals, the continual desire of Western peoples for commodities which they themselves could not produce (one thinks especially of silk, cotton, spices, tea, porcelain, and lacquer), and the inherently divisive tendencies of alphabetic script, which permitted the growth of numerous warring nations with centrifugal dialects or barbarian languages. By contrast China was a coherent agrarian land-mass, a unified empire since the third century B.C. with an administrative tradition unmatched elsewhere till modern times, endowed with vast riches both mineral, vegetable, and animal, and cemented into one by an infrangible system of ideographic script admirably adapted to her fundamentally monosyllabic language. (Needham 1969: 119)

So, the competition among the European states may actually have *contributed to* innovation and creativity based on curiosity. China's territorial unity, which is often touted as one of the country's major achievements, may have been a factor inhibiting the development of innovation and of science.

Some scholars, notably Karl August Wittfogel (1896–1988), have attached very great importance to the physical environment as a driver of Chinese civilisation. Wittfogel wrote widely on this subject, especially in his 1957 book *Oriental Despotism*, basing much of his argument on Karl Marx's Asiatic mode of production theory.[4] He proposed that China was despotic because of the need for water control, in particular the need to build dykes, prevent flooding and in general control the Yellow River on the great northern plain. The link is that water control on a vast scale requires great organization, which can only be provided by a highly professionalized bureaucracy supervising enormous and subservient supplies of manpower. Wittfogel called this society 'hydraulic' and despised it as changeless and cruel. He summed up the response of people living under this despotism as follows: 'To the demands of total authority common sense recommends one answer: obedience' (Wittfogel 1957: 149).

Needham and Wang (1959) reviewed *Oriental Despotism*. In his review, he attacked Wittfogel for the 'naïve assumption' that Marxism could not develop and that all Marxisms were the same. He denied that China was despotic and criticized Wittfogel for ignoring good features of its civilization, such as the development of science and technology that put it generally ahead of Europe until the fifteenth century. He attacked Wittfogel for reductionism and for regarding the need for water control as the only source of China's bureaucracy.

On the other hand, Needham acknowledged Confucian bureaucracy as an obstacle to scientific development. He also praised China for its ability to control water and regarded this as a potential source of power; for instance, he is on record as saying that the Qin dynasty of the third century BCE built its power very largely 'on extensive irrigation works' (Needham et al. 1971: 227).

Clearly, Needham saw a role for the physical environment in explaining the lack of a scientific breakthrough such as the one that occurred in Europe. He shared some points with Wittfogel, but his overall interpretation had none of the latter's harsh condemnation. Instead, he was appreciative and admiring of Chinese tradition and achievements.

In considering the other main material factor inhibiting Chinese scientific development—the economic—we might also suggest a major comparison with how things happened in Europe. An early but still interesting theory concerning the development of modern science is that of the Austrian pioneer of the sociology of science Edgar Zilsel (1891–1944).

A Jewish Marxist, Zilsel fled Austria after the Anschluss, first to England and then to the USA. The 'Zilsel thesis' argues in essence that science of the kind that led to the modern world could only take firm root when capitalism emerged in Western society: 'The whole process was imbedded in the advance of early capitalistic society, which weakened collective, magical thinking, and belief in authority and which furthered causal rational and quantitative thinking' (Zilsel 2000: 7). He posited cooperation between university scholars and superior artisans, which was possible only from about the beginning of the seventeenth century.

Sharing a Marxist approach with Zilsel, Needham was attracted to his theory, in particular the notion that the breakdown of the gap between the merchant class and intellectuals may have contributed to the rise of modern science. The hierarchy dictated by Confucianism actually put merchants quite low in the social hierarchy and thus prevented the kind of cooperation between the merchant and intellectual classes that occurred in Europe. This would certainly be a factor inhibiting the rise of modern science in China (Cohen 2001: 23–24).

3.2 Non-Material Factors: Philosophy and Culture

One of the great divides in Chinese tradition is that between Confucianism and Daoism. The former came to be dominant and was the philosophy that lay beneath the bureaucracy and controlled the state.

It was an ideology that talked not about abstract thinking so much as society, not about nature but about human affairs and governance. It was heavily rationalist, text-oriented and rigidly conservative. It persisted throughout Chinese history and probably inhibited the spirit of enquiry necessary for a scientific revolution.

One can hardly claim that it saw no innovations, because the Song dynasty (960–1279) spawned a new approach to Confucianism, including new ideas, that is known to history as Neo-Confucianism. However, socially Neo Confucianism also moved Chinese society towards more rigidity in the form of greater oppression of women and stereotypical family relationships. Moreover, the Mongol conquest of the thirteenth century destroyed much of what the Song dynasty created that was new, such as the growth of cities and commercial development.

Needham was harshly critical of Confucianism's role in the development of Chinese science and technology. His views are succinctly expressed in a shortened version of his great work:

> Confucianism has little connection with the history of science. A religion without theologians, it had no one to object to the intrusion of a scientific view on its preserves, but in accordance with the ideas of its founding fathers, it turned its face away from Nature and the investigation of Nature, to concentrate on a millennial interest in human society, and human society alone. (Ronan 1978: 84)

On the other hand, philosophical Daoism was notable for its love of nature and respect for the natural world. It was much more receptive to science and technology than Confucianism, much more open to new ideas and less hidebound and conservative. Daoism remained an influential force throughout Chinese history, but it was always subordinate to Confucianism. Men who had entered the bureaucracy and failed to achieve their career goals or stirred up trouble by disagreeing with powerful people often retreated into Daoist creativity. This is the impulse that led to some of China's most enduring artistic creations, such as the landscape paintings of the Song dynasty.

Needham was very attracted to Daoism and its positive attitude towards nature. In particular, he admired Daoism's most famous doctrine of *wuwei* (inaction). He believed that *wuwei* 'implied learning from Nature by observation' (Ronan 1978: 98).

Daoism raises other questions. A crucial one is whether humankind *ought to* try and conquer nature or cooperate with it, and *wuwei* might imply the latter. Modern science puts the emphasis on using the natural world by recognizing the law of nature; it relies on practical experiment, evidence and the natural law. On the other hand, science also wants to conquer nature in the interests of humankind. Traditional Daoist thinking in China would imply opposition to the extent of interference with nature that the modern world has produced.

Some scholars have contested Needham's excessive emphasis on Daoism as a motor for scientific development in China. They point out that Buddhism and even Neo-Confucianism have elements that absorb observation of the natural world, with ideas on nature that approached contributing to science. Ho Peng Yoke (1926–2014), the distinguished historian of Chinese science who was for a decade the honorary director of the Needham Research Institute, refers to the main Neo-Confucianists as 'philosophers of science' but 'not scientists' (Ho 2005: 180). He describes a conference held in Cambridge shortly before Needham's death and attended by many distinguished scholars, at which the theme was whether Daoism was the only philosophical stream contributing to Chinese science, with most contributors adopting a negative position (Ho 2005: 196–197). To be fair, Needham himself was clearly impressed with Chinese cosmology, which draws not only on Daoism but also on other philosophical strains. He is on record as characterizing the Chinese worldview as seeing a 'harmonious co-operation of all beings … because they were all parts in a hierarchy that formed a cosmic pattern' (Ronan 1978: 306).

Earlier we noted the importance of Confucian bureaucracy in Chinese history, as well as the connection with the physical environment and Confucian philosophy. The state was extremely powerful in dynastic China, with the emperor and his mandarins holding considerably more power than was the case in Europe. Perhaps the Confucian bureaucratic state was just a bit *too* powerful, to the exclusion of other sources of influence that might have made for a wider variety of creative initiatives. Perhaps Alexis de Tocqueville (1805–1859) was right when he famously remarked that despotism makes people look 'coldly on one another: it freezes their souls' (de Tocqueville 2010: ix).

A social connection can also be found in the main way in which men were chosen for entry into the bureaucracy that ran this authoritarian state. This was a complex system of examinations, which was based on the Chinese classics and involved much more emphasis on rote-learning than on analysis. The examinations bestowed enormous social status on those who were able to pass them and are relevant to China's failure to produce a scientific revolution in several ways.

Two of these deserve emphasis. One is that the examinations exercised a stultifying impact on the educated elite. This meant that the most intelligent and educated people within society failed to be innovative because the spirit of creation contributed nothing to their chances of doing well in society. It is not that they were unable to analyse, but that they were never given the chance to do so. Second, the sons of the merchant classes tried to raise themselves in society not by increasing their wealth, but by attempting to enter the bureaucracy through passing the examinations. The very power that proved so crucial to the development of science in Europe was stifled in China.

We might add another social phenomenon in passing. The examinations were open only to men and not to women. About half of society was never given the chance to contribute. One cannot put too much emphasis on this factor, because it applied everywhere in those days, not merely in China. What we *can* perhaps claim is that women were considerably more oppressed in China than in Europe and were kept even more firmly out of the ranks of those who might contribute intellectually to society.

In the passage where Needham comments on the difference between the physical environments of Europe and China, we noticed in passing a reference to language, especially script. A major scholar to see the scientific spirit as lacking in pre-modern China was the eminent American Sinologist Derk Bodde (1909–2003). Among the many factors that he believed inhibited the development of scientific thinking was a written language ill-adapted to the expression of scientific ideas (Bodde 1991: 133). Interestingly enough, Bodde's 1991 book was actually the result of three years in Cambridge working with Joseph Needham (Le Blanc 2006: 164). Needham was generally much less interested in this factor than Bodde and even came later on to discard it as irrelevant (Cohen 2001: 22). In the light of Needham's exposition of so many scientific ideas expressed in Chinese, my own view is that to discard Chinese language as ill-adapted to the expression of scientific ideas is going too far.

4 Is the Needham Question Worth Asking?

The Needham question has been criticized as being excessively negative. To ask why something did *not* happen in a particular country may be less interesting than asking why it *did* happen. This would mean that we should not ask the question why modern science *did not* emerge in China, but rather why it *did* do so in Europe.

This is a reasonable formulation. However, there are grounds for supporting the validity of the Needham question. Cohen writes (1994: 381) that, in pragmatic terms, knowledge of non-Western science would have been very much smaller without Needham's work: 'After all, Joseph Needham's *Science and Civilisation in China* owes both its origin and the guiding thread holding its many tomes together to the confident expectation that sensible answers can be given to this very question.'

All this does is to tell us what we would have missed had the question not been asked. It does not really lend academic validity to posing the question. However, my own view is that the question is far from irrelevant in academic terms. This is because Needham posed it in the context of China having been a long way ahead of Europe until the sixteenth century, when one might have expected that the great breakthrough that led to modern science could readily have occurred in China.

Another relevance of the Needham question is to ask not so much why China failed, but why no other culture joined effectively in the pursuits of this science for so long. After all, it was centuries after the scientific revolution before China, or indeed other cultures, really joined in the scientific advance. As one scholar notes, 'the Needham question is not about an exercise in what-if history, but it's about favorable cultural infrastructure for science' (Gorelik 2012).

And, from the point of view of the present chapter, it is perhaps just as important to note that Needham raises questions of the utmost importance for global history. As we have seen above, Needham and those who discuss him make constant comparisons between China and Europe, comparisons that involve not only science and technology but also the nature of the physical environment and economic history, as well as philosophy and society.

5 Conclusion

The Needham question is essentially too big to answer. However, I think the tentative suggestions that Needham himself raised contain a lot of sense. In particular, I doubt very much indeed that there is anything essential or 'genetic' in Chinese civilization or people that would make the development of modern science impossible in China. Also, I see a great deal of sense in asking whether cultural, social, economic and political circumstances affect phenomena like the development of science and its use for practical purposes. The question why developments took place at particular historical stages or why they did *not* take place at others is important and definitely worth further research.

We live in the shadow of modern science and it has served human development well on the whole. On the other hand, now we are entering the post-modern world, it may be useful to rethink the overall patterns of modern science. Can modern science help us cope with the new problems of environmental deterioration? At the World Conference on Science, held in Budapest in 1999, the Chinese scholar Liu Dun from the Chinese Academy of Social Sciences posed the question in the following way:

> Can people really find a way of keeping harmony between mankind and nature, science and society, industrial development and a healthy ecological environment, global economic integration and cultural diversity? This is a crucial question for mankind in the new century. In this sense, the 'Needham question' will continue to evoke divergent responses from different parts of the world; and of course, its significance will extend far beyond the more specific matter of science and China.

What becomes obvious is that 'the Needham question' retains global relevance and is likely to do so for the foreseeable future. The relationship between science and modernity still matters, both in China and globally. Science will be able in major ways to help humankind into the indefinite future.

Notes

1. For a well-known and comprehensive biography of Needham, see Winchester (2008).
2. Volume 6, Part 4: Métailie 2015.

3. See Needham's biography on the website of the Needham Research Institute: 'Joseph Needham, 1900–1995,' http://www.nri.org.uk/joseph.html.
4. China is rarely central to Marx's arguments. The 'Asiatic mode' relies more on India than China. Marx believed that, due to the 'climate and territorial conditions, especially the vast tracts of desert' in India, the despotic government must carry out public works, organizing 'artificial irrigation by canals and waterworks,' which form the 'basis of Oriental agriculture' ('The British Rule in India' in Marx and Engels 1969–1970: 489). For a full-length study of the Asiatic mode of production, see Sawer (1977).

References

Bodde, Derk. 1991. *Chinese Thought, Science, and Society: The Intellectual and Social Background of Science and Technology in Pre-Modern China*. Honolulu: University of Hawaii Press.

Cohen, Hendrik Floris. 1994. *The Scientific Revolution, A Historiographical Inquiry*. Chicago: The University of Chicago Press.

———. 2001. Joseph Needham's Grand Question, and How to Make It Productive for Our Understanding of the Scientific Revolution. In *Science and Technology in East Asia, Vol. 9, The Legacy of Joseph Needham*, ed. A. Arrault and C. Jami, 21–31. Turnhout: Brepols.

———. 2010. *How Modern Science Came into the World Four Civilizations, One 17th-Century Breakthrough*. Amsterdam: Amsterdam University Press.

De Tocqueville, Alexis. Trans. John Bonner. 2010. *The Old Regime and the French Revolution*. Mineola, New York: Dover Publications.

Elman, Benjamin A. 2005. *On Their Own Terms: Science in China, 1550–1900*. Cambridge, MA: Harvard University Press.

Fung, Yu-lan. 1922. Why China has no Science—An Interpretation of the History and Consequences of Chinese Philosophy. *International Journal of Ethics* 32 (3): 237–263.

Gorelik, Gennady. 2012. How the Modern Physics was Invented in the 17th Century, Part 1: The Needham Question. *Scientific American*, 6 April, web version. http://blogs.scientificamerican.com/guest-blog/how-the-modern-physics-was-invented-in-the-17th-century-part-1-the-needham-question/. Accessed 12 June 2016.

Ho, Peng Yoke. 2005. *Reminiscence of a Roving Scholar: Science, Humanities and Joseph Needham*. Singapore: World Scientific.

Keightley, David N. 1972. 'Benefit of Water': The Approach of Joseph Needham. *Journal of Asian Studies* 31 (2): 367–371.

Le Blanc, Charles. 2006. Derk Bodde. *Proceedings of the American Philosophical Society*, 150 (1) March: 161–165.

Liu, Dun. 1999. A New Survey of the Needham Question. Paper delivered at the World Conference on Science, Budapest, September, web version at http://wenku.baidu.com/view/6b87585077232f60ddcca1f5.html?from=rec&pos=0&weight=1. Accessed 19 June 2014.

Mackerras, Colin. 1989. *Western Images of China*. Hong Kong: Oxford University Press.

Marx, Karl, and F. Engels. 1969–1970. *Selected Works*, 3 vols. Moscow: Progress Publishers.

Métailie, Georges. 2015. *Biology and Biological Technologies: Traditional Botany: An Ethnobotanical Approach*. In *Science and Civilisation in China*, vol. 6, Part 4, ed. Joseph Needham. Cambridge: Cambridge University Press.

Needham, Joseph, and Ling Wang. 1954. *Science and Civilisation in China, Volume I, Introductory Orientations*. Cambridge: Cambridge University Press.

———. 1959. Review of K. A. Wittfogel's *Oriental Despotism*. *Science and Society* 33 (1): 58–65.

———. 1969. *The Grand Titration. Science and Society in East and West*. London: Allen & Unwin.

——— et al. 1971. *Science and Civilisation in China, Volume IV, Physics and Physical Technology, Part 3, Civil Engineering and Nautics*. Cambridge: Cambridge University Press.

Needham Research Institute. Joseph Needham, 1900–1995. http://www.nri.org.uk/joseph.html.

Ronan, Colin A. 1978. *The Shorter Science and Civilisation in China Volume I*. Cambridge: Cambridge University Press.

Sawer, Marian. 1977. *Marxism and the Question of the Asiatic Mode of Production*. The Hague: Martinus Nijhoff.

Sivin, Nathan. 2015. The Needham Question. *Oxford Bibliographies. An online bibliography*. doi:10.1093/OBO/9780199920082-0006. New York: Oxford University Press.

Winchester, Simon. 2008. *The Man Who Loved China: The Fantastic Story of the Eccentric Scientist Who Unlocked the Mysteries of the Middle Kingdom*. New York: HarperCollins.

Wittfogel, Karl A. 1957. *Oriental Despotism: A Comparative Study of Total Power*. New Haven: Yale University Press.

Zilsel, Edgar. 2000. *The Social Origins of Modern Science. Boston Studies in the Philosophy of Science*, vol. 200. Dordrecht: Kluwer Academic Publishers.

Open Access This chapter is licensed under the terms of the Creative Commons Attribution 4.0 International License (http://creativecommons.org/licenses/by/4.0/), which permits use, sharing, adaptation, distribution and reproduction in any medium or format, as long as you give appropriate credit to the original author(s) and the source, provide a link to the Creative Commons license and indicate if changes were made.

The images or other third party material in this chapter are included in the chapter's Creative Commons license, unless indicated otherwise in a credit line to the material. If material is not included in the chapter's Creative Commons license and your intended use is not permitted by statutory regulation or exceeds the permitted use, you will need to obtain permission directly from the copyright holder.

RETRACTED CHAPTER: Encounter and Coexistence: Portugal and Ming China 1511–1610: Rethinking the Dynamics of a Century of Global–Local Relations

Harriet Zurndorfer

The editor(s) and author have retracted this chapter because the editors and publishers were unable to obtain the required copyright consent for publication. The editors and the author have agreed to this retraction.

RETRACTED CHAPTER

RETRACTED CHAPTER

RETRACTED CHAPTER

RETRACTED CHAPTER

RETRACTED CHAPTER

RETRACTED CHAPTER

RETRACTED CHAPTER

RETRACTED CHAPTER

RETRACTED CHAPTER

RETRACTED CHAPTER

RETRACTED CHAPTER

RETRACTED CHAPTER

RETRACTED CHAPTER

RETRACTED CHAPTER

RETRACTED CHAPTER

Challenging National Narratives: On the Origins of Sweet Potato in China as Global Commodity During the Early Modern Period

Manuel Perez Garcia

This research has been sponsored and financially supported by the GECEM ('Global Encounters between China and Europe: Trade Networks, Consumption and Cultural Exchanges in Macau and Marseille, 1680–1840') project hosted by the Pablo de Olavide University, UPO (Seville, Spain). The GECEM project is funded by the ERC (European Research Council)-Starting Grant, under the European Union's Horizon 2020 Research and Innovation Programme, ref. 679371, http://www.gecem.eu. The P.I. (Principal Investigator) is Professor Manuel Perez Garcia (Distinguished Researcher at UPO). I am grateful to comments and suggestions on the earliest version of this chapter by Professor Harriet Zurndorfer (Leiden University), who are outstanding specialists in the field of East Asian and Chinese Studies. Any mistakes and errors in this chapter are under author's responsibility.

M. Perez Garcia (✉)
Shanghai Jiao Tong University, Shanghai, China

© The Author(s) 2018
M. Perez Garcia and L. de Sousa (eds.), *Global History and New Polycentric Approaches*, Palgrave Studies in Comparative Global History, https://doi.org/10.1007/978-981-10-4053-5_4

1 Introduction

The introduction of American cereal crops is probably one of the most important events in China's agricultural history, having a great effect on the agriculture production, national life (He Bingdi 1979), the transformation of consumer behaviour and, to some extent, the nationalization of consumption. The sweet potato (*Ipomoea Batatas L.*), in Chinese gānshǔ 甘薯, is a staple food crop for ancient Chinese society. Today it still plays an important role in Chinese daily life, as well as guaranteeing national food security. Sweet potato and other crops from American origin such as corn (yùmǐ 玉米), potato (shǔ 薯), chili (làjiāo 辣椒) and dragon fruit or pitalla (huǒlóng guǒ 火龙果) were introduced through the Manila-Acapulco galleons in the last phase of Ming dynasty, transforming the Chinese economy, improving cultivation techniques and forming an important part of the peasant-farmer's basket of crops (Marks 1998). The analysis and impact on the Chinese economy of such crops—in this chapter the focus is on the case of sweet potato—might shed light to the debate of the great divergence and the question posed by Pomeranz (2000) and Bin Wong (1997) on what were the forces that prevent China to escape from Malthusian constraints. As we can see in the data provided in this chapter, the rise in consumption of crops such as sweet potato contributed to the rapid increase of the Chinese population. This is an important factor in comprehending the economic transformation of China during the last period of the Ming dynasty, as well as the Qing dynasty.

In addition, another important dimension of the analysis is the nationalization of these American crops that entered China. The current debate in Chinese academia as to whether sweet potato is indigenous to China or from American origin is notable proof of such a process of nationalization that Chinese historiography during recent years has attempted to reinforce within a solid national narrative. 'There is nothing we don't have that we need from you'—this statement was made by Emperor Qianglong to Lord Maccartney during his mission to China in 1792–1793, whose aim was to show to Western powers, mainly England, the self-sufficiency of the Chinese economy (Waley-Cohen 1993; Berg 2006).

The powerful meaning of such an affirmation still echoes nowadays in Chinese academia within the re-affirmation of the long-standing history and cultural roots of Chinese civilization, which attempts to re-affirm its uniqueness. For this reason, the main aim of this chapter is to analyse the origins, channels of diffusion, distribution and impact of the sweet potato in Chinese economy by making an overview of Chinese historiography to observe how this topic has been analysed. Thus, it is important to comprehend how this subject has evolved since the early days of the foundation of the People's Republic of China (PRC) and whether the studies on sweet potato in the field of economic history has been framed as a new national narrative. A survey has been made in the main academic database of China, CNKI (China National Knowledge Infrastructure)[1] and Chaoxing,[2] from 1958 to 2015. It is acknowledged that the search is as comprehensive as the material databases provided and inevitably the author's own judgement is reflected in this literature review due to the current constraints in terms of accessing original Chinese sources, and the obvious limits of the research on the topic due to political pressures in China during the second half of the twentieth century until today.

The analysis of the introduction of global commodities of American origin in China—in this case the origins and distribution of sweet potato—represents a valuable example of how global history is penetrating into Chinese academic circles and how it is implemented conceptually and methodologically. Such an example might illustrate the real challenges of global history mainly in an academic context very much influenced by political and ideological constraints, in which the role of history is certainly to foster the new patriotic and national effervescence and to maintain the unification of the diverse population of China (which comprises around 55 ethnic minorities). The major aim is therefore to present the uniqueness of Chinese civilization and history. This is the main objective of the current neo-Confucian policies, from which the field of social sciences and humanities is not absent (Huang and Gove 2012; Tu 1998). The form of writing history—we might say the patriotic historicism—reflects such political and ideological practices. An apparently irrelevant topic—for example, the study of the introduction of new agricultural crops of American origin in China, such as sweet potato, chili or potato—is not as trivial as we might believe. Certainly, as will be seen in the following pages, a process of 'nationalization of consumption' or 'nationalizing global history' can be demonstrated in the way in which an important group of Chinese scholars believe that sweet potato is indigenous to China.

Therefore, Chinese academic circles, the traditional Marxist school of China has a strong influence in presenting history to the general and non-academic audience and the public consciousness (Liu Shuang 2002; Qian Chengdan 2001). This makes difficult to put global history in practice (Northrop 2012) since the main challenge and obstacle is to overcome such nationalistic and patriotic myopias (Yu Pei 2006; Wu Xiaoqun 2005). For real practitioners of global history, the confrontation of such ideological and political apparatus entails some methodological problems, since the lack of infrastructure and an international academic environment prevents the creation of a core curriculum, courses, seminars and workshops by which global history could be deeply discussed methodologically and theoretically (An Changchun 1993; Liang Zhan-Jun 2006; Liu Beicheng 2000). A pedagogical turn is more than necessary—in other words, making a public pedagogical function to bring about an academic consciousness to institutionalize global history by which internationalization, mobility and diversity should be firmly rooted at the department, faculty and university levels.

2   Towards a New National Narrative: The Evolution on Studies of Sweet Potato in Chinese Historiography

For the overview of the Chinese research on the introduction and distribution of sweet potato in China, the Chaoxing and CNKI databases have been employed, searching keywords such as fānshǔ (番薯), gānshǔ (甘薯), hóngshǔ (红薯), chuán rù (传入), which means introduction of sweet potato, to analyse the early origins of sweet potato. The research has been completed and limited to the scarce articles and journals related to the topic. The total number of journal articles is 168 (see Fig. 1). All retrieved articles have been examined to find those that focused particularly on the introduction and distribution of sweet potato in the Ming and Qing dynasties. The total number for the literature review related to the economic and agricultural history of China is 31, and each of these has been fully reviewed.

Some academic circles have also shown a continuous solicitude for the origins of sweet potato in China since the establishment of the PRC, with a relatively stable number of academic articles and even several research milestones (Fig. 1). Researchers have come to recognize the importance of the introduction of American cereal crops in China. Three major research phases can be established for this topic.

The first phase is from 1949 to 1966, starting with Hu Xiwen 胡锡文 (1958), who conducted a relatively complete discussion about the origin, distribution and cultivation techniques of sweet potato based on the agricultural books from the Ming and Qing dynasties and zhōngguó dìfāng zhì 中国地方志—Local Gazetteers of China. Thereafter, notable articles, which were published successively on material culture and the introduction and

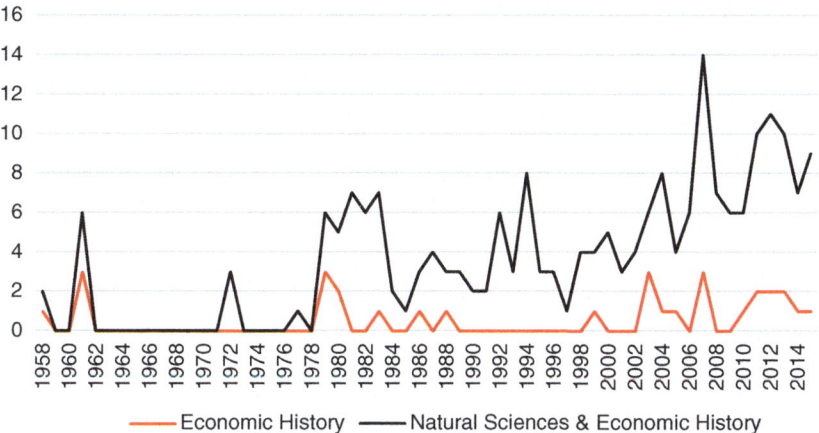

Fig. 1 The trend of academic articles on the research of the introduction of sweet potato (1958–2015). *Source* http://ss.zhizhen.com/s.do?sw=番薯+传入&go=q

origins of sweet potato by Wang Jiaqi 王家琦 (1961), Xia Nai 夏鼐 (1961) and Wu Deduo 吴德铎 (1961), stirred up a debate about whether sweet potato is indigenous to China. However, the analysis of this research in this phase was still in its early stages. It did not provide enough in-depth exploration, and the field of research and the number of articles was also limited.

The second phase is from 1966 to 1978. The whole of Chinese academia became bogged down because of some obvious political factors, due to the negative effects of the Cultural Revolution, and the research on sweet potato also declined without any further progress being made. The third phase started in 1978 and flourished in the 1980s with more representative publications on the introduction and distribution of American crops (mainly corn, potato and sweet potato) in China and their influence in the economy; consequently, research by He Bingdi 何炳棣 (1979),[3] Chen Shuping 陈树平 (1980), Guo Songyi 郭松义 (1986) and Cao Shuji 曹树基 (1988) stood out. This new type of analysis contributed to some improvement in terms of the quality and results in the research. By the 1990s, researchers were focusing on the cereal crops' overall influence on the whole of society with multi-angle and multi-level considerations, which was shown in the works of Min Zongdian 闵宗殿 (1991), Zhang Jian 张箭 (2001), Lan Yong 蓝勇

(2001) and Li Yingfa 李映发 (2003). From the first phase until today, scholars have further studied the introduction of American crops in China providing more historical evidence. However, academic debates are still ongoing on some important problems and limits in the research. This chapter briefly reviews the academic research in this field with the aim of first introducing the existing results and debates of four perspectives of the primary research and then concluding with a discussion for further studies.

Debin Ma has made a great contribution in terms of reviewing the evolution on economic studies and models of economic growth in Chinese academic circles, mainly from the second half of the twentieth century until now (Ma 2004a, b). Ma's work offers a major revisionist thesis on economic growth in China for the eighteenth and nineteenth centuries, incorporating within the analysis traditional social and political institutions in order to understand the path of long-term economic growth or stagnation in China.

As can be observed in Fig. 1 and as attested to by Debin Ma (2004a), in the 1980s, studies on Chinese economic history reached a more mature phase. This was a period of recovery and new intellectual blossom after the shock of the Cultural Revolution (Xu Dixin and Wu Chengming 1993). Such a period of openness was also evidenced through a renewed interest by several overseas scholars in the study of the uniqueness and evolution of long-term economic growth in China. This opened the door for the California School, several scholars specializing in the Chinese economy mainly led by Pomeranz, Blaut, Lee, Goody, Marks, Bin Wong and Von Glahn, among others (Vries 2010), centering the debate on the revisionist thesis on the economic growth of China during the eighteenth century. However, as Debin Ma recalled in his paper (Ma 2004a: 260), such debates generally took place outside China. Even though the 1980s saw a relaxation in the control over scholarly works and intellectuals, the constraints within Chinese academia were still rigid. For this reason, rather than focusing on the evolution of Chinese studies in general,[4] the pioneering works being produced by overseas scholars, this chapter centres more on the analysis of the evolution of studies on sweet potato in Chinese historiography. The field of humanities and history has been traditionally relegated to a secondary position in Chinese society. However, in recent years we have witnessed a renaissance in the area of historical studies, whose major purpose is to follow mainstream and government policies. Such policies emphasize the implementation of the concept of 'soft power' and culture to present in the international arena the long-lasting and unique Chinese civilization. A new national history (or histories) in China has gained new ground, an example of this are the current projects of the Chinese government on the New Silk Road, referred to as 'One Belt, One Road' yīdài yīlù 一带一路. Such a project aims not only to develop investments and infrastructures, but also to promote Chinese culture in line with Chinese 'soft power' policies.

Revisionist theories on China's long-term stagnation, mainly published in Chinese by Li Bozhong, argue that the obsession in searching 'sprouts of capitalism' in China, by which the European exceptionalism and economic model applied to China might be observed, has misled the analysis of the Chinese economy (Li Bozhong 1998). I agree with Li's (1998) explanation mentioning that such an obsession could be explained by 'a profound inferiority complex, qíngjié (情结), developed in the Chinese public psyche from China's perceived backwardness relative to the West since the mid-nineteenth century' (Li Bozhong 2002). The perception of Western aggression in China has contributed to perpetuating in the Chinese public psyche the idea of blaming Westerners for the failure to modernize the country. Such perception mainly took place after the Opium Wars and the failures of China to modernize and internationalize the country in the same way than Japan did during the Meiji Restoration by successfully maintaining its traditional East Asian essence. The Tongzhi Restoration in China failed to fully implement its reforms (Westad 2012). The imposition of unfair treaties and local uprisings from northern to southern regions, provoking disunity and instability in the country from the nineteenth to the twentieth centuries, contributed to forming a nationalist narrative. Such patriotic schemes took form following the May Fourth Movement of 1919, in which we find for the first time the modern use of China as a national concept. Today this national renaissance can be observed through Xi Jinping's policy of the 'Chinese Dream', zhōngguó mèng 中国梦, which has notable echoes in academic circles.

Such perceptions, framed by an obvious national and patriotic mindset, were reinforced in the years after the foundation in 1949 of the PRC through two major periods of great disaster and economic instability: the Great Leap Forward (1958–1960) and the Cultural Revolution (1966–1976). These years form the benchmark of the CCP consolidation, political control and repression of intellectuals (Fairbank and Goldman 2006: 343). This obviously created the psychological ground regarding any intellectual form of 'Western characteristics' as potentially damaging for the nation. Some Chinese intellectual circles, through overseas experiences, have shaken off such a traditional mentality. This mindset, with some nuances, still exists today in Chinese academia and its own road to engaging internationalization within 'Chinese characteristics', zhōngguó tèsè 中国特色 (Li Wang 2014). This gives some insights into observing the penetration of global history in China at two levels: (1) totally ignoring the field, not repressing or banning it explicitly as in past times, but using other levels of repression, such as not funding projects on global history and relegating the field to a marginal level; or (2) in relation to those who pay attention to global history are hugely criticized by the Chinese Marxist School. Traditional Marxists of China see the field of global history as 'neo-colonialist strategy' that can potentially contaminate the meaning, concept and narrative of Chinese history and civilization. For this reason, global history is constantly transformed and manipulated within a nationalistic agenda (Wang Yunlong 2002: 121).

Such preconceptions and theoretical frameworks might give us some clues as to why studies and analysis within a clear global perspective have been transformed within a national narrative. This is the case for the analysis of circulation and diffusion of overseas commodities such as the introduction of agricultural crops of American origin to China, and in particular the case of sweet potato. Analysis of the period from the 1950s to the 1970s emphasizes the fact that such crops are indigenous to China. New narratives follow this pattern, stressing the importance of national consumption through a process of nationalizing overseas commodities such as sweet potato, which contributed from dynastic times up to the present day to the development of the Chinese national economy and agriculture.

3   The Origin of Sweet Potato in China

Generally, academia acknowledges that sweet potato was introduced to China under the Ming dynasty. However, opinions were divided about whether sweet potato was indigenous to China before the introduction and whether the gānshǔ (甘薯) in the ancient books is same as sweet potato. Most scholars (Ding Ying 1928; Hu Xiwen 1958; Liang Jiamian 1980; Cao Ling 2003) regard them as different species; sweet potato was introduced from America in a relatively short time. On the contrary, some researchers (Wang Jiaqi 1961; Zhou Yuanhe 1983) insisted that they are the same.

For those who believe that sweet potato is indigenous, the ancient books are the most important source. Wang Jiaqi (1961) held the opinion that China had historical evidence about sweet potato even before the Ming dynasty and that the earliest source was in Yangfu's *The Yiwu Zhi* (异物志, literally, Record of Foreign Matters) in the Eastern Han dynasty and in Jihan's *The Nanfang Caomu Zhuang* (南方草木状, literally, *Plants of the Southern Regions*). The *Yiwu Zhi* said: "*The sweet potato is like taro, and its flesh is white as fat… The southern people regarded them as rice.*" In *Nanfang Caomu Zhuang*, it is clearer that: "*The sweet potato tastes like Dioscorea Opposita.*" These records do not only name it as "*sweet potato*", but also provide an unambiguous description of its shape, size, feature, planting and harvesting, which proved that was not recorded as *"Dioscorea Opposita"*. Zhou Yuanhe (1983) carried out a similar analysis and inferred that sweet potato enjoyed a long history in China, even back to the Han and Jin dynasties. Yuanhe (1983) mentioned that during the Jin dynasty some improvements were introduced for the cultivation of this crop. This is naturally the literature that, mainly from the 1960s onwards, echoing the political mainstream prompted by the Cultural Revolution movement, tended to build a national narrative in terms of historical analysis.

Nevertheless, in recent decades within the framework of the period of political openness, scholarship embraced new theories and, therefore, more evidence seems to support the opinion that sweet potato was introduced to China from overseas. The two strongest pieces of supporting evidence for this are from modern science and the ancient Chinese scholar Xu Guangqi 徐光启 (1562–1633). At the beginning of the seventeenth century, Xu returned to his hometown, Shanghai, and, as Needham suggested (1984), he experimented with Western techniques of irrigation to cultivate sweet potato. The scientists found wild relatives of sweet potato in Mexico and Guatemala, which had been crops as early as 3000 BCE. In the 1960s, some root block relics of sweet potato were discovered in Peru (Zheng Nan 2013). This case demonstrates that the origins of sweet potato is from the New World. In addition, Xu Guangqi, the pioneer of promoting the planting of sweet potato in China, made a scientific summary that *"there are two kinds of potato (shu), one is the Dioscorea fordii Prain et Burk (mountain potato) which is indigenous in Guangdong and Fujian, the other one is the Ipomoea batatas (sweet potato), which is introduced from overseas"*.

Based on irrefutable evidence, most scholars tend to support the position that sweet potato was not indigenous to China, but was introduced under the Ming dynasty. However, some disputes on its origin remain, which is important for further research and discussion (Fig. 2).

3.1 Introduction: The Timing and Route of Sweet Potato

The knowledge of the Americas in China, through travellers, seafarers, stories or myths describing the first contacts with the New World, more specifically New Spain (Mexico), was casual and without any delimited plan for a conquest, as was the case for the European enterprise towards the Americas. Despite the possible introduction of Chinese material culture and contacts in the Americas before the arrival of Columbus, this does not mean that there was a 'Chinese discovery' of the Americas. It was through the Manila-Acapulco galleons that knowledge and communication between both continents was stimulated through the circulation and introduction of new commodities such as sweet potato, among others. These accounts provide evidence that sweet potato was introduced in China at the end of the Ming dynasty in 1594 (Goodrich 1937). In fact, consciously or unconsciously, Chinese scholarship has acknowledged 1594 as the year of the introduction of sweet potato in China following the suggestions made in the pioneering work of Goodrich (1937). Goodrich also suggested that sweet potato likely entered China from the island of Luzon, Malaysia or the South Seas. However, he did not give much empirical evidence to prove this (Goodrich 1937). Having this research as a point of departure, Fujian (福建) and Guangdong (广东) provinces have been widely accepted as the main areas where crops of American origin, such as sweet potato, entered China.

There is unanimity in the opinion that sweet potato was brought into Fujian (福建) territory through maritime trade. A re-examination of this theory through Fujian (福建) and Yunnan (云南) historical sources suggests that there was an early introduction of sweet potato via the Yunnan (云南) region (Ping-Ti Ho 1955). One of the major reasons why the year of 1594 has been widely recognized as the year of the introduction of sweet potato in China is because a famine took place that year. Therefore, this crop attracted the attention of political authorities and the governor of Fujian (福建). The governor distributed pamphlets on methods for extensive cultivation to eradicate famine (Ping-Ti Ho 1955). Consequently, in early scholarly research of the twentieth century

CHALLENGING NATIONAL NARRATIVES: ON THE ORIGINS ... 63

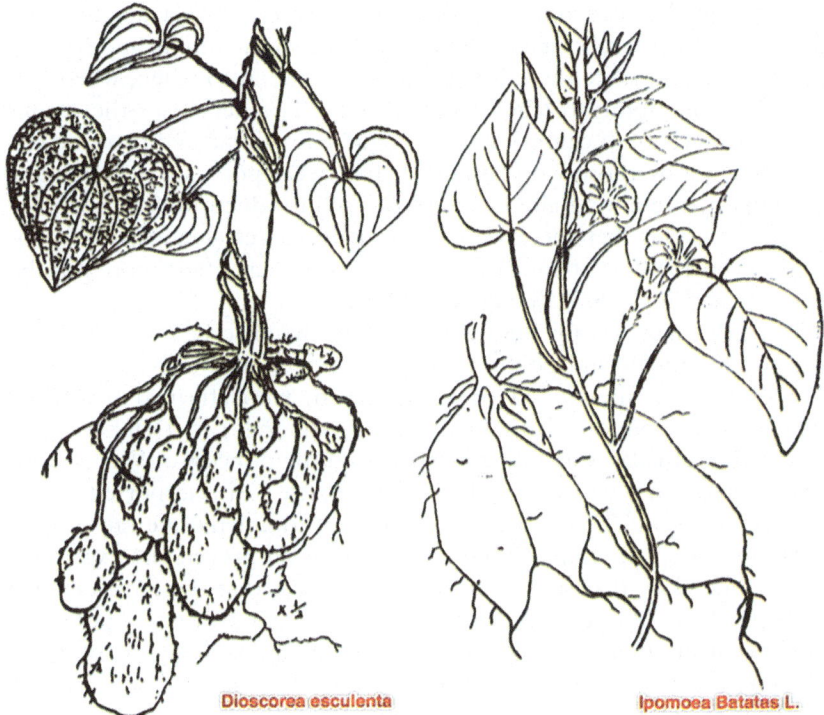

Fig. 2 Two kinds of potato: Dioscorea Esculenta and Ipomoea Batatas. *Source* Liang Jiamian, Qi Jingwen (1980)

(Goodrich 1937; Ping-Ti Ho 1955), two main channels for the introduction of sweet potato into Jiangsu (江苏) and Fujian (福建) provinces were widely accepted. The route of Fujian (福建) province is the one that has gained more support: i. in Changle (长乐) county, in Fujian (福建) province, near Fuzhou (福州), sweet potato was introduced through merchants from Luzon (Philippines). ii. another route for the introduction of sweet potato was through the urban area of Changzhou (常州), in southern Jiangsu (江苏) province. Locals claimed that the first introduction of sweet potato was into this locality and was kept a secret. There are no sources to corroborate this evidence or the year when it was introduced in Changzhou (常州); therefore, this cannot be considered a plausible option.

Based on the consensus that there was a type of sweet potato introduced into China, scholars should focus more on the timing and route of its introduction, since there is still a lively debate as to when, where and how this commodity reached inland China. The debate in the second half of the twentieth century was covered by a national and patriotic narrative mainly by those who sustained that sweet potato was indigenous to China by presenting alternative routes of introduction. Some scholars tend to consider that there were three main routes (Liang Jiamian and Qi Jingwen 1980), but another group of researchers offers more possible routes (Cao Ling 2003; Zheng Nan 2010).

Liang Jiamian and Qi Jingwen (1980) analysed several ancient books and county annals and pointed out that there were three main routes. The first one is mentioned by Lin Huailan, who affirmed that sweet potato was introduced from Vietnam (Jiaozhi 交趾) to Dianbai (电白) county. Lin Huailan was a doctor who saved the princess of Vietnam and was granted food, which included sweet potato. Lin transported it back to China secretly. There was even a temple to commemorate Lin (*Annals of Dianbai county; Annals of Guiping county*). However, the experience was so legendary that some scholars also suspect that these records may be far-fetched. The second one is the transportation of sweet potato by Chen Yi from Vietnam (Jiaozhi 交趾) to Dongguan (东莞). In 1580, Chen Yi travelled to Vietnam (Annan 安南) by boat and was encountered sweet potato. He obtained the seeds by bribing the chief of a tribe and escaped back in 1582 to Dongguan (东莞) county, Guangdong (广东), because sweet potato was banned from export as it can be observed in the genealogy of Chen in Fenggang (凤岗) village. The third one was Chen Zhenlong's attempt, which was also the most influential one. Chen lived in the Philippines (Lv Song 吕宋) for a long time and knew that sweet potato was good to improve the standards of living in the same way as the five cereals. Thus, he brought it back to Fujian (福建) in 1593 and planted it successfully. In addition, it is important to mention that sweet potato was distributed to other provinces in China with the help of the government and Chen's descendants (Li Yuan 2011).

Cao Ling (2003) and Zheng Nan (2010) mentioned more possible routes, quoting other ancient books. One route was from the Philippines to Changzhou (常州) in the mid-Wanli era mentioned in the book Min Xiaoji by Zhou Lianggong 周亮工 (1612–1672). Another route was from overseas to Nan'ao (南澳) and Quanzhou (泉州) in 1584–1585.

Gongsun Jian also clarified a similar opinion about two alternative routes. Besides the sea route, a land route also seemed helpful to the introduction of sweet potato. Based on the records in the *General Annals of Yunnan* (1574) and the *Annals of Dali* (1563), He Bingdi (1979) deduced that sweet potato could be introduced into China from Burma at that time (Table 1).

Traditional Chinese scholarship has insisted in this via for the introduction of sweet potato in China (Ping-Ti Ho 1955). This is an overland route from India and Burma, by which Chinese scholarship remarks that sweet potato reached Yunnan (云南) province before 1594. The local history of Yunnan (云南) suggests that sweet potato is indigenous to this region. Local sources mentioned that sweet potato was under the name of red tuber, hóngshǔ (红薯) or red taro, hóng yù (红芋), "*in contrast to native Chinese yam, which was clearly identified as dioscorea (shān yáo 山瑶)*" (Ping-Ti Ho 1955). Ping-Ti Ho (1955) makes this clear affirmation, suggesting that this yam was indigenous to China, and later he contradicts himself, suggesting that there is no clear evidence of the year and routes of introduction, whether from Fujian (福建) or Yunnan (云南). In addition, in the event that sweet potato was introduced from Yunnan (云南) via Burma and India, it is plausible to consider that it reached these areas via maritime trade from the Philippines through the Manila-Acapulco galleons.

Although scholars have arrived at a consensus on the existence of several routes for the introduction of sweet potato into China, only Chen Zhenlong's efforts received recognition from the whole of academia. The existence of five other complementary routes was questioned for the following three reasons: (1) the records in the local annals and genealogy probably exaggerated the facts (Cao Ling 2004), so it would be scientifically unsustainable to recognize an alternative route for the introduction of sweet potato without any other supporting material—in this case, Liu Huailan and Chen Yi's introduction of sweet potato from Vietnam around 1582 called for more circumstantial evidence; (2) the transcription of historical books is usually accompanied by anachronisms, even though the first recorder's account was based on solid fact—for example, the description of sweet potato in Zhou Lianggong's *Min Xiaoji* was not written by himself, but was derived from He Yuanqiao's *Min Book*. Zhou only changed some words, but according to his writings it is very

Table 1 Period and areas of introduction of sweet potato in China during the Ming Dynasty

Time	Place	Name	Original record
Before 1582	Dongxia village, Dianbai county, Guangdong province	Lin Huailan	*Annals of Dianbai county*, *Annals of Guiping county*
1582	Fenggang village, Dongguan county, Guangdong province	Chen Yi	Genealogy of Chen in Fenggang village
1593	Changle county, Fujian province	Chen Zhenlong	*Instructions for Practical Living of the Sweet Potato* (金薯传习录 Jinshu Chuanxilu)

Source Liang Jiamian and Qi Jingwen (1980)

difficult to establish the timing in which sweet potato was introduced; (3) the records might mistake *Dioscorea Opposita* as sweet potato. For instance, Li Debing and He Baolin do not agree with He Bingwen's thesis of Burma as main route for the introduction of sweet potato because Bingwen fails in identifying different typologies of potato. Furthermore, researchers are still not certain about the existence of sweet potato in Burma at that time. To sum up, there are six possible routes for the introduction of sweet potato based on ancient books, but only the route suggested by Chen Zhenlong has gained recognition. The other five routes, and their possible chronologies, require more research and empirical evidence to support them.

3.2 The Distribution of Sweet Potato

In relation to the distribution of sweet potato, researchers focused on different aspects. In 1980s, He Bingdi (1979), Chen Shuping (1980) and Guo Songyi (1986) concentrated more on the progress of the distribution from a macro-perspective based on the local annals. Similarly, Zhou Yuanhe (1983) summarized several routes. From the 80s onwards, scholars emphasized the progress of the distribution in different provinces and the research went further (Guo Songyi 1986). The following lines will first offer general information on the progress of the distribution of sweet potato, then will describe the map routes, and finally will provide some discussion about the dynamics of its circulation.

There is agreement among most scholars that it did not take much time for sweet potato to be accepted by Chinese communities once it was introduced. It had become widely planted in Fujian (福建) and Guangdong (广东) province at the end of Ming dynasty. It was introduced into Jiangxi (江西) province, Hunan (湖南) province, Zhejiang (浙江) province and Jiangsu (江苏) province in the latter half of the seventeenth century. In the mid-eighteenth century, it had spread over all southern provinces and had extended its range to the Yellow River basin and the northern provinces.

In this case, there were four channels for the internal diffusion of sweet potato from Guangdong (广东) province and Fujian (福建) province to the west and north (see Map 1). The first channel (the red line on the map) could be labelled as the coastal route from Fujian (福建) reaching inner China. This route went from Quanzhou (泉州) to Changle (长乐), the Yuhuan island (玉环岛), Wenzhou (温州), Taizhou (台州), Danxian (郸县), Zhoushan (舟山), Shanghai (上海), Shangdong (山东), Henan (河南) and up to Hebei (河北). The second channel (the yellow line on the map) could be named the Guangdong-Jiangxi route (广东-江西), and it went from Dianbai-Guangzhou (电白-广州) to Shaoguan (韶关), Meiling (梅岭), Dayu (大余), Ganzhou (赣州) and Nanchang (南昌). The third channel can be named Guangzhou-Zhongyuan (广州-中原) following the Central Plain route; see the blue line on the map) and it went from Guangzhou (广州) to Shaoguan (韶关), Pingshi (坪石), Chenxian (郴县), Hengyang (衡阳), Changsha (长沙), Yueyang (岳阳), Wuchang (武昌), Nanchang upland (南昌高地) and to the Central Plain (中原区域). Finally, the fourth channel, the Guangzhou-Guizhou (广州-贵州) route (the purple line on the map), went from the Zhujiang River Basin (珠江流域) to Guangxi (广西) province and Guizhou (贵州) province. Zhou Yuanhe also suggested an alternative route, as mentioned earlier, from Burma and Vietnam to Yunnan (云南), Guizhou (广州) and north to Sichuan (四川), which was not documented clearly, and no other scholars support this theory. The east coastal channel from Fujian (福建), reaching the inner regions of China, has been established as the main route.

After the introduction and distribution of this crop, the range of cultivation of sweet potato had spread across a very large area at the end of the Qing dynasty. Nevertheless, there was an obvious centralized distribution in Guangdong (广东) province and Fujian (福建) province, the

Map 1 Routes of Distribution of Sweet Potato in Ming China. *Source* Archive of Matteo Ricci Institute of Macau (Archivum Romanum Societatis Jesu), Jap. Sin. 181, Epistola Sinarum, f. 001

southern hill region in Fujian (福建) province, Zhejiang (浙江) province, Jiangxi (江西) province and Anhui (安徽) province, the mountainous area in Hubei (湖北) province and Hunan (湖南) province, the Sichuan (四川盆地) Basin and the southern centre of Shandong (山东) province.

Looking back at the process and timeline of the introduction and distribution of sweet potato, there are two important factors that contributed to its rapid diffusion: (i) the rising levels of consumption for this commodity in the areas where it was first introduced; and (ii) its growth enriched the farming land and allowed improvements in the techniques of cultivation. For the introduction of sweet potato in the period of Emperor Wanli (万历) during the Ming dynasty, academia generally agrees that there are four factors which fostered its diffusion (Zheng Nan 2010; Chen Lili 2007; Ouyang Chunlin 2012; Luo Shujie 2014): (i) the channels of transportation were relatively developed compared to previous generation and the number of international contacts had multiplied; (ii) it was a commodity that due to its rich nutrients, such as carbohydrates, improved standards of living, provoking a growth in the population; (iii) the annexation of land by imperial elites and the power of the despotic gentry became more violent, having as a result the loss of lands by peasants (Zheng Nan 2010; Chen Lili 2007; Luo Shujie 2014). This factor might be somehow simplistic, and made by traditional PRC scholars, since obviously for landlords and imperial elites, the management and entire tenancy of land represented a strong instrument for the exercise of power through heavy bureaucracy and institutions. Such scholarship should insist more on the negative effect of the role of institutions and bureaucracy rather than the linear and obvious result of elites obtaining more land and peasants losing it; (iv) in Guangdong (广东) province and Fujian (福建) province, the grain fields were much smaller in size because of the massive planting of cash crops and a food shortage emerged, which finally prompted people to look for other heavy yielders and to plant them on a large scale. However, the social unrest at the end of the Ming dynasty and the overwinter problem of sweet potato in the northern area hindered the spread of it at that time.

When it comes to the factors for the concentrated distribution of sweet potato in the Qianlong and Jiaqing periods (乾嘉时期), opinions are divided. Some scholars hold that the spread of sweet potato was the crucial watershed for population growth and improvements in cultivation techniques in China (He Bingdi 1979; Cao Ling 2003, 2005; You Xiuling 2003; Chen Zhongqi 2012). There are some factors which might explain it. First, the high pressure of population growth and the resulting increase in demand for food. For instance, migration during the Qing dynasty played an important role in the distribution of sweet potato in Sichuan (四川) province. The high yield of sweet potato and its great help in times of drought were fully recognized by the government, which also prompted its distribution. The improvement in overwinter techniques of cultivation was another important reason for the planting of sweet potato in the Yellow River basin.

Conversely, Wang Baoning (2013), who focuses his research on the distribution of sweet potato in Shandong (山东) province, claimed that the main reason for its rapid diffusion was to combat natural disasters. But he did not relate this directly to the high pressure exerted by the growth in population. In addition, the scale of planting sweet potato only extended in some local areas. In this case, Wang argues that there were not sufficient conditions for the effective distribution of sweet potato. In general, the main debate on the distribution of sweet potato has focused on factors that contributed to its rapid assimilation in the territories where it was first introduced, improving local economies. Different assumptions such as its influence on the population pressure and disaster relief might need further discussion.

4 The Influence of Sweet Potato on Agricultural Production and the Social Economy

There is a lacuna in the academic writing on the influence of sweet potato in China. Nevertheless, some discussion can also be found in articles on the introduction and distribution of American-originated crops, which are mainly concerned with their influence on Chinese agriculture, the social economy, population and the ecological environment. He Bingdi (1979) deemed that the introduction of corn and sweet potato led to a systemic long-term change in Chinese land utilization and grain production, and this marked the second revolution in Chinese grain production history. The book *Grain Yield per Mu of the Qing Dynasty* (Zhao Gang et al. 1995) showed the role of corn and sweet potato in boosting the grain production in the late Ming and early Qing dynasties and the consequential damage caused to the environment, which in turn brought about the decline in grain production later.

The introduction of American crops increased the farmland in central and south-western China during the Qing period. For instance, the characteristics of sweet potato, such as flood resistance, endurance of drought and high adaptability, made it survive in coastal sandy land and poor mountain soil, which meant more land could be used for its cultivation. Other crops such as corn and potato have the same quality. Table 2 shows that the farmland in central and south-western China in the Qianlong (乾隆) and Jiaqing (嘉慶) periods nearly doubled compared to the early Qing dynasty. At that time, corn and sweet potato were rapidly distributed in these provinces (Ma Xueqin 1999; Wang Shengpeng 2015). Thus, corn and sweet potato played an important role in the expansion of the cultivated area. The use of farmland did not increase much from Jiaqing (嘉慶) to Guangxu (光緒) periods due to the decline in population and limited expansion of new land. In addition, American crops have high yielding per *mu* improving the land-use mainly in areas non-specialized in agriculture (Table 3). Thus, the gross output of grain of China increased dramatically at that time.

Chen Shuping (1980) analysed the influence of American crops on the socio-economic development of Chinese territory. On the one hand, the introduction of sweet potato raised grain production and extended the plantation area. On the other hand, it also contributed greatly to the planting of cash crops and the commercialization of food production, which promoted the handcraft industry and commerce.

The introduction of sweet potato seemed to have some negative effects on the long-term Chinese socio-economic development (Huang Fuling 2011; Song Junling 2007). Lan Yong (2001) focused on the

Table 2 The field area statement in Central China and Southwestern China in the Qing Dynasty (units: 1000 *Mu*)

	Shunzhi 18 years (1661)	Qianlong 18 years (1753)	Jiaqing 17 years (1812)	Guangxu 13 years (1887)
Hunan & Hubei	79,335	90,755	92,100	93,950
Sichuan	1188	45,957	46,547	46,417
Yunnan	5211	7543	9315	9319
Guizhou	1074	2573	2766	2765
Total	86,808	146,828	150,728	152,451

Source Liang Fangzhong (1980). *Mu* is a Chinese unit of land area equivalent to approximately one-sixth of an acre

Table 3 The yield and increment of corn and sweet potato in the Qing Dynasty

	Yield per Mu	Increment per Mu
Corn	180 *Jin* (equivalent to 2 *Dan* of millet)	10.37 *Jin*
Sweet Potato	About One Thousand *Jin* (equivalent to 3.84 *Dan* of rice and 3.09 *Dan* of millet)	10.77 *Jin*

Source Zhang Gang (1955). *Jin* and *Dan* is a Chinese mass unit equivalent approximately to 600 grams

Chinese subtropical mountain areas. This scholar considers that the introduction of American high-yielding crops led to a continuous population growth (see Fig. 3), which initiated the mountain exploitation under the Qing dynasty and later caused the structural poverty and limited commercial economy in these areas. During the Ming-Qing transition in the first quarter of the seventeenth century, an important decline in population occurred due to wars and a dynastic crisis, which resulted in famines, floods, economic chaos and rebellions (Bin Wong 1997). However, as it can be observed in Fig. 3, a steady growth in the Chinese population continued following the introduction of sweet potato at the end of the sixteenth century until the nineteenth century. He Bingdi (1979) held the opinion that the introduction of American crops, the revolution of the grain production and the population explosion jointly interacted as causes and effects. Wang Yumin and Jiang Tao sustain the same argument. Ge Jianxiong considered these agricultural improvements as the significant reason for the population miracle (Song Junling 2007). Zhang Jian (2001, 2013) and Zhang Gang (1955) recalled that the negative effect of the high-yielding crops on the environment should not be ignored. Zhang Gang (1955) stated that the exploitation of the mountain led to the fatal destruction of the ecological balance, including the deforestation, soil erosion, farmland desertification and frequent

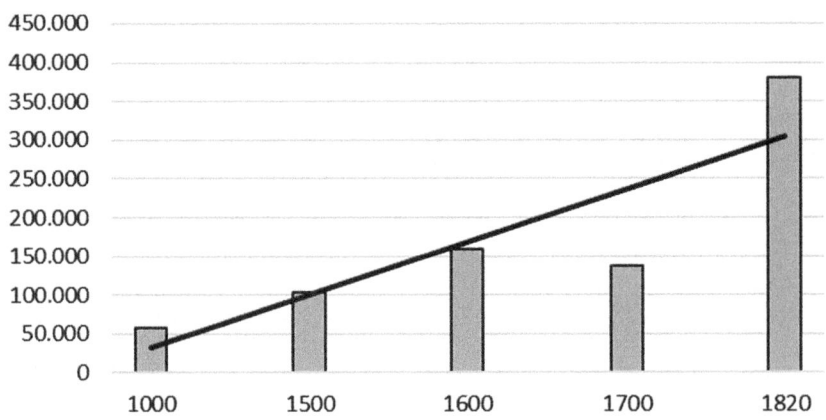

Fig. 3 Population growth in China from 1000 to 1820. *Source* Maddison Project, http://www.ggdc.net/maddison/maddison-project/home.htm, 2013 version; Maddison (1995, 2001, 2003)

floods, which finally resulted in a decreasing grain yield (Cao Ling 2004).

5 Conclusions

Based on the literature review, it can be considered that Chinese academia still has a long way to go in terms of further analysing the introduction and distribution of sweet potato in China. Some disputes remain, as it has been mentioned above, since patriotic narratives aim to nationalize commodities that entered China from the Americas and therefore to make them indigenous.

Nevertheless, the research and discussion on the role of sweet potato in early modern China could be deepened. An important group of scholars still focuses on American high-yield crops and has given little consideration to the influence of sweet potato itself (Cao Ling 2004; Song Junling 2007). In addition, there is a lack of long-term historical analysis that can provide a fuller perspective. Current research also separates China from its global connections by only concentrating on the Chinese internal agricultural revolution and economy, with the clearly nationalistic and patriotic aim of presenting the long-standing civilization and uniqueness of China. However, relying on the influence of sweet potato and other cereal crops introduced from the Americas, the analysis of the different models of economic growth in China and the West and the great divergence debate could be enriched by observing how China's consumers, market and political choices affected its development and destiny in the early modern era when Europe forged ahead during the first Industrial Revolution.

The most important reason for this inefficiency is the lack of multidisciplinary research and analysis, as well as the void in international academic communication, as most researchers have focused on this issue through the study of Chinese agricultural history, mainly due to the political context that existed from the 1960s to the early 1980s. Obviously, I am referring here to PRC scholarship and not to that carried out by Chinese overseas and Western scholars, whose work has been fruitful in terms of results and academic discussions. Therefore, in Chinese scholarship achievements nowadays, the scope of research is still quite limited. In this case, more effort should be made to promote interdisciplinary research embracing global history without 'Chinese national characteristics', which obviously obscures pure academic results without any type of manipulation, revealing new perspectives and diverse realities.

Notes

1. The concept of the CNKI was proposed by the World Bank in 1998. The main objective of the CNKI is to create a database to share knowledge and resources with the whole of society, as well as value-added for applicable research to spread information to all public and private economic sectors. This project was initiated in June 1999 by Tsinghua University, with the strong support of the party and state leaders, the Ministry of Education, the Central Propaganda Department, the Ministry of Science and Technology, the General Administration of Press and Publication, the State Copyright Bureau and the State Planning Commission. Thus, it involves academic, educational, publishing, library and information circles, as well as the CNKI Engineering Group. The creation of this national and political-orientated leading digital library aims to include largest full-text information, CNKI Digital Library, China Knowledge Resources and CNKI Grid Resource Sharing Platform to find solutions of current economic, political and social issues of China. This database stands out as a good source to observe how global history, and the analysis of the concept of being global in China through the introduction of foreign crops such as sweet potato, is penetrating in academic circles and challenging the current nationalist and patriotic agenda of the Chinese government.
2. Chāoxīng 超星 is a database providing library sources, with an orientation towards both an academic and a non-academic audience, to provide services for education and scientific research in China. The Ministry of Education supports this platform, which has similar objectives to the CNKI.
3. The work by He Bingdi 何炳棣 or Ping-Ti Ho is included here in Chinese scholarship since his research on the introduction of American crops in China, published in 1979 in the Chinese journal 世界农业 *Shìjiè nóngyè*, is a review of his former work published in 1955 in the *American Anthropologist* journal. He was an accomplished Chinese-American scholar who conducted outstanding work on Chinese history, mainly on demography and plant history. I will refer to him here as He Bingdi and will only refer to his name Ping-Ti Ho when quoting his work published in *American Anthropologist*.
4. For the sake of not repeating a long list of works, I will mention some of the most relevant, such as: Perkins (1975), Rawski (1989), Zurndorfer (1989), Wright (1992), Von Glahn (1996; 2016), Wong (1997), Maddison (1998), Deng (1999), Pomeranz (2000) and Ma (2004a).

References

An, Changchun. 1993. Cong shijieshiguan kan woguo shijieshi xueke jianshe [The Construction of the Field of World History in our Country regarding the Concept of World History]. *Wuhan daxue xuebao (Journal of Wuhan University)* 4: 13–18.

Berg, M. 2006. Britain, Industry and Perceptions of China: Matthew Boulton, 'Useful Knowledge' and the Macartney Embassy to China 1792–94. *Journal of Global History* 1: 269–288.

Cao, Ling. 2003. *Meizhou liangshi zuowu de chuanru, chuanbo ji qi yingxiang chuanbo* [Study on the Introduction, Spread and Affection of American Cereal Crops]. Master Thesis of Nanjing Agricultural University.

Cao, Ling. 2004. Ming Qing meizhou liangshi zuowu chuanru zhongguo yanjiu zongshu [The Overview of the Studies on the Introduction of American Cereal Crops in Ming Qing Dynasty]. *Ancient and Modern Agriculture* (2): 95–103.

Cao, Ling. 2005. Meizhou liangshi zuowu de chuanru dui woguo nongye shengchan he shehui jingji de yingxiang [Influence the Introduction of American Cereal Crops on Agricultural Production and Social Economy of China]. *Ancient and Modern Agriculture* (3): 79–88.

Cao, Shuji. 1988. Yumi he fanshu chuanru zhongguo luxian xintan [A New Investigation on the Path of the Introduction of Corn and Sweet Potato]. *Research of Chinese Social and Economic History* (4): 62–74.

Chen, Lili. 2007. Yuanyang taoci maoyi yu fanshu de yinzhong [The Ocean Trade of Ceramics and the Introduction of Sweet Potato]. *Agricultural Archa* (3): 26–31.

Chen, Shuping. 1980. Yumi he fanshu zai zhongguo chuanbo qingkuang yanjiu [The Studies on the Distribution of Corn and Sweet Potato in China]. *Social Sciences in China* (3): 187–204.

Chen Zhongqi. 2012. Shi lun Ming, Qing shiqi ganshu zai xinan diqu de chuanbo yu yingxiang [On the Distribution and Influence of Sweet Potato in Southwestern Area During Ming and Qing Dynasty]. *Journal of Fuling Teachers College* (11): 11–15.

Deng, Gang. 1999. *The Premodern Chinese Economy: Structural Equilibrium and Capitalist Sterility*. London and New York: Routledge.

Ding, Ying. 1928. Ganshu, jian suozhe "zuowu ming shi kao" di yibufen. *Nong sheng* (123).

Fairbank, J. K., and M. Goldman. 2006. *China: A New History*, 2nd ed. Cambridge, USA: Harvard University Press.

Goodrich, L.C. 1937. The Introduction of Sweet Potato into China. *China Journal* 27: 206–208.

Guo, Songyi. 1986. Fanshu zai Zhejiang de yinzhong he tuiguang [The Introduction and Distribution of Sweet Potato in Zhejiang Province]. *Zhejiang Academic Journal* (3): 45–49.
He, Bingdi. 1979. Meizhou zuowu de yinjin, chuanbo ji qi dui zhongguo liangshi shengchan de yingxiang [On the Introduction, Distribution of American Crops and their Influence on Chinese Agricultural Production]. *World Agriculture* (4): 21–41.
Ho, Ping-Ti. 1955. The Introduction of American Food Plants into China. *American Anthropologist*, New Series, Vol. 57, No. 2, Part 1 (Apr.): 191–201.
Hu, Xiwen. 1958. Ganshu laiyuan he women laodong zuxian de zaipei jishu [The Origin of Sweet Potato and Cultivation Technique of Chinese Forefather]. *Journal of Agricultural Heritage* (2): 21–32.
Huang, Fuling. 2011. *Ming Qing shiqi fanshu yinjin zhongguo yanjiu* [The Study on the Introduction of Sweet Potato into China during Ming and Qing Dynasty]. Master Thesis of Shandong Normal University.
Huang, Hui-Cheng, and M. Gove. 2012. Confucianism and Chinese Families: Values and Practices in Education. *International Journal of Humanities and Social Science* 2 (3) (February): 10–14.
Lan, Yong. 2001. Ming qing meizhou nongzuowu yinjin dui yaredai shandi jiegou xing pinkun xingcheng de yingxiang [The introduction of the Ming and Qing American Crops on the formation of subtropical mountain structural poverty]. *Zhongguo nong shi (Chinese Agricultural History)* (4): 3–14.
Li, Bozhong. 1998. *Agricultural Development in Jiangnan, 1620–1850*. New York: St. Martin's Press.
Li, Bozhong. 2002. *Lilun, Fangfa, Fazhan Qusi* [Theory, methodology and developmental trends]. Beijing: Tsinghua University Press.
Li, Wang. 2014. Internationalization with Chinese Characteristics: The Changing Discourse of Internationalization in China. *Chinese Education and Society* 47 (1) (January-February): 7–26.
Li, Yingfa. 2003. Qing chu yimin yu yumi ganshu zai sichuan diqu de chuanbo [Migration in Early Qing Dynasty and the Transmission of Maize and Sweet Potato in Sichuan]. *Zhongguo nong shi (Chinese Agricultural History)* (2): 7–13.
Li, Yuan. 2011. Ming Qing shiqi ganshu de yinzhong ji qi zai Shandong de tuiguang [The Introduction of Sweet Potato in Ming and Qing Dynasty and its Distribution in Shandong Province]. *Journal of Shandong Agricultural University (Social Science Edition)* (2): 82–87.
Liang, Fangzhong. 1980. *The Statistics of the Household, Farmland and Land Tax of All the Past Dynasties in China*. Shanghai: Shanghai People's Publishing House.
Liang, Jiamian, and Qi Jingwen. 1980. Fanshu yinzhong kao [On the Introduction of Sweet Potato]. *Journal of South China Agricultural College* (3): 74–79.

Liang, Zhan-Jun. 2006. Quanqiu shi yu shijie shi yitong chuyi [Comparing World History and Global History: a Chinese Scholar's View]. *Shoudu shifan daxue xuebao shehui kexue ban* [Journal of Capital Normal University] (Social Sciences Edition) 3: 1–5.

Liu, Beicheng. 2000. The Challenges of Reconstructing World History. *Shixuelilunyanjiu (Historiography Quarterly)* 4: 67–69.

Liu, Shuang. 2002. The View of History and Methodology in the Process of Globalization. *Xuexiyu Tansuo (Study and Exploration)* 4: 121–126.

Luo, Shujie. 2014. Qingdai yumi fanshu zai guangxi de chuanbo chayi yuanyin xinjie [A New Interpretation of the Reasons of Diverse Spread of Corns and Sweet Potatoes in Guangxi During Qing Dynasty]. *Journal of Guangxi University for Nationalities* (5): 105–108.

Ma, Xueqin. 1999. Mingqing shiqi yumi, fanshu zai henan de zaizhong yu tuiguang [The Planting and Distribution of Corn and Sweet Potato in Henan Province in Ming and Qing Dynasty]. *Ancient and Modern Agriculture* (1): 49–53.

Ma, D. 2004a. Growth, Institutions and Knowledge: A Review and Reflection on the Historiography of the 18th–20th Century China. *Australian Economic History Review* 44 (3) (November): 259–277.

Ma, D. 2004b. Why Japan, not China, was the first to develop in East Asia: Lessons from sericulture, 1850–1937. *Economic Development and Cultural Change* 52: 369–394.

Maddisson, A. 1998. *The Chinese Economic Performance in the Long-Run*. Paris: OECD Development Centre.

Maddisson, A. 1995. *Monitoring the World Economy 1820–1992*. Paris: OECD Development Centre.

Maddisson, A. 2001. *The World Economy: A Millennial Perspective*. Paris: OECD Development Centre.

Maddisson, A. 2003. *The World Economy: Historical Statistics*. Paris: OECD Development Centre.

Marks, Robert B. 1998. *Tigers, Rice, Silk & Silt: Environment and Economy in Late Imperial South China*. Cambridge: Cambridge University Press.

Min, Zongdian. 1991. Haiwai nongzuowu de chuan ru he dui woguo nongye shengchan de yingxiang [The introduction of overseas crops and the impact on China's agricultural production]. *Gujin Nongye (Ancient and Modern Agriculture)* 1 issue: 1–11.

Needham, Joseph. 1984. *Science and Civilisation in China:* Volume 6, Biology and Biological Technology, Part 2: Agriculture. Cambridge: Cambridge University Press.

Northrop, D. 2012. Introduction: the challenge of World History. In *A Companion to World History*, ed. D. Northrop, 1–13. Oxford: Wiley-Blackwell.

Ouyang, Chunlin. 2012. *Fanqie de yinzhong yu Ming Qing Fujian yanhai shehui (1594–1911)* [Introduction of Sweet Potato and Social Change in Fujian Coastal Communities in Ming and Qing Periods (1594–1911)]. Master's Thesis of Fujian Normal University.

Perkins, D.H. 1975. *China's Modern Economy in Historical Perspective*. Stanford: Stanford University Press.

Pomeranz, K. 2000. *The Great Divergence: China, Europe, and the Making of the Modern World Economy*. Princeton: Princeton University Press.

Qian, Chengdan. 2001. Probing into the Idea of 'Global History': An Impression of the 19th Congress of the International Historical Sciences. *Shixue Yuekan (History Monthly)* 2: 145–150.

Rawski, T.G. 1989. *Economic Growth in Prewar China*. Berkeley: University of California Press.

Song, Junling. 2007. *Ming Qing shiqi meizhou nongzuowu zai zhongguo de chuanzhong ji qi yingxiang yanjiu* [Studies on Spreading and Growing and Influences of Crops Originated in American During Ming and Qing Dynasties: Focusing on Maize, Sweet potato and Tobacco]. Doctoral Dissertation of Henan University.

Tu, W.M. 1998. Confucius and Confucianism. In *Confucianism and the family*, ed. W.H. Slote, and G.A. de Vos, 3–36. New York: State University of New York Press.

Von Glahn, R. 1996. *Fountain of Fortune: Money and Monetary Policy in China, 1000–1700*. Berkeley: University of California Press.

Von Glahn, R. 2016. *The Economic History of China: From Antiquity to the Nineteenth Century*. Cambridge: Cambridge University Press.

Vries, P. 2010. The California School and Beyond: How to Study the Great Divergence? *History Compass* 8 (7) (July): 730–751.

Waley-Cohen, J. 1993. China and Western Technology in the Late Eighteenth Century. *The American Historical Review* 98 (5) (Dec): 1525–1544.

Wang, Baoning. 2013. Qianlong nianjian Shandong de zaihuang yu fanshu yinzhong [Famine and the Introduction of Sweat Potatoes in Shandong in Qianlong Era]. *Agricultural History of China* (3): 9–26.

Wang Jiaqi. 1961. Lue tan gan he gan shu lu. [Slight Discussion about Sweet Potato and Record of Sweet Potato]. *Cultural Relics* 3: 27–30.

Wang, Shengpeng. 2015. Qingdai Sichuan meizhou liangshi zuowu de chuanzhong ji dui yinshi chansheng de yingxiang [The Introduction of American Crops in Sichuan in Qing Dynasty and Its Influence on Diet]. *Journal of Sichuan Higher Institute of Cuisine* (4): 6–9.

Wang, Yunlong. 2002. From Modernization to Globalization. *Xuexiyu Tansuo [Study and Exploration]* 3: 121–125.

Westad, O.A. 2012. *Restless Empire: China and the World since 1750*. Philadelphia, USA: Basic Books.

Wong, R.B. 1997. *China Transformed: Historical Change and the Limits of European Experience*. Ithaca and London: Cornell University Press.
Wright, T. (ed.). 1992. *The Chinese Economy in the Early Twentieth Century: Recent Chinese Studies*. New York: St. Martin's Press.
Wu, Deduo. 1961. Guanyu ganshu he jinshu chuanxi lu [On the Sweet Potato and its Instruction]. *Cultural Relics* 8: 60–61.
Wu, Xiaoqun. 2005. Do We Really Need a 'Global View of History'? *Xueshu Yanjiu (Academic Research)* 1: 22–27.
Xia, Nai. 1961. Lüe tan fanshu he shuyu [Slight Discussion about the Sweet Potato and Dioscorea Opposita]. *Cultural Relics* (8): 58–59.
Xu, Dixin, and Chengming Wu (eds.). 1993. *Xin Minzhuzhuyi Geming Shiqi de Zhongguo Zibenzhuyi* [Development history of Chinese capitalism]. Beijing: People's Publishing House.
You, Xiuling. 2003. Qing chu yimin yu yimi ganshu zai Sichuan diqu de chuanbo [The Migrants in the early Qing Dynasty and the Distribution of Corns and Sweet Potato in Sichuan]. *Agricultural History of China* 22 (2): 6–22.
Yu, Pei. 2006. Global History and National Historical Memory. *Shixuelilunyanjiu* [Historiography Quarterly] 1: 18–30.
Zhang, Gang. 1955. *The Research on the Yield of Crops in Qing Dynasty*. Beijing: China Agriculture Press.
Zhang, Jian. 2001. Lun meizhou liang shi zuowu de chuanbo [On the spread of food crops in the Americas]. *Zhongguo nong shi (Chinese Agricultural History)* (3): 89–95.
Zhang, Jian. 2013. Nongzuowu chuanboshi yanjiu de lizuo: du meizhouzuowu zai zhongguo de chuanbo ji qi yingxiang yanjiu [A Masterpiece to Research the History of Crop's Spreading-Book Review on the Introduction of American-Originated Crops into China and their Long-Term Influence]. *Agricultural History of China* (2): 138–144.
Zhao Gang, Liu Yongcheng and Deng Bianzhu. 1995. *Grain Yield per Mu of the Qing Dynasty*. Jiangsu: China Agriculture Press.
Zheng, Nan. 2010. *Meizhou yuanchan zuowu de chuanru ji qi dui zhongguo shehui yingxiang wenti de yanjiu* [On the Introduction and Influence of American Native Crops on Chinese Society]. Doctoral Dissertation of Zhejiang University.
Zheng, Nan. 2013. Meizhou zuowu fanshu de chuanru ji zai Heilongjiang diqu de yinzhong yu zaipei [The Introduction of Sweet Potato and Its Cultivation in Heilongjiang]. *Journal of Chuxiong Normal University* 28 (8): 4–11.
Zhou, Yuanhe. 1983. Ganshu de tusheng, chuanru, chuanbo yu renkou [The Indigenous, Introduction and Distribution of Sweet Potato in Population]. *Agricultural History of China* 3: 75–88.
Zurndorfer, H. 1989. *Change and Continuity in Chinese Local History: The Development of Hui-chou Prefecture, 800 to 1800*. Leiden: Brill.

Open Access This chapter is licensed under the terms of the Creative Commons Attribution 4.0 International License (http://creativecommons.org/licenses/by/4.0/), which permits use, sharing, adaptation, distribution and reproduction in any medium or format, as long as you give appropriate credit to the original author(s) and the source, provide a link to the Creative Commons license and indicate if changes were made.

The images or other third party material in this chapter are included in the chapter's Creative Commons license, unless indicated otherwise in a credit line to the material. If material is not included in the chapter's Creative Commons license and your intended use is not permitted by statutory regulation or exceeds the permitted use, you will need to obtain permission directly from the copyright holder.

Economic Depression and the Silver Question in Nineteenth-Century China

Richard von Glahn

The last decade of the eighteenth century marked a crucial transition in China's economic fortunes. After a century of steady growth in production, population and prosperity that had begun in the 1680s, a sudden reversal occurred in the 1790s. Prices tumbled amid widespread reports of economic distress and deteriorating trade. The White Lotus Rebellion (1796–1805) devastated a large swath of western China, forcing the Qing imperial government to empty its treasuries in costly military campaigns. The final suppression of the rebellion brought some respite, but not a return to prosperity. In 1815, the eruption of the Tambora volcano in Indonesia—the largest volcanic eruption in recorded history—triggered several years of global climatic disturbances, drastically disrupting agriculture as far away as New England and Ireland. Catastrophic flooding in the 1820s—including the devastating Yellow River floods of 1824–1826—precipitated famines in both northern and southern China, fomenting peasant unrest and urban food riots. The deflationary spiral triggered in the 1810s intensified in subsequent decades. The worst years

R. von Glahn (✉)
University of California, Los Angeles, USA

coincided with the reign of the Daoguang Emperor (r. 1820–1850), and thus this era has become known as the Daoguang Depression.

The Daoguang Depression also coincided with the two most traumatic events in the history of nineteenth-century China: the Opium War fiasco (1839–1842) and the onset of the Taiping Rebellion (1850–1864). The immediate economic effects of the Qing's ignominious defeat in the Opium War were minor compared to the cost to the imperial court's prestige. The Taiping Rebellion, in contrast, left much of the central and lower Yangzi River basins—the economic heartland of China—in ruins. Estimates of the loss of life over the course of the rebellion range from 20–50 million to as many as 90 million people. The Taiping Rebellion abruptly ended the long surge that had increased China's population from roughly 150 million in 1680 to an estimated 436 million in 1850, a level that would not be reached again until the 1920s. These events transformed the image of China in Western eyes, indelibly branding it as a poor and backward country just at the moment that the West began to enjoy the first fruits of the self-sustaining economic growth that accompanied the Industrial Revolution.

The stark contrast between the 'prosperous age' (as contemporaries themselves described it) of the eighteenth century and the dramatic regression of the nineteenth century raises important questions about the nature of the pre-modern Chinese economy. Recent scholarship seeking to frame the economic torpor of nineteenth-century China in a long-term perspective has proposed three principal explanations: (1) neo-Malthusian models that emphasize the distinctive features of China's 'peasant economy'; (2) dependency theories—rooted in the older 'imperialism of free trade' paradigm—that assert the deleterious consequences of China's growing integration into a global trade system; and (3) a neo-Smithian perspective that underscores the ecological limits to economic growth and the diminishing returns to market expansion found in all pre-modern agrarian societies (not just China).

Neo-Malthusian models provide structural explanations for the inherent limits of the small-farm peasant economy that has prevailed in China for most of its imperial history, and certainly throughout the late imperial era. Kang Chao has postulated that the continuous fragmentation of landholdings under China's equal inheritance laws and the worsening labour/land ratio that accompanied unrestrained population growth resulted in steadily decreasing returns to agricultural work. Philip Huang's 'involution' thesis likewise emphasizes that the rationality of peasant self-sufficiency and strategies of household reproduction favoured a labour-intensive mode of production rather than capital-intensive managerial farming. Ironically, the expansion of markets in the late imperial era provided enhanced opportunities for family survival through production for the market, but at the cost of diminished labour productivity that stifled wage-based and capital-intensive forms of economic organization. Both Chao and Huang agree that labour productivity in Chinese agriculture had peaked in the Song dynasty and diminished steadily afterwards (Chao 1988; Huang 1990).

In the eyes of dependency theorists, the emergence of a world economy since 1500 resulted in the incorporation of the non-European world into a capitalist system dominated by European nations. Commodity flows and capital investment forged links that fostered the economic subordination of peripheral satellite regions to the hegemonic powers of the capitalist core. The sociologist Frances Moulder, a student of Immanuel Wallerstein, was among the first to apply this analysis to China (Moulder 1977: 91–127). In her view, China's economic incorporation into the world capitalist system began in around 1800, although it intensified after the Opium War, which marked the beginning of China's political incorporation. In a different vein (quite distinct from Wallerstein's world-systems analysis), William Atwell has argued that China had already become economically dependent on the global trading system in the seventeenth century. According to Atwell, the growth of domestic commerce in the late Ming period, which was fuelled by massive imports of foreign silver, rendered the Chinese economy vulnerable to disruptions in global trade. The abrupt decline in European overseas trade in the middle decades of the seventeenth century drastically reduced the flow of silver to China, wreaking economic turmoil that contributed directly to the collapse of the Ming state and the Manchu conquest of China in 1644 (Atwell 1986, 2006). Manhoung Lin claims that the Chinese economy in the nineteenth century likewise was dependent on the global trading system, and especially imports of foreign silver, to sustain its prosperity. The combination of economic depression in Europe—resulting in the evaporation of demand for Chinese tea and silks—and a crisis in worldwide silver production not only halted the flow of silver to China, but also reversed that flow. In her view, this haemorrhage of silver was the principal cause of the Daoguang Depression (Lin 2006).

Both Huang's neo-Malthusian 'involution' thesis and the dependency models express the idea that rather than improving economic welfare, market integration acted as a catalyst for the immiseration of the Chinese populace. A much more positive view of the role of the market in China's late imperial economy has been advanced by the so-called 'California School' of revisionist economic history.[1] From this perspective, similar Smithian dynamics of market expansion and specialization of labour animated economic growth in the main regions of advanced economic development across the world in the early modern era, including the Jiangnan region of China, the Kantō Plain in Japan, Bengal, and the leading European economic regions of England and the Low Countries. However, as Smith himself had prophesied, given the limitations of pre-modern technology in what remained fundamentally agrarian economies, by the end of the eighteenth century, all of these regions had begun to encounter diminishing returns to labour and capital investment. Ecological constraints—maximal exploitation of arable land, deforestation and the growing ecological costs of intensive land use—inhibited further economic improvement. Only through a revolution in energy production—the invention of steam-powered mechanization utilizing fossil fuels in place of human and animal labour and inefficient water and wind power—could liberation from the 'biological old regime' be achieved. By the turn of the nineteenth century, just such a great leap forward in energy production was well under way in Britain, paving the way for the Industrial Revolution. In China and other advanced economic regions, however, the productive potential of traditional technologies had already been exhausted, impeding further economic development (Pomeranz 2000; Marks 2002). Hence, a 'Great Divergence' emerged between England's path to self-sustaining economic growth and the 'high-level equilibrium' of pre-modern economies elsewhere.

This chapter will examine evidence for population, prices, wages and income, standards of living, silver flows and money supply in China during the first half of the nineteenth century in order to elucidate the causes and consequences of the Daoguang Depression. The findings present here do not support the neo-Malthusian and dependency hypotheses outlined above. Instead, the neo-Smithian analysis of the California School provides the most satisfactory explanatory model for the economic distress China suffered in this period. In addition, the Daoguang Depression should be seen as part of a long-term pattern of cyclical conjunctures of economic expansion and contraction that had determined the basic rhythm of economic life not only in late imperial China, but in early modern Europe as well.

1   Measuring Economic Performance: GDP and Real Wages

Economic historians have responded to Kenneth Pomeranz's bold assertion that income levels in eighteenth-century Jiangnan were on a par with the most advanced economic regions of Europe (England and the Netherlands) by making a concerted effort to develop quantitative measures to compare the economic performance of late imperial China with other advanced economies in Europe and Asia. The two principal measures currently utilized in making such comparisons have been estimates of Gross Domestic Product (GDP) and real wage rates. To be sure, there are significant empirical challenges to calculating GDP and real wages as well as theoretical problems regarding their utility as measures of comparison, and the results of such exercises must be viewed with caution.[2]

The late Angus Maddison was the pioneer in developing GDP estimates to measure and compare long-term economic performance on a global scale. Maddison estimated that China's per capita GDP had reached a high level ($600 in 1990 international dollars) in 1700— slightly less than two-thirds of the level of Europe, but ahead of both Japan and India. Maddison also asserted that aggregate GDP growth in China outpaced Europe between 1700 and 1820, with the result that in 1820 China's share of global GDP reached 33%, eclipsing that of Europe (27%). But this increase resulted from China's huge population expansion, not economic development; on a per capita basis, China's GDP had stagnated since 1700, in contrast to sustained improvement in Europe. By Maddison's calculation, China's per capita GDP in 1820 had sunk to only 55% of the European level (Maddison 2001: 42–48, 2007, 44, Tables 2.1–2.2c).

Most efforts to quantify the size of the economy in late imperial China have been responses to Maddison's methods and results.

Maddison's technique, it should be noted, was relatively crude and presumed that per capita output remained unchanged from the end of the Song dynasty to the nineteenth century (Table 1). William Liu has derived his estimates—which show a very high per capita GDP in the Song that fell precipitously in the Ming and only partially recovered in the Qing—from calculations of soldiers' real wages as a proxy for per capita income. However, there are substantial problems with Liu's methodology, and his estimates of GDP cannot be considered reliable.[3] Liu Ti, who was among the first scholars to utilize national accounting analysis, has arrived at strikingly different results. He argues that agriculture generated a mere 54% of GDP in 1600, in contrast to 34% produced by industry and construction, and thus his estimates of Ming GDP are far higher than those of William Liu. By Liu Ti's calculations, nominal GDP grew fivefold between 1600 and 1840, but the increase in real terms (constant prices) was far more modest, and per capita real GDP declined by roughly 20% over that period. Part of this decline can be explained by the reduced share of the industrial sector, which in Liu's analysis declined by nearly half, to 20% of total GDP, by 1840 (agriculture, in contrast, rose to 69%). The size of the service sector remained constant (around 11–12% of the total), but its composition changed radically: Liu Ti suggests that finance comprised a third of the service sector in 1840 compared to only 4% in 1600, while the government spending's share of the service economy fell from 45 to 22% (Liu 2009).

A recent analysis by Stephen Broadberry and his collaborators concurs with William Liu's view that per capita GDP peaked in the Northern Song, but then declined continuously thereafter. The Broadberry team's figures indicate a steady equilibrium throughout the Ming period at the same level as the Northern Song, followed by a steep plunge in the Qing period. By their calculations, population growth had sharply curtailed per capita GDP already by 1750, with a further decline by 1850 to a level roughly 60% that of the Song peak. These findings largely reflect the failure of grain yields to keep pace with population growth from the Song period onwards and thus echo Kang Chao's analysis (Broadberry et al. 2017).[4] Shi Zhihong and his collaborators arrive at slightly lower (by roughly 10%) per capita GDP figures from 1661 to 1850 than Broadberry et al., but the trend they chart is virtually identical. The key new argument proposed by the Shi Zhihong group is that the decline in per capita GDP largely resulted from the relative decline in

Table 1 Estimates of Chinese GDP

Maddison 2007		William Guanglin Liu 2015		Liu Ti 2009			Shi Zhihong et al. 2014		Broadberry et al. 2017	
Year	P.C GDP (1990$)	Year	P.C. GDP (tls.)	Year	P.C. GDP (tls.)	P.C. GDP (1990$)	Year	P.C. GDP (1990$)	Year	P.C. GDP (1990$)
960	450	1080	7.5						1090	1204
1300	600	1420s	0.73–0.98						1400	960
		1580s	2.88	1600	4.5	388			1600	977
1700	600			1650	4.1	360	1661	938		
				1750	3.8	340	1766	626	1750	685
1820	600	1880s	7.63	1840	3.4	318	1850	545	1850	594
1952	538									

Sources (Maddison 2007: 44, Tables 2.1–2.2c; Guanglin Liu 2015: 266, Table F-4; Shi Zhihong et al. 2014: 11, Table 10; Liu Ti 2009: 153, appendix Table 1; Broadberry, Guan and Li 2017: 34, Table 6)

the high-income service sector (especially the government) from 1650 to 1900 (Shi et al. 2014: 6–7).

Thus, recent efforts to calculate GDP for the Ming and Qing periods have produced divergent results, largely because of different premises about the relative weights of agriculture, industry and services in the Chinese economy. Most of these scholars agree, however, that the surge in population growth during the Qing period steadily reduced per capita GDP. There is also general agreement that Chinese per capita GDP was already far lower than the levels of England and the Netherlands in 1600, and fell even further behind by 1800. Shi Zhihong et al., for example, estimate that China's per capita GDP in 1812 was a mere 28% of that of England (Shi et al. 2014: 11, Tables 10–11).[5] Although Liu Ti diverges from others in portraying China's per capita GDP as roughly constant during the Qing dynasty, he concludes that it had declined to less than 20% of the British level by 1840. Liu Ti's absolute figures for Chinese per capita GDP are surely too low, but his analysis of the composition of GDP and the long-term trend in per capita GDP seem more plausible.

Given the severe limitations of the data and the necessity of making very large and tentative assumptions, these efforts to analyse the size and structure of GDP in pre-modern China can only be regarded as heuristic exercises. Of course, as Pomeranz has persuasively argued, comparing the whole Chinese Empire, with its vast disparities in economic development, to European countries such as Britain mixes together highly dissimilar and unequal units of analysis. Instead, Pomeranz has insisted on the necessity of comparing the most advanced economic regions of roughly equal size, such as England, the Netherlands, Jiangnan and the Kantō Plain in Japan. This principle is the cornerstone of the collaborative study by Li Bozhong and Jan Luiten van Zanden, which compares GDP and labour productivity in the Netherlands and two counties (Huating and Lou) in Songjiang prefecture (near Shanghai) in the 1820s (Li and Van Zanden 2012).[6] The geography of the two regions is similar (low-lying plains with ready access to both inland and overseas water transport), and they both were characterized by high rates of urbanization and commercialization (Li estimated that 80% of output and 67% of consumption in Hua-Lou passed through the marketplace). But the regional economies differed in significant ways: Hua-Lou, the heart of the Jiangnan cotton industry, had a much higher proportion of the workforce engaged in manufacturing, whereas commerce and banking employed a much greater share of the Dutch population. Li and van Zanden find that labour productivity in agriculture was very high in both regions, but wages from artisanal and industrial work in Hua-Lou were far lower than in the Netherlands, reflecting the fact that Hua-Lou's industrial workforce consisted overwhelmingly of women spinners and weavers. Consequently, there was a large disparity in per capita income between the two regions: the Dutch level was 81 per cent higher (86% higher when measured in purchasing power parity (PPP) terms) than in Hua-Lou. The authors attribute this gap to greater Dutch capital investment in labour-saving technologies in industrial production, transport and to some extent agriculture. Low wage rates and high interest rates and capital costs acted as brakes on such investment in Hua-Lou. Li and van Zanden calculate that Hua-Lou's per capita GDP in 1820 was $988, or about 83% of the level of Western Europe as a whole, but only 54% of that of the Netherlands. In contrast to Pomeranz and studies that have focused on consumption, Li and van Zanden find a large gap in GDP between Jiangnan and the advanced economic regions in Europe. But Li and van Zanden's estimate for Hua-Lou's per capita GDP is 70–80% higher than the estimates of Broadberry et al. ($598) and Shi Zhihong et al. ($545) for China as a whole in 1850.[7]

Economic historians commonly utilize real wages as an index of the standard of living, based on the logic that since wage earners occupied a marginal niche within pre-modern economies, their wages can serve as a proxy for marginal labour productivity in general. Robert Allen's comparison of real wages in China and Europe has found that wage rates in Ming-Qing China were substantially lower than in England and the Netherlands, although comparable to other parts of Europe such as Germany and Italy (Allen 2009). Drawing primarily on Li Bozhong's data (with adjustments) and converting income data to PPP exchange rates, Allen concluded that the labour productivity of Jiangnan farmers was already high in 1600 and remained unchanged in 1800 at a level comparable to the richest agricultural regions in England. Farm work was vastly more intensive in Jiangnan: labour intensity (days worked per unit of land) was eight times greater in Jiangnan than England, but output in Jiangnan was nine times higher. In the early seventeenth century, Jiangnan's farming families earned substantially higher incomes than English farm workers. But the net income (measured in rice) of female textile workers fell by half between the seventeenth and nineteenth centuries. By Allen's calculations, family income in Jiangnan declined by 42% from 1620 to 1820, largely due to falling prices for textiles and the sharp reduction in farm size. To be sure, the income of Jiangnan farm families c. 1820 was no worse than that of English farm workers. But Allen concludes that population growth and the worsening land/labour ratio had resulted in growing impoverishment even in Jiangnan.[8]

In another study, Allen and a group of collaborators have sought to compare the real wages of unskilled workers in Beijing, Suzhou and Guangdong with other European and Asian cities (Allen et al. 2011). They conclude that real wages in Chinese cities were already far below (barely half) the level of London and Amsterdam in the first half of the eighteenth century, although on a par with Central and Southern European cities well into the nineteenth century. But the utility of such comparisons is questionable. Compared to Europe, a far smaller percentage of the Jiangnan workforce consisted of full-time wage labourers—perhaps 10–15%, in contrast to more than half in England and the Netherlands. Wage labourers in Jiangnan earned only 30–40% of the income of tenant farmers with security of tenure, and even less compared to smallholders (Pomeranz 2008: 84–85; Xu and Wu 2000: 37).[9] The earnings of such wage labourers—the vast majority of whom were single men—barely sufficed for their own upkeep and could not support a family. The disparity in proletarian wages adduced by Allen and his collaborators is not incompatible with closer parity in family incomes and living standards in general.

Nonetheless, recent efforts to quantify economic performance in Ming-Qing China suggest that per capita output declined steadily from 1600 to 1810—with the most precipitous fall occurring during the eighteenth century—and then stabilizing (at a very low level) that persisted until the 1940s (Liu Ti suggests that this plateau was reached earlier in around 1770). These studies thus portray Qing China as caught in the Malthusian scissors of rising population growth exceeding productive capacity. There is considerable evidence that the Chinese economy had begun to exhaust its productive capacities by 1800. But whether the depression of the early nineteenth century was driven by Malthusian factors requires further investigation.

2 Population, Prices and Money Supply

Between the pacification of Taiwan in 1683 and the outbreak of the White Lotus Rebellion in 1796, China enjoyed a century of remarkable domestic tranquility that fostered unprecedented population growth. By the end of the seventeenth century, China's population had returned to its Ming peak of 150 million. Over the course of the eighteenth century, the empire's population doubled, with the most pronounced increase occurring during the first half of the eighteenth century (Table 2). While economic growth in the late Ming period had been concentrated in the southeastern coastal provinces, during the early and middle Qing period, the most striking increases in population and agricultural production were found in the interior provinces of the south (Hunan, Hubei and especially Sichuan), the Central Plain and the southwestern frontier provinces. Much of this increase resulted from the advance of Chinese settlement and agriculture into the remote upland regions of the interior. As Fig. 1 shows, between 1776 and 1820, the rate of increase was significantly higher in the sparsely inhabited provinces in the west (Sichuan and Shaanxi above all).

Contemporary observers fully recognized this remarkable population increase, and as early as 1748 leading statesmen expressed fears that population growth—which had always been seen as a sign of good governance—was outstripping food production, creating a disequilibrium that drove up prices and posed an endemic threat to subsistence and survival (Will 1994: 866–868; Marks and Chen 1995: 141–142; Dunstan 2005: 307–462). Certainly, the eighteenth century was also marked by a secular rise in the price level. The sharpest increases occurred in rice-deficit areas such as Jiangnan and Guangdong in 1730–1758, but prices moderated thereafter, and even fell in the 1790s.[10] The most comprehensive evidence for price inflation comes from rice prices (Fig. 2), but the prices

Table 2 Population of Qing China

	Population (in millions)
1680	150
1776	311
1820	383
1850	436

Source Cao Shuji (2000: 704, Table 16–2)

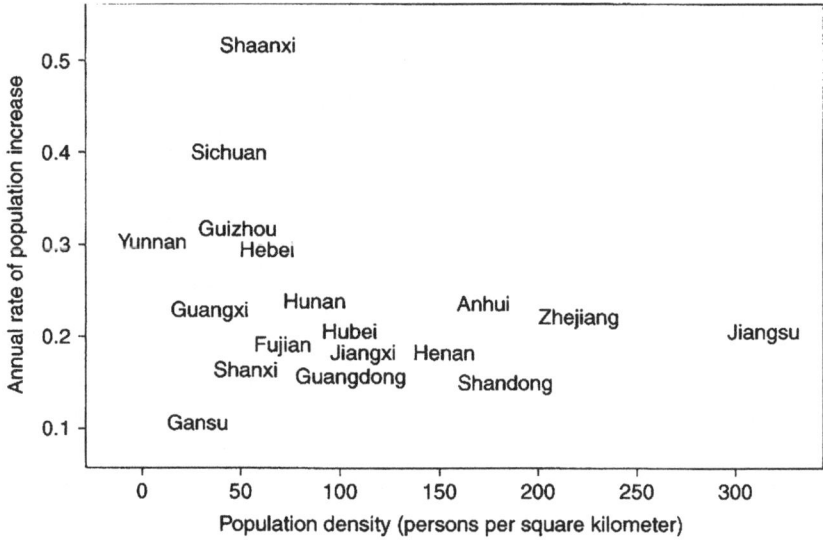

Fig. 1 Population density and rates of growth, 1776–1820. *Source* Peng Kaixiang (2006: 61, Fig. 5.4)

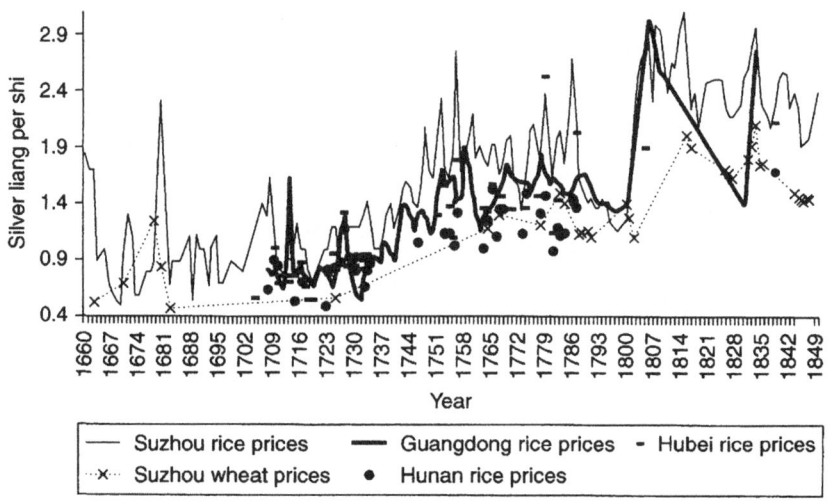

Fig. 2 Grain prices in South China, 1660–1850. *Source* Peng Kaixiang (2006: 33, Fig. 3.1)

of other grains, cotton, silk and various consumer goods (clothing, fuel, liquor, medicine and paper) also exhibit similar trends during the eighteenth century (Kishimoto 1997: 138–153; Peng 2006: 34–36; Chen 2005: 158–161). Thus, relative prices remained fairly stable.

Although the strain imposed on the environment and productive resources by population growth became increasingly severe, the evidence does not suggest that China had reached the point of a Malthusian demographic crisis. To be sure, sharp spikes in mortality occurred on a regular basis. In 1813–1814, a severe drought caused grain prices in Hebei to double and culminated in a genuine mortality crisis, with the state powerless to relieve starvation and suffering. Hebei again suffered severe harvest failures in the early 1820s (Li 2007: 255–266). Demographic research on rural Liaoning (Manchuria) has demonstrated

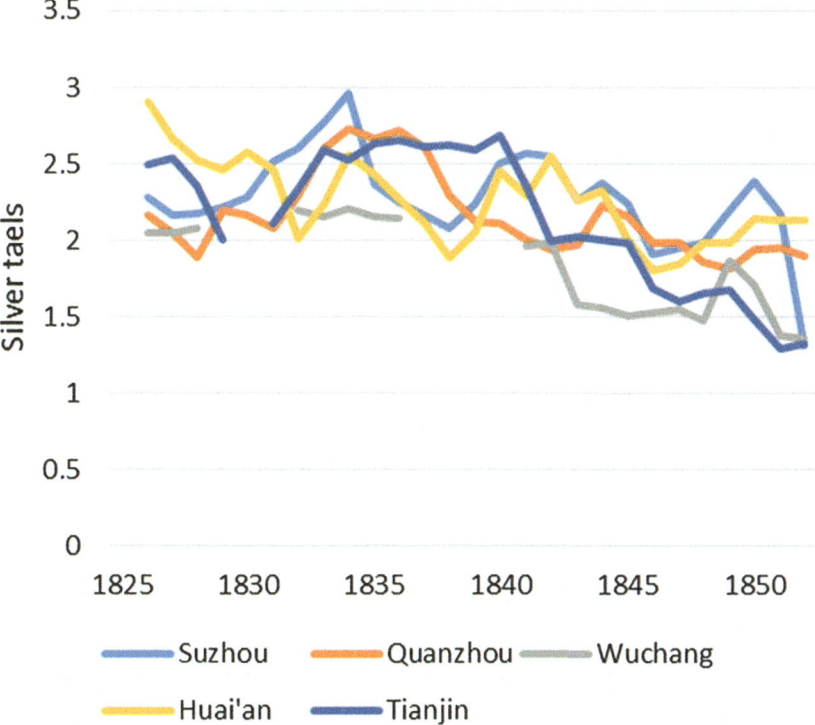

Fig. 3 Rice prices in five major markets, 1826–1852. *Source* Wang Yeh-chien (1996: 266, Table 3)

definite correlations between vitality and short-term price movements: marriages and births declined during years of high food prices and increased when prices were low, while conversely deaths rose and fell in tandem with the rise and fall of grain prices. Population growth certainly exacerbated the economic pressure on the poor. Long-term trends in Liaoning show no increase in male mortality during the period 1800–1850, but household formation, marriages and births declined, suggesting a society under demographic stress (Lee and Campbell 1997: 31–39).

But long-term correlations between prices and population change are less evident. Following the steady increase in grain prices across the eighteenth century, prices plunged in the 1790s and then rose after 1800. Grain prices spiked sharply in both the north and the south in the 1810s, but abated in most areas in the 1820s. From 1835 to the early 1850s, grain prices trended downwards in all major commercial regions of China (Fig. 3).[11] According to the ledgers of the Tongtaisheng, a

Fig. 4 Prices of agricultural and manufactured goods in Ningjin (Hebei), 1800–1850. *Source* Ningjin Tongtaisheng ledgers; Peng Kaixiang (2006: 90, Fig. 5.4)

general goods merchandising firm based in Ningjin, Hebei, the nominal prices of both agricultural and manufactured goods rose in the 1810s and then declined in the 1820s (with a sharp drop in the early 1830s), before returning to their previous level (Fig. 4). But in terms of silver (converted from prices originally recorded in coin), the prices of both agricultural and manufactured products as well as wages decreased steadily from 1815 to 1850, apart from a brief recovery in the mid-1830s (Fig. 5). Other data corroborate these trends. The welfare ratios for Beijing, Suzhou and Guangzhou wage workers postulated by Allen and his collaborators declined slowly across the eighteenth century, abruptly rose in 1780–1795 and then fell even more sharply in 1795–1820. Subsequently, the welfare ratio in Beijing (the only city for which they have data for the 1820s–1840s) continued to decline (Allen et al. 2011: 27–28, Figs. 5–6). However, when measured in grain rather than silver, wages of unskilled labourers were relatively stable in Beijing during the period 1807–1838. Nominal daily wages paid in coin (the typical

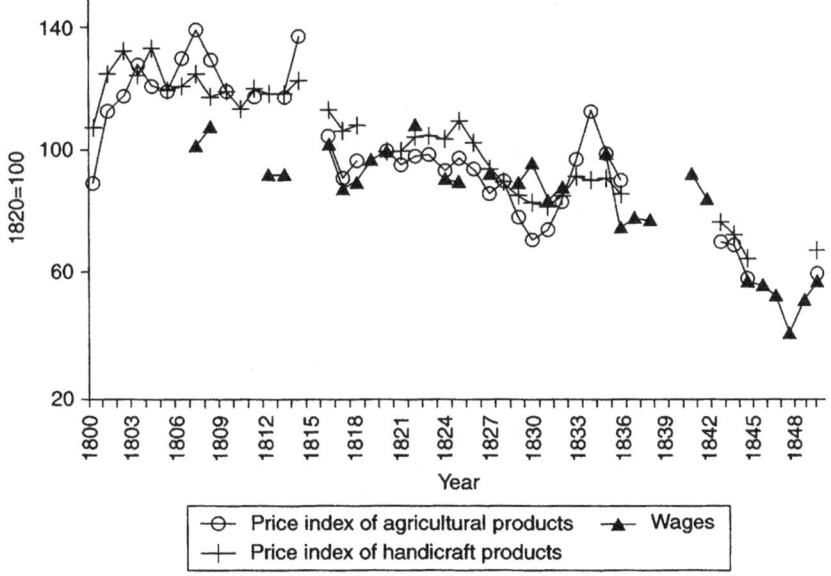

Fig. 5 Prices and wages (Silver equivalents) in Ningjin (Hebei), 1800–1850. *Source* Ningjin Tongtaisheng ledgers; Peng Kaixiang (2006: 37, Fig. 3.5)

practice in Beijing) rose slightly during this period, but purchasing power measured in silver fell significantly (Fig. 6). The Daoguang Depression years of 1820–1850 thus witnessed static or declining real prices and wages—and in silver terms, steep deflation—even as China's population continued to grow at a steady rate. These price trends are not consistent with a Malthusian scenario of intensifying pressure on food supply, which should have had inflationary consequences.

It is more likely that the price inflation of the eighteenth century reflected the substantial growth of the money supply rather than the

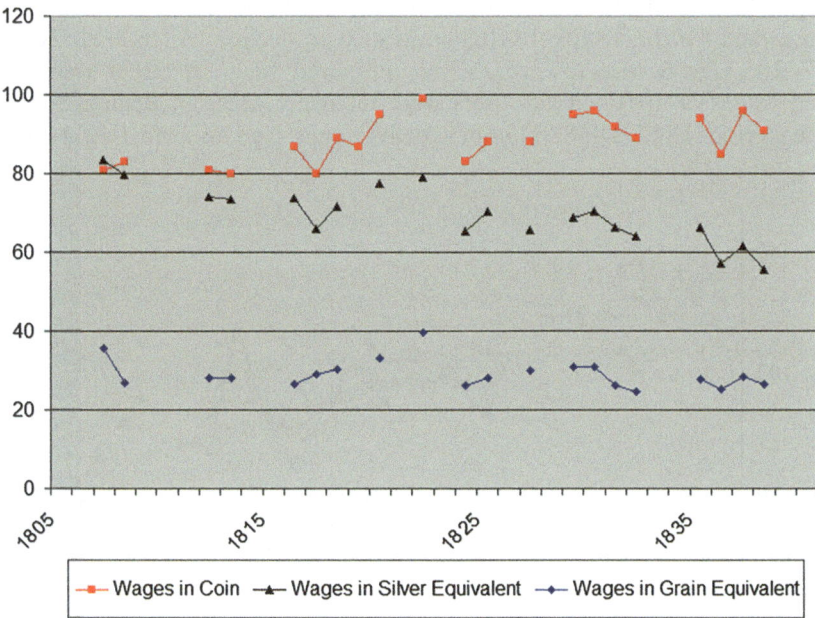

Fig. 6 Daily wages of unskilled labourers in Beijing, 1807–1838. Wages in coin: *wen*/day (based on Buck). Wages in silver equivalent: *li*/day (based on exchange ratios in Tongtaisheng ledgers). Wages in grain equivalent: *shao*/day (based on Jiangnan rice prices). *Source* Li Longsheng (2010: 174, Table 3.17)

stress of overpopulation.[12] The keen attention given to China's imports of foreign silver has obscured the fact that the major force driving the growth of the money supply in the eighteenth century was a dramatic increase in the minting of bronze coin. Although silver imports in the early eighteenth century had fallen from their peak level of a century earlier, imports of Japanese copper and the rapid development of copper mining in Yunnan from the 1730s to the 1790s enabled the Qing state to raise the output of state mints nearly tenfold compared to the late seventeenth century.[13] During the period 1740–1785, the average annual output of bronze coin was equivalent in value to 125 tons of silver at a time when silver imports averaged 50 tons per year (Fig. 7). The demand for bronze coin was most acute in highly commercialized regions such as Jiangnan, where bronze coin displaced silver as the monetary standard

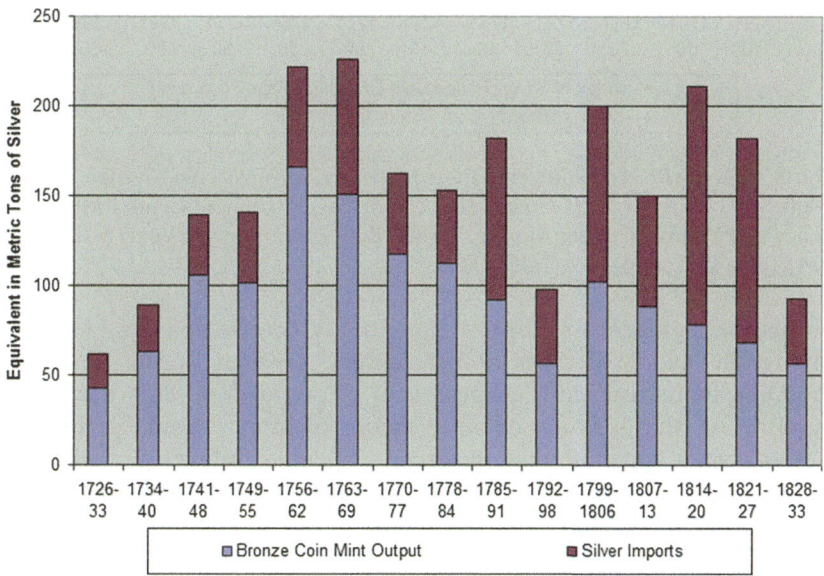

Fig. 7 Growth of the money supply, 1726–1833 (annual averages). *Sources* Bronze coin mint output: Vogel n.d.: 606–640, Appendix D.4. Silver imports: Dermigny (1964, 2: 735) Coin-silver exchange ratios: Vogel (1987: 17–23, Appendix 3)

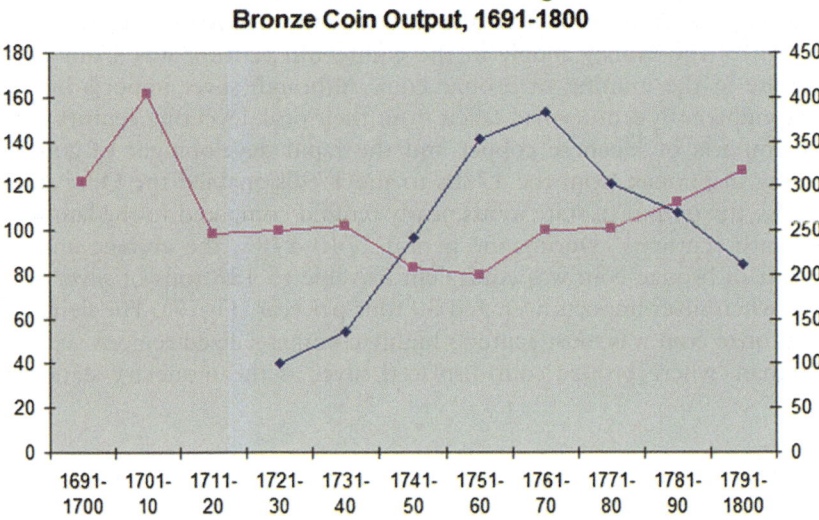

Fig. 8 Silver: Bronze coin exchange ratios and bronze coin output, 1691–1800. 1721–1730 = 100. *Source* Hans Ulrich Vogel, 'Chinese Central Monetary Policy and Yunnan Copper Mining, 1644–1800' (unpub. ms.), Vogel n.d.: 414–424, Table C. 1, 606–632, Table D4.2

in the mid-eighteenth century.[14] Significantly, bronze coin rose in value during the middle decades of the century, precisely at the time that the Qing mints reached their peak level of output (Fig. 8)—exactly the opposite of what a crude quantity theory of money would predict. It is also readily apparent that the trends in eighteenth-century silver to bronze coin exchange ratios show no correlation with the fluctuations in imports of foreign silver. The value of silver rose in the last two decades of the eighteenth century even as silver imports surged to new highs.

3 The Silver Question

It has been argued that the chief cause of economic depression in the early nineteenth century was the massive outflow of silver during these years, a reversal of the centuries-long pattern of silver flowing into China as a result of surging opium imports (Mann Jones and Kuhn 1978: 130; Peng 1983: 25–26). This argument traces back to contemporary Chinese officials and statesmen: as early as 1820, the influential policy advisor Bao Shichen warned that opium smuggling by foreign merchants was causing 100 million silver taels to drain out of China every year (Rowe 2010, 72).[15] A large body of modern scholarship likewise has attributed the 'drain of silver' to the dramatic increase in opium imports. Manhoung Lin has modified the standard explanation for the drain of silver, de-emphasizing the effects of the import of opium and instead attributing the outflow of silver to a global crisis in the production of precious metals and a worldwide economic depression that eroded demand for Chinese exports such as tea (Lin 2006). With the revival of gold and silver production and rapid growth of tea and silk exports in the 1850s, silver once again began to flow into China. At the same time, Lin, like earlier scholars, depicts the Chinese economy as having developed an unhealthy dependency on imports of foreign silver that left it vulnerable to the vicissitudes of the global capitalist economy.

Since the pioneering work of Hosea Morse in the early twentieth century, the reversal in the flow of silver has been dated to the late 1820s. However, in her book, Lin Man-houng developed a new quantitative study of China's balance of trade that proposed a new dating for the onset of the reversal in the flow of silver beginning in 1808 (Table 3). According to Lin's calculations, China's net silver exports during the period 1808–1856 amounted to 384 million pesos (10,070 metric tons). But she went on to emphasize that silver began to flow back into China in substantial quantities after 1857, while imports of opium reached unprecedentedly high levels and accounted for an even greater proportion of

Table 3 Lin Man-houng's estimates of net silver flows in and out of Qing China. Unit: millions of silver pesos

Years	Net inflow	Net outflow
1721–1740	68	
1752–1800	105	
1808–1856		384
1857–1866	187	
1868–1886	504	

Source Lin (2006: 95)

China's imports. She concluded that the import of opium alone cannot explain the outflow of silver in the first half of the nineteenth century.

Lin's calculation that the net outflow of silver began as early as 1808, rather than from 1826 as indicated by Morse's data, certainly was a startling new finding. However, Kishimoto Mio has drawn attention to errors in Lin's calculations that seriously misrepresent the export of silver from China (Kishimoto 2009: 93–95). Subsequently Lin acknowledged the errors and modified her data, lowering her estimate for the net outflow of silver during the period 1808–1856 from 384 million pesos to 327 million pesos. Most importantly, her revised figures indicate that the reversal in the flow of silver began in the late 1820s, a re-affirmation of the dating originally proposed by Morse (Lin 2011: 17, Fig. 10). In my view, however, Lin's data is still flawed, because she relies on balance of trade statistics rather than actually measuring the flow of silver. My own estimate of China's silver imports and exports during the period 1818–1854 (Table 4) indicates that China experienced a net loss of 134 million pesos, or 3576 tons of silver, rather than the 308 million pesos projected by Lin for these years.

Although Lin Man-houng's analysis shifts the focus away from opium, she still views the outflow of silver as the proximate cause of economic depression in China. But I believe this thesis is untenable.[16] Contrary to Lin's claims, there was no crisis of silver production following the demise of Spanish colonial rule in Latin America in the 1810s. Coin output in Mexico did decline from the historical high of 18 million pesos minted in 1810, but by 1827, when the outflow of silver from China began,

Table 4 Net flow of silver from China, 1818–1854 (all figures in millions of pesos)

	A Silver imports	B Silver exports	Net flow of silver (A–B)
1818–20	19.31	9.42	+9.89
1821–25	26.13	5.12	+21.01
1826–30	12.72	25.68	−12.96
1831–35	5.17	24.98	−19.81
1836–40	2.77	32.26	−29.49
1841–45	2.34	53.67	−51.33
1846–50	0.24	30.82	−30.57
1851–54	0.82	21.51	−20.69
Total	69.51	203.46	−133.95

Source von Glahn (2013: 50, Table 2.10)

output had returned to a minimum of 10 million pesos per year. China's maximum imports of silver never exceeded three million pesos in a year, so there was ample supply to accommodate Chinese demand. Nor is it true that China's exports of tea and silk declined during this period; on the contrary, exports of tea and silk reached an unprecedented high level in the early 1830s (Fig. 9).[17] Chinese exports then levelled off until the dramatic surge to far higher levels that occurred in the 1850s.

Other recent estimates of the silver outflow by Chinese scholars—although higher than my figures—have largely downplayed the magnitude of the drain of silver in the first half of the nineteenth century. The economist He Liping, for example, has calculated that net silver exports averaged 1.86 million *liang* per year during the 22 years between 1817 and 1839, for a total net loss of 40.84 million *liang* (1523 metric tons) (He 2007: 70). He concludes, based on estimates of China's total silver stock c. 1800 that range from 600 million to 1.1 billion *liang*, that the net outflow of silver during this period amounted to only 3.6–6.7% of

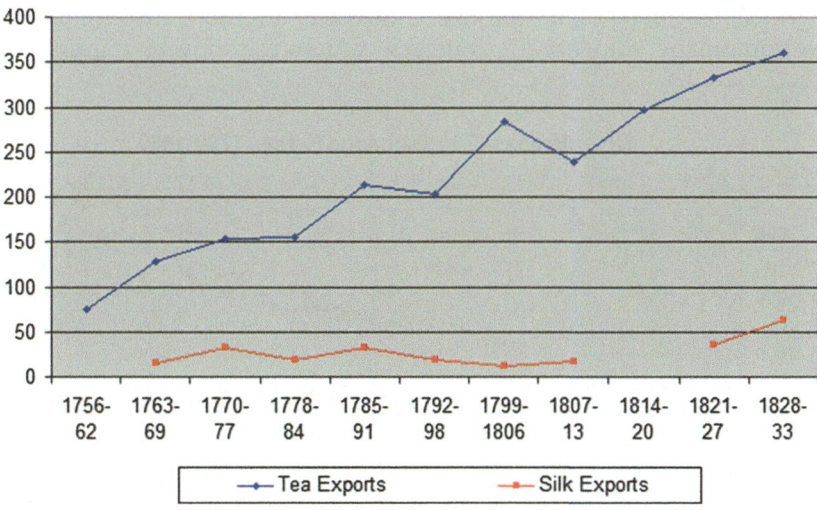

Fig. 9 Tea and silk exports, 1756–1833. (annual averages; tea exports in thousands of piculs; silk exports in hundreds of piculs): Silk data is incomplete and no silk data is available for 1756–1762 and 1814–1820. *Source* Dermigny 1964: 2, 549–553

China's total silver stock. If we use instead Hamashita Takeshi's estimate of 1.67 billion *yuan* (equivalent to 1.16 billion *liang*) for China's total silver stock in the 1850s, the net outflow of silver before 1839 based on He's figures would have been only 3.5% (Hamashita 1984: 391).[18] The stock of money is obviously relevant for understanding bullion movements because the significance of fluctuations of silver imports will depend on the size of the existing stock. From the perspective of stock demand, I fully concur with He's conclusion that this magnitude of silver export could not have caused the drastic effects commonly ascribed to it.

The principal evidence for a shortage of silver in China during the first half of the nineteenth century is the sharp appreciation of silver (relative to bronze coin) beginning in the mid-1830s (Fig. 10). Contemporary Chinese statesmen attributed the falling value of bronze coin to the widespread use of foreign silver pesos as a means of exchange and exhorted the court to halt the circulation of foreign coin. Undoubtedly the greater utility of a silver coin of standard weight and purity such as the Spanish peso contributed to the diminished value of bronze coin, but bronze coin also depreciated relative to uncoined sycee silver. Debasement of the bronze coin issued by the state—confirmed by numismatic evidence—encouraged widespread private minting of

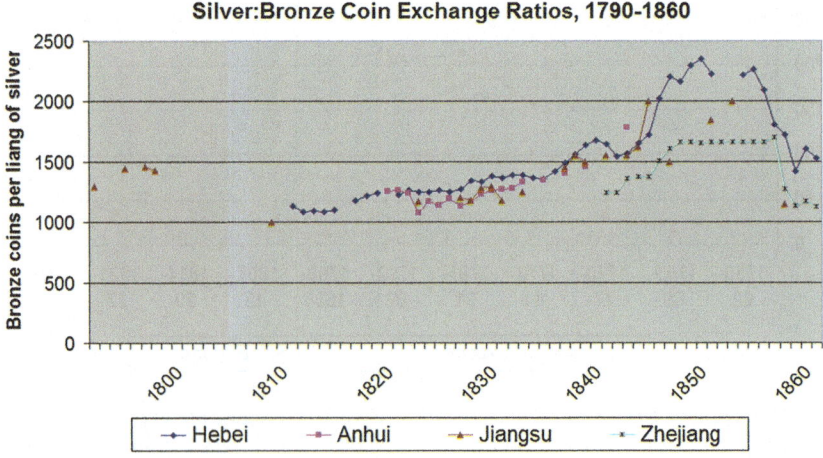

Fig. 10 Silver: Bronze coin exchange ratios, 1790–1860. *Source* von Glahn (2013: 55, Fig. 2.20)

heavily adulterated coin (Burger 2015; Wang 2003: 196–199). Thus, the increasingly inferior quality of bronze coin contributed to its fall in value. Another new development that contributed to the depreciation of bronze coin was the growing issue of bronze coin-denominated paper notes (*qianpiao*) by the private banks (*qianzhuang* and *yinhao*) that began to proliferate from the end of the eighteenth century, especially in North China (Wang 2003: 180–184; von Glahn 2013: 55–57).[19]

Surprisingly, Fig. 10 reveals that the depreciation of bronze coin appears to have been significantly more severe in North China, traditionally a region more dependent on bronze coin, rather than in Jiangnan, where silver was in more common use and the Spanish peso coin (the Carolus dollar) had become widely employed as a means of exchange. Oscillations in the silver–bronze coin exchange ratios reflected the differential demand for each type of currency, and not simply a shortage of silver. As Kuroda Akinobu persuasively argues, the fragmentary structure of currency circulation in late imperial China and the high seasonality of monetary demand resulted in a disproportionate demand for means of payment, especially bronze coin, within local markets. In the Qing period this demand was increasingly satisfied by money substitutes such as *qianpiao*. In Kuroda's view, China suffered from shortages of bronze coin, not silver. Given the lack of integration between local-level and upper-level markets, the influx of foreign silver did not fundamentally alter the autonomy of local currency circuits (Kuroda 2000, 2008: 187–198).

In my view, a key feature of the Chinese monetary system throughout the entire imperial era has been endemic shortages of money. Since the establishment of the bronze coin monetary standard in the Qin and Han dynasties, the state was unable to supply sufficient quantities of low-value bronze currency to meet the needs for a means of exchange. This problem became increasingly acute during the late imperial era with the growing penetration of the market in all regions of the Empire. Even during the peak period of mint output in the late eleventh century, when the Northern Song dynasty minted over five billion coins per year, contemporaries complained of shortages of money severe enough to be called 'coin famines' (*qianhuang*). Over and over again, in Chinese history we see a strong preference for the more abundant currency. Thus, bronze coin tended to rise in value at times when the state minted large quantities of coin (in the Northern Song and the mid-Qing) and fall when mint output slackened (in the Southern Song and the Ming).

The adoption of new monetary standards—such as the Song *huizi* paper money and the Carolus silver peso in the nineteenth century—above all was premised on having a sufficient supply of currency to meet the demand for currency. This demand preference contradicts the simplistic assumptions of the fairly crude versions of the quantity theory of exchange that all too often have been employed uncritically by historians. Moreover, the value of bronze coin hardly rose once silver began to flow into China in even greater quantities after 1855. On the contrary, according to the records of the Imperial Maritime Customs, the value of bronze coin remained below the average values of the 1820s for the rest of the century (Fig. 11).

We also find a parallel trend in the depreciation of coin relative to silver during the early nineteenth century in Vietnam, where the value of silver rose sharply in the late 1820s, with another steep increase occurring in the 1840s (Fig. 12). Ironically, the appreciation of silver in Vietnam was mostly attributed to exports of silver to China (estimated at two million *liang*/*lạng* per year in the 1830s) as well as the debasement of the Dai Viet kingdom's coinage, which from 1813 was minted from zinc rather than copper (Fujiwara 1960: 42–48). It is worth noting that the second quarter of the nineteenth century was a period of economic

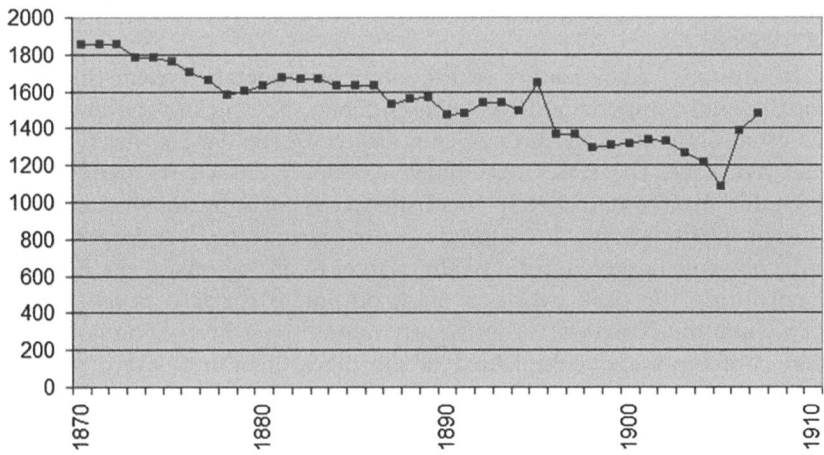

Fig. 11 Silver–Bronze coin exchange ratios, 1870–1906. *Source* Peng Xinwei (1965: 848)

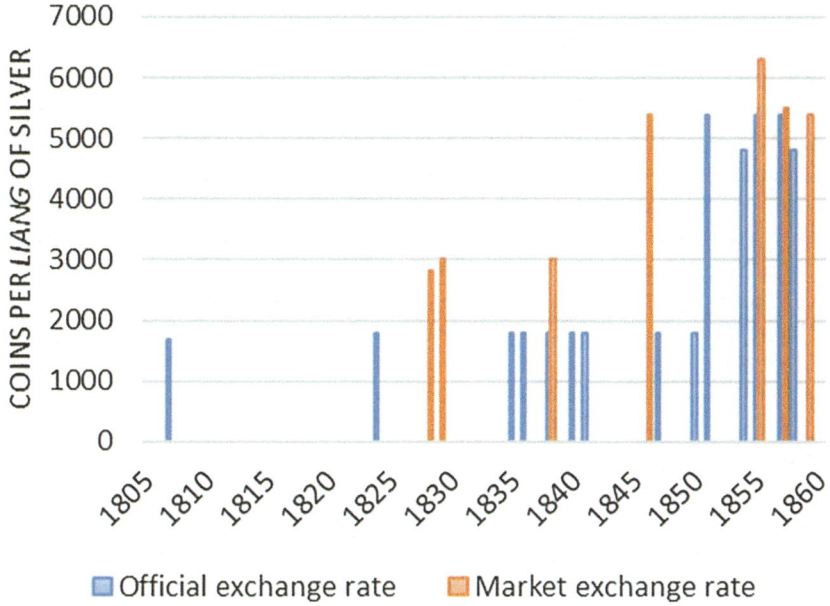

Fig. 12 Silver: Coin exchange ratios in Vietnam, 1807–1860. *Source* Taga 2015: 10–13, Tables 2 and 3

depression and deflation not only in China, but in other parts of Asia as well.[20] In India, price deflation (including a steep erosion in the prices of export goods) persisted throughout these decades despite the growing infusions of silver from China. Economic distress was most acute during the crisis years of 1830–1833, when the East India Company repatriated enormous quantities of silver to Britain, but the malaise continued even after robust net inflows of silver returned from 1834 (Siddiqi 1983: 253–254, 1995, 16–25).[21] In India, as in China, the causes of economic depression cannot be attributed to silver shortages alone.

The silver price deflation in China in the early nineteenth century thus cannot be correlated either with population trends or fluctuations in silver imports (or in foreign trade generally). There appears to be a closer correlation with the money supply. After the long secular increase of the eighteenth century, prices abruptly fell in the 1790s, when new infusions of money, both coin and silver, contracted sharply due to the White Lotus uprising and the curtailment of European overseas trade following the French Revolution and the outbreak of the Napoleonic Wars. But the correlation is inexact, especially during the period 1818–1827, when silver prices fell even as silver imports peaked. The deflationary trend that commenced c. 1815 cannot be explained by variations in the money supply. Moreover, the standard estimates of money supply fail to account for the spreading use of paper substitutes such as *qianpiao* and the 'silver notes' (*yinpiao*) that were widely used in South China. Li Longsheng has gone so far as to propose that the volume of silver notes in circulation (which he estimates at 61 million taels) fully replaced the net outflow of silver (62 million taels, by his estimate) during the period 1820–1851 (Li 2010: 179–180, Table 3.20). However, in the absence of more explicit evidence for the volume of notes in circulation, this hypothesis remains speculative.

As the pronounced dip in grain prices in the 1790s indicates (and the outbreak of the White Lotus Rebellion confirmed), China's domestic economy was displaying signs of serious strain. We lack data to measure changes in output and trade with any precision, but reports from inland and maritime customs depots are revealing. Table 5 shows the revenues reported by the four largest customs depots. The data indicate that trade volume peaked in domestic commercial centres such as Huai'an (lynchpin of the Grand Canal, and the salt trade in particular), Suzhou (hub of the national rice market) and Jiujiang (a major Yangzi River port and gateway to the Middle Yangzi tea-producing regions) in the 1770s–1790s and declined thereafter. In contrast, maritime trade at Guangzhou soared in the late eighteenth century; beginning in 1802, the maritime customs revenue of Guangzhou surpassed

Table 5 Customs revenues, 1725–1831. (thousands of silver taels)

Huai'an Inland		Xupu (Suzhou) Inland		Jiujiang Inland		Guangzhou Maritime	
1725	84	1727	353	1731	252	1727	91
1736	484	1738	382	1739	352	1742	310
1753	325	1753	495	1753	354	1753	515
1773	557	1764	542	1776	662	1765	600
1818	441	1791	583	1801	539	1804	1642
1828	302	1818	427	1820	585	1812	1375
1831	324	1831	391	1829	600	1831	1462

Source Wu Chengming (2001: 271, Table 18)

the total revenues of the three largest inland customs stations, testifying both to the vitality of overseas trade and the torpor into which domestic trade had descended. Customs revenues at Guangzhou and Jiujiang held relatively steady from the turn of the century up to the Opium War (although the Jiujiang receipts remained below their eighteenth-century peak). Customs revenue figures at Suzhou and Huai'an reveal a downward trend across the first half of the nineteenth century well below late eighteenth-century levels.

Although the economic expansion of the eighteenth century initially fostered a more integrated national market centred on Jiangnan, by the end of the century a strong centrifugal trend towards regionalization and rustification had emerged. Migration to the marginal agricultural regions of the interior arrested growth in labour productivity. Crop yields continued to improve in Jiangnan, but overall agricultural productivity probably declined. In North China, production of cotton and other non-food crops fell after 1750, reflecting a shift towards subsistence farming to meet the needs of the region's still rapidly growing population (Pomeranz 2000: 140–141). The proportion of the total population living in cities declined to about 5% in the mid-nineteenth century, less than half the urbanization rate of the Southern Song (Skinner 1977: 229).[22] Jiangnan's share of the national population shrank from 14% in 1391 to 7.6% in 1776.[23]

Jiangnan's pre-eminent role in the national economy diminished as well. For example, rural households in Hubei began to manufacture coarse cotton cloth which they exchanged for rice from the more productive agricultural regions of Hunan and Sichuan. Subsequently, Sichuan developed its own 'native cloth' (*tubu*) industry that marketed its products within Sichuan and in the outlying frontier provinces of Yunnan and Guizhou. The growth of rural industry in the interior came at the expense of core areas such as Jiangnan, which produced better-quality but more expensive cloth. As the market for Jiangnan textiles in the interior dried up, the flow of rice, timber and other raw materials down the Yangzi River ebbed (Yamamoto 1991; Pomeranz 2000: 242–249). This pattern of domestic 'import substitution' curtailed interregional trade (as we see in Table 5), resulting in greater regional autarky.

Jiangnan, China's most commercially developed region, was therefore particularly vulnerable to these structural changes in the Chinese economy. By the early nineteenth century, Jiangnan's economy bore little resemblance to the agrarian order that prevailed throughout most of

China. According to Li Bozhong's reconstruction of the Hua-Lou local economy in the 1820s, manufacturing employed 56% of adult workers and generated 33% of total added value, in contrast to 27% and 31% respectively for agriculture. The Hua-Lou area had an urbanization rate as high as 40%, and nearly 30% of its gross product (consisting almost entirely of cotton goods) was exported to external markets (Li 2010, 2013). But the cotton industry was by no means flourishing. According to Li's figures, cotton manufacture absorbed 43% of total employment in Hua-Lou, but generated only 9% of its aggregate product. Price data for the cotton industry is extremely fragmentary, but the few figures that do exist suggest a substantial decline compared to the eighteenth century. Data on Chinese cotton exports show that in the early 1830s, the price of cotton cloth (predominantly Songjiang 'nankeens') at Guangzhou had fallen 28% compared to the average price of the 1810s (Wu 2001: 267). A treatise on Songjiang agriculture published in 1834 observed that the market for Songjiang cloth had been distressed for more than a decade, and poor cotton harvests since 1829 had made raw cotton prohibitively expensive.[24]

4 Conclusion

Economic depression in early nineteenth-century China was marked by a sustained decline in silver prices beginning in c. 1815. The Daoguang Depression coincided with an ecological crisis: climatic disturbances, harvest failures and catastrophic floods, particularly during the period 1815–1835. Conventional explanations for China's economic troubles have emphasized either: (1) China's incorporation into a capitalist world economy on unfavourable terms, resulting in a massive drain of silver abroad, primarily to pay for opium imports; or (2) a Malthusian crisis of subsistence triggered by unsustainable population increases that overtaxed the productive capacity of the Chinese economy. Yet neither of these theses is satisfactory.

In the first place, the onset of economic depression pre-dated the reversal in the flow of silver bullion. As Li Bozhong has observed, complaints of economic distress and widespread impoverishment of rich and poor alike were already being aired by 1820, well before the outflow of silver and bronze coin depreciation had become severe (Li 2007: 173–178). Moreover, any assessment of the impact of silver flows on the Chinese economy must consider questions of demand as well as supply.

As Kishimoto Mio has shown, the penetration of foreign silver as shown by the adoption of the Carolus peso as a monetary standard varied extensively by region, and even by type of transaction (Kishimoto 2011: 13–17). For example, in Jiangnan, the Carolus peso was widely used as the common currency of trade and finance by the beginning of the nineteenth century, yet land sale contracts continued to be denominated in bronze coin well into the nineteenth century. The complexity of China's domestic monetary system at this time—which included Carolus pesos, copper and silver notes, and bronze coin as well as bullion silver—is still not sufficiently well understood. Given the present state of knowledge, we should beware any theories that treat the Chinese monetary system—or, for that matter, the Chinese economy—as an undifferentiated whole.

The new evidence for a Malthusian crisis from recent research—falling per capita GDP and real wages—is encumbered by methodological problems and questionable theoretical assumptions. The reversal of price trends in c. 1815—resulting in steep deflation in silver prices, but a steady level in relative prices—and the continuous population expansion down to the outbreak of the Taiping Rebellion belie a Malthusian narrative. Of course, given the massive scale of the Chinese Empire, regional variations were undoubtedly significant. The decline of cotton cloth manufacture in Jiangnan during the second quarter of the nineteenth century was related to structural and long-term conjunctural shifts in China's domestic economy. The concentration of population growth in poorer regions in western China and the increasing rustification of handicraft production had adverse effects on urban manufacture in regions such as Jiangnan, which could no longer compete with cheaper cotton goods produced in the interior regions.

The economic depression in early nineteenth-century China should be seen in the context of a long-standing pattern of conjunctural oscillation of economic expansion and contraction typical of advanced pre-modern economies. In the classic formulation of François Simiand, a long wave of economic expansion—the A-phase of population growth, expanding output and rising prices—was inevitably followed by an equally long B-phase of high mortality, deflation and stagnant output (Simiand 1932). Jack Goldstone has argued that the A-phase of commercial growth and economic prosperity that germinated across Eurasia in the early sixteenth century ultimately culminated in the economic distress, social conflicts and political crises that erupted in Ming China, Western Europe and the Ottoman Empire in the mid-seventeenth century. The subsequent B-phase of economic contraction lasted until the early eighteenth century before the Chinese and European economies regained momentum, inaugurating a new A-phase (Goldstone 1991). In my view, although we can find some parallels in the cyclical trends of growth and decline in China and Europe in the period 1500–1800, there were crucial differences as well.[25] In the case of China, the long A-phase that lasted from the 1690s down to the 1790s did not end in a demographic collapse, but rather a precarious equilibrium. It is quite possible that eighteenth-century China experienced an 'industrious revolution' not unlike that hypothesized for contemporary Japan and Europe, in which population expansion was accompanied by the intensification of work and increased non-agricultural production in the countryside that, together with the development of horizontal exchange within local and regional markets, led to economic specialization and productivity gains equalling or exceeding demographic growth.[26] Despite the apparent synchronicity of the Daoguang Depression and the B-phase of deflation and economic contraction in Europe during the period 1817–1850, fundamental differences between the economies of China and Europe had emerged by this time.[27]

In addition, the role of silver imports in the Chinese economy had changed since the 'Silver Century' of 1550–1650. The primacy of silver—a cardinal feature of the A-phase of 1500–1650—became attenuated as bronze coin displaced silver bullion as the monetary standard in many local markets in the eighteenth century. Moreover, the economics of the silver trade had changed dramatically, as the arbitrage profits that orchestrated the global movements of silver during the 'Silver Century' vanished. Just as the causes of the Daoguang Depression are to be found in China's domestic economic conditions rather than the global economy, the reduced demand for money (silver and bronze coin alike) during these decades was a symptom, not the cause, of this economic distress.

Notes

1. For an introduction to the revisionist approach and basic arguments of the 'California School', see Goldstone (2000).
2. For an incisive argument asserting the fallacy of GDP as a measure of economic productivity in pre-modern societies, see Du and Jin (2011). GDP is intended to measure all goods, labour and services that entered the marketplace, but much of the gross product of pre-modern societies was

not marketed. Conversion of values into universal measures for purposes of comparison such as 1990 US dollars also requires a standard index for prices (usually gold, which had no monetary function in China) that may not actually reflect real market values. On the technical problems of price calculations for GDP estimates, see Peng Kaixiang (2011).
3. For more details on the deficiencies of Liu's methodology, see my review of his book in *T'oung Pao* 102.4–5 (2016): 566–70.
4. The authors conclude that their findings confirm Huang's involution thesis, but their model does not provide an adequate test of that thesis.
5. The authors calculate that China's per capita GDP in the eighteenth century was far below the levels of Spain and Italy as well.
6. The 1820s were a period of economic torpor, if not depression, in both regions.
7. Debin Ma (2008) calculates that per capita GDP in Jiangsu-Zhejiang in the early twentieth century was roughly 50 per cent higher than the average for China as a whole. He also points out that per capita tax revenue (which perhaps can be taken as a rough proxy for income) was also 50% higher in Jiangsu-Zhejiang during the eighteenth century.
8. Allen concludes that the golden age for Jiangnan farming/weaving families came in the early seventeenth century, but of course his study skips over the intervening two centuries. If one substitutes the much higher cotton cloth prices that prevailed in the late eighteenth century in place of the extremely depressed prices of the 1820s, I suspect that the golden age continued down to 1800 irrespective of population growth.
9. Xu Dixin and Wu Chengming estimated that only 1–2% of the Ming population were wage labourers.
10. For Jiangnan prices, see Yeh-chien Wang (1992); for Guangdong, see Marks and Chen (1995). Wheat prices in Zhili (Lillian Li 1992) and rice prices in Hunan (Wong and Perdue 1992) rose very gradually from 1740 to 1790.
11. For further data on grain prices in the north which show the same trends, see Lillian Li (2007: 196–220) and Lee and Campbell (1997: 27–39).
12. This is also the conclusion of Peng Kaixiang (2006).
13. From 1738 to 1810, Yunnan copper mines produced an average of 6000 tons of copper annually, reaching a peak of 9000 tons in 1764 (Vogel 1987: 32–33).
14. On the return to a bronze coin monetary standard in Jiangnan in the mid-eighteenth century, see Kuroda (1987); Kishimoto (1997: 353–363).
15. Needless to say, Bao's hyperbolic figures are hardly credible.
16. For more detailed critiques of Lin's analysis, see Irigoin (2009) and von Glahn (2013: 49–58).

17. As Wang Jingyu (2006: 497) observes, the appreciation of silver in China—at a time when silver was depreciating in the London market—should have been favourable to Chinese exports.
18. Hamashita's figure, based on an 1850 report from the British governor in Hong Kong, seems preferable to the figures cited by He.
19. Provincial officials roundly blamed the excess of *qianpiao* notes for contributing to the depreciation of bronze coin.
20. A preliminary assessment of the common trend of deflation and economic distress in Southeast Asia during the first half of the nineteenth century was presented in Ōhashi (2015).
21. For the data on silver imports and exports to India, see Chaudhuri (1966: 358–359, Tables 4 and 5). Although Indian opium and cotton exports surged during 1830–1833, the East India Company delivered its silver bullion proceeds from China directly to Britain rather than to India. See Bowen (2010: 473).
22. Skinner estimated China's urbanization rate in 1843 at 5.1%.
23. For population data for the eight core prefectures of Jiangnan for 1391 and 1776, see respectively Li Bozhong (2003: 142, Table 5.3) and Cao Shuji (2000: 87–88, Table 3–5, 113, Table 3–15).
24. Cited in Li Bozhong (2010: 492).
25. For a detailed analysis, see von Glahn (2003).
26. On the concept of 'industrious revolution'—which has been applied in somewhat different ways to eighteenth-century Japan and Western Europe, see Hayami (1979) and de Vries (2008). The studies of Pomeranz (2000) and Li Bozhong (2010) implicitly suggest that just such an 'industrious revolution' occurred in Qing China.
27. On the dating of a B-phase of economic contraction in Europe to 1817–1850, see Vilar (1974: 397–399).

REFERENCES

Allen, Robert C. 2009. Agricultural Productivity and Rural Incomes in England and the Yangtze Delta, c. 1620–c. 1820. *Economic History Review* 62 (3): 525–550.

Allen, Robert C., Jean-Pascal Bassino, Debin Ma, Christine Moll-Murata, and Jan Luiten Van Zanden. 2011. Wages, Prices, and Living Standards in China, 1738–1925: In Comparison with Europe, Japan, and India. *Economic History Review* 64, supplement 1: 8–38.

Atwell, William S. 1986. Some Observations on the 'Seventeenth-Century Crisis' in China and Japan. *Journal of Asian Studies* 45 (2): 223–244.

———. 2006. Another Look at Silver Imports into China, ca. 1635–1644. *Journal of World History* 16 (4): 467–489.

Bowen, H.V. 2010. Bullion for Trade, War, and Debt Relief: British Movements of Silver to, around, and from Asia, 1760–1833. *Modern Asian Studies* 44 (3): 445–475.

Broadberry, Stephen, Hanhui Guan, and David Daokui Li. 2017. China, Europe, and the Great Divergence: A Study in Historical National Accounting, 980–1850. In: www.lse.ac.uk/economicHistory/pdf/Broadberry/China8.pdf.

Burger, Werner. 2015. Silver is Expensive, Cash is Cheap: Official and Private Cash Forgeries as the Main Cause for the 19th Century Monetary Turmoil. In: *Money in Asia (1200–1900): Small Currencies in Social and Political Contexts*, eds. Jane Kate Leonard and Ulrich Theobald, 141–154. Leiden: Brill.

Cao, Shuji 曹树基. 2000. *Zhongguo renkou shi: Qing shiqi* 中国人口史, vol. 5, 清时期. Shanghai: Fudan daxue chubanshe.

Chao, Kang. 1988. *Man & Land in Chinese History: An Economic Analysis*. Stanford: Stanford University Press.

Chaudhuri, K.N. 1966. India's Foreign Trade and the Cessation of the East India Company's Trading Activities, 1828–40. *Economic History Review* 19 (2): 346–363.

Chen, Chunsheng 陳春聲. 2005. *Shichang jizhi yu shehui bianqian: 18 shji Guangdong mijia fenxi* 市場機制與社會變遷:18世紀廣東米價分析. 2nd ed. Taipei: Daoxiang chubanshe.

Dermigny, Louis. 1964. *La Chine et l'occident: le commerce à Canton au XVIIIe siècle*. Paris: S.E.V.P.E.N.

De Vries, Jan. 2008. *The Industrious Revolution: Consumer Behavior and the Household Economy, 1650 to the Present Day*. Cambridge: Cambridge University Press.

Du, Xuncheng 杜恂诚 and Li Jin 李晋. 2011. Zhongguo jingji shi 'GDP' yanjiu zhi wuqu 中国经济史"GDP"研究之误区. *Xueshu yuekan* 学术月刊 43 (10): 74–81.

Dunstan, Helen. 2005. *State or Merchant? Political Economy and Political Process in 1740s China*. Cambridge: Harvard University Asia Center.

Goldstone, Jack A. 1991. The Causes of Long Waves in Early Modern Economic History. *Research on Economic History*, supplement 6: 51–92.

———. 2000. The Rise of the West—or Not? A Revision to Socio-Economic History. *Sociological Theory* 18 (2): 175–194.

Fujiwara, Riichirō 藤原利一郎. 1960. Genchō shita ni okeru kinginka no mondai 阮朝下における金銀価の問題. *Shisō* 史窓17–18: 35–50.

Hamashita, Takeshi. 1984. Foreign Trade Finance in China, 1810–1850. In: *State and Society in China: Japanese Perspectives on Ming-Qing Social and Economic History*, eds. Linda Grove and Christian Daniels, 387–435. Tokyo: University of Tokyo Press.

Hayami, Akira 速水融. 1979. Kinsei Nihon no keizai hatten to 'Industrious Revolution'. 近世日本の経済発展と 'Industrious Revolution'. In: *Kindai ikōki no Nihon keizai* 近代移行期の日本経済, eds. Shinbō Hiroshi 新保博 and Yasuba Yasukichi 安場保吉, 3–14. Tokyo: Nihon keizai shimbunsha.

He, Liping 贺力平. 2007. Yapian maoyi yu baiyin wailiu guanxi zhi zai jiantao—jianlun guonei huobi gongji yu duiwai maoyi guanxide lishi yanbian 鸦片贸易与白银外流关系之再检讨–兼论国内货币供给与对外贸易关系的历史演变. *Shehui kexue zhanxian* 社会科学战线 2007. 1: 63–80.

Huang, Philip C.C. 1990. *The Peasant Family and Rural Development in the Yangzi Delta, 1350–1988*. Stanford: Stanford University Press.

Irigoin, Alejandra. 2009. The End of a Silver Era: The Consequences of the Breakdown of the Spanish Peso Standard in China and the United States, 1780s–1850s. *Journal of World History* 20 (2): 207–243.

Kishimoto, Mio 岸本美緒. 1997. *Shindai Chūgoku no bukka to keizai hendō* 清代中国の物価と経済変動. Tokyo: Kembun shuppan.

———. 2009. New Studies on Statecraft in Mid- and Late-Qing: Qing Intellectuals and their Debates on Economic Policies. *International Journal of Asian Studies* 6 (1): 93–95.

———. 2011. Foreign Silver and China's Domestic Economy. Presented at the Third European Congress on World and Global History. London, 14–17 April, 2011.

Kuroda, Akinobu 黒田明信. 1987. Kenryū no senki 乾隆の銭貴. *Tōyōshi kenkyū* 東洋史研究 45 (5): 692–723.

———. 2000. Another Monetary Economy: The Case of Traditional China. In: *Asia-Pacific Dynamism, 1500–2000*, eds. A.J.H. Lathan and Heita Kawakatsu, 187–98. London: Routledge.

———. 2008. Concurrent but Non-Integrable Currency Circuits: Complementary Relationships among Monies in Modern China and Other Regions. *Financial History Review* 15 (1): 17–36.

Lee, James Z., and Cameron Campbell. 1997. *Fate and Fortune in Rural China: Social Organization and Population Behavior in Liaoning, 1774–1873*. Cambridge: Cambridge University Press.

Li, Bozhong 李伯重. 2003. Was There a 'Fourteenth-Century Turning Point? Population, Land, Technology, and Farm Management. In: *The Song-Yuan-Ming Transition in Chinese History*, eds. Paul Jakov Smith and Richard von Glahn, 135–175. Cambridge: Harvard University Asia Center.

———. 2007. Daoguang xiaotiao yu guiwei dashui 道光萧条与癸未大水. *Shehui kexue* 社会科学 2007. 6: 173–178.

———. 2010. *Zhongguode zaoqi jindai jingji: 1820 niandai Huating-Louxian diqu GDP yanjiu* 中国的早期近代经济:1820年代华亭—娄县地区 GDP 研究. Beijing: Zhonghua shuju.

———. 2013. An Early Modern Economy in China: A Study of the GDP of the Huating-Lou Area, 1823–1829. In: *The Economic History of Lower Yangzi Delta in Late Imperial China: Connecting Money, Markets, & Institutions*, ed. Billy K.L. So, 133–145. London: Routledge.
Li, Bozhong, and Jan Luiten Van Zanden. 2012. Before the Great Divergence? Comparing the Yangzi Delta and the Netherlands in the Beginning of the Nineteenth Century. *Journal of Economic History* 72 (4): 956–989.
Li, Lillian M. 1992. Grain Prices in Zhili Province, 1736–1911: A Preliminary Study. In: *Chinese History in Economic Perspective*, eds. Thomas G. Rawski and Lillian M. Li, 69–99. Berkeley: University of California Press.
———. 2007. *Fighting Famine in North China: State, Market, and Environmental Decline, 1690s–1990s*. Stanford: Stanford University Press.
Li, Longsheng 李隆生. 2010. *Qingdaide guoji maoyi: baiyin liuru, huobi weiji he Wan Qing gongyehua*. 清代的國際貿易: 白銀流入,貨幣危機和晚清工業化. Taipei: Xiuwei zixun keji.
Lin, Man-houng. 2006. *China Upside Down: Currency, Society, and Ideologies, 1808–1856*. Cambridge: Harvard University Asia Center.
———. 2011. Latin America Silver and Early Nineteenth-century China. Presented at the Third European Congress for World and Global History. London, April 14–17, 2011.
Liu, William Guanglin. 2015. *The Chinese Market Economy, 1000–1500*. Albany: State University of New York Press.
Liu Ti 刘逖. 2009. "1600–1840 nian Zhongguo guonei shengchan zongzhi gusuan" 1600-1840 年中国国内生产总值估算. *Jingji yanjiu* 经济研究 2009. 10: 144–155.
Ma, Debin. 2008. Economic Growth in the Lower Yangzi Region of China in 1911–1937: A Quantitative and Historical Analysis. *Journal of Economic History* 68 (2): 355–392.
Maddison, Angus. 2001. *The World Economy: A Millennial Perspective*. Paris: OECD Publications.
———. 2007. *Chinese Economic Performance in the Long Run, 960–2030 AD*. Rev. ed. Paris: OECD Publications.
Mann Jones, Susan, and Philip Kuhn. 1978. Dynastic Decline and the Roots of Rebellion. In: *The Cambridge History of China*, vol. 10, *Late Ch'ing, 1800–1911*, ed. John K. Fairbank, 1: 107–162. Cambridge: Cambridge University Press.
Marks, Robert B. 2002. *The Origins of the Modern World: A Global and Ecological Narrative*. Lanham: Rowman & Littlefield.
Marks, Robert B., and Chunsheng Chen. 1995. Price Inflation and its Social, Economic, and Climatic Context in Guangdong Province, 1707–1800. *T'oung Pao* 81 (1–3): 109–152.

Moulder, Frances V. 1977. *Japan, China, and the Modern World Economy: Toward a Reinterpretation of East Asian Development ca. 1600 to ca. 1918*. Cambridge: Cambridge University Press.

Ōhashi, Atsuko. 2015. An Era of Deflation and Southeast Asia: The First Half of the 19th Century. Presented at the XVII World Economic History Congress. Kyoto, 3–7 August, 2015.

Peng, Kaixiang 彭凯翔. 2006. *Qingdai yilaide liangjia: lishixuede jieshi yu zaijieshi* 清代以来的粮价:历史学的解释与再解释. Shanghai: Shanghai renmin chubanshe.

———. 2011. Lishi GDP gusuan zhongde jijia wenti chuyi 历史GDP估算中的计价问题刍议. *Zhongguo jingji shi yanjiu* 中国经济史研究 2011. 4: 53–60.

Peng, Xinwei 彭信威. 1965. *Zhongguo huobi shi* 中國貨幣史. 2nd ed. Shanghai: Shanghai renmin chubanshe.

Peng, Zeyi 彭泽益. 1983. *Shijiu shiji houbanqide Zhongguo caizheng yu jingji* 十九世纪后半期的中国财政与经济. Beijing: Renmin chubanshe.

Pomeranz, K. 2000. *The Great Divergence: China, Europe, and the Making of the Modern World Economy*. Princeton: Princeton University Press.

———. 2008. Chinese Development in Long-Run Perspective. *Proceedings of the American Philosophical Society* 152 (1): 83–100.

Rowe, William T. 2010. Money, Economy, and Polity in the Daoguang-Era Paper Currency Debates. *Late Imperial China* 31 (2): 69–96.

Shi, Zhihong, Ni Yuping, and Bas van Leeuwen. 2014. Chinese National Income, ca. 1661–1933. Centre for Global Economic History (Utrecht University). Working Paper Series, no. 62. http://www.cgeh.nl/sites/default/files/WorkingPapers/CGEHWP62_ShiXuyiNiVanLeeuwen.pdf.

Siddiqi, Asiya. 1983. Money and Prices in the Earlier Stages of Empire: India and Britain, 1760–1840. *Indian Economic and Social History Review* 18 (3–4): 231–262.

———. 1995. Introduction. *Trade and Finance in Colonial India, 1750–1860*. New Delhi: Oxford University Press.

Simiand, François. 1932. *Recherches anciennes et nouvelles sur le mouvement general des prix du 16ᵉ au 19ᵉ siècle*. Paris: Domat Montchrestien.

Skinner, G. William. 1977. Regional Urbanization in Nineteenth-Century China. In: *The City in Late Imperial China*, ed. G. William Skinner, 212–49. Stanford: Stanford University Press.

Taga, Yoshihiro. 2015. The Development of the Silver Economy in Nineteenth Century Vietnam. Presented at XVII World Economic History Congress. Kyoto, 3–7 August, 2015.

Vilar, Pierre. 1974. *Or et monnaie dans l'histoire*. Paris: Flammarion.

Vogel, Hans Ulrich. 1987. Chinese Central Monetary Policy, 1644–1800. *Late Imperial China* 8 (2): 1–52.

———. n.d. Chinese Central Monetary Policy and Yunnan Copper Mining, 1644–1800. Unpublished manuscript.

von Glahn, Richard. 2003. Money-Use in China and Changing Patterns of Global Trade in Monetary Metals, 1500–1800. In: *Global Connections and Monetary History, 1470–1800*, eds. Dennis O. Flynn et al. 187–205. UK: Ashgate Press.

———. 2013. Cycles of Silver in Chinese Monetary History. In: *The Economic History of Lower Yangzi Delta in Late Imperial China: Connecting Money, Markets, & Institutions*, ed. Billy K.L. So, 17–71. London: Routledge.

———. 2016. Review of William Guanglin Liu, The Chinese Market Economy. *T'oung Pao* 102 (4–5): 566–570.

Wang, Jingyu 汪敬虞. 2006. Guanyu yapian zhanzhenghou shinianjian yingui qianjian yingxiangxia Zhongguo dui waimao wentide shangque. 关于鸦片战争后十年间银贵钱贱影响下中国对外贸问题的商榷. In: *Zhongguo shehui jingji shi luncong: Wu Chengming jiaoshou jiushi huadan jinian wenji* 中国社会经济史论丛:吴承明教授九十华诞纪念文集, ed. Fang, Xing 方行, 492–506. Beijing: Xinhua shudian.

Wang, Yeh-chien 王業鍵. 1992. Secular Trends of Rice Prices in the Yangzi Delta, 1638–1935. In: *Chinese History in Economic Perspective*, eds. Thomas G. Rawski and Lillian M. Li, 35-68. Berkeley: University of California Press.

———. 1996. Shijiu shiji qianqi wujia xialuo yu Taiping tianguo geming 十九世紀前期物價下落與太平天國革命. In: *Shibian, qunti, yu geren: diyijie quanguo lishixue xueshu taolunhui lunwenji* 世變,群體,與個人:第一屆全國歷史學學術討論會論文集, 259–284. Taipei: Taida lishixi.

———. 2003. Zhongguo jindai huobi yu yinhangde yanjin (1644–1937) 中國近代貨幣與銀行的演進. *Qingdai jingji shi lunwenji* 清代經濟史論文集, 161–274. Taipei: Daoxiang chubanshe.

Will, Pierre-Étienne. 1994. Développement quantitatif et développement qualitatif en Chine à la fin de l'époque impériale. *Annales: Histoire, Sciences Sociales* 49 (4): 863–902.

Wong, R. Bin and Peter Perdue. 1992. Grain Markets and Food Supplies in Eighteenth-Century Hunan. In: *Chinese History in Economic Perspective*, eds. Thomas G. Rawski and Lillian M. Li, 126–144. Berkeley: University of California Press.

Wu, Chengming 吴承明. 2001. Shiba yu shijiu shiji shangyede Zhongguo shichang 18与19世纪上叶的中国市场. *Zhongguode xiandaihua: shichang yu shehui* 中国的现代化:市场与社会, 238–288. Beijing: Sanlian shudian.

Xu, Dixin, and Wu Chengming. 2000. *Chinese Capitalism, 1522–1840*. London: Macmillan.

Yamamoto, Susumu 山本進. 1991. Shindai Shisen no chiiki keizai: inyū daitai mengyō no keisei to Ha-ken gagyō 清代四川の地域經濟:移入代替棉業の形成と巴県牙行. *Shigaku zasshi* 史學雜誌 100 (12): 2005–2035.

Open Access This chapter is licensed under the terms of the Creative Commons Attribution 4.0 International License (http://creativecommons.org/licenses/by/4.0/), which permits use, sharing, adaptation, distribution and reproduction in any medium or format, as long as you give appropriate credit to the original author(s) and the source, provide a link to the Creative Commons license and indicate if changes were made.

The images or other third party material in this chapter are included in the chapter's Creative Commons license, unless indicated otherwise in a credit line to the material. If material is not included in the chapter's Creative Commons license and your intended use is not permitted by statutory regulation or exceeds the permitted use, you will need to obtain permission directly from the copyright holder.

Kaiiki-Shi and World/Global History: A Japanese Perspective

Hideaki Suzuki

1 Introduction

'Kaiiki-shi (海域史)' certainly establishes a position in historical studies in Japan today. Kaiiki-shi is well included, for example, in the scope of Iwanami series of world history and that of Japanese history; both have a good reputation as a distinguished collection of historical studies in Japan. The latest series of world history has a volume entitled *Islam and Indian Ocean World, 16th to 18th Centuries*,[1] and that of Japanese history consists of several Kaiiki-shi-related chapters.[2] Furthermore, a number of projects are ongoing and new publications come out annually.

Kaiiki-shi is very hard to translate into English. It is literally the history of 'kaiiki (海域)'. 'Kaiiki' can be divided into 'kai (海)', which means ocean or sea, and 'iki (域)', which means region or area. However, historians generally do not intend to include some spatially limited nuance in this term of 'kaiiki-shi' in a strict sense. A common translation for 'kaiiki-shi' in English is 'maritime history'. Although maritime history has a variety of definitions, this translation can be fair if we follow the

H. Suzuki (✉)
Nagasaki University, Nagasaki, Japan

manner of Frank Broeze, who regarded maritime history as a study covering various relationships between humans and the sea.[3] Indeed, nowadays, various human activities in the sea are discussed in the framework of Kaiiki-shi. However, we need to note that the similarity of Kaiiki-shi to maritime history in this manner is a rather new trend which covers last decade or two. Rather than seeking for a conclusive definition of Kaiiki-shi, this chapter aims at explaining what Kaiiki-shi is in its development in Japanese historiography in order to examine my second aim, which is discussed in the following paragraph. Its development is not straightforward, and I do not intend to make a long list to cover all the publications related to this field.[4] My description of the development of Kaiiki-shi eventually meets world/global history. Thus, only limited references related to this direction are mentioned in the following argument.

The second aim of this chapter is to argue both consistency and inconsistency between Kaiiki-shi and world/global history. Obviously, in the last decade and a half, historians in Japan become much keener to world/global history, and many of them seek for the breakthrough in Kaiiki-shi towards world/global history. However, at the same time, scholarly efforts to encourage Kaiiki-shi ironically seem to close the bridge between two. This observation of Japanese academia will shed light on the future possibilities and obstacles of world/global history which can be applied even beyond Japanese academia.

2   Earlier Works

The origin of Kaiiki-shi would be a topic highly arguable. Some trace its origins back to the early twentieth-century Japanese oriental historians, when 'tōzai kōshō-shi (東西交渉史)' attracted scholarly attention. 'Tōzai kōshō-shi' literally means 'history of East–West relations'. Its main focus was initially land communications, notably the Silk Road; however, gradually scholars began to explore maritime communications as well, particularly those across Asian seas. Several studies produced in this field are still regarded as classics for Kaiiki-shi. Many place identifications are still useful and so too are detailed monographs such as *Sō-matsu no teikyosihaku saiiki-jin ho jukō no jiseki* (宋末の提擧市舶西域人蒲壽庚の事蹟 *Vestige of Teikyoshihaku Ho Jukō, a man from the western region of China in the late Song period*) by Jitsuzō Kuwabara (桑原隲藏).[5] Kuwabara traced the life of Ho Jukō (蒲壽庚 Po Siukeng), an Arabian Muslim port official of the Song dynasty in detail, and closely examined commercial history between Middle East and China in this period as well as Arabo-Persian settlement in coastal China.

Taihoku Imperial University (台北帝国大学) played a significant role in this direction. At the time it was founded, it offered Nanyō-shi (南洋史) course, which encouraged Japanese historians' maritime interests. The Nanyō-shi course was established as a unique course of the Taihoku Imperial University, because no other Japanese universities had the course focusing on 'nanyō-shi,' the history of maritime Southeast Asia and the South Pacific at that time.[6] Takio Izawa (伊沢多喜男), a politician who influenced the foundation of Taihoku Imperial University enormously, seemed to have expected the Nanyō-shi course to become a strong driving force for the university along with other Nanyō studies.[7] As Li Donghua (李東華) points out, Nanyō-shi was expected to contribute to establish Dai Tōa Kyōei Ken (大東亜共栄圏 Greater East Asia Co-Prosperity Sphere).[8]

Li's comment about its contribution to Greater East Asia Co-Prosperity Sphere is undeniable; however, it is also true that its academic contribution is also significant till today. Some of the works published by the faculties are still influential among Kaiiki-shi scholars and even beyond. Naojirō Murakami (村上直次郎) served as the first chair of the Nanyō-shi course. Murakami was a specialist on the history of Japan–Western relations. He was fluent in Dutch, Spanish, Portuguese and some other European languages[9] and his publications include the history of Japanese relations with European countries and also the history of Christianity in Japan, the history of overseas Japanese, and even Taiwanese history.[10] Seiichi Iwao (岩生成一) and Kenji Yanai (箭内健次) also taught the course. Particularly, a classic for Kaiiki-shi is Seiichi Iwao's *Nanyō nihon-machi no kenkyū* 南洋日本町の研究 (*Study on Japantowns in Southern Sea*),[11] which traces the development and expansion of Japanese overseas communities in Asian seas in the early modern period. Scholars in this generation did not use the term 'kaiiki-shi'; however, as mentioned above, several works in this period are still found in bibliographies of modern works on Kaiiki-shi. Certainly they cultivated the field from which kaiiki-shi later emerged.

Another body of Kaiiki-shi to emerge is taigai kōshō-shi (対外交渉史). This is a part of Japanese history that focuses especially on Japanese foreign relations. We need to mention, when we trace its development, Shiryō Hensanjyo (史料編纂所 the Historiographical Institute). This institute has its roots in the Wagaku kōdanjyo 和学講談所 (Institute of Japanese Studies) established by Hokiichi Hanawa 塙保己一 (1746–1821), a Kokugaku scholar. It was financially supported by the Tokugawa Shogunate and eventually, at the end of the nineteenth century, under the Meiji government, it was integrated into Tokyo Imperial University. The main focus of this institute was on compiling and publishing fundamental source materials for Japanese history.[12] In 1906, it took over from the Ministry of Foreign Affairs the project to compile documents related to foreign countries during the late Tokugawa period. Since then, the institute has been home to specialists on the history of Japanese foreign relations up to the present day. Seiichi Iwao moved from this institute to Taihoku Imperial University.

The crisis of Taigai kōshō-shi arrived after the end of the Second World War. Shōsuke Murai (村井章介) states that Taigai kōshō-shi was:

> eventually degraded as if it had a deserted air under criticism to old regime which made Emperor pinnacled and also Marxist history which was now free from oppression reached its peak. The main concern in historians was to prove that the historical law of Marxism theory can be even applied to Japan which had been 'the land of gods which is unequalled in any other country.' Therefore, it was natural that historians got interest in socio-economic history as field, particularly they devoted themselves to analyze the relations of production as well as those of social classes, both were base of society. Assuming any nation states follow the same path of development, they tended to fix the focus of their research on "national" history.[13]

This can be applied not only to Taigai kōshō-shi, but also to Tōzai kōshō-shi. Indeed, many historians in Japan tended to be involved in historical materialism, while Taigai kōshō-shi and Tōzai kōshō-shi became unpopular under criticism of pre-war overseas expansion. Only a small group of young scholars got an interest in Taigai kōshō-shi. Blowing in the post-war wind, this field was hanging almost by a thread. One good piece of fortune was that the Historiographical Institute still retained a section on foreign relations, which was a sort of shelter for these scholars in post-war generation. In particular, Takeo Tanaka's (田中健夫) contribution was huge. He was a specialist on medieval and early modern Japan–foreign relations in service to the institute. While he produced a number of original works which are still influential, he guided scholars in the younger generation, such as Shōsuke Murai and Yasunori Arano (荒野泰典), who played a central role in establishing Kaiiki-shi in the field of Japanese history.

3   The Emergence of Kaiiki-Shi

The other flow which eventually confluent with the above mentioned flows to form Kaiiki-shi was emerged among oriental historians who succeeded the interest of Tōzai kōshō-shi. Notably, Hikoichi Yajima (家島彦一) advocated the concept of 'indo-yō kaiiki-sekai

(インド洋海域世界 Indian Ocean Kaiiki World)' as early as the end of the 1960s.[14] He tried to capture the entire Indian Ocean (which historically extends from the East African coast to the East China Sea) as one historical unit.[15] He was supervised by Shinji Maejima (前嶋信次), a pioneer of Middle Eastern history in Japan. Maejima was a student of Toyohachi Fujita (藤田豊八) and followed Fujita to Taihoku Imperial University, where he obtained a position as assistant on the Nanyō-shi course.

While Yajima's foresight is remarkable, the period between the late 1980s and the early 1990s was an important turning point for the development of Kaiiki-shi studies. Yajima published his anthology entitled *Umi ga tsukuru bunmei* (海が創る文明 *The Ocean Created Civilization*) in 1993.[16] This was his second book after *Isulām sekai no seiritsu to kokusai shōgyō* (イスラーム世界の成立と国際商業 *Establishment of the Islamic World and International Commerce*).[17] His concept of 'indo-yō kaiiki-sekai' has been refined through projects organized in his institute, the Research Institute for Languages and Cultures of Asia and Africa, Tokyo University of Foreign Studies.[18] His 'indo-yō kaiiki-sekai' is based on network theory. Regarding ports as nodes, and human beings, trading goods and information as flow, he drew a large web of networks across the Indian Ocean. In Japan, this sort of network theory has been largely developed in the project entitled 'Urbanism in Islam' (1987–1991; Principal Investigator Yūzō Itagaki (板垣雄三), Professor of Middle Eastern Studies at the University of Tokyo), in which Yajima was also involved.[19]

Similarly, in 1992, a six-volume series of *Ajia no naka no nihon-shi* (アジアのなかの日本史 *Japanese History in Asia*) was completed, which was edited by Arano, Murai and Masatoshi Ishii (石井正敏), an ancient Japanese historian who also studied under Takeo Tanaka. According to the short memoir about this project by Arano, their main aim was 'to self-demolish and reconstruct of Japanese historians by Japanese historians'.[20] These editors criticized conventional nation-centred Japanese history and tried to reconsider Japanese history in Asian context.[21] This is a milestone for Taigai kōshō-shi, because this project finally clearly shows a new way of contributing to the wider academia after a long struggle in post-war circumstance. Their Asian perspective was supported by Takeshi Hamashita's (濱下武志) work. As a specialist in Chinese economic history, he clarified the tribute system, which strongly influenced diplomacy and international commerce in East Asia and beyond.[22] In particular, in the framework of economic history, he explained the significance of tribute system as the medium between the world economy and the state economy.[23] He also applied network theory to explain this medium, while he was certainly aware of the limit of nation-centred perspective when he argued tribute system.

A remarkable point about this period is that scholars in different fields referred to each other and gradually their focus on the maritime sphere overlapped with each other. They also shared criticism of national history, and therefore they equally sought more efficient units of history that would be larger than nation states but not as large as the entire world. Such a coincidence should be understood within the context of this new era when a new perspective on the world is urgently required after the end of the Cold War regime. In addition, the economic historian Heita Kawakatsu (川勝平太) and Takashi Shiraishi (白石隆), an expert in the field of international politics, also published Kaiiki-shi-related works.[24] It was also in 1993 that 'Kaiiki ajia-shi kenkyū-kai (海域アジア史研究会)', a circle of scholars including MA and PhD students from the Osaka area who were interested in Kaiiki-shi, began. This circle is still very active, holding monthly seminars, and its core members contributed to *Kaiiki ajia-shi kenkyū Nyūmon* (海域アジア史入門 *Kaiiki Asian History Reader*), as will be mentioned in the following section. To conclude this section, I need to mention the publication of Japanese translation of Fernand Braudel's *La Méditerranée*.[25] This long-awaited volume activated interaction among scholars in different areas further.[26]

4   Kaiiki-Shi in KAKENHI Projects and the Terminology of 'Kaiiki'

Academic trend of Kaiiki-shi can be glimpsed when we examine the database of Grants-in-Aid for Scientific Research (KAKENHI). KAKENHI is the largest funding source for Japanese academia in general. Thus, an analysis of this database enables us to see the academic trend to a certain degree. Due to frequent changes of items, only the titles of adopted projects can be searched for in the database. Thus, while it is obvious that many Kaiiki-shi-related projects have been conducted under the title without the term 'kaiiki,' such as those projects about port towns, it is unable to pick up these projects. However, at least this search allows us to grasp the rough trends of Kaiiki-shi. Searching for projects including the term 'kaiiki' in title regardless of the field, the database produces 738 results of projects between 1966 and 2016, of which 85 are related to historical studies. The first history project in the database appears in 1984, which was 'Chū-kinsei ni okeru kan shina-kaiiki kōryū-shi no kenkyū' (中近世における環シナ海海域交流史の研究 'Study on Exchange History across East China Sea Kaiiki in the Medieval and Early Modern Period') (Principal Investigator: Tadashi Nakamura (中村質), Professor of Japanese Medieval History in Kyushu University). On the other hand, the term 'kaiiki' was used for a long time before historians began to use it in their project titles. The 738 'kaiiki' projects include various fields such as fisheries, oceanology, natural geography, marine engineering, environmental studies, etc. as well as results from the humanities and social sciences. These non-humanities and social sciences projects tend to use the term 'kaiiki' in a literal sense. In other words, 'kaiiki' in these project titles implies some certain limited oceanic space which the project focuses on, such as 東部ベーリング海域における中層魚類の研究 'tōbu bēringu-kaiiki ni okeru chūsō-gyorui no kenkyū' ('Study on Mesopelagic Fish in the Eastern Bering Sea').

'Kaiiki' projects in the humanities and social sciences include those in area studies, archaeology, history, etc. In relation to area studies, many of 'kaiiki' projects were on Southeast Asia in the beginning and later on East Asia. Some of these social science projects seem to have used 'kaiiki' in a literal sense in the same way as non-social scientists did. But many others do not. Especially historians consciously use the concept of 'kaiiki,' in order not to argue some limited oceanic space itself, but to propose alternative historical perspective to the conventional ones. Those historians using 'kaiiki' are often very critical of conventional perspective of history which is heavily land-centred as they criticize. Instead of accepting this conventional perspective, they are eager to emphasize 'kaiiki' to capture those which have been largely overlooked.

However, the term 'kaiiki' is confusing due to its various usages, particularly in the non-humanities and social sciences fields, as if 'kaiiki' indicates that they focus on some limited space. Thus, some projects recognize such limits of nuance in the term 'kaiiki', so they add '-sekai' (世界 world), '-kōryū' (交流 exchange) and some other words to it in order to avoid such misunderstandings. There are several reasons why historians keep on using 'kaiiki' despite this very fuzzy terminology. Probably the biggest reason is that they imply their resistance against land-centred history by using this term. And Kaiiki-shi historians see nation-centred history behind this land-centred history. In Japanese, 'region' is generally called 'chiiki (地域)' which can be divided into 'chi' (earth, land) and 'iki'. Thus, 'kaiiki' ('kai' [ocean] and 'iki') is generally easily accepted as a kind of antonym of 'chiiki'.

5 The Booming of Kaiiki-Shi

Figure 1 shows that the number of Kaiiki-shi projects which have been adopted by KAKENHI increased in the 2000s. The rise of scholarly interest in world/global history contributes largely to the boom of Kaiiki-shi in this period. In Japan since the 2000s, world/global history began to attract historians. In Japanese academia, inter-regional approaches and some mega or supra-regional history are widely accepted as part of world/global history. Kaiiki-shi is frequently mentioned as one notable example of these.[27]

A significant physical impact was made by several large projects. One notable example is a five-year project from 2005 entitled 'Higashi-ajia no kaiiki kōryū to nihon dentō bunka no kēsē: ninpō wo shōten to suru gakusaiteki-sōsē' (東アジアの海域交流と日本伝統文化の形成——寧波を焦点とする学際的創生 'Maritime Cross-cultural Exchange in East Asia and the Formation of Japanese Traditional Culture') organized by Tsuyoshi Kojima (小島毅), a specialist on the history of Chinese thought. This project, widely known as 'nin-puro', brought together a large number of scholars in various fields and investigated the origins of Japanese traditional culture in historical maritime communication in East Asia. This multi-disciplinary project extended the field of Kaiiki-shi.

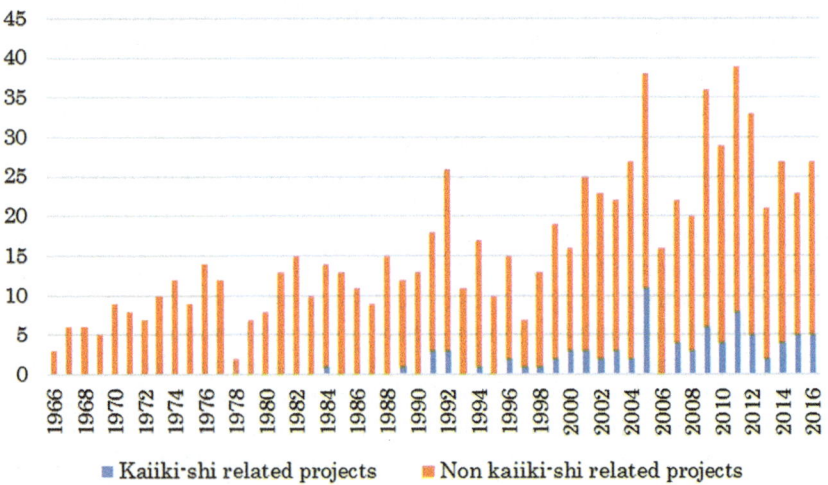

Fig. 1 The number of accepted KAKEN-HI projects under the title including "Kaiiki"

Multi-disciplinary projects existed prior to this project; however, these were basically project mainly aiming at publication[28] while this project had a five-year research period and eventually involved various scholars in related fields to a greater extent and let them communicate more intensively. 'Nin-puro' consisted of 34 smaller projects and published two series, totalling 26 volumes. For example, *Umi kara mita rekishi* (海から見た歴史 *History Viewed from the Ocean*) was published as a part of a series and was written by almost 30 co-authors.[29] Many of these were young scholars, and many of them are currently driving Kaiiki-shi. Not a few principal investigators for Kaiiki-shi projects adopted as KAKENHI after 2005 are those who joined the above-mentioned project ('nin-puro'). Until the project started, Kaiiki-shi was not a common subject in adopted KAKENHI projects, as Fig. 6.1 shows; however, since 2007, at least two projects a year were adopted and this tendency has continued up to the time of writing (summer 2016).

Furthermore, 'Kaiiki ajia-shi kenkyū-kai' published *Kaiiki ajia-shi kenkyū nyūmon* in 2008.[30] This handbook for Kaiiki-shi featured 32 contributors, some of whom also contributed to *Umi kara mita rekishi*. A detailed literature review on various topics on Kaiiki-shi is given in this book. Despite the fact that it largely focuses on East and Southeast Asian Kaiiki-shi, it is certainly another huge achievement for Kaiiki-shi. Through the above-mentioned development, Kaiiki-shi has finally achieved a certain position in historical studies in Japan today.

6 Potentials and Limits: The Dilemma of Kaiiki-Shi

As we have seen, Kaiiki-shi has multiple origins. Thus, there is no absolute definition of it. However, we are still able to see some shared features: an obvious contribution of Kaiiki-shi of conventional understanding of history is to criticize land-centred understanding and to connect histories which were previously constrained by national boundaries. Kaiiki-shi clearly proves the reality that the obstacle of national boundaries does not come from historical facts, but from the imaginations of historians. The more that the Kaiiki-shi perspective unveils various cross-boundary communications through history, the more we can break spell imposed on the field by national boundaries. In other words, Kaiiki-shi makes historians and their readers realize that a rich 'world' existed in history across borders conventionally recognized today. This would be a very powerful criticism towards our conventional understanding of history in Japan. As Masashi

Haneda (羽田正) notes, a general understanding of world history in Japan, which is highly influenced by education given in schools, is based on national and regional histories.[31] In other words, world history consists of various divided parts of the world, such as Chinese history, American history, British history, Japanese history, Southeast Asian history, etc., and these are basically regarded as being able to be narrated individually from ancient times up to the present day. Thus, one of the main objects for Japanese world/global historians is to deconstruct the nation state-centred perspective. Here we can find the bridge between Kaiiki-shi and world/global history in Japanese academia.

However, there are several problems in creating a bridge between these two. One is an epistemological problem. In other words, when Kaiiki-shi breaks conventional boundaries, it simultaneously creates another new boundary. The more we describe and narrate Kaiiki-shi, the more Kaiiki-shi forms a certain boundary to distinguish itself from others. Establishing courses and organizations is without doubt favourable for Kaiiki-shi historians, because these prove significance of Kaiiki-shi as well as these assure their position in academia. However, simultaneously this direction of development certainly formalizes Kaiiki-shi, which fosters the logic of exclusion. My attempt in this chapter—to describe the development of Kaiiki-shi—would surely contribute to this end. Another epistemological issue is as follows. Needless to say, we are unable to recognize anything without a name. Thus, when we discuss some 'kaiiki', we need to give it a proper name. Once some 'kaiiki' is recognized by a particular name, we are likely to define it and this definition always requires distinguishing it from others. In this process of definition, its geographical extent is always a focus. Thus, many Kaiiki-shi add some regional indicators in front of 'kaiiki', such as "'indo-yō' kaiiki" or "'ajia' kaiiki". Often historians repeatedly caution readers that the geographical extent of 'kaiiki' can enlarge and shrink from time to time and it is impossible to show its extent statistically on a map. However, it is also impossible for historians to develop the argument without any explanation of its geographical extent. Then, once historians show its extent, even without forgetting the above caution, the readers follow the argument bearing that extent in mind.

Kaiiki-shi historians have not yet found a way to sweep this minefield. Could history be narrated without any geographical limitations? Actually, some do. For instance, historians of diasporas are able to describe the unity of diasporic people without placing a strong emphasis on geography. Their focus is on diasporic people, but on geography. Unfortunately, Kaiiki-shi historians cannot follow their manner. Largely this is because actors in

Kaiiki-shi are too fluid and too diverse. Thus, so far, Kaiiki-shi historians need to set their focus on some geographical space (port towns are good examples) and observe it to catch various flows and interactions. This is not only an issue for Kaiiki-shi historians; the matter is more general. Here we need to think about specialities. Historians tend to be discreet once they go beyond the area where they specialize. Speciality is largely created by both extensive knowledge in a particular area and language ability. Especially in Japan, even long before the current movements of world/global history, world history has been a subject in high school and historians are familiar with it. But this world history is no more than the combination of national and regional histories. In this context, production of world history can be well described as a sort of division of labor. A combination of specialists would make it possible to write this sort of world history. On the contrary, current world/global historians in Japan are not satisfied with this sort of world history, partly because they notice that a lot of things are missed in such a framework and some even claim that a historical perspective in such a framework prevents the development of a global imagination, which is required by the human beings living in the current world. However, under the current system of historical studies, we need to choose some particular speciality. This is a dilemma that not only kaiiki-shi historians but also world/global historians in Japan are now facing.

7 Conclusion

This chapter has traced the development of kaiiki-shi. Kaiiki-shi does not confine itself to a static definition; we can understand the aim and scope of Kaiiki-shi through observing its multi-faceted character and following its transformation. So what is the position of Kaiiki-shi now? It is now that kaiiki-shi historians are noticing its limits. No longer does mere criticism of land-centred history satisfy readers. Often the criticism of land-centred history forms an ocean-centric history. This tendency is accelerated by a formalization of Kaiiki-shi and also professionalism of historian. Furthermore, persistence in specialization encourages division of Kaiiki-shi. Because the ocean is the sphere where a variety of people come across, under the conventional logic of historical studies, generally historians are required to focus on some particular language for analysis. This is a totally reasonable strategy; however, indeed the borderless character of Kaiiki-shi ironically disappears when confronted by the professionalism of historians and it even creates borders between different forms of 'Kaiiki'. However, several Kaiiki-shi historians already began to challenge these limitations. For example, Shinji Yamauchi (山内晋次) examined early modern East Asian Kaiiki while comparing and connecting with neighbouring Kaiiki, such as Southeast Asian Kaiiki and Indian Ocean Kaiiki.[32] In addition, there was a joint session entitled 'Rekishi no nakano kaiiki: Umi ga tsunagu, hedateru sekai' (歴史の中の海域——海がつなぐ/隔てる世界 'Kaiiki in History: the World connected/disconnected by the Ocean') at the annual meeting of the Historical Science Society of Japan in 2013, and there specialists on ancient Rome, the medieval Mediterranean, the early modern Caribbean and the modern Indian Ocean gathered and discussed each other's fields.[33] As such, certainly, Kaiiki-shi historians are now well aware of its connections with world/global history and struggle with its limitations.

Most realistic and certain steps for Kaiiki-shi historians to take in relation to world/global history is to follow the above-mentioned two methods, i.e. comparison and connection. As Shinji Yamauchi does, Kaiiki-shi historians carefully look around their neighbouring areas and seek any opportunity to connect and compare with these. At this moment, we cannot escape from specialization. Certainly, historians need to have extensive knowledge and language skills of a particular geographical area. However, this does not deny historians' efforts to connect with other specialists. Connecting each historian's visibility with each other can then efficiently challenge conventional world history in Japan, which is a mere addition to divided histories. Of course, this chain needs to include historians working mainly on land. This challenge will eventually deconstructs Kaiiki-shi itself. Once it realizes, Kaiiki-shi as challenger of land-centred history is no longer needed and historians also recognize that there are various mediums on land which function in the same way as those in Kaiiki does. Then, Kaiiki will complete its task while we can achieve a solid foundation for world/global history.

Notes

1. *Isulāmu/kan-Indo-yō sekai 16–18 seiki*, Tokyo: Iwanami shoten, 2000.
2. For instance, Shinji Yamauchi, 'Higashi ajia kaiiki ron' ('On East Asian Kaiiki') in *Iwanami kōza nihon rekishi*, vol. 20, Tokyo: Iwanami shoten, 2014, pp. 89–114.
3. Frank Broeze, 'From the Periphery to the Mainstream: The Challenge of Australia's Maritime History', *The Great Circle* 11(1) (1989), pp. 1–14.
4. The following works are worth reading for those who like to know more details on Kaiiki-shi-related studies: Hiromu Nagashima, 'Ajia kaiiki tsūshō

ken ron: Indo-yō sekai wo chūshin ni' ('On Asian Kaiiki Commercial Zone: Featuring Indian Ocean World') in Rekishigaku kenkyūkai (ed.), *Rekishigaku ni okeru houhouteki tenkai (Methodological Turns in Historical Thinkings)*, Tokyo: Aoki shoten, 2002, pp. 21–36; Shiro Momoki (ed.), *Kaiiki ajia-shi kenkyū nyūmon (Kaiiki Asian History Reader)*, Tokyo: Iwanami shoten, 2008; Takayuki Ito, 'Nihon ni okeru higashi ajia kaiiki kōryū-shi kenkyū no genjō to dōkō' ('Present Situations and Trends of Studies on East Asian Kaiiki-shi in Japan') in Shoji Yamada and Guo Nanyan (eds), *Kōnan bunka to nihon (Jingnan Culture and Japan)*, Kyoto: International Research Centre for Japanese Studies, 2012, pp. 139–151.
5. Jitsuzō Kuwabara, *Sō-matsu no teikyosihaku saiiki-jin ho jukō no jiseki*, Shanghai: Tōa kōkyū-kai, 1923.
6. For the Nanyō-shi course in Taihoku Imperial University, see Yoshiro Matsuda and Yu Chan, 'Taihoku teikoku daigaku bunsei-gakubu nanyō-shigaku no seiritsu to tenkai' ('Establishment and Development of Nanyō history in the Department of Literature and Law, the Taihoku Imperial University') in Tetsuya Sakai and Toshihiko Matsuda (eds), *Teikoku nihon to shokuminchi daigaku (Imperial Japan and Colonial Universities)*, Tokyo: Yumani shobo, 2014, pp. 251–284. In addition, the Oriental History course was taken by Toyohachi Fujita, former Professor of Oriental History in Tokyo Imperial University, who was a leading scholar on Tōzai kōshō-shi at that time. Fujita had numerous publications including translation and annotation of *Dao yi zhi lue*, geographical work in Yuan period. He moved from Tokyo Imperial University to Taihoku Imperial University to hold the chair of Oriental history as well as dean of the department in 1928 when the university was founded. However, he died soon after his arrival.
7. Yu Chin, 'Nihon tōchika no Taihoku Teikoku Daigaku ni tsuite' ('On Taihoku Imperial University under Japanese Occupation'), *Tōyō Shihō* 10 (2004), p. 68.
8. Li Donghua, *Guang fu chu qi tai da xiao shi yan jiu, 1945–1950 (A Study of the Early History of National Taiwan University, 1945–1950)*, Taipei: National Taiwan University Press, 2014, p. 173.
9. Yeh Pi-ling, 'Murakami Naojirō de taiwan shi yanjiu' ('Murakami Naojirō's Study of Taiwan History'), *Bulletin of Academia Historica* 17 (2008), p. 8.
10. For his works, see Anonymous, 'Murakami Naojirō-sensei ryakureki, kōgi, kōen, chosho, ronbun mokuroku' ('Biographical Note and List of Publications by Dr. Murakami'), *Jōchi Shigaku* 13 (1968), pp. 3–13.
11. Seiichi Iwao, *Nanyō nihon-machi no kenkyū*, Tokyo: Minami ajia bunka kenkyūjyo, 1940.
12. See http://www.hi.u-tokyo.ac.jp/english/about_hi/message-e.html for details of the Historiographical Institute (last viewed 8 November 2017).
13. Shōsuke Murai, 'Kaisetsu', in Takeo Tanaka (ed.), *Wakō: umi no rekishi*, Tokyo: Kodansha, 2012, pp. 250–251.

14. His detailed explanation of the earlier concept of the Indian Ocean world is available in Hikoichi Yajima, 'Maritime Activities of the Arab Gulf People and the Indian Ocean World in the Eleventh and Twelfth Centuries', *Journal of Asian and African Studies* 14 (1977), pp. 195–208. As I will discuss, his concept of the Indian Ocean world has developed since then.
15. More correctly, he sets several small-kaiiki and examines connections among them. His concept of 'indo-yō kaiiki-sekai' is a unit which consists of these inter-related small-kaiikis, while it has a certain autonomy as a whole. See Hikoichi Yajima, *Kaiiki kara mita rekishi: Indo-yō to chicyū-kai wo musubu kouryū-shi (History Seen from Kaiiki: The History of Exchange Connecting the Indian Ocean and the Mediterranean)*, Nagoya: Nagoya University Press, 2006, pp. 17–25.
16. Hikoichi Yajima, *Umi ga tsukuru bunmei*, Tokyo: Asahi Shimbun Sha, 1993.
17. Hikoichi Yajima, *Isulām sekai no seiritsu to kokusai shōgyō*, Tokyo: Iwanami shoten, 1991.
18. Masato Iizuka and Hikoichi Yajima, 'Fīrudo wāku kara no shiten' ('Observation from Fieldwork'), *Field Plus* 12 (2014), pp. 22–27.
19. See e.g. Hikoichi Yajima, 'Toshi nettowāku wo megutte: indo-yō nishi-kaiiki ni okeru dau sen chōsa ni motozuku' ('On Urban Networks: Based on Research on Dhow in the Western Indian Ocean Kaiiki'), *Isuramu no toshi-sei kenkyū-hōkoku* 8 (1988), pp. 1–16.
20. Yasunori Arano, '*Ajia no nakano nihon-shi* (zen 6 kan) no henshu wo oete' ('After Editing *Japanese History in Asia* (6 vols))', *Shien* 54(1) (1993), p. 122.
21. Arano, '*Ajia no nakano Nihon-shi*', p. 121.
22. Takeshi Hamashita, *Kindai chūgoku no kokusai-teki keiki: chōkō bōeki shisutemu to kindai ajia (International Momentum for Modern China)*, Tokyo: University of Tokyo Press, 1990.
23. Takeshi Hamashita, *Chōkō bōeki shisutemu to kindai ajia (Chinese Tribute Trade System and Asian Modernization) Kokusai Seiji* 8 (1986), p. 42.
24. Heita Kawakatsu, *Kaiyō no bunmei-shikan (A Maritime Historical View of Civilization)*, Tokyo: Chuo Koron-sha, 1997; Takashi Shiraishi, *Umi no teikoku: Ajia wo dou kangaeruka (Empire of the Sea: How Do We Think about Asia?)*, Tokyo: Iwanami Shoten, 2000.
25. Fernand Braudel, *Chichū-kai*, trans. by Masami Hamana, 5 vols, Tokyo: Fujiwara shoten, 1991–1995.
26. See Heita Kawakatsu (ed.), *Umi kara mita rekishi: Burōdel Chichū-kai wo yomu (A Maritime View of History)*, Tokyo: Fujiwara shoten, 1996.
27. See e.g. Tsukasa Mizushima, 'Gurōbaru hisutorī kenkyū no chōsen' ('Challenges of Global History Studies') in Tsukasa Mizushima (ed.), *Gurōbaru hisutorī no chosen (Challenges of Global History)*, Tokyo: Yamakawa shuppan sha, 2008, pp. 15–16; Shigeru Akita, 'Gurōbaru

hisutorī no chōsen to seiyou-shi kenkyū' ('Challenge of Global History and Studies of Western History in Japan'), *Journal of History for the Public* 5 (2008), p. 35; Haneda, *Atarashii sekai-shi e (Towards New World History)*, Tokyo: Iwanami Shoten, 2011, pp. 140–143.
28. In this respect, it is worth mentioning two series. One is *Daikōkai jidai sōsho* (The Age of Discovery Series) published by Iwanami Shoten, which covers numerous travelogues, ethnographies and voyages written by Europeans during the Age of Discovery. These have been translated into Japanese and 42 volumes have been published over 27 years since 1965. This is a huge project involving not only historians, but also scholars of literature, anthropologists and specialists in other related fields. The other is six-volume series, called *Umi no Ajia* (Seas of Asia; edited by Keiichi Bimoto, Takeshi Hamashita, Yosinori Murai and Hikoichi Yajima, published by Iwanami Shoten, 2000–2001), is also multi-disciplinary series while not a few contributors are historians.
29. Masashi Haneda (ed.), *Umi kara mita rekishi (History Viewed from the Ocean)*, Tokyo: University of Tokyo Press, 2013.
30. Momoki (ed.), *Kaiiki ajia-shi kenkyū nyūmon*.
31. Masashi Haneda, 'Atarashii sekai-shi to chiiki-shi' ('New World History and Regional History') in Masashi Haneda (ed.), *Gurōbaru hisutorī to higashi ajia-shi (Global History and East Asian History)*, Tokyo: University of Tokyo Press, 2016, pp. 19–22.
32. Yamauchi, 'Higashi ajia kaiiki ron'.
33. See the special feature in *Rekishigaku kenkyū* 913 (2013).

Open Access This chapter is licensed under the terms of the Creative Commons Attribution 4.0 International License (http://creativecommons.org/licenses/by/4.0/), which permits use, sharing, adaptation, distribution and reproduction in any medium or format, as long as you give appropriate credit to the original author(s) and the source, provide a link to the Creative Commons license and indicate if changes were made.

The images or other third party material in this chapter are included in the chapter's Creative Commons license, unless indicated otherwise in a credit line to the material. If material is not included in the chapter's Creative Commons license and your intended use is not permitted by statutory regulation or exceeds the permitted use, you will need to obtain permission directly from the copyright holder.

PART II

Trade Networks and Maritime Expansion in East Asian Studies

The focus of this part goes from the micro to the macro perspective, embracing the so-called 'jeux des échelles', in order to analyse the inner dynamics of the trade between Japan, China and Southeast Asian areas in the context of a global network system through the crucial role of socioeconomic agents such as local and private traders of Chinese and Japanese origin, as well as those from Europe. Reviewing from a wide perspective the role of geostrategic port cities in East Asia, and reducing the scale to a more local context, we might observe: (1) local flows of trade and capital through the study of the tribute system and the transformation of such a system during the Ming dynasty; (2) typologies or categories of commerce such as the illegal form with the 'barbarians' of South China Sea trade, the so-called nanban (南蛮) trade and the official shuinsen (朱印船) commerce; (3) social agents, mainly the Jewish trade networks of Portuguese origin in Japan and China; (4) the models of navigation systems, which were crucial for the development of commerce, long-distance communication and market integration.

The Structure and Transformation of the Ming Tribute Trade System

Gakusho Nakajima

1   Introduction

In this chapter, I attempt to investigate whether we can summarize the foreign trade system during the Ming era as a single concept of the 'tribute trade system' or 'the mutual trade system'. Needless to say, the term 'tribute system' was commonly used for conceptualizing the traditional diplomacy and foreign trade system of the Ming-Qing Empire based on the 'Chinese world order', in contrast to the 'treaty system' introduced by the Western powers after the Opium War (Fairbank 1968). Further, Hamashita Takesi conceptualized a historical system of international trade network developed under the tribute system of the Ming-Qing Empire as the 'tribute trade system' (Hamashita 1990, 1997). Recently, scholars such as Iwai Shigeki 岩井茂樹 and Ueda Makoto 上田信 have proposed categorizing the foreign trade system from the late Ming onwards as a 'mutual trade system' (*hushi tizhi*; Jp. *goshi taisei* 互市體制) rather than a 'tribute trade system', because during this period, foreign trade was mainly conducted in the form of

G. Nakajima (✉)
Kyushu University, Fukuoka, Japan

'mutual trade' (*hushi* 互市) between private Chinese merchants and foreign merchants, and tribute trade accounted for no more than a limited portion of foreign trade (Iwai 2004: 132–134, 2005: 121–124, 2009: 30–38, Ueda 2005: 249–262).

This concept of the 'mutual trade system' is essentially proposed as an antithesis to a prevailing discourse that summarizes foreign trade in the Ming-Qing period as the 'tribute trade system'. On the other hand, Iwai and Ueda also have not given a clear definition of 'mutual trade' at the moment, and sufficient investigation of institutions and actual practices of the 'mutual trade' from the late Ming onwards remains to be done (Okamoto 2007). Can we really summarize the foreign trade system throughout the late Ming and the Qing period as a single concept of the 'mutual trade system'?

In this chapter, I have investigated and will describe the various types of trade that occurred in both maritime and inner Asia, and will also sketch a series of historical events that had critical meanings for the formation of a new system at the end of this period. Looking at the various types of trade that actually took place between the 1360s and the 1570s, we can conclude that it would be more appropriate to talk about a 'tribute and trade system' rather than a 'mutual trade system', at least in relation to the late Ming and the early Qing period. The trade order in East Asia at the time can be said to have been in a fluid and transitional state, moving from the earlier unitary tribute trade system to a system in which various forms of trade, such as tribute trade, mutual trade and visiting trade, coexisted in accordance with the political and economic relations in existence between the Ming and its trading partners.

2 THE TEMPORAL TRANSFORMATION OF THE MING TRIBUTARY TRADE SYSTEM

Da Ming huitian 大明會典 (1587 edn) comprehensively enumerated all the tributaries of the Ming dynasty.[1] Here I provisionally categorize tributaries of the Ming listed in *Da Ming huitian* into six zones (Fairbank 1968: 1–4; Banno 1973: 83–85).[2] At first, I include Korea, Japan and Ryukyu in the 'Eastern Zone', and will then group the Southeast Asian tributaries into the 'Southern Zone', and tributaries in India and West Asia into the 'Indian Ocean Zone'. On the other hand, I will group tributaries belonging to the Mongols and the Jurchens together as the 'Northern Zone', will call the tributaries in Central Asia the 'Western

Zone' and will group tributaries belonging to Tibet and Southwest China into the 'Southwestern Zone'.[3] Further, I will group the tributaries belonging to the Eastern, the Southeastern and the Indian Ocean Zone into the 'Maritime Asia', while the Northern, the Western, and the Southwestern Zone will comprise the 'Inner Asia' (Mancall 1968: 72–75).[4] In Table 1, I have classified all tributaries listed in *Da Ming huitian* into the six zones mentioned above.[5]

The tribute trade system that was established in the late fourteenth century had expanded in the early fifteenth century, but it began to decline as early as the mid-fifteenth century and actually collapsed by the mid-sixteen century. Here I will roughly survey the temporal transformation of the Ming tributary trade by dividing the 200 years between the 1360s and the 1560s into six major periods, while broadening our horizons to the inner, as well as maritime, Asia (Fairbank and Têng 1941:

Table 1 Tributaries of the Ming listed in *Ta-Ming huitian* 大明會典 (1587 edn)

Region		Names of the tributaries
East Asia (Eastern Zone)		朝鮮 (Korea)・琉球 (Ryukyu)・日本 (Japan)
South-east Asia (Southern Zone)	Mainland	安南(Vietnam)・真臘 (Cambodia)・暹羅 (Siam)・占城 (Champa)
	Malay peninsula	彭亨 (Pahang)・滿剌加 (Melaka)・急蘭丹 (Kelantan)・古里班卒 (Panchor?)
	Sumatra	三佛齊 (Palembang)・須門達那 / 蘇門答剌 (Samudra)・覽邦 (Lampong)・阿魯 (Aru)・碟里 (Deli)・南巫里 / 喃渤里 (Lamuri)・合貓里 (Komoring?)
	Java	爪哇 (Java)・百花 (爪哇西部?)・淡巴 (Demak?)・日羅夏治 (Gresik?)・千里達 (Cirebon?)
	Eastern islands.	浡泥 (Burnei)・婆羅 (Borneo)・蘇祿 (Sulu)・呂宋 (Luzon)・古麻剌 (Kumalarang)
Indian Ocean (Indian Ocean Zone)	East India	瑣里 / 西洋瑣里(Cola)・榜葛剌・彭加那 (Bengal)・招納樸兒 (Janupur)
	Malabar coast	古里 (Calicut)・小葛蘭 (Quilon)・柯枝 Cochin)・甘把里・坎巴夷替 (Coyampadi)・加異勒 (Cail)
	Gujarat	宿察尼 (Kutch)・烏涉剌踢 (Gujarat)・奇剌尼 (Lar?)・捨剌齊 (Surat?)・夏剌比 (Valabhi?)
	Indian Ocean	錫蘭山 (Ceylon)・溜山 (Maldives)
	West Asia	佛菻 (Byzantium)・忽魯謨斯 (Hormuz)・魯密 (Rum)・黑葛達 (Bagdad)
	Arabia peninsula	祖法兒 (Zufal)・阿丹 (Aden)・剌撒 La'sa)・天方 (Mekka)・默德那 (Medina)
	East Africa	麻林 (Malindi)・不剌哇 Brawa)・木骨都束 (Mogadishu)
	Unidentified	八可意・打回・阿哇・沙里灣泥

Table 1 (continued)

Region		Names of the tributaries
North Asia (Northern Zone)	Mongol	蒙古 (Mongol)・瓦剌 (Oirad)
	Uriyangkhad	兀良哈 (Uriyangkhad) 三衛（朵顏衛・福餘衛・泰寧衛）
	Manchuria	海西女直 (Haixi Jurchen)・建州女直 (Jianzhou Jurchen)・野人女直 (Yeren Jurchen)
Central Asia (Western Zone)	Hami & Shazhou	哈密衛 (Hami guard)・安定衛 (Anding guard)・阿端衛 (Aduan guard)・罕東衛 (Handong guard)・罕東左衛 (Handong left guerd)・赤斤蒙古 (Chijin Mongol guard)・曲先衛 (Quxian guard)
	Eastern Turkistan	亦力把力 (Ilibalik)・土魯番 (Turfan)・火州 Karakhodja)・柳陳城 (Lukchak)・于闐 (Khotan)・哈失哈兒 (Kashgar)・別失八里 (Bishbalik)・俺力麻 (Almalik)・察力失 Chalish)・苦先 (Kucha)・牙兒干 (Yarkand)・阿速 (Aksu)
	Western Turkistan & Afganistan	哈烈／黑婁 (Herat)・撒馬兒罕 (Samarkand)・哈的蘭 (Khatran)・掃蘭 (Sairam)・把丹沙／八答黑商 (Badakshan)・把力黑 (Balkh)・脱忽麻 (Togmak)・卜哈剌 (Bokhara)・克失迷兒 (Kashmir)・火壇／火占 Khodjend)・沙六海牙 (Sharokia)・俺都淮 (Andkhui)
	Iran & West Asia	失剌思 (Shiraz)・你沙兀兒 Nishapur)・帖必力思 (Tabriz)・亦思弗罕 (Isfahan)・魯迷 (Rum)・天方 (Arabia)
	Unidentified	哈三・哈烈兒沙的蠻・乜克力・幹失・怕剌・果撒思・牙思・戎・白・兀倫・耶思成・坤城・捨黑・擺音・克即乩・哈辛
Southwest Plateau (Southwestern Zone)	Tibetan sects	闡教王 (*Chanjiao wang*)・闡化王 (*Chanhua wang*)・輔教王 (*Fujiao wang*)・贊善王 (*Zanshan wang*)・護教王 (*Hujiao wang*)・大乘法王 (*Dachengfa wang*)・大寶法王 (*Dabaofa wang*)
	Amdo & Kham & Western Sichuan	長河西魚通寧遠宣慰司 (Zhanghexi-Yüdong-Ningyuan *xuanweishi*)・雜道長官司 (Zadao *zhangguansi*)・朵甘思宣慰司 (Duogansi *xuanweishi*)・直管招討司 (Zhiguan *zhaotaosi*)・董卜韓胡宣慰司 (Dongbuhanhu *xuanweishi*)・別思寨按撫司 (Biesizhai *Anfusi*)・加渴瓦寺 (Jiahewa temple)・金川寺番僧 (Tibetan monks of Jinchuan temple)・雜谷按撫司 (Zagu *anfushi*)・打喇兒寨 (Dalaer stockade)・達思蠻長官司 (dasiman *zhangguansi*)・長寧按撫司 (Zhangning *anfusi*)・韓胡碉怯列寺 (Hanhudiaoqielie temple)・洮岷等處番僧 (Tibetan monks in Tao-Min area)・洮岷等處番族 (Tibetan tribes in Tao-Min area)
	Southwestern aboriginal offices	Aboriginal offices in Sichuan, Guizhou, Guangxi, Yunnan, and Huguang Provinces 土司 (military aboriginal office such as 軍民府 *junminfu*・按撫司 *anfusi*・長官司 *zhangguansi* 宣慰司 *xuanweisi* ；土官 (civil aboriginal office of perfestures and counties)

Source *Daming huitian* (1587 edn), Ch. 105–108, libu 禮部 63–66, chaogong 朝貢 1–4
Main reference works: Fairbank and Têng (1941), 'Index of tributaries listed in six editions of the collected statues'; Liu Jiafang 陸家榮, Xie Fang 謝方, and Liu Junling 陸峻嶺 eds. (1986); Zhong Xinglin 鍾興麟 ed. (2008); Geoff Wade, 'Some southeastern Asian polities mentioned in the MSL,' in *Southeast Asia in the Ming Shi-lu* (http//epress.nus.edu.sg/msl/)

Table 2 The number of tributes by main tributary states in the Ming (1368–1566)

	Tributary states	I 1368–1402	II 1403–1435	III 1436–1464	IV 1465–1509	V 1510–1539	VI 1540–1566	Total
East Asia	Korea	60	158	87 + α	135 + α	90 + α	81 + α	611 + α
	Ryukyu	54	105	63	37	20	16	295
	Japan	10	10	1	4	3	1	29
Southeast Asia	Vietnam	25	6	27	23	4	4	89
	Siam	39	26	11	10	1	4	91
	Champa	23	31	22	10	3	1	90
	Cambodia	12	7	0	0	0	0	19
	Melaka	0	20	7	5	2	0	34
	Samudra	0	16	0	0	0	0	16
	Parenbang	6	4	0	0	0	0	10
	Java	11	34	18	3	0	0	66
	Burnei	1	9	0	0	0	0	10
Central Asia	Hami	0	94	84	56	14	7	255
	Turfan	0	25	5	40	14	8	92
	Bishbalik	1	10	1	0	0	0	12
	Ilibalik	0	15	18	1	0	0	30
	Samarkand	9	26	14	15	14	4	82
	Herat	0	14	5	1	0	0	20
	Arabia	1	1	0	2	11	4	18
	Rum	0	3	0	0	3	5	11

Sources Korea: Li Yunquan 李雲泉 (2004), pp. 75–76; Ryukyu: Noguchi Tetsurō 野口鐵郎 (1977), pp. 186–206.日本: Hashimoto Yū 橋本雄 (2002), pp. 10–11; Southeast Asia: Qiu Xuanyu 邱炫煜 (1995), pp. 128; 180–184; 294–295; Central Asia: Watanabe Hiroshi 渡邊宏 (1971), pp. 1–39

156–157; Ptak 2003: 157–191).[6] In Table 2 below, I have provisionally collected statistics on the tributes made by the main tributary states of the Ming, after consulting some useful secondary literature.

3 THE FIRST PERIOD: 1368–1402

Immediately after his enthronement in 1368, the first Ming Emperor, Hongwu 洪武, positively dispatched embassies to the surrounding states to persuade them to send tributary missions to the Ming. In response to them, more than a dozen polities of East and Southeast Asia send tributes to the Hongwu court. They were bestowed with the title of king and accepted the suzerainty of the Ming Empire (*cefeng* 冊封) and were allowed to engage in tribute trade with the Ming (Ōsumi 1982; Sakuma 1992: 3–24; Li 2004: 61–133).

On the other hand, the early Ming government strictly prohibited coastal populations from making private overseas voyages. In 1374, when the Ming government further abolished the Maritime Trade Supervisorates (*shibosi* 市舶司), both overseas voyages by Chinese merchants and visits to China by foreign merchants became impossible, and overseas trade was restricted only to interstate trade between the Ming and tribute states. Thus, during the early Ming, the tribute system and the maritime exclusion policy were indivisibly integrated, and the Ming government assumed monopolistic control not only over diplomatic relations but also over foreign trade with the surrounding states under the tribute trade/maritime exclusion system (Sakuma 1992: 25–39; Danjō 1997, 2004; Zheng 2004: 7–56; Chao 2005: 30–50; Li 2007: 29–54). In overland trade too, private foreign trade was severely restricted (Serruys 1975: 72–83).

The cornerstone of the tribute trade was of course the tribute goods presented by tributaries and the gifts awarded by the Ming emperor. But in practice, the greater part of the tribute trade consisted of transactions in the additional goods brought in by tribute envoys and the accompanying merchants. These additional goods were either taken without compensation or were purchased by the government, after which another cargo could be offered to the market for 'mutual trade' (*hushi* 互市), which was permitted at the entry point and the guesthouse for foreign envoys (*huidongguan* 會同館) in the capital (Serruys 1975: 47–83; Sakuma 1992: 3–24; Chao 2005: 50–58). In this way, the Ming Empire created a centripetal trade system managed by the central government, and the overriding principle of the Ming's trade policy was the unity of tribute and trade (*gongshi yiti* 貢市一體), which meant that there could be no trade without tribute.

But as for overland trade, the early Ming state exceptionally provided for some official markets along the inland border, where foreigners were permitted to engage in 'mutual trade' with Chinese government agencies and private merchants to acquire military and courier horses. The 'Horse Trade Offices' (*chamasi* 茶馬司) were established along the peripheries of Shaanxi (陝西) and Sichuan (四川) provinces in the late fourteenth century, where the Central Asians and the Tibetans were allowed to exchange their horses for Chinese tea (Tani 1972: 55–98; Rossabi 1998: 245–258).

In the Hongwu period, most of the tribute states were part of East and Southeast Asia. In particular, Korea (Koryŏ 高麗 and Chosŏn 朝鮮 Kingdom) and Ryukyu (Zhongshan 中山 and two other kingdoms) were two most important tribute states of the Ming from the beginning. On the other hand, the tribute relationship with Japan was unstable because of domestic disturbances and the intensified activities of *wokou* 倭寇 (Sakuma 1992: 43–96). Besides, Vietnam, Siam, Champa, Cambodia and Java also often sent tributary missions to the Ming. From the Indian Ocean, only two missions from the South India were recorded. In addition, tribute missions from Inner Asia were severely limited because of continuing political confrontations with the Mongol polities, except that missions of Tibet and Samarkand repeatedly arrived. Further, in 1394, the Hongwu Emperor issued an order to break off diplomatic and trade relations with overseas countries except for Ryukyu, Cambodia and Siam, so at the very end of the fourteenth century, tributaries of the Ming were almost limited to Korea, Ryukyu and some Southeast and Inner Asian states, and, combined with a maritime seclusion policy, foreign trade was reduced to a low level (Li 2004: 64–65; Zheng 2004: 47–51).

4　The Second Period: 1403–1435

Yongle 永樂, the emperor who ascended the throne in 1403, promoted an extremely positive foreign policy, actively dispatching large-scale fleets and envoys, represented by Zheng He's expedition, both to maritime and Inner Asia. As a result, the tributaries of the Ming rapidly expanded to a vast range in the Indian Ocean, in North and West Asia, as well as in East and Southeast Asia (Ōsumi 1984). To manage tribute trade with maritime Asian polities, the Ming court reopened the Maritime Trade Supervisorates in Guangzhou, Quanzhou and Ningbo in 1403, and repositioned them as agencies dealing with tribute trade rather than as agencies for controlling private trade, as had previously been the case.

In the Eastern Zone, Korea and Ryukyu send outstandingly numerous missions in all tributaries, and Japan also sent missions almost every year from 1401 to 1411 (Sakuma 1992: 97–140; Nakajima 2003). In the Southern Zone, except for the main tributary states such as Siam, Champa, Melaka and Java, many states and port cities sent tributes in response to Zheng He's voyage. In addition, from the Indian Ocean Zone, many polities in India, West Asia, Arabia and East Africa sent missions along with the return voyages of Zheng He's fleets. It is especially noticeable that important ports along the main sailing routes that linked Eastern and Western Eurasia, such as Melaka, Sumatra, Lamuri, Ceylon, Cochin, Calicut, Hormuz and Aden, repeatedly sent tributes and engaged in tribute trade with the Ming court (Qiu 1995: 135–203).

Zheng He's fleets not only performed the role of diplomatic and military power display, but also achieved the aims of large-scale trading missions (Yajima 1993: 243–274). They positively conducted trade at every calling port, exported Chinese goods and imported tropical products such as pepper and sappanwood (Ptak 2003: 165–170; Wada 1967, 1981).[7] Zheng He's expedition brought about the revival of long-distance trade in maritime Asia, which had once flourished under Mongol rule, but had declined during the 'fourteenth century general crisis'. On the other hand, under the strict maritime exclusion policy, no one was permitted to engage in private overseas trade, though illicit private trade did not cease, even in the heyday of the tribute trade in the early fifteenth century.

Tribute trade with Inner Asian states, which was operated only on a limited scale in the first period, also expanded considerably in the second period. In the Northern Zone, the Yongle emperor founded the Regional Military Commission (*dusi* 都司) in Manchuria and organized the Jurchen tribes belonging to Haixi 海西, Jianzhou 建州, and Yeren 野人 Nuzhen 女真 into the military guard (*wei* 衛) system, bestowing nominal titles of military offices on the chieftains of those tribes. These Jurchen chieftains, who were bestowed these titles, sent tribute missions in every year, along with the chieftains of the Mongolian tribes in Western Manchuria, who were organized into three guards units known as the three Uriyanghad guards (*Wuliangha sanwei* 兀良哈三衛).

The Jurchen and Uriyanghad tribes not only carried out tributary trade, but also engaged in 'mutual trade' in the 'horse markets' (*mashi* 馬市) founded in Guanning 廣寧 and Kaiyuan 開原 in Liaodong 遼東, where the Jurchens and the Uriyangkhad (one of the Mongols mainly living in Manchuria) brought horses and other products such as ginseng, and bought various Chinese products (Serruys 1967: 3–7, 113–126, 1975: 92–103; Ejima 1999: 153–181, 217–244). On the other hand, in the Mongol plateau, the Yongle emperor bestowed seals and the title of Prince (*wang* 王) on the leaders of the Mongols and the Oirads. However, tribute relationships between the Ming with the Mongols and the Oirads remained unstable, and so the Yongle emperor led five militarily expeditions to the Mongolian plateau. In spite of such military confrontations, Chinese goods were indispensable for the Mongols and the Oirads, so the Mongol leader Arughtai sent tribute missions as many as 44 times during the second period, and the Oirats leaders also sent missions almost every year after 1408 onwards (Serruys 1967: 5–9, 126–127).

In the Western Zone, the Yongle emperor organized the Mongol princes residing between the Hexi 河西 corridor and the Tarim basin into seven military guards, and let them send tributes. In particular, the Mongol prince of Hami, which was a gateway for the caravan trade along the Silk Road, was bestowed with the title of '*Zhongshun wang* 忠順王'. And Hami was positioned as the key point for controlling diplomatic and commercial relations with Central Asia (Nagamoto 1963; Rossabi 1998: 246–250). In addition, from Eastern Turkistan, which was under the influence of the Moghulistan Khanate, some locales such as Bishbalik, Ilibalik and Turfan sent tributes to the Ming. Further, from Western Turkistan and Iran, which were within the territory of the Timurid Empire, various missions from Samarkand, Herat and other cities along the Silk Road routes, in which many caravan merchants accompanied, were dispatched to the Ming court and engaged in tribute trade (Rossabi 1998: 246–250; Zhang 2006).

Besides, Yongle invited leaders of the main sects of Tibetan Buddhism to the capital, bestowed upon them the title of religious prince (*fawang* 法王, *jiaowang* 教王, etc.) and incorporated them into tribute relations, although the Tibetan monks perceived the Ming emperor as their religious patrons rather than their sovereign (Satō 1986: 173–320; Rossabi 1998: 241–245). In addition, the Tibetan tribes and temples in the Eastern Tibetan plateau (the Amdo and Kham regions) were incorporated into the military system of the Ming, were bestowed with nominal military titles and engaged in horse-tea trade at the Horse Trading office, as well as tribute trade (Tani 1972: 55–70; Yi 2000: 166–204, 247–255).

5   The Third Period: 1436–1464

In this period, the Ming court, which was severely pressed by excessively heavy financial burden accompanied with tributary trade, changed its extremely positive foreign policy in the early fifteenth century into a far more passive one, and as a result, the number and scale of the tribute trade with the maritime Asian countries declined rapidly. Nevertheless, tribute trade with Inner Asia, especially with the Oirads, strikingly expanded beyond the control of the Ming court (Ōsumi 1986).

In maritime Asia, Korea and Ryukyu steadily continued tribute trade, and Vietnam (Lê 黎 Kingdom), which had recovered independence from the Ming in 1427, also often sent tribute missions (Yamamoto 1975: 253–269), although the frequency of the tributes from Japan was restricted to once every ten years from 1453 onwards (Hashimoto 2002: 3–9). On the other hand, tribute missions from the Southern Zone decreased rapidly. Many port states that had repeatedly sent tributes to the Ming in the second period ceased to send envoys, and only the four countries of Champa, Shiam, Meleka and Java continued to send tribute, although the Ming court restricted the frequency of tributes of these four countries to once every three years until the mid-fifteenth century. The decline in tribute missions from the Indian Ocean Zone was far more drastic and finally came to an end with a tribute mission from Ceylon in 1459 (Qiu 1995: 223–234). The decline of the tribute trade with the maritime Asian countries was partly compensated by intermediary trade by the Ryukyu kingdom and growth of the smuggling trade of Chinese merchants in the South China Sea (Ptak 2003: 171–177).

In contrast, in Inner Asia, Esen, the leader of the Oirads, markedly extended his tribute trade with the Ming. In the 1540s, he unified the Mongol plateau and extended his power over Uriyangkhad eastwards. Further, he brought the Hami and Hexi corridor under his control, and commanded the caravan trade with Central Asia. In order to obtain Chinese goods exported to Central Asia, he aggressively extended tribute trade with the Ming, and the number of men on each mission of the Oirads, which was only 267 in 1437, surged to over 2000 in the 1440s and reached over 2500 in 1448, of which 752 were occupied by Muslim merchants. Seeing this excessive expansion of the Oirads' tribute trade, the Ming court tried to curtail its scale, but conflicts between Esen and the Ming over this led to Esen's invasion of China and resulted in the Tumu 土木 incident in 1449 (Serruys 1967: 128–134; Hagiwara 1980: 47–98).

In the Western Zone, Hami, which was under the control of Esen, sent tributes as many as 84 times. In addition, Ilibalik and Turfan in Eastern Turkistan and Samarkand and Herat in Western Turkistan continuously sent missions. Further, in the Southwestern Zone, with the

Ming emperor's indulgence in Tibetan Buddhism as a background, the scale of the tributes missions of Tibet notably expanded (Yi 2000: 223–244).

6   The Fourth Period: 1465–1509

During the late fifteenth and early sixteenth centuries, tribute trade with the Ming from maritime Asia continuously declined in the long term, while tribute trade with Inner Asia still remained relatively important. In the Eastern Zone, Korea steady sent tributes in this period too, but in Japan the Muromachi 室町 Shogunate lost its control over tribute trade, and the two powerful lords in Western Japan, the Hosokawa 細川 and the Ōuchi, 大內, struggled over the initiative of the tribute trade (Sakuma 1992: 141–157).

In the Southern Zone, tribute trade with the Ming continued to decline. Though Vietnam, Siam, Champa, Melaka and Java dispatched tribute missions, this was done with less frequency than the once every three years regulated by the Ming (Qiu 1995: 223–234). In addition, the intermediary trade by the Ryukyu kingdom that had compensated for the decline of tribute trade also rapidly decreased from the 1460s, and Ryukyuan official trade with Java and Sumatra was also disrupted by the 1460s. Furthermore, the Ming court restricted the frequency of Rykyuan tribute trade, which had been every year, to once every two years in 1474 (Kobata 1942: 126–172; Okamoto 2010: 17–22, 34–41).

Despite the long-term declines in both tribute trade with Southeast Asian polities and intermediary trade of the Ryukyu kingdom, the total scale of Sino-Southeast Asian trade seems not to have decreased. It must be consistent growth of credential trade in the South China Sea, which seems to well exceed the decline of tributary trade. In this period, the maritime exclusion policy enforced in the early Ming period gradually slackened, allowing more and more Chinese smugglers to make trading voyages from Fujian and Guangdong to Southeast Asia (Sakuma 1992: 212–219; Ptak 2003: 177–179). In addition, foreign trading vessels that were not official tribute missions began to arrive at Guangzhou Bay and engaged in 'mutual trade' (*hushi* 互市) with the Chinese merchants there. The local authorities of Guangdong also overlooked such unofficial trade in Guangzhou Bay and collected customs from trading vessels arriving there (Pires 1944: 116–128).

In Inner Asia, the hegemony of the Oirads collapsed after the death of Esen in 1454, and various powers among the Mongols and the

Oirads continued to engage in internal conflicts, as a result of which their tribute trade dropped sharply. But in the 1480s, Toghon, the leader of the Mongols, expanded his power and resumed large-scale tribute trade with the Ming, with the cooperation of Muslin merchants (Serruys 1967: 134–139; Hagiwara 1980: 171–193). In the Western Zone, the Ming court intended to curtail the tribute trade with Central Asia and restricted the frequency of tributes of the Hami to once a year, and that of Ilibalik and Turfan to once three or five years in 1465 (Haneda 1974: 418).

In the late fifteenth century, the Moghulistan Khanate moved its base from the Ili region to the Tarim basin, and one of its princes, Ahmad, who ruled the Turfan basin, promoted tribute trade and repeatedly made inroads into the Hami and Hexi corridor. In 1493, Ahmad attacked Hami and captured its king, who had been enthroned by the Ming, but the Ming court stopped tribute trade with Turfan as a countermeasure, so Ahmad was obliged to retreat from Hami four years after (Rossabi 1972: 215–222). Besides that, the Ming court restricted the frequency of tributes by Tibetan sects and tribes to once every three years and restrained the number of missions to 150 men or fewer in 1470, but in fact these regulations seem not to have been necessarily adhered to (Yi 2000: 237–144).

As mentioned above, the mutual trade between foreign trading vessels and Chinese merchants gradually increased in Guangzhou Bay from the late fifteenth century; simultaneously in Inner Asia, up to the late fifteenth century, mutual trade between the Central Asian caravan traders and Chinese merchants had appeared at Suchou 肅州, which was a gateway to caravan routes on the western edge of Gansu 甘肅. In 1495, the Mekrid tribe that had immigrated to suburbs of Suchou asked the Ming court to participate in the 'mutual trade' that was held every season at Suzhou, and its request was approved by the Ming (Serruys 1975: 45). It is noticeable that until the late fifteenth century, gateways of mutual trade were opened both in coastal and inland border regions beyond the framework of the tribute trade system.

7   The Fifth Period: 1510–1539

From the late fifteenth century, while tributary trade continuously declined, the smuggling trade of Chinese merchants and 'mutual trade' between foreign and Chinese merchants gradually expanded, both in maritime and Inner Asia. Further, from the 1510s onwards, contradictions between the stiff principles of the tributary trade system and the actual extension of foreign trade out of the framework of the tribute system caused armed conflicts both in the coastal and inland peripheries of the Ming Empire.

In maritime Asia, the Portuguese occupied the Melaka kingdom, which was the largest centre of trade network in Southeast Asia, and forced their way into the trading sphere in the Asian seas. As a result, many Muslim, Chinese and Ryuykuan merchants who had arrived at Melaka hitherto changed their destination to other ports in the Malay Peninsula, Sumatra and Java, then function of entrepôt in Southeast Asia was dispersed (Suzuki 1998: 198–200; Ptak 2003: 179–182). From the late 1510s onwards, the Portuguese fleets participated in 'mutual trade' at Guangzhou Bay and sent a further mission to the Ming court to establish official trade. But their negotiations ended in failure, and the Ming court issued an order strictly prohibiting the mutual trade at Guangzhou Bay that had hitherto been overlooked. The Portuguese fleets were then forcibly excluded from Guangzhou Bay until 1522 (Wan 2001: 77–113; Iwai 2004: 110–144; Li 2007: 220–231).

In this period, the tribute trade in maritime Asian all the more declined. In the Eastern Zone, while Korea and Ryukyu continued to regularly send tributes, in Japan confrontation over the initiative of tribute trade between the Hosokawa and the Ōuchi escalated into armed conflicts involving the two missions dispatched by both sides in Ningbo in 1523 (Sakuma 1992: 157–164). In the Southern Zone, in addition to the fall of the Melaka kingdom, tributes from Siam and Champa also decreased sharply (Qiu 1995: 291–295).

In Inner Asia, disturbances over the tribute trade was getting more and more obvious. In the Northern Zone, Dayan Khan, who had unified the Mongol plateau in 1511, frequently made raids into the Ming northern peripheries, and tribute trade was broken off from the 1510s (Serruys 1967: 8–9; Hagiwara 1980: 190–193). Furthermore, in the Western Zone, Sultan Mansūr, who now ruled Turfan as the successor to his father Ahmad, repeatedly made inroads into the Hami and Hexi corridor. The Ming court again prohibited his tribute trade as a countermeasure, but he only intensified his raids, and the Ming were obliged to approve his possession of Hami and in the end allowed him to resume trading. As a result, the Ming almost lost its initiative over the tribute trade with Central Asia, and so restricted the frequency of Hami and

Turfan's tribute trades to once every five years (Rossabi 1972: 222–225). The Ming court's loss of control over Hami indicates that traditional diplomatic measures controlling surrounding states by integrating the tribute system and foreign trade reached an impasse up to the early sixteenth century.

8 THE SIXTH PERIOD: 1540–1566

Armed conflicts over the tribute trade, which had escalated both in the coastal and inland peripheries of the Ming Empire, rapidly intensified from the 1540s and extended throughout the whole length of the southeast coast and northern border, as raids and plunder by *wokou* 倭寇 in the southeast and by the Mongols in the north, namely '*beilu nanwo* 北虜南倭' or 'the Northern Mongols and the Southern Japanese'.

In the Eastern Zone, during 1540, a base of credential trade had grown at the Shuangyu 雙嶼 port in the Zhoushan 舟山 islands, where Chinese smugglers, Portuguese private merchants and Japanese seafarers gathered to engage in trade during the 1540s and exchanged Chinese goods for Japanese silver and tropical products. The destruction of the smuggling base of Shuangyu by the Ming navy in 1548 brought about a further proliferation of raids and plunderers along the southeast coast (Sakuma 1992: 258–294; Ptak 1998; Zheng 2004: 127–184).

Meanwhile, in the Southern Zone, mutual trade between foreign trading vessels and Chinese merchants gradually revived, and in the 1550s the local authority of Guangdong permitted foreign vessels to call on Guangzhou and engage in mutual trade with specific Chinese merchants as official brokers, through whom the foreign merchants paid customs. Thus, in the mid-sixteenth century, while smuggling, piracy and plunder were increasingly rampant in the East China Sea, in the South China Sea, credential trade and plunder were gradually absorbed into mutual trade in Guangzhou (Wan 2001: 77–113; Iwai 2004; Li 2007: 249–277).

When the activities of *wokou* spread along the southeastern border, the inroads and plunder by the Mongols led by Altan Khan intensified markedly in the northern border along the Great Wall. Altan, a grandson of Dayan Khan, repeatedly claimed the resumption of tribute trade and the opening of 'horse markets' to the Ming, but the Ming court rejected his claim, so he repeatedly made large-scale inroads into north China and surrounded Beijing in 1550. As a result, the Ming court approved the revival of tribute trade and opening of the 'horse market' in 1551, but both of these were disrupted in the next year, so that Altan again repeated his raids and plunder into the Ming periphery up to the mid-1560s (Serruys 1975: 149–161; Matsumoto 2001: 177–217).

In Manchuria, the Ming court restricted the total number of men in tribute missions dispatched by the Jurchens to within 1500. This restriction brought about fierce competition over obtaining licences for engaging in this tribute trade and participation in the 'horse market' (Ejima 1999: 178–179, 185–200). In Central Asia, the Hami and Turfan relatively followed the regulation that restricted the frequency of tributes to once every five years (Rossabi 1990).[8] However, besides the tribute missions that reached Beijing, it seems that more numerous caravan merchants arrived at the northwest border of the Ming to engage in mutual trade. For example, a Persian merchant, Haji Muhammad, participated in a caravan and arrived at Suzhou 肅州 about 1550, but because no one except for missions to Daiming Khan (the Ming emperor) were allowed to advance into the interior of China, he merely bought rhubarb at the market of Suzhou, and then transported this crude drug to Venice and sold it (Yule 1916: 291–293; Sawada 2008: 57–58). His testimony reveals that 'mutual trade' between the Chinese and foreign merchants in the border region was grown not only at Guangzhou Bay in the southeast, but also Suzhou in the northwest.

9 The Formation and Structure of the '1570 System'

As sketched out above, the Ming tribute trade system was transformed by following a mostly parallel trajectory and was eventually reconstructed by 1571 as the result of the relaxation of the strict ban on private foreign trade, both in the southeastern and northwestern peripheries. Some Japanese scholars called this reconstructed foreign trade system the 'mutual trade system' (Iwai 2004, 2005, 2009; Ueda 2005). But I feel some hesitation in summarizing the foreign trade system throughout the late Ming and Qing periods as a 'mutual trade system', because the structure of foreign trade in the late Ming had a more plural and fluid character than that of the mid-Qing period. Here I rather want to provisionally call it quite simply the '1570 system'.

In a following passage, I will sketch a series of historical events that had critical meanings for the formation of the '1570 system':

- *The late 1560s*: a crucial step of the sublation of the tribute trade system was, of course, the relaxation of the embargo on overseas trade in the early Longqing 隆慶 reign (1567–1572), as a result of which the Chinese merchants were permitted to make trading voyages from the Haicheng 海澄 county of southern Fujian to Southeast Asia. They needed to obtain licences (*wenyin* 文引), the number of which was fixed by quota, and paid customs levied on their ships, cargos and licences (Sakuma 1992: 322–324; Li 2007: 312–345).[9] In contemporary sources, maritime trade from Haicheng to Southeast Asia was sometimes called 'visiting trade' (*wangshi* 往市), as opposed to 'mutual trade'.
- *1570*: the Ryukyu kingdom dispatched its last official trading ships to Siam. At this point, the Ryukyu kingdom's intermediary trade between Southeast and Easy Asia, which flourished in the fifteenth century, finally came to an end as a result of the rapid expansion of the Chinese merchant's trading voyages to Southeast Asia (Takara 1980: 224–235).
- *1571*: this was a year of multiple significance, in which the following critical historical events occurred that opened up a new phase of the international trade system in both maritime and inland East Asia:

1. The founding of Manila: the Spaniards founded Manila as the capital of the Spanish Philippines in 1571. Thereafter, the Spanish galleons shipped an enormous amount of New World silver, the production of which in Potosí and other mines rapidly increased in the 1570s, from Acapulco to Manila across the Pacific in every year. The New World silver brought to Manila was exchanged with Chinese products such as silk, cotton cloth and porcelain, which was imported by the Fujian merchants and then flowed into the Chinese market (Schulz 1939; Sugaya 2001; Nakajima 2007a).
2. The opening of Macao-Nagasaki trade: in 1571, the Portuguese 'Great Ship' entered the port of Nagasaki 長崎 for the first time and thereafter the intermediary trade between Macao and Nagasaki became a mainstay of the Portuguese local trade in the Asian seas. Through Macao-Nagasaki trade conducted by the Portuguese, enormous amounts of Japanese silver flowed into Chinese markets via Macao, in exchange for Chinese products, especially silk and silk yarn (Boxer 1959; Oka 2008).

Table 3 The structure of the 1570 system in the late sixteenth century

I Maritime Asia

Zones	States	Entry points of tribute trade	Mutual trade/Visiting trade
The Eastern Zone	Korea	Liaodong: Fenghuangcheng,	Border trade in Liaodong.
	Japan	<Tribute trade was suspended in 1549>	Macao-Nagasaki trade> <Smuggling by the Chinese>
	Ryukyu	Fuzhou Maritime Supervisorate	<Smuggling by the Chinese>
The Southern Zone	Vietnam Siam	Guangxi: Pingxiang, Guangzhou Maritime Supervisorate	Visiting trade from Haicheng (the late 1560's-)
	The other states	<No official tribute trade was recorded after 1543>	Mutual trade in Guangzhou Bay
The Europeans	Portugal	<Negotiations for interstate trade ended in failure >	Mutual trade at Macao (1557-)
	Spain		Visiting trade from Haicheng To Manila (1573-)

II Inner Asia

Zones	States	Entry points of tribute trade	Mutual trade/ Visiting trade
The Northern Zone	The Mongols	Shanxi: Datong	Horse markets along the Great Wall (1571-)
	The Uriya-ngkhad	Bei Zhili: Xifengkou	Horse/wood markets in Liaodong
	The Jurchens	Liaodong: Kaiyuan	Horse/wood/ mutual trade markets in Liaodon
The Western Zone	Hexi corridor States in Central Asia	Gansu: Jiayuguan From Hami to Jiayuguan	Horse trade office in Shaanxi
The South–western Zone	Tibet, Amdo, Kham	Shaanxi and Sichuan	Horse trade office in Shaanxi and Sichuan
	Abboricginal offices	Sichuan, Yunnan, Guizhou, Guanxi, Huguang	<Trade with the Chinese merchants>

3. The Longqing peace agreement: as a result of a peace agreement between the Ming court and the Altan Khan, the Ming granted the Altan the title of king (*Shunyi wang* 順義王) and permitted him to send tribute missions annually. Altan was allowed to bring 500 horses as an annual tribute and could receive Chinese products in return. In addition, the Ming court allowed the opening of 'mutual trade' markets with the Mongols along the Great Wall. There the Mongols brought their horses in the main and obtained various Chinese products in return (Serruys 1967: 64–93; 1975: 162–254; Ono 1996: 61–106).
4. The growth of 'mutual trade' in Liaodong: in 1571, two 'wood markets' (*mushi* 木市) were opened in western Liaodong, then in 1576 three 'mutual markets' (*hushichang* 互市場) were opened in eastern Liaodong. The increase in these markets, where the Jurchens and the Uriyanghad were allowed to exchange their local products with Chinese commodities, brought about the further growth of 'mutual trade', together with existing 'horse markets' (Ejima 1999: 374–387, 399–404).

As shown above, the tribute trade system going back to the early Ming dynasty was reorganized as a result of changes in the East Asian trade order, and the way was open for the adaptation of the ossified tribute system to the actual trade order, both in the maritime and inland Asia. In the former, the reconstructed Ming international trade system consisted of the following three trade sectors: (1) the tribute trade sector: tribute trade conducted periodically by Korea and Ryukyu, and sporadically by Vietnam and Siam; (2) the visiting trade sector: Fujian (Haicheng)-Southeast Asia trade carried out by the Chinese private trading ships, through which New World silver shipped by the Spanish galleons flowed into China via Manila; (3) the mutual trade sector: Chinese merchants' trade with the Portuguese at Macao, through which Japanese silver was imported, and that with the Southeast Asians at Guangzhou bay that had gradually developed from the late fifteenth century onwards; (4) the smuggling sector: Chinese merchants' illegal voyages to foreign countries, especially these to Japan, through which Japanese silver was directly imported.

On the other hand, in the case of the northwestern crescent, the trade system consisted of the following three sectors: (1) the tribute trade sector: tribute trade conducted by the Mongols, the Jurchens, some states in Central Asia, the monasteries in Tibet and tribal chieftains in the southwest periphery; (2) the mutual trade sector: private trade with the Mongols at markets along the Great Wall, with the Jurchens at markets in Liaodong, and with the Central Asians and the Tibetans at the Horse Trading Offices in Shaanxi; (3) the smuggling sector: illegal trade with the Mongols, the Jurchens and the others conducted by Chinese smugglers.

Table 3 gives a summarized structure of the 1571 system. It shows that the Ming's neighbours enjoyed trade relations with the Ming that involved one, two or, as in the case of Annam and Siam, all three possibilities, i.e., tribute trade, mutual trade and visiting trade. The sole exception was Japan, which was not granted access to any of these trade options, except for the smuggling sector and intermediary trade such as Macao-Nagasaki trade (Nakajima 2007b: 129–133).

10 Conclusion

When we summarize the structure of the foreign trade system as stated above, is it adequate to conceptualize it as the 'mutual trade system'? It seems that the term 'mutual trade system' is not necessarily appropriate to represent the whole structure of it, at least for the late Ming period. There is no doubt, of course, that 'mutual trade' with the Mongols and the Jurchens developed in the northern periphery, and trade with the Portuguese carried out at Macao increasingly came to account for a larger part of the whole Ming international trade. On the other hand, the trading voyage from Haicheng bound for Southeast Asia was often called 'visiting trade' (*wangshi* 往市) in contemporary sources, distinct from 'mutual trade'.

Further, the tribute trade sector still had a considerable importance in the late Ming foreign trade system. In the Southern Zone, tribute trade certainly came to have only a marginal role. On the other hand, as for the Eastern Zone, to states such as Korea, Ryukyu and Vietnam, tribute trade remained a mainstay of trade with China, even in the late Ming period. And in the Northern Zone, tribute trade continued to be an important form of the Ming-Mongol trade after the Longqing peace agreement (Serruys 1967: 64–93), and the Jurchen chieftains also struggled to obtain licences to engage in tribute trade as much as possible (Ejima 1999: 189–200). Some states in the Western Zone too periodically sent tribute trade missions, although many of them were private trading caravans that disguised themselves as official missions (Rossabi 1998: 253). Further, in the Southwestern Zone, the Ming court relaxed the restrictions on the number of tribute envoys sent by Tibetan sects and tribes, which had been restrained to 150 men or fewer, and allowed up to 1000 men to join in any single mission from the 1570s onwards.[10]

In general, the tribute trade sector still accounted for no small portion of the entire foreign trade, even in the late Ming period. Generally speaking, the foreign trade system in the late Ming seems to be far more pluralized than that of the mid-Qing. Provisionally, I would like to call this East Asian trade system (namely, the '1570 system') the 'tribute and trade system' (*gongshi tizhi* 貢市体制), encompassing tribute trade on the one hand, and mutual trade and visiting trade on the other. The trade order in East Asia at the time can be said to have been in a fluid and transitional state, moving from the earlier unitary tribute trade system to a system in which various forms of trade, such as tribute trade, mutual trade and visiting trade, coexisted in accordance with the political and economic relations in existence between the Ming and its trading partners.

The relaxation of the exclusive maritime policy, and the opening of the Macao-Nagasaki and Acapulco-Manila-Fujian trade in the southeast periphery and the Longqing peace agreement in the northern periphery, all of which comprised the mainstay of the '1570 system', were a series of historical events generated in the causal relationship with the 'birth of the global economy' in the late sixteenth century (Atwell 1998; Flynn and Giráldez 2006), and the development of 'the China's silver century' (Von glahn 1996). And the formation of the '1570 system', which was characterized by a plural and fluid structure and showed a sharp contrast with the previous unified and rigid tribute trade/maritime exclusion system in the early Ming period, further promoted the expansion of the foreign trade boom in the peripheral regions. Up to the early seventeenth century, powerful leaders who combined commercial profits and military forces were growing up among the booming situation in the periphery of the Ming Empire (Iwai 1996), whose representatives were Nurhaci in the northwestern crescent and Zheng Zhilong 鄭芝龍 in the southeastern crescent (Kishimoto 1998a: 39–48; 1998b: 18–31).

Notes

1. Da Ming huitian (*Collected Statutes of the Great Ming*, 1587 edn), Chapter 105–108, libu 禮部 55–58, chaogong 朝貢 1–4.
2. K. Fairbank grouped the tributary states of the Qing dynasty listed in Da Qing huitian 大清會典 (*Collected Statutes of the Great Qing*, 1818 edn) into three main zones, namely the Sinic Zone, the Inner Asia Zone and the Outer Zone. Later, Banno Masataka 板野正高, by following

Fairbank's grouping, classified the tribute states of the Ming dynasty that are listed in the *Collected Statutes* into three zones, namely the Sinic Zone, the Inner Asia Zone and the Outer Zone.

3. Da Ming huitian grouped the tributaries in the Eastern Zone, the Southeastern Zone and the Indian Ocean Zone together as the 'Southeast barbarians' (dongnan yi 東南夷). In contrast, it called the tributaries belonging to the Mongols the 'Northern barbarians' (beidi 北狄), while the Jurchens in Manchuria were called the 'Northeast barbarians' (dongbeiyi 東北夷). Then it included the tributaries belonging to the Central Asia and Tibet into a category of 'Western barbarians' (xirong 西戎) and listed tribal chieftains in Southwest China under the category of the 'aboriginal offices' (tuguan 土官).

4. Mark Mancall divided the tributaries of the Qing into two categories, namely the 'northwestern crescent' and the 'southeastern crescent'. In this chapter, 'Maritime Asia' and 'Inner Asia' roughly correspond to Mancall's 'southeastern crescent' and 'northwestern crescent' respectively.

5. Since many tributaries sent tribute missions to the Ming only in the early fifteenth century, this table by and large shows the spatial structure of the Ming tribute trade system in the early fifteenth century, when the Ming tribute system maximally expanded.

6. Formerly, J.K. Fairbank and S.Y. Têng divided the temporal transition of the Ming tribute system into five major periods. Roderich Ptak also presents the six periods on the transition of the Ming maritime trade with Southeast Asia from the late fourteenth century to the 1360s to the late 1560s. In order to formulate my own periodization of the Ming tribute trade system, I consulted the periodization presented by them.

7. These trades were often operated by Muslim and Chinese (including Chinese Muslim) merchants who engaged in internal trade in maritime Asia. Especially in Archipelago Southeast Asia, immigrant Chinese formed some communities, cooperated with local polities, and engaged in internal and tribute trade. Some of them further acted as diplomatic and trade envoys to East Asian countries such as Ryukyu, Japan and Korea.

8. Besides, it is generally regarded that the Central Asian caravan trade declined in the sixteenth century because of the development of sailing routes that directly linked Western and Eastern Eurasia and political disturbances on the caravan route (Rossabi 1990); nevertheless, some tribute missions had arrived at the Ming court from Samarkand, Arabia and Rum.

9. In 1589, 44 licences were issued respectively for the 'eastern oceans' (dongyang 東洋; continental Southeast Asia, Sumatra and Java) and the 'western oceans' (dongyang 西洋; the Philippines and the Sulu zone), and later the total number was increased to 137 by 1597. Although a ban on trade with Japan was still restrained , smuggling by Chinese merchants into Japan had steadily increased (Nakajima 2007a: 75–83).

10. Da Ming huidian, Chap. 108, libu 66, chaogong 4, Xirong xia 西戎下.

REFERENCES

Atwell, William. 1998. Ming China and Emerging World Economy, c. 1470–1650. In: *Cambridge History of China*, Vol. 8, The Ming Dynasty, 1368–1644, pt. 2, Cambridge: Cambridge University Press.

Banno, Masataka 坂野正高. 1973. *Kindai Chūgoku seiji gaikōshi: Vasuko da Gama kara goshi undō made* 近代中国政治外交史:ヴァスコ・ダ・ガマから五四運動まで. Tokyo daigaku shuppankai.

Boxer, Charles R. 1959. *The Great Ship from Amacon: Annals of Macao and Old Japan Trade, 1555–1640*. Lisbon: Centro de Estudos Historicos Ultramarinos.

Chao, Zhongchen 晁中辰. 2005. *Mingdai haijin yu haiwai maoyi* 明代海禁與海外貿易. Beijing: Renmin chupanshe.

Danjō, Hiroshi 檀上寛. 1997. Minsho no kaikin to chōkō: Minchō sensei sihai no rikai ni yosete 明初の海禁と朝貢:明朝専制支配の理解に寄せて. In: *Min Shin Jidaishi no kihon mondai* 明清時代史の基本問題, ed. Mori Masao 森正夫 et al. Tokyo: Tokyo Kyūko shoin.

———. 2004. Mindai kaikin gainen no seiritsu to sono haikei: ikin gekai kara kakai tūban he 明代海禁概念の成立とその背景:違禁下海から下海通番へ. *Tōyōshi kenkyū* 東洋史研究 63 (2).

Ejima, Hisao 江嶋壽雄. 1999. *Mindai Shinsho no Jochokushi kenkyū* 明代清初の女直史研究. Fukuoka: Chūgoku shoten.

Fairbank, John King, and S.Y. Têng. 1941. On the Ch'ing Tributary System. *Harvard Journal of Asiatic Studies* 6 (2): 135–246.

Fairbank, John King. 1968. Preliminary framework. In: *The Chinese World Order: Traditional China's Foreign Relations*, ed. John King Fairbank. Cambridge, MA: Harvard University Press.

Flynn, Dennis O., and Arturo Giráldez. 2006. Globalization Began in 1571. In *Globalization and Global Economy*, ed. Banry K. Gills and William R. Tompson. New York: Routledge.

Hagiwara, Junpei 萩原淳平. 1980. *Mindai Mōkoshi kenkyū* 明代蒙古史研究. Kyoto: Dōhōsha.

Hamashita, Takeshi 濱下武志. 1990. *Kindai Chūgoku no kokusaiteki keiki: Chōkō bōeki shisutemu to kindai Ajia* 近代中国の国際的契機:朝貢貿易システムと近代アジア. Tokyo: Tokyo daigaku shuppankai.

Hamashita, Takeshi. 1997. *Chōkō shisutemu to kindai Ajia* 朝貢システムと近代アジア. Tokyo: Tokyo daigaku shuppankai.

Haneda Akira 羽田明. 1974. *Mindai Seiiki shiryō* 明代西域史料. Kyoto: Mindai Seiikishi kenkyūkai.

Hashimoto Yū 橋本雄. 2002. Kenminsen no haken keiki 遣明船の派遣契機. *Nihonshi kenkyū* 日本史研究, 479.

Iwai, Shigeki 岩井茂樹. 1996. Jūroku jūnana seiki no Chūgoku henkyō shakai 十六・十七世紀の中国辺境社会. In: *Minmastu Shinsho no shakai to bunka* 明末清初の社会と文化, ed. Ono Kazuko. Kyoto: Kyoto daigaku jinbun kagaku kenkyūjo.

———. 2004. Jūroku seiki Chūgoku ni okeru kōeki chitsujo no mosaku: goshi no genjitsu to sono ninshiki 十六世紀中国における交易秩序の模索:互市の現実とその認識. In: *Chūgoku kinsei shakai no chitsujo Keisei* 中国近世社会の秩序形成, ed. Iwai Shigeki. Kyoto: Kyoto daigaku jinbun kagaku kenkyūjo.

———. 2005. Mindai Chūgoku no reisei haken shugi to Higasi Ajia no chitsujo 明代中国の礼制覇権主義と東アジアの秩序. *Tōyō bunka* 東洋文化 85.

———. 2009. Teikoku to goshi: 16–18 seiki higashi Ajia no tūkō 帝国と互市: 16–18 世紀東アジアの通交. In: *Teikoku to Ajia nettowaku: Chōki no jūkyū seiki* 帝国とアジア・ネットワーク: 長期の 19 世紀, ed. Kagotani Naoto 籠谷直人 and Wakimura Kōhei. Tokyo: Sekai sishōsha.

Kishimoto, Mio. 1998a. *Higashi Ajia no kinsei* 東アジアの「近世」. Tokyo: Yamakawa shuppansha.

———. ed. 1998b. *Higasi Ajia Tōnan Ajia dentō shakai no keisei* 東アジア・東南アジア伝統社会の形成. Tokyo: Iwanami shoten.

Kobata, Atsushi 小葉田淳. 1942. *Chūsei nantō Tsūkō bōekishi no kenkyū* 中世南島通交貿易史の研究. Tokyo: Tōkō shoin.

Li, Qingxin 李慶新. 2007. *Mingdai haiwai maoyi zhidu* 明代海外貿易制度. Beijing: Shehui kexue wenxian Chubanshe.

Li, Yunquan 李雲泉. 2004. *Chaogong zhidu shilun: Zhongguo gudai duiwai guanxi tizhi yanjiu* 朝貢制度史論: 中國古代對外關係體制研究. Beijing: Shehuikexue Chubanshe.

Liu, Jiafang 陸家榮 et al. 1986. *Gudai Nanhai diming huishi* 古代南海地名匯釋. Beijing: Zhonghua shuju.

Mancall, Mark. 1968. The Ch'ing Tributary System: An Interpretative Essay. In: *The Chinese World Order*, ed. Fairbank.

Nakajima, Gakushō 中島楽章. 2003. Eiraku nenkan no Nichi-Min chōkō bōeki 永楽年間の日明朝貢貿易. *Shien* 史淵, 140.

———. 2007a. Jūroku seikimastu no Fukken-Firipin-Kyūshū bōeki 十六世紀末の福建-フィリピン-九州貿易. *Shien* 史淵, 144.

———. 2007b. Hōwa to Tsūkō: Sen gohyaku kyūjū yonen no Ninpō kaikō mondai wo megutte 封倭と通貢————一五九四年の寧波開貢問題をめぐって————. *Tōyōshi kenkyū* 東洋史研究: 66–2.

Nagamoto, Hisanori 永元寿典. 1963. Minsho no Hami ōke ni tsuite: Seiso no Komuru keiei 明初の哈密王家について: 成祖のコムル経営. *Tōyōshi kenkyū* 東洋史研究: 22–1.

Noguchi Tetsurō 野口鐵郎. 1977. *Chūgoku to Ryukyū* 中國と琉球. Tokyo: Kaimei shoin.

Oka, Mihoko 岡美穂子. 2008. Kinsei shoki no Nanban bōeki no yushutsunyūhin nit suite: Sebirya Indo monjokan shozou siryou no bunseki kara 近世初期の南蛮貿易の輸出入品について：セビーリャ・インド文書館所蔵史料の分析から. *Tokyo daigaku shiryō hensanjo kenkyū kiyō* 東京大学史料編纂所研究紀要, 18.

Okamoto, Hiromichi 岡本弘道. 2010. Ryukyū ōkoku kaijō kōshōshi kenkyū 琉球王国海上交渉史研究. Naha: Yōju Shoin.

Okamoto, Taikashi 岡本隆司. 2007. Chōkō to goshi to kaikan 朝貢と互市と海関. *Shirin* 史林 90 (5).

Ono, Kazuko 小野和子. 1996. *Minki tōshakō: Tōrintō to Fukusha* 明季党社考:東林党と復社. Kyoto: Dōhōsha shuppan.

Ōsumi, Akiko 大隅晶子. 1982. Minshoi Kōbuki ni okeru chōkō ni tsuite 明初洪武期における朝貢について. *Museum* 371.

———. 1984. Mindai Eirakuki ni okeru chōkō ni tsuite 明代永楽期における朝貢について. *Museum* 398.

———. 1986. Mindai Sentoku Tenjunki no chōkō ni tsuite 明代宣徳~天順期の朝貢について. *Museum* 421.

Pires, Tomé. Trans. by Armando Cortesao. 1944. *The Suma Oriental of Tome Pires*, vol. 1. London: Hakluyt Society.

Ptak, Roderich. 1998. Sino-Japanese Maritime Trade, Circa 1550: Merchants, Ports and Networks. In: *China and the Asia Seas: Trade, Travel, and Visions of the Other (1400–1750)*. Aldershot: Ashgate.

———. 2003. Ming Maritime Trade to Southeast Asia, 1368–1567: Visions of a 'System'. In: *China, the Portuguese, and the Nangyang: Oceans and Routes, Regions and Trade (c. 1000–1600)*. Aldershot: Ashgate.

Qiu, Xuanyu 邱炫煜. 1995. *M' ing Diguo yu Nanhai Zhufanguo Guanxi de Yanbian*. 明帝国与南海諸蕃国関係的演変. Taibei: Lantai Chubanshe.

Rossabi, Morris. 1972. Ming China and Turfan, 1406–1517. *Central Asiatic Journal* 16 (3).

———. 1990. The 'Decline' of the Central Asian Caravan Trade. In: *The Rise of Merchants Empires: Long-Distance Trade in the Early Moredn World, 1350–1750*, ed. James D. Tracy. Cambridge: Cambridge University Press.

———. 1998. The Ming and Inner Asia. In: *Cambridge History of China. Vol. 8, The Ming Dynasty, 1368–1644, Part 2*, ed. Denis Twitchett and Frederick W. Mote. Cambridge: Cambridge University Press.

Sakuma, Shigeo 佐久間重男. 1992. *Nichi Min kankeishi no kenkyū* 日明関係史の研究. Tokyo: Yoshikawa kōbunkan.

Satō, Hisashi 佐藤長. 1986. *Chūsei Tibettoshi kenyū* 中世チベット史研究. Kyoto: Dōhōsha shuppan.

Sawada, Minoru 澤田稔. 2008. Jūroku seiki zengo no Chūō Ajia ni okeru tsūshō nettowaku 一六世紀前後の中央アジアにおける通商ネットワーク. In:

Kaiiki sekai no nettowakuto jūsōsei 海域世界のネットワークと重層性, ed. Kawamura Tomotaka 川村朋貴 et al. Tokyo: Katsura shobō.

Schurz, William Lytle. 1939. *The Manila Galleon*. New York: Dutton.

Serruys, Henry. 1967. *Sino-Mongol Relations During the Ming II: The Tribute System and Diplomatic Missions (1400–1600)*. Brussels: Institute berge des hautes etudes Chinoises.

———. 1975. *Sino-Mongol Relations During the Ming III, Trade Relations: The Horse Fairs (1400–1600)*. Brussels: Institute berge des hautes etudes Chinoises.

Sugaya, Nariko 菅谷成子. 2001. Supein ryō Firipin no seiritsu スペイン領フィリピンの成立. In: *Tōnan Ajia kinsei no seiritsu* 東南アジア近世の成立, ed. Ikehata Yuikiho 池端雪浦 et al. Tokyo: Iwanami shoten.

Takara, Kurayosi 高良倉吉. 1980. *Ryūkyū no jidai: Ōinaru rekisizō wo motomete* 琉球の時代:大いなる歴史像を求めて. Tokyo: Chikuma shobō.

Tani, Mitsutaka 谷光隆. 1972. *Mindai basei no kenkyū* 明代馬政の研究. Kyoto: Tōyōshi kenkyūkai.

Ueda, Makoto 上田信. 2005. *Umi to teikoku: Min Shin jidai* 海と帝国:明清時代. Tokyo: Kōdansha.

Von Glahn, Richard. 1996. *Fountain of Fortune: Money and Monetary Policy in China, 1000–1700*. Berkeley: University of California Press.

Wada, Hisanori 和田久徳. 1967. Jūgo seiki shotō no Sumatora ni okeru kakyō shaki 十五紀初頭のスマトラにおける華僑社会. *Ochanomizu daigaku jinbun kagaku kiyo* お茶の水大学人文科学紀要, 20.

———. 1981. Jūgo seiki no Jawa ni okeru Chūgokujin no tūshō katsudō 十五世紀のジャワにおける中国人の通商活動. In: *Ronshū: Kindai Chūgoku kenkyū* 論集: 近代中国研究. Tokyo: Ymakawa shuppannsha.

———. 2001. *Zhong-Pu zaoqi guanxishi* 中葡早期関係史. Beijing: shehui kexue wenxian chupanshe.

Wan, Ming and Hikoichi Yajima 家島彦一. 1993. *Umi ga tsukuru bunmei: Indoyō kaiiki sekai no rekishi* 海が創る文明:インド洋海域世界の歴史. Tokyo: Asahi sinbunsha.

Yamamoto, Tatsurō 山本達郎 ed. 1975. *Betonamu Chūgoku kankeishi: Kyukushi no taitō kara Shinhushu sensōmade* ベトナム中国関係史: 曲氏の台頭から清仏戦争まで. Tokyo: Yamakawa shuppansha.

Yi, Weixian 伊偉先. 2000. *Mingdai Zangzushi yanjiu* 明代蔵族史研究. Beijing: Minzu shupanshe.

Yule, Henry. 1916. *Cathay and the Way Thither, Being a Collection of Medieval Notices of China*, vol. I. London: Hakluyt Society.

Watanabe Hiroshi 渡邊宏. 1971. Mindai kaikyō shokoku chōkōhyō 明代回教諸國朝貢表. In Ajia Ahurika bunka kenkyūjo kenkyū nenpō.

Zhang, Wende 張文徳. 2006. *Ming yu Tiemuer wangchao guanxishi yanjiu* 明与帖木児王朝関係史研究. Beijing: Zhonghua shuju.

Zheng, Yongchang 鄭永常. 2004. *Laizi haiyang de chaoxuan: Mingdai haimao zhengce yanbian yanjiu* 來自海洋的挑戰: 明代海貿政策比較研究. Taibei: Daoxiang chupanshe.

Zhong Xinglin 鍾興麟. 2008. *Xiyu diming kaolu* 西域地名考錄. Beijing: Guojia tushuguan chupanshe.

Open Access This chapter is licensed under the terms of the Creative Commons Attribution 4.0 International License (http://creativecommons.org/licenses/by/4.0/), which permits use, sharing, adaptation, distribution and reproduction in any medium or format, as long as you give appropriate credit to the original author(s) and the source, provide a link to the Creative Commons license and indicate if changes were made.

The images or other third party material in this chapter are included in the chapter's Creative Commons license, unless indicated otherwise in a credit line to the material. If material is not included in the chapter's Creative Commons license and your intended use is not permitted by statutory regulation or exceeds the permitted use, you will need to obtain permission directly from the copyright holder.

The *Nanban* and *Shuinsen* Trade in Sixteenth and Seventeenth-Century Japan

Mihoko Oka

1 Background to the *Nanban* Trade

Traditionally, the word *nanban* (南蛮 lit. 'southern barbarian') meant vaguely the uncivilized peoples belonging to the south of China. In sixteenth-century Japan, this word probably signified the general area in the Indochina peninsula of modern Thailand and Cambodia. When the Japanese first encountered people from the Iberian Peninsula, they called them 'nanban-jin' (南蛮人 southern barbarians) because they had arrived along with the people traditionally so called from Indochina and because they brought goods associated with those areas.

In 1498, the Portuguese were the first European power to round the Cape of Good Hope, the southernmost point of Africa, entering the Indian Ocean with the guidance of Islamic sailors who were thoroughly familiar with the sea lanes, to successfully join in the Indian Ocean trade. They established fortresses at important points in order to protect that trade. While maintaining a delicate balance with local ruling powers, they

M. Oka (✉)
University of Tokyo, Tokyo, Japan

developed a trade network structured around points and lines. This was the so-called *Estado Português da Índia*, or Portuguese India.[1]

The Portuguese Age of Discovery has been commonly conceived of as an absolute maritime dominance of the Indian Ocean as far as the seas around Indochina, but that is simply an impression. In reality, the fortresses were mostly nothing more than corners in major Asian ports, built with the permission of the local authorities. In other words, these were not colonies at all.

The soldiers sent from Portugal to defend these fortresses would become merchants soon after their military service ended and were scattered among the ports throughout Asia engaging in trade. Thus, with almost no relation to the interests of the Kingdom of Portugal, many Portuguese involved in trading operations came to live in the Coromandel region of the Bay of Bengal on the eastern coast of India, the trading ports of Pegu, Arakan, Cambodia and Siam on the continental portion of Southeast Asia, or the many port cities of the islands of Southeast Asia. In later years many Portuguese also lived in Batavia where the Dutch East India Company had its base, functioning as intermediaries with local peoples in Dutch trading activities (Souza 1986: 129–145).

2   The Dispersion of Portuguese Merchants

The recent spread of Chinese and Indian overseas settlers has been called a diaspora. Diaspora is a word derived from Greek that was originally used to signify the scattering of the Jews by the Roman Empire after the destruction of the Temple of Jerusalem and the colonization of Judea. In the study of history and sociology in modern society, this word is used to indicate the phenomenon of the movement of a particular people to another region due to some circumstances, their forming a community there, and the group maintenance of their culture by the participation of large numbers of people. In that sense, during the Age of Discovery, the phenomenon of the Portuguese dispersing themselves abroad and establishing communities in all the major ports of Asia did not arise from a Portuguese dominance of the seas, but instead more strongly had the trappings of a diaspora.[2] Moreover, many of the Portuguese people who made up this diaspora were Sephardim (Iberian Jews) who had escaped the clutches of the Inquisition, which was rampaging through the Iberian Peninsula of the sixteenth century. This is not just a jargon phrase here, but based on the findings of recent studies this phenomenon was, in a real sense, a diaspora.³

To give an overview, when the Portuguese traders living in Asian ports arrived in Japan, they did so in the company of Southeast Asians, and it is thought that they were contextualized by the pre-existing concept of *nanban* as applied to Southeast Asians. The ship that arrived at Tanegashima in 1543 was owned by the Chinese Wang Zhi 王直.⁴ There were over 100 foreigners aboard that ship besides the Portuguese, and so to Japanese eyes, the ship was full of a rare assortment of 'southern barbarians'.⁵ What clearly set the Portuguese apart from the Southeast Asian 'southern barbarians' was the early modern European culture and civilization they came from, their superior military technology in firearms, and their Christianity as followers of a religion then almost unknown in Asia.

3 The *Nanban* (Southeast Asian) Trade in the Age of Civil Wars

Japan was substantially open to the world during the Age of Civil Wars (*sengoku jidai*) compared with the following period. In the sixteenth century, Japan had overseas trade relationships, including such well-known events and occurrences as: the tally trade with Ming China, the prosperity of Sakai 堺 and Hakata 博多,⁶ the disruption of diplomacy and trade due to the Ningbo Incident 寧波の乱 (1523), the Ōuchi 大内 clan monopoly on the tally trade, the activities of *wokou* (mixed-race smugglers mainly comprising Chinese merchants) late in the period and the activities of the Kyushu lords dispatching ships in unofficial trade with China. In addition, Ōtomo Yoshishige 大友義鎮, the lord of Bungo province, not only sent ships to China but also established a close trade and diplomatic relationship with Cambodia (Kage 2015: 164–187).

The Ōtomo clan established diplomatic relations with a king of Cambodia, whose name is rendered as 浮喇哈力汪加 [pinyin; fu-la-ha-li-wang-jia]. This is probably King Sathta (1570s–1595s) of the Longvek era. Cambodia at that time was constantly being invaded by the Ayutthaya kingdom of neighbouring Siam, but took advantage of the distraction of the Ayutthaya in their conflict with the Toungoo Dynasty of Burma to expand its own influence (Groslier 2006: 40–42). Around the time of King Satha's reign, Cambodia was growing wealthy from trade with other regions based at the ports of the Tonlé Sap river.

There was thus a need to resist the Ayutthaya, so the Cambodian kings increased the number of Portuguese mercenaries in their employ. In the hope of military support, they pursued diplomatic relations with Spain, which was then expanding its influence in the Philippines (Groslier 2006: 26). King Satha sent an envoy to the Ōtomo with the intention of increasing the power of Cambodia, coinciding with the period when Cambodia was pursuing policies of national enrichment through trade with various regions.

The King of Cambodia had received an envoy from the Ōtomo before 1579 with gifts from them including 'beautiful women', and in return sent an elephant to Bungo Funai (the capital of Bungo). However, the ship was seized by the Shimazu 島津 en route, and the diplomatic messages and gifts of the King of Cambodia addressed to Ōtomo Yoshishige ended up with the Shimazu.[7] What happened to the elephant after that is not known (Kage 2015: 168).

In the following Edo period, many *shuinsen* 朱印船 ('red seal ships' or officially approved ships) sailed to Cambodia, and the major goods imported from Cambodia to Japan were sugar, deerskins, incense and so on. It is said that the Japanese word for pumpkin (*kabocha*), derived from the name 'Cambodia', originates from the time of Ōtomo Yoshishige, when pumpkins were brought from Cambodia to Bungo Funai by the Portuguese. This cannot be proven from primary historical sources, but because in Ōtomo Yoshishige's time there were friendly relations with both the Cambodians and the Portuguese in Bungo Funai, these factors may have been woven together.

Other than those with Ōtomo Yoshishige, from 1570s to the 1590s, relations between Kyushu and Siam and Cambodia can be inferred.[8] In 1577, a Chinese named Guo Liuguan 郭六官, identified as an envoy of the King of Ayutthaya, entered the port of Hirado of the Matsura 松浦, and the next year the ship of Wu Lao 呉老 arrived. Through them the Matsura sought out trade with the Kingdom of Ayutthaya (Kage 2015: 164–167). In addition, in 1563 a Siamese ship entered Yokoseura in the Ōmura 大村 domain, and in 1565 another Siamese ship entered the port of Fukuejima on the Gotō islands. The ship that arrived at Yokoseura was captained by a Portuguese, while the ship that came to Gotō was captained by a Chinese with several Portuguese aboard.

During the latter half of the sixteenth century, the image of Portuguese arriving in Japanese ports is strong, but from the above it can be seen that among the lords of Kyushu, trade was becoming popular with Southeast Asian mainland countries such as Siam and Cambodia. At the same time, the *nanban* trade with the Portuguese based in Macao was also beginning, and to entice Portuguese vessels, it became necessary to allow missionary activities in their domains and to protect the missionaries, even though they may not have converted to Christianity themselves (Elison 1998).

In the sixteenth century, what the Japanese most desired among the goods these traders brought were military supplies such as lead, saltpetre as an ingredient of gunpowder, and guns and cannons. The demand for raw silk and textiles arose in the following period after society stabilized. In other words, in order to obtain Southeast Asian lead and Chinese saltpetre, it was necessary to use Portuguese intermediaries.

It has been pointed out in recent years that, in return for these goods, not only silver, which was dramatically increasing in production at the time, but also human resources may have been sent.[9] The 'beautiful women' Ōtomo Yoshishige sent to the King of Cambodia as a gift have already been mentioned. It is interesting that when Toyotomi Hideyoshi 豊臣秀吉, the ruler of unified Japan, handed down his order expelling the Jesuit missionaries in 1587, one of the reasons given for its promulgation was that the Portuguese were exporting slaves from Japan as they did with the Siamese and Cambodians (Frois 1983: 402).

4 Merchants at the Time of the Opening of Nagasaki Port

To give an overview of the changing times, commercial relations with Southeast Asia arose during the Age of Civil Wars, and on that premise, Edo period Japanese ships that had received a government licence for foreign trade (*shuinsen*) often sailed to Southeast Asia. Such merchants and their crews holding a charter to sail abroad did not suddenly appear in the Edo period. It is posited that during the latter half of the sixteenth century or even earlier in a different form, trade and ocean-going transportation was undertaken.[10] Influential Nagasaki merchants or *shuinsen* traders throughout the Muromachi 室町 period were often involved with the trading capitals of Sakai and Hakata that had grown prosperous from the Ming trade. The Suetsugu 末次 family were early modern trade magnates who had fixed their base of operations in Nagasaki, which was opened in 1571, achieving tremendous influence in the seventeenth century. They had their origins in Hakata and had expanded their trade greatly by backing the Jesuits and the *nanban* trade (Oka 2001).

5   The Life of a Christian Merchant

Suetsugu Kōzen 末次興膳 was the first to settle in Nagasaki and do business there. A passage in the *Historia do Japam* of Luís Fróis dated 1563 and quoting a letter from Luís de Almeida states the following about a person thought to be Suetsugu Kōzen (Christian name Cosme):

> Hibiya Ryōkei 日比屋了珪 sent messengers to me (Luís de Almeida) and a Japanese friar, and also to a man taking care of all the things for us in Japan. He is a wealthy and very good Christian. His name is Cosme Cojen. (Frois 1981: 31)

While very brief, this passage shows that Suetsugu Kōzen was intimate with the Hibiya 日比屋 family, the representative Christian merchants of Sakai, was affluent and possessed a network capable of assisting the Jesuits throughout Japan (probably meaning a range with Kyoto as the northern limit). Kōzen-machi 興膳町 in Nagasaki is derived from his name.

Chōshō-ji 長生寺 temple (Sōtō-shū 曹洞宗) in Akizuki (modern-day Asakura-shi, Fukuoka) was founded by the Buddhist monk Kuten Zenryō 玖天全良 in 1600 with extensive contributions from Suetsugu Kōzen.[11] Fróis in the *Historia do Japōo* for 1590, about 10 years earlier, states as follows.

> When we arrived in Akizuki the missionaries were met by Cosme Kōzen, an elderly and outstanding Christian long known to us. He is quite the master of Hakata, and the father of many Christian children of renown. He is affluent and involved in large business transactions. His original home is in Hakata, but he had many houses elsewhere. One of those many houses was in Akizuki, and there he was treated with great importance by Lord Akizuki Tanezane秋月種実 ... Although the good Cosme Kōzen was past seventy, he came all the way from his home in Hakata just to meet the padres and have them stay in his house there. (Frois 1984; 276)

In other words, in 1590 Kōzen was a good Christian. At that time he lived in Hakata rather than Nagasaki. Why did he contribute to the building of a Sōtō-shū Buddhist temple in Akizuki in his later years?

Kōzen also had the Buddhist name Zennyū 善入. If, for example, he had abandoned the Christian faith following the order expelling the Jesuits (1587) out of fear of Hideyoshi's intentions, then in 1590 he would no longer have been a Christian. Nevertheless, Hideyoshi's banishing of Christian missionaries was aimed at preventing the ruling elite of greater than a specific *kokudaka* 石高 (annual stipend) from becoming Christians, and had nothing to do with merchants like Kōzen. Murayama Antonio Tōan 村山等安, a favourite vassal of Hideyoshi and Nagasaki Daikan 長崎代官 (Magistrate of Nagasaki), was a Christian when he was appointed to that post, so it seems unlikely that Kōzen abandoned his faith out of fear of what Hideyoshi might do.

6 Japanese Religious Culture and the Jesuit's Response

The author has previously pointed out the theory that early Japanese Christians were unable to make a clear distinction between Buddhism and Christianity, and even though the missionaries forbade faith in other religions, they might not have felt the need to abandon them so easily (Oka 2014b). When Francis Xavier first came to Japan, he made use of the Japanese of one Anjirō, originally who had sufficient knowledge on Shingon Buddhism 真言宗, in explaining Christian doctrine, and so the omnipotent Deus of Christianity was translated as Dainichi 大日 (Mahāvairocana), and in general Christian terminology borrowed from Buddhist terminology (Kishino 1998). The result was that Christianity was understood and accepted as a form of Buddhism. When Francisco Cabral came to Japan in 1570 as the Superior, he searched for a way to rectify this situation. He decided on such policies as using Portuguese for religious terminology, but the Visitor of Missions, Alessandro Valignano, an Italian, espoused the idea of 'cultural accommodation' with local customs in missionary work, and it is thought that Christianity and Buddhism became superficially impossible to distinguish to the ordinary faithful.

The following appears in Valignano's *Advertimentos e avisos acerca dos costumes e catangues de Japão*[12] written in 1581:

> The Fathers and Brothers are like the Buddhist monks of Christianity. Those who are given the greatest respect among all the religions and sects of Japan, and who are familiar to all the Japanese of every social caste are

the monks of Zen Buddhism. It would be advantageous for us to occupy a position of the same status as they.

Besides this passage, the recommendation that Jesuit priests adopt the manner of Zen monks for missionary work can be inferred throughout this work, and it was for that reason that the traditional tea ceremony (*cha-no-yu*) was introduced to churches. In other words, this means that Christian missionaries adopted an outward appearance closely resembling that of Buddhist monks. Regarding conversions, it is conjectured that, for the lords and powerful people with a strong enough influence to provide the basis for the missionaries' existence, they permitted considerable compromise in the conditions for their conversions. If that was the case, a Christian convert who also takes refuge in Buddhism would not only be possible but also in a sense unavoidable. This is, however, extremely difficult to prove from the letters of the missionaries, because allowing people in authority to have a two-layered faith conflicts with the strict Christian prohibition against idolatry and so could not be put into writing.

For someone engaged in trade and commerce in Nagasaki, for example, to gain greater profits, it would have been necessary to become close to the missionaries, which is to say to become a Christian. It is worth noting the fact that Kōzen had already achieved a good relationship with the Jesuits as early as 1565. When he participated in the *nanban* trade begun by the Jesuits for their financial support, he served as a trade agent for distributing goods within Japan, possibly expanding his financial power and network.

Kōzen's son, the first Suetsugu Heizō Masanao 末次平蔵(政直), was successful in removing Murayama Tōan in 1619, and himself became the Magistrate of Nagasaki. Before that, Heizō had received an official charter to sail abroad from the Edo Bakufu, and from 1604 to 1634 sent out trading ships a total of 10 times. Suetsugu Heizō was a hereditary name, and it is thought that in 1630, Masanao, the first of that name, passed it on to the second of that name, Shigesada, and so those voyages lasted for two generations. The Suetsugu vessels were bound for quite a wide area, including Siam, Luzon, Taiwan, Cochinchina and Tonkin.

7   Early Nagasaki Headmen and Trade

Beginning with the town construction of Nagasaki in 1571, the position of Headman in overall charge of the town was fixed. After Hideyoshi seized the city and appointed Terasawa Shima no kami as Magistrate of Nagasaki, the Headmen were appointed from among the town elders. The town elders at the time were Takagi Ryōka 高木了可, Gotō Sōtarō 後藤宗太郎 (Sōin 宗印), Machida Sōka 町田宗加 and Takashima Ryōetsu 高島了悦, all Christians, and at the time having already achieved wealth through trade.

Their birthdates and backgrounds were all unclear in the Japanese records, but their ages in 1601 are given in Spanish materials kept at the Mexican General National Archive (De Sousa 2015). According to that source, Gotō Sōin (baptismal name Thomé) was 44, Takagi Ryōka (baptismal name Luís) was 47 and Machida Sōka (baptismal name João) was 45. There is no information given for Takashima Shirobei Ryōetsu (baptismal name Jeronimo). In the same records Machida Sōka (known in Portuguese and Spanish materials as Moro João) was a sea captain from the 1580s sailing between Macao and Nagasaki and also owned a house in Macao. It is unclear if Sōka captained a Japanese ship or a ship within a Portuguese fleet, but at that time many of the Portuguese *nanban* ships sailing between Macao and Nagasaki had numerous Japanese among their crews, and Sōka is thought to have been in charge of those Japanese sailors (De Sousa 2010).

Gotō Sōin was also a sea captain sailing his own ship to Manila. In the Edo period, he was active in *shuinsen* trade and received official charters for voyages to Brunei in 1606, and to Siam in the following year (Iwao 1983). Compared with his activities in sixteenth-century overseas trade, there is no indication that Machida Sōka prepared any *shuinsen*. Takagi Sakuemon 高木作右衛門 (either Ryōka 了可 or the second, Tadatsugu 忠次) sent out a *shuinsen* in 1616 to the Moluccas (Iwao 1983), and in 1628 a *shuinsen* of Sakuemon was burned by a Spanish ship while docked in Ayutthaya.[13] The year before that, an official charter for Siam is thought to have also been granted to him (Iwao 1983: 220).

All of these people were Christians with a deep connection with the Jesuits, and are thought to have been certainly influential in the town administration of Nagasaki.[14] With the Edo period ban on Christianity, Takagi Sakuemon immediately abandoned his beliefs, and the Takashima family followed suit. The Takagi and Takashima families maintained their regional control over Nagasaki until the closing days of the Tokugawa government in nineteenth-century.

Among the four original organizers of Nagasaki, Machida Sōka and Gotō Sōin were actual seafarers themselves who were personally familiar with overseas areas. They did not abandon Christianity even after the government ban and were banished from Nagasaki. It is interesting that the Takagi family and the Takashima family, who were not seamen but trading merchants on the land, obeyed the government restriction and continued to play an important role in the Nagasaki administration until the end of the Edo period. Christian relics have been unearthed from the site of the Takashima family house located where the Nagasaki Family Court stands today, and so it is possible that the Takashima family preserved their faith in some form after they had officially abandoned it.

8   The Jesuits and *Nanban* Trade

In order to expand their missionary work in Japan, the Jesuits needed large amounts of capital. They gradually came to depend on the profits received from the *nanban* trade for maintaining their missionary work, as has been pointed out in the studies of Takase Kōichirō.[15] A historical document that clearly and concretely demonstrates this is the testimony of the Franciscan friar, Sebastian de San Pedro, denouncing the trade of the Jesuits as one reason for the Tokugawa banning Christianity, along with the Provincial of the Jesuit mission in Japan, de Carvalho's refutation of that (Takase and Kishino 1988). The following is a passage by San Pedro detailing Jesuit involvement in the *nanban* trade:

> The Jesuit Fathers who loaded galleons and other vessels with raw silk and other goods from Macao bound for Japan did not only hold these goods in large quantity but also obtained all the raw silk other traders had brought to sell at prices they themselves set called *pancada*.[16] After that they distributed these among Japanese merchants at a special price, gaining a great many friends. Trading was their means for preaching the word of God among them, and they used the profits not only for cathedrals and maintaining *collegios* for Japanese preachers but also gave great amounts of charity to destitute Christians, and also thus obtained funds for other expenses incurred along with missionary work among non-Christians. (Takase and Kishino 1988: 271–272)[17]

According to this passage, through contracts with the markets in Macao, the Jesuits loaded ships from Macao with 50 *pico*s (approximately three tons) of raw silk, and also bought raw silk from other Portuguese traders in Nagasaki, acting as brokers for sales to the Japanese. They used the following concrete method in their operations:

> In Nagasaki their (the Jesuits) monasteries were like customs houses, and were not houses (*casa*) of prayer. Trading ships arrived each year from Macao in China loaded with raw silk and goods, and it is common knowledge that those ships were a large measure of what they brought to Japan. They had a business office next to their *casa*, and there their sales representatives to the Japanese market weighed out their goods. They were there to measure the imported raw silk. Eventually two friars came to live in the business office, and all they did was carry out that business. (Takase and Kishino 1988: 324)[18]

To summarize, in the early period of early modern Nagasaki, nearly all of the raw silk brought by vessels led by the *Capitão Mor* from Macao passed through the hands of the Jesuits to be distributed among Japanese merchants. Following the above passage is a description of how Japanese merchants, administrators and senior officials all consigned their capital to Portuguese ships through the Jesuit friars in order to buy the goods they sought. In other words, the core of the *nanban* trade was a system in which goods from Portuguese ships and Japanese capital were exchanged though the brokerage of the Jesuits (Oka 2010b).

9 THE MUTUAL COMPLEMENTARITY OF THE PORTUGUESE SHIPS AND *SHUINSEN*

At the beginning of the early modern period, another kind of trade developing at Nagasaki was the *shuinsen* trade, which from San Pedro's testimony cited above can be conjectured to have been in a mutually complimentary relationship with the *nanban* trade using Portuguese ships:

> The Portuguese [of Macao], particularly when their *nau* (carracks) were not sailing to Japan, brought their own goods to the Japanese traders [that had arrived in Macao] and secretly loaded them onto their ships ... He (the *procurador*[19] of Japan) immediately and for that purpose procured

goods for the representative of the Jesuit Fathers residing in Macao. This was because his property was never carried by the regular *nau*, but rather on Japanese ships. The Japanese had made this their custom, and it was possible ... As soon as it arrived in Japan, the Fathers took the property to their *casa* or to their business office, so that they might sell it when they wished.

The commonly held view is that after the affair of *Nossa Senhora da Graça* (1609–1610), which caused a severe conflict between the Portuguese and Japanese authorities at the port of Nagasaki, there were no more *shuinsen* bound for Macao. The reason is given as the strong insistence of the Portuguese to the Tokugawa government that the Japanese, who had caused a disturbance in Macao, would be forbidden from entering the port of Macao. However, due to the following complete ban on Christianity by the Tokugawa government and the ending of missionary activities, it is recognized as having been necessary to eliminate the *shuinsen* too, which were returning to Japan loaded with Jesuit goods.

10 Portuguese Merchants Living in Nagasaki

Among the powerful citizens of Nagasaki were those who had provided the rented houses used by the Portuguese. The Portuguese who did not return to Macao lived throughout Nagasaki interspersed among the Japanese. Most of them were temporary residents, but some with Japanese wives and also children were permanent residents engaging in trading activities. Some also had obtained official charters from the Tokugawa government and were involved with the *shuinsen* trade.

According to Iwao Sei'ichi's studies, the names of the traders who appear to be Portuguese of Nagasaki involved in chartered overseas trade were given as *Karasesu, *Gonsarubesu, *Ahonzo, *Gonsaru Biera and *Rodorigesu (Iwao 1983: 220). From other European sources, these names in probable proper Portuguese are António Garces, Manuel Gonçalves, Afonso (family name unknown), Gonçalo Vieira and Manuel Rodrigues. According to Iwao, Manila was their major trading port and some among them may be identified as Spaniards, but from the 1601 document written by Luis de Cerqueira, Bishop of Japan, they are known to be Portuguese (De Sousa 2010: 77–115).

At the time, the trade between Japan and Manila was mostly carried out by Portuguese in Nagasaki. Among them, in 1613 Manuel Gonçalves went to Siam, and the next year to Cochinchina(Nguyễn dynasty) with ships granted a charter. In 1618, Gonçalves' ship returned from Manila to Nagasaki, with a Jesuit and mendicant order missionary smuggled aboard (Pages 1869). Interestingly, this Manuel Gonçalves appears in *Genna kōkai ki* 元和航海記 by Ikeda Yoemon 池田与右衛門 as a master of seamanship. The fact that as an ordinary person he engaged in information and cultural exchange between the Portuguese and the Japanese provides a new perspective to the awareness that Western knowledge came mainly through the schools of the Jesuits and from missionaries.

Also, António Garces was from a powerful family in Macao, and Manuel Rodrigues was already living in Nagasaki in 1601 and was a resident of Hirado. It is worth noting that while they were Portuguese, they were involved in the Japan–Manila trade. After 1580, Philip II was King of both Spain and Portugal, but in practice the two countries were administered separately. This was also true of the overseas colonies and settlements. In order to avoid a negative impact on the profits of both countries, Philip II banned passage between Spanish and Portuguese territories. In other words, travel between Macao and Manila was forbidden. Nevertheless, smuggling was carried out between both areas, and private merchants conducted trade (De Sousa 2010).

For Japan, Manila was an exporter of deerskins, gold dust and Chinese goods via Fujian merchants. For Manila, Japan was a necessary trading partner in the area of food supplies. The Portuguese, who were familiar with the sea lanes and were linguistically able to barter with the Spanish, were advantageous to the Japan–Manila trade.

11   Christians and Southeast Asia

With the Tokugawa government's ban on Christianity in 1614, the leading Japanese Christians along with the missionaries were banished to Macao and Manila. Records show that in that year about 300 Christians left Japan (Borao 2005; Teixeira 1993), but the *shuinsen* trade itself continued for nearly 20 years after that, so it is thought that among those who sought religious freedom, some went to live in the Japanese towns in Macao and Southeast Asia. The Japanese who moved to Asian ports sooner or later intermingled and merged with the local populations, and in order to maintain their faith, the Jesuits expanded their churches and missionary activities in Southeast Asian ports.[20]

The Tokugawa government was aware that the ports of Southeast Asia were the haunts of Japanese Christians. After 1624, when the trade with Spanish Manila and the English ended, the Tokugawa government gradually restricted the range of their trading methods. Despite this, it was difficult to cut off trade with the Portuguese of Macao, who offered great quantities and varieties of excellent goods, and they were sceptical of the competitiveness of the Dutch East India Company and the Chinese ships. Also, because of the conflict in Taiwan with the Dutch caused by the *shuinsen* of Suetsugu Heizō, it was necessary to ascertain their trustworthiness.

After the abrogation of trade with Portuguese vessels and the Shimabara and Amakusa uprisings (known as the Shimabara Rebellion), the Tokugawa government was less concerned with stabilizing the domestic economy than with the need to annihilate the Christians. This was clearly realized in 1639, but why did the complete ban on overseas travel for Japanese ships and Japanese persons happen before that, in 1635? The author posits that travelling abroad from Japan to Macao and the ports of Southeast Asia, where the crew would come into contact with missionaries and Japanese Christians living abroad, was seen as dangerous.

In reality, there was an incident in which it was discovered that a *shuinsen* bound for Cochinchina (Vietnam) called at Macao and the crew came into contact with a Japanese priest named Paulo dos Santos living in Macao. It is known that the Japanese involved was connected with the Kagaya, one of Dejima merchant[21] in Nagasaki. In other words, the Tokugawa government understood that a connection was being maintained between Japan and the Christians through the *shuinsen*. Also, Jesuit missionary activities were expanding in the 1620s in the ports of Southeast Asia, and there was a danger that missionaries could be smuggled into Japan from Manila or Macao.

In reality, after ending trade with Portuguese vessels, inspections of ships were strictly carried out even when the rapidly increasing Chinese ships arrived, and at times Christian-related items were found. The Chinese came not only from the Chinese mainland, but long-distance ships called *okufune* 奥船 also arrived sailing from Southeast Asia. These peaked in the mid-seventeenth century and gradually diminished for contentious reasons, but perhaps one reason was the Tokugawa government's awareness of the danger of the expanding Christian missionaries in Southeast Asia and the strengthening of searches of the *okufune*.

According to the *Nagasaki yawakusa* 長崎夜話草, in 1656 an envoy from the Ayutthaya dynasty arrived in Japan bearing an official letter, but the Tokugawa government was suspicious that a missionary might also be onboard the ship and refused passage. As long as there were Japanese Christians and missionaries, a ship coming to Japan from a port in Southeast Asia was the object of severe caution. In 1675, a smuggling incident was uncovered involving Kageyama Kyūdayū 陰山九太夫, a servant of the fourth Suetsugu Heizō Shigetomo 末次平蔵茂朝, who conspired with the Chinese interpreter Shimoda Yasōemon 下田弥惣右衛門 to hire a Chinese ship and captain to engage in smuggling with Cambodia (Morinaga 1993). This was after a large-scale smuggling incident in 1667 involving a relative of the Suetsugu family, Itō Kozaemon 伊藤小左衛門, an official merchant to the Fukuoka domain, so the Nagasaki Suetsugu family must have been sufficiently cautious. Even after the closing of Japan, the hiring of foreigners for smuggling (or investing in it) may have continued in secret to some degree in Nagasaki. After this, the Suetsugu family disappears from the stage of Japanese history. It is ironic that the cause of their misfortune was trade with Southeast Asia, which was how they originally accumulated their wealth.

12   Conclusion

The primary momentum for the *nanban* trade was the need for importing military *matériel* in the Age of Civil Wars. Japanese history merged with the great trends of world history, probably leading to many social changes. In this period, Japan and Southeast Asia were linked by many routes through many intermediaries, and the trade between Macao and Japan was probably one of them.

The opening of the port of Nagasaki provided the opportunity for linking Japan with the world beyond Southeast Asia, and the imprints of the activities of those traders deeply remain in modern Japan in the form of *nanban* culture, with resonances in food, clothing, art and so on.

The analysis in this chapter clarifies that many individual figures/players were involved in trading activities during the latter half of the sixteenth century and the early seventeenth century, as well as explaining the structure of Japanese trade in that era. In previous Japanese studies on this period, Portuguese *nanban* trade, *shuinsen* trade and new participants VOC and EIC have tended to be examined by different historians taking into account their 'territories'. However, I suggest that future research should study these trading forces more comprehensively, rather than by each individual factor, in order to more effectively clarify the role of Japan in international surroundings from the perspective of global history.

Notes

1. Recently many books and articles about Portuguese India have been published. However, there is limited research on the relationship of Portuguese with local regimes or the Portuguese presence viewed from a broad perspective based on an understanding of maritime Asia. Basic knowledge about Portuguese India presented in this chapter is mainly taken from three monographs: Pearson 1976; Souza 1986; and Subrahmanyam 1990.
2. The term 'Portuguese diaspora' has gained greater recognition after the publication of Stefan Halikowski Smith's *Creolization and Diaspora in the Portuguese Indies: The Social World of Ayutthaya 1640–1720*.
3. James Boyajian was the first author who pointed out the importance of *converso* or *marrano* in the Portuguese Indies. See Boyajian (2008). Lucio de Sousa's recent works on Portuguese converso merchants in East Asia, especially in Macao, Japan and the Philippines, based on detailed analysis using Inquisition records, are remarkable. See de Sousa (2010, 2015).
4. Concerning the arrival of Portuguese to Tanegashima, Japanese scholarship after the 1970s conducted highly developed research on it as part of wokou's activity. Cf. Murai Shōsuke 村井章介, Sekaishi no Naka no Sengoku Nihon 世界史の中の戦国日本 [Japan in the age of Civil Wars Viewed from the World History], Chikuma Shobo (Tokyo), 2012.
5. Nanpo Bunshi 南浦文之, Teppo-ki 鉄炮記 in Nanpo Bunshu 南浦文集, 1625.
6. The most remarkable Japanese scholar on tributary trade between Ming China and Japan is Tanaka Takeo 田中健夫. Tanaka's works has been developed recently by Hashimoto Yu 橋本雄. Hashimoto has published many books and articles on the topic. Cf. Hashimoto (2005).
7. Shōshi 頌詩 [Odes], Kennin-Ji Reiun-in 建仁寺霊雲院.
8. This information is taken from *Cartas que os Padres e Irmãos da Companhia de Jesus escreverão de Japão & China...* (Evora, 1598). Cf. Oka (2014).

9. The first argument was made by Okamoto Yoshitomo 岡本良知 in his monograph *16 Seiki Nichi-Ou Kotsu Shi no Kenkyu 16世紀日欧通交史の研究* [*Study on Japan–European Relations in the Sixteenth Century*] (Rokko shobo, 1942). Recently a comprehensive study using newly found records was written by Lucio de Sousa (2014).
10. A study on the *shuinsen* trade has been developed by the Japanese historian Iwao Sei'ichi 岩生成一. At present, there are no studies that go beyond this work.
11. Chieslik, Hubert, Akizuki no Kirishitan秋月のキリシタン [Kirishitan in Akizuki], Kyobunkan, 2000. Chieslik argues that this Kozen, the founder of the Buddhist temple, might be a son of Kōzen, the Nagasaki merchant. However, according to records kept in the temple, the founder Kōzen was 85 years old when he built this temple in 1600. Based on this evidence, Kōzen, the founder of the temple and the person mentioned in Frois' record, might be considered the same person.
12. This text appears in Josef Franz Schütte, Schütte, *Il Cerimoniale per i Missionari del Giappone: 'Advertimentos e avisos acerca dos costumes e catangues de Jappão' di Alexandro Valignano*: Edizioni di Storia e letterature, 1946.
13. This affair greatly influenced the diplomatic policy of Tokugawa Japan. The red-seal ship trade soon faded out. Cf. Iwao (1934).
14. Gotō Sōin is known to have had a printing office in Nagasaki for the Society of Jesus.
15. Takase Kōichirō 高瀬弘一郎 has published many monumental works on the Society of Jesus in Japan and their involvement in the Portuguese trade. Cf. Takase Kōichirō, Kirishitan Jidai no Kenkyuキリシタン時代の研究 [Study on the Era of Kirishitan], Iwanami Shoten, 1977. Ibid, Kirishitan Jidai Taigai Kankei no Kenkyuキリシタン時代対外関係の研究 [Study on the International Affairs of Japan in Christian Century], Yoshikawa kobunkan, 1994. Kirishitan Jidai no Bōeki to Gaikōキリシタン時代の貿易と外交 [The Trade and Diplomacy in the Kirishitan Era], Yagui shoten, 2002.
16. The word 'pancada' originally means 'hitting'. Here it means 'wholesale price'. The word is estimated to have originated from the act of using a gavel.
17. The original documents is conserved in the Biblioteca de la Real Academia de la Historia, Cortes 566, ff.184–189. The transcribed and edited text can be found in Willeke (1984).
18. The original document is conserved in the Biblioteca de la Real Academia de la Historia, Cortes 566, ff.354–377v. The transcribed text by Bernward H. Willeke is in *Archivum Franciscanum Historicum*, An. 78, 1985, 51–97.

19. Procurador in the Society of Jesus in Japan took care of trading activity, financial matters and material support for the missionary work. Cf. Oka (2006).
20. Regarding Jesuit activity in Southeast Asia, a long report written by Francisco Cardim S.J. is the most comprehensive. Cf. Cardim (1894).
21. Dejima was built as a residential area for Portuguese merchants in 1636. Twenty-five specially appointed merchants who were allowed to trade with the Portuguese were called 'Dejima-Chonin' 出島町人. Kagaya 加賀屋 was known to be a Dejima Chonin. This means that Kagaya was strongly connected with Portuguese trade and was a powerful merchant. Cf. Oka (2010).

References

Borao, J. E. 2005. La Colonia de Japoneses en Manilla en el Marco de las Relaciones de Filipinas y Japón en los siglos XVI y XVII. *CUADERNOS CANELA*, No. 17: 25–53.

Boyajian, James. 2008. *Portuguese Trade in Asia under the Habsburgs, 1580–1640*. Baltimore: The Johns Hopkins University Press.

Cardim, António Francisco (ed. Luciano Cordeiro). 1894. In: *Batalhas da Companhia de Jesus, na sua gloriosa província do Japão*. Lisbon: Imprensa Nacional.

De Sousa, Lucio. 2010. *The European Presence in China, Japan, the Philippines and Southeast Asia, the Life of Bartolomeu Landeiro*. Macao: ICM.

———. 2014. *Escravatura e Diáspora Japonesa nos Séculos XVI e XVII*. Braga: NICPRI. University of Minho.

———. 2015. *The Jewish Diaspora and the Perez Family Cases in China, Japan, the Philippines and the Americas*. Macao: ICM.

Elison, George. 1988. *Deus Destroyed: The Image of Christianity in Early Modern Japan*. Cambridge, MA: Harvard University Press.

Frois, Luis. 1976–1984. In: *Historia do Japam*, ed. José Wicki S.J. 5 vols. Lisbon: Biblioteca Nacional Lisboa.

Groslier, Bernard P. Trans. Michael Smithies. 2006. *Angkor and Cambodia in the Sixteenth Century [Angkor et le Cambodge au XVIe siècle d'après les sources portugaises et espagnoles]*, 40–42. Bangkok: Orchid Press.

Hashimoto Yu 橋本雄. 2005. *Chusei Nihon no Kokusaikankei* 中世日本の国際関係-東アジア通交圏と偽使問題 [International Relations of Medieval Japan]. Tokyo: Yoshikawa Kōbunkan.

Iwao, Sei'ichi 岩生成一. 1934. Matsukura Shigemasa no Luzon tou Ensei Keikaku 松倉重政の呂宋島遠征計画 [Plan for Conquest of Luzon by Matsukura Shigemasa]. *Shigaku Zasshi* 史学雑誌, 45: 9.

———. 1983. *Shinhan Shuinsen Bōekishi no Kenkyu* 新版朱印船貿易史の研究 [New Edition A Study on the Red Seal Ship Trade]. Tokyo: Yoshikawa Kōbunkan.

Kage, Toshio 鹿毛敏夫. 2015. *Ajia no Naka no Sengoku Daimyō* アジアの中の戦国大名 [Sengoku Daimyō in Asia]. Tokyo: Yoshikawa Kōbunkan.

Kishino, Hisashi 岸野久. 1998. ザビエルと日本 [Xavier and Japan]. Tokyo: Yoshikawa kobunkan.

Morinaga, Taneo 森永種夫. 1993. *Hankacho* 犯科帳──長崎奉行の記録 [Record of Crimes: Record of the Nagasaki Magistrate]. Tokyo: Iwanami shoten.

Oka, Mihoko 岡美穂子. 2001. A Great Merchant in Nagasaki in 17th Century. Suetsugu Heizô II and the System of Respondência. *Bulletin of Portuguese/Japanese Studies*, no. 2.

———. 2006. A Memorandum by Tçuzu Rodrigues: The Office of Procurador and Trade by the Jesuits in Japan. *Bulletin of Portuguese/Japanese Studies*, no. 13. Lisbon: CHAM-UNL.

———. 2010a. Investment of Japanese Silver in XVII Century Macao-Japan Trade. In *O Estado da India e os Desafios Europeus*, eds. João Paulo Oliveira e Costa and Vitor Luis Gaspar Rodrigues, 119–138. Lisbon: CHAM & CEPCEP.

———. 2010b. *The Nanban Trade: Merchants and Missionaries*, 281–321. Tokyo: University of Tokyo Press.

———. 2014a. 16 seiki kohan no Ayutaya koeki to Nihon, 16世紀後半のアユタヤ交易と日本" [Ayutthaya Trade and Japan in the Latter Half of the 16th Century]. In: *Daikokaijidai no Nihon to Kinzoku koeki* 大航海時代の日本と金属交易 [Japan and Metal Trade in the Age of the Great Voyages], ed. Hirao Yoshimitsu 平尾良光. Kyoto: Shibunkaku Shuppan.

———. 2014b. Kirishitan to Tōitsu Seiken キリシタンと統一政権 [Christians and Unified Government]. In: *Iwanami Kōza Nihon Rekishi, Kinsei*, vol.1 岩波講座日本歴史 [*Iwanami's Japanese History, Early Modern* 1]. Tokyo: Iwanamishoten.

Pages, Leon. 1869. *Histoire de la Religion Chretienne au Japon*, vol. 1. Paris : C. Douniol.

Pearson, M. 1976. *Merchants and Rulers in Gujarat: the Response to the Portuguese in the Sixteenth Century*. Berkeley: University of California Press; New Delhi: Munshiram Manoharlal.

Souza, George Bryan. 1986. *The Survival of Empire: Portuguese Trade and Society in China and the South China Sea 1630–1754*. Cambridge MA: Cambridge University Press.

Subrahmanyam, Sanjay. 1990. *Improvising Empire: Portuguese Trade and Settlement in the Bay of Bengal 1500–1700*. Oxford: Oxford University Press.

Takase, Kōichirō 高瀬弘一郎 and Hisashi Kishino 岸野久. 1988. イエズス会と日本 [The Society of Jesus and Japan], vol. 2. Tokyo: Iwanami Shoten.

Teixeira, Manuel. 1993. *Os Japoneses em Macau*. Macau: Instituto Cultural de Macau/Comissão Territorial para as Comemorações dos Descobrimentos Portugueses, 29.

Willeke, Bernward H. 1984. *Franziskanische Studien* 66 (Münster): 176–181.

Open Access This chapter is licensed under the terms of the Creative Commons Attribution 4.0 International License (http://creativecommons.org/licenses/by/4.0/), which permits use, sharing, adaptation, distribution and reproduction in any medium or format, as long as you give appropriate credit to the original author(s) and the source, provide a link to the Creative Commons license and indicate if changes were made.

The images or other third party material in this chapter are included in the chapter's Creative Commons license, unless indicated otherwise in a credit line to the material. If material is not included in the chapter's Creative Commons license and your intended use is not permitted by statutory regulation or exceeds the permitted use, you will need to obtain permission directly from the copyright holder.

The Jewish Presence in China and Japan in the Early Modern Period: A Social Representation

Lucio de Sousa

Abbreviations

AGI	Archivo General de Indias. Seville, Spain.
AGN	Archivo General de la Nación. Mexico City, Mexico.
AGS	Archivo General de Simancas. Simancas, Spain.
ARSI Jap-Sin	Archivum Romanum Societatis Iesu, Japonica-Sinica. Rome, Italy.
BA	Biblioteca da Ajuda. Lisbon, Portugal.
BNC	Biblioteca Nazionale Centrale. Rome, Italy.
BNP	Biblioteca Nacional. Lisbon, Portugal.
IAN/TT	Arquivo Nacional Torre do Tombo. Lisbon, Portugal.

In the course of this work I shall use specific terminology. The word *Converso*, which was widely used by Spanish and English historiography, and the word *Cristão-Novo* (New Christian), extensively utilized in Portuguese historiography, have the same meaning. Both refer to Sephardic Jews or descendants of Sephardic Jews who converted/were forced to convert to Christianity (i.e., Catholicism) in Spain and Portugal. These Sephardic Jews, and their descendants,

L. de Sousa (✉)
Tokyo University of Foreign Studies, Tokyo, Japan

are usually divided into two types: those who converted to Christianity and who effectively cut their ties with Judaism; and those who, despite having converted/being forced to convert to Catholicism, secretly practised (some sort of) Judaism. In the Far East, the terms *Converso* and *Cristão-Novo* may be confused with Chinese and Japanese neophytes who converted to Catholicism. Documental sources often use these terms. Therefore, I do not believe that it is appropriate to use these terms within an Asian context. Hence, in order to disentangle the different backgrounds of Jewish 'converts' to Christianity, I have chosen to use the term *Judeo-converso* (Portuguese for a Sephardic Jew forced to convert to Catholicism) for people of Sephardic Jewish origin.

Professor Lucio de Sousa is leading the Board of Advisors of GECEM project. GECEM ('Global Encounters between China and Europe: Trade Networks, Consumption and Cultural Exchanges in Macau and Marseille, 1680–1840') project hosted by the Pablo de Olavide University, UPO (Seville, Spain). The GECEM project is funded by the ERC (European Research Council)-Starting Grant, under the European Union's Horizon 2020 Research and Innovation Programme, ref. 679371, www.gecem.eu. The P.I. (Principal Investigator) is Professor Manuel Perez Garcia (Distinguished Researcher at UPO).

1 Introduction

Judeo-conversos played a very important role in the Atlantic trade carried out by Portugal and Spain in the sixteenth and seventeenth centuries; yet, their presence in China and Japan, barring some specific cases, has remained unknown. The first reason for this absence is due to the fact that the inquisitorial records collected in Goa and covering the Portuguese communities established in these regions have not survived. The second reason is related to the very morphology of this group commonly known as *Nação Portuguesa* (Portuguese nation: this is how the Portuguese Jews would refer to themselves). Spread over several continents and empires, managing to stay socially connected, the *Judeo-conversos* who participated and created commercial networks as their diaspora extended from the Iberian Peninsula to Macau and Nagasaki also developed various strategies to remain hidden.

This chapter is divided into three sections. The first section will study the formation and establishment of the *Judeo-conversos* in Macau since the establishment of this Portuguese enclave in China (1557) until the revolt against the Portuguese authorities in 1611. The second section will investigate the *Judeo-converso* community in Japan and its relationship with the Society of Jesus. The third and final section will examine the cognitive perceptions of *Judeo-conversos* in China and Japan in the early modern period (c. late fifteenth century to c. late eighteenth century).

The Sephardic presence in Asia between 1498 and 1611 can be divided into four main phases. The first is the opening of the sea route to India by Vasco da Gama (1460–1524) in 1498. Many Jewish descendants participated either in commercial activities or in the Portuguese Diaspora to India. Since at this time the Inquisition had not yet been established in Goa (1560–1774; 1778–1812), it is very difficult to identify the Jewish origin of many of these participants.

The second Diaspora starts in around 1548 with the foundation of the Inquisition in Portugal (1536–1821). The Portuguese inquisitorial court, contrary to what had happened with other inquisitorial courts of the Iberian Peninsula, had as its main target the descendants of the Iberian Jews, i.e., the Sephardic Jews of Portuguese and Spanish descent. This event marks a new Diaspora for many *Judeo-conversos* to Asia, thus forming the first community of *Judeo-conversos* in India of Iberian origin: the community of *Judeo-conversos* of Kochi.[1] These *Judeo-conversos* established important relations with the Jewish commercial networks in the region, especially with the communities of Hormuz, and with many Sephardic Jewish communities who also settled in North Africa and the Ottoman Empire. The prestige of the Kochi community ended in 1558, when it was accused of having committed several acts against the Catholic faith. The main figures of this community were arrested and, along with their relatives, they were then sent to Lisbon for trial. As can be inferred from the Inquisition archive files, the dismantling of this community was rampant. Many of its members chose essentially three escape routes: Hormuz, the Bay of Bengal and Malacca.

The third dispersion movement began in 1560[2] with the official foundation of the Inquisition Court in Goa as well as with the official settlement of the Portuguese in Macau (1557). Within a few years, this city became a haven not only for *Judeo-conversos* but also for all merchants and European mercenaries who for some reason wanted to escape the control of the Portuguese authorities in Goa.

The fourth diasporic movement occurred after the fusion of the Portuguese and Castilian crowns (1580–1640). This political event resulted in two important Diasporas: a first one composed of Portuguese *Judeo-conversos* who settled in the neighbouring kingdom of Castile, thus escaping the Portuguese Inquisition, the latter being considered more repressive than its Spanish counterpart[3]; and a second Diaspora also composed of Portuguese *Judeo-conversos* who chose to move to Spanish America. Many members of the Portuguese community, in Mexico City and Acapulco, initiated significant investments in the trade with China through the Manila colony.[4] This circulation between the Portuguese and Spanish Empires made the inquisitorial persecution against the *Judeo-conversos* more difficult.

2 The Sephardic Presence in Macau

2.1 The First Community of Sephardic Origin in Macau

The official European settlement in the Macau peninsula occurred in 1557. This settlement was the culmination of numerous failed attempts to obtain from the Chinese authorities a place where the Portuguese could disembark, wait and prepare their ships for their commercial trips in the area and beyond. The European settlement in this geostrategic place was not the product of mere coincidence as Portuguese traders were looking for a safe haven near Canton where ships could dock for many decades. The Macau Peninsula met all these requirements (Loureiro 1996).

Initially, China had possession of the land and Portugal was the administrative power of the community; yet, gradually it became impossible to disentangle the administrative sovereignty of Macau. Hence, today people tend to say that it was a shared administration, negotiated between the Portuguese and Chinese authorities. Perforce, the local community, consisting of a mixture of nations that considered itself as being Portuguese, was subjugated to various interests. As for the *Judeo-conversos* settled in Macau, they used numerous strategies to survive the religious persecution of the time (de Sousa 2010: 1–11).

In order to rule the local population, the position of Head Captain was created. The latter was the official representative of the Portuguese authorities before the Chinese and Japanese and, simultaneously, was also the highest judicial authority in Macau. Nevertheless, this presence was more symbolic than effective, since in reality the private traders who organized all trade bound for Japan by paying a percentage to the Head Captain were actually in charge of the Portuguese enclave in China (Souza 1986: 18–22; ARSI Jap-Sin 14 II: 341–342).

As for the presence of *Judeo-conversos* in Macau, prohibiting merchants of Jewish descent from settling in this region dates back to 31 January 1545, when the queen regent Catherine of Portugal (1507–1578) ordered the 13th Governor/4th Viceroy of India, João de Castro (1500–1548), to cancel all previous laws that allowed the *Judeo-conversos* to travel in the Portuguese Armada to India, declaring that from that moment on, they were to be prevented from travelling to Asia (Andrade, Luíz 1835 [1651]: 422). This law continued with a new edict issued by King Sebastian of Portugal (1554–1578), dated 15 and 20 March 1568, in which it was stated that 'any New Christian can go or shall go to the region of India without my permission, signed by me, under penalty of doing the contrary be arrested and lose all their properties, half for those who accuse him and the other part for my Treasury' (Pato 1884, II: 216).

Thus, we can conclude that the presence of *Judeo-conversos* in Macau, under Portuguese law, was considered illegal and any identified citizen of Jewish descent should be sent to Goa or Lisbon for trial. This judicial context would contribute to the fact that the *Judeo-converso* community in Macau had to remain hidden and silent during the first two decades of the founding of the city. However, this presence would be unveiled on 15 November 1579, when the Jesuit Francisco de Meneses wrote an important letter to his Superior in Rome, the priest Mercurian, of the intention of the local *Judeo-converso* community to build a synagogue in Macau: 'a housing and a secret place where they could worship'. This information appears to be genuine, given that the Mandarins of Canton, being consulted by some Portuguese with this request, did not understand the need to build a 'new church', as he could not identify the difference between the *Judeo-conversos* and the remaining Christian merchants (de Sousa 2010: 72–73).

The same letter also states that in this city lived '600 neighbours' of Portuguese origin, which in the sixteenth century meant '600 householders,' and half of them, i.e., 300 citizens, were *Judeo-conversos* who had fled from the Inquisition in Goa. If we associate a family with every *Judeo-converso* householder (although some could be single), the number of citizens of Jewish ancestry would be even higher. Although I have not found any information regarding the outcome of the negotiations, the answer seems to be in the negative and that the survival of this community in Macau was in danger because of this letter.

Unfortunately, I did not find additional references to the *Judeo-conversos* living in Macau during this time. The Portuguese Inquisition, established in Goa in 1560, focused its activities primarily on India. It did not send any representatives to ascertain the Sephardic presence in Macau (AGN, Inquisición vol. 237: 488f.).

Only in 1583, for the first time in the history of Macau, a Head Captain representing the political and commercial interests of the crown, also represented the interests of the Goa Inquisition. The Head Captain General elected Aires Gonçalves de Miranda, who had a legal warrant issued by the Inquisition to capture and imprison all *Judeo-conversos* living in Macau and to send them to Goa to be judged. Ironically, this warrant did not prevent the carrack of Aires Gonçalves de Miranda from travelling with *Judeo-conversos* on their way to China.[5]

I am unaware of what type of negotiations had been initiated by the Head Captain General and the local community once the former arrived in the city. However, Head Captain Aires Miranda Gonçalves' plan to imprison all *Judeo-conversos* did not materialize. The main merchants remained in the city; only those with little or no political or economic clout were captured: Luís Pardo (1582); Francisca Teixeira (1585) and the priest Francisco de Azurara (1585); António Nóbrega (1586); and Pêro Fernandes d'Arias (1587).[6] Unfortunately, the content of these court files did not survive. Of the accused, only two were indicted for Judaizing (Luís Pardo and Francisca Teixeira). Three of the accused may also be included in one case. When Francisca Teixeira was accused of Judaizing, her husband Pêro Fernandes d'Arias, also a *Judeo-converso*, bribed the priest Francisco Azurara and received secret information about the legal procedures taken by the Goa Inquisition against his wife.

Upon being discovered, they were both arrested: the priest Francisco de Azurara was sentenced for revealing the inquiries carried out in Macau to the person who was guilty, and Pêro Fernandes d'Arias was sentenced for bribing 'certain people who brought the proofs against his wife for this Holy Inquisition' (Lourenço 2007: 224–227).[7] As for Francisca, we know that she was born in Macau, daughter of Manuel Teixeira and Inês Gomez, both Portuguese of Jewish descent. His father also had a brother named Estêvão Gomez who lived in India. Three of her sisters were also born in Macau: Leonor da Fonseca (in 1567), who was also captured by the Goa Inquisition in 1594 (IAN/TT, *Inquisição de Lisboa*, n. 13360); Mécia Leitoa, who married Rui Boto (a *Judeo-converso*); and Ana Mascarenhas, who married Adrião Almada (a *Judeo-converso*) and later, a second time, a Portuguese named António Ferreira (a Christian), a householder in Chaul.[8] There was also a fourth brother named Pedro Teixeira.[9]

Francisca was later sentenced to life imprisonment for Jewish practices.[10] Her husband Pêro Fernandes d'Arias was released and forced to pay a fine of 11 *pardaos*.[11] Unfortunately, Luís Pardo's court files did not survive; hence, it is not possible to reconstruct his social network in Macau.

Except for Francisca and Luís Pardo, none of the remaining Macau *Judeo-conversos* were captured or tried by the Inquisition; thus, the Portuguese enclave in China remained temporarily impregnable.

As a way to solve the 'Jewish problem' in China and defeat the opposition against the Inquisition in Macau, the Religious Court began to restructure the Macau inquisitorial hierarchy and its members, as evidenced by the correspondence between the Inquisitor of Goa and the Holy Office of the General Council of 24 December 1585:

> there are many years that neither from China [Macau] nor from Malacca arrives a prisoner, nor denunciation to this table having those regions reputation of having many [*Judeo-conversos*], where I do not know if I dare claim to be more of service for God and benefit to the souls not to grant to the aforementioned bishops of those places jurisdiction over the Inquisitorial things is at least in China [Macau], but rather their power should be restricted by His Holiness, and these evil places would be remedied and would work much better if Your Reverence send some Inquisitor – if you have two – visit them, and if you do not, you should send a reliable and honest deputy. (Baião 1930, II: 102; Lourenço 2012, I: 218).

In 1586, the new Inquisitor, Tomás Pinto, emphasized again the need to ascertain the purity of blood in Malacca and China:

> Your Highness will see how Judaism is quiet, since it is more probable that [Judaism] is concealed because the People of the Nation [i.e., the Portuguese Jews] are spread in some parts of the state [of Portuguese India] like China [Macau], Malacca, Cochin, and the fortresses in the North, where there are many signs that they make their ceremonies and people do not dare denounce them to the vicars because of the abovementioned things. (Baião 1930: 119; Sousa 2004: 24)

This passage clearly shows that although there are indications of *Judeo-conversos* living in several Portuguese trading posts in India, Southeast Asia and China, the Inquisition found it extremely difficult to penetrate these spaces. Additionally, the Portuguese Christians who had settled in those regions did not denounce the *Judeo-conversos*. In 1587, despite the impossibility of sending an Inquisitor to Macau, the Religious Court decided to be represented in Macau by sending Captain João Gomes Fayo.[12] This was the second attempt of the Inquisition to capture *Judeo-converso* merchants in Macau. Upon his arrival, Fayo presented to the local authorities an ordinance issued by the Goa Inquisition Court to arrest all *Judeo-conversos* who practised Judaism, promising to give any denouncer half of the confiscated property. As for the other half of the confiscated property, it would go to the Goa Inquisition Treasury (AGN, Inquisición vol. 237: 457f). The justification presented was the prohibition of 1568, in which King Sebastian stated that no *Judeo-converso* could travel to Malacca, China or Japan (AGN, Inquisición 1601, vol. 263, exp. 1U: 140).

In Macau, the arrival of Captain João Gomes Fayo immediately generated a huge controversy among Jewish merchants and a major revolt of the *Judeo-conversos* traders against the Inquisition (AGN, *Inquisición*, vol. 237: 457f; de Sousa 2015: 70). The negotiations that followed, and their key players, remain unknown. Also unknown is the outcome of this confrontation (AGN, *Inquisición*, vol. 237: 457f). However, we can state that the Macau *Judeo-conversos* won, since no individual of Jewish ancestry from the community was captured or sent to Goa.[13] This occurrence also demonstrates the cohesion and real importance of this Sephardic community, which had managed to obtain protection from the Christian community against these anti-Jewish sentiments and actions. This episode is also omitted in the letters written by the members of the Society of Jesus to Europe.

Besides the failed attempt by the Inquisition to penetrate Macau, the year 1587 also marked the arrival of an important family of *Judeo-conversos* persecuted by the Lisbon and Goa Inquisitions: Rui Perez and his two sons.[14]

Rui Perez was born in Viseu in the late 1520s or early 1530s to a family of Jewish origin.[15] Contemporary testimonies claim that he and his family had been persecuted by the Inquisition; hence, he left Europe for India without his wife and with only two children (AGN, *Inquisición*, vol. 237: 457).

Unfortunately, there are many elements that obscure the true past of the Perez family. In their diaspora this family used many different names to hide its ancestry. For example, Rui Perez also used a second family name: Rui Fernandes (AGN, Inquisición, 1601, vol. 263, exp. 1U: 140). His children also changed names during the time they lived in China and Japan. The oldest was known by three different names (António Rodrigues, Francisco Rodrigues and João Rodrigues), whereas the youngest son used the names Manuel Fernandes and Luís Rodrigues (AGN, *Inquisición*, 1601, vol. 263, exp. 1U: 137, 138v, 140). This concern in erasing traces that could reveal their true origin, possibly to protect other family members living in Portugal or Asia, suggested a turbulent relationship with the Inquisition.

Being newcomers, and with no ties within the community, the Perez family members were the ideal victims. Therefore, when the representative of the Goa Inquisition, Captain João Gomes Fayo, started persecuting them, they did not receive any assistance from the community; as such, they were formally charged for being Jews before the judicial magistrate Damião Gonçalves, who then represented the judicial power of the crown in the city (Braga 1998: 78). Simultaneously, Bishop Leonardo de Sá O.C. (1581–1597), who was living in the city, also decided to persecute them. The eldest son of Perez was the first victim. Arrested on the orders of the Bishop, going by the name António Rodrigues, he negotiated with the authorities his conditional release by paying a bail, only to participate in a Macau-Japan commercial journey. Instead of returning to Macau, he fled to Nagasaki, never to return to China (AGN, *Inquisición*, vol. 237: 460).

The second victim was Rui Perez himself, who was eventually aided by the most unsuspected person of the entire city, Head Captain Jerónimo Pereira. Pereira, the official representative of the Portuguese crown and the highest authority of the city, hid Rui Perez in the annual trade carrack destined for Japan. It is also through this trail that we catch a glimpse of the Sephardic community living in Nagasaki. The case of the Perez family is an example of how the Macau *Judeo-converso* community was particularly adverse to the *Judeo-conversos* persecuted by the Inquisition. Probably the city residents were afraid that these unexpected arrivals could cause major and profound religious investigations by the Inquisition in Goa and decided not to cooperate with or assist the newcomers.

The same would happen to the *Judeo-converso* António Díaz de Cáceres, who in 1589, in order to recover his fortune (Adler 1896: 29; Cohen 1970: 172–175, 2001: 29; Gitlitz 2002: 69) travelled from the port of Acapulco to the Philippines and Macau (Liebman 1970: 171). He departed on 29 December 1589, as captain of the ship *Nuestra Señora de la Concepción*, also known by the name *San Pedro* (AGI, *Inquisición*, 1596, vol. 159, exp. 1: 83), while his wife, Catalina de Léon y de la Cueva, and his relatives were arrested by the Mexican Inquisition. As for the commercial journey, the historical evidence we have, mainly from Díaz de Cáceres' own diaries, testify that a trading company formed by Díaz de Cáceres (Cohen 1970) and his partner António de los Cobos was purposely created for the realization of this trip. The ship *Nuestra Señora de la Concepción/San Pedro* was property of the slave merchant Manuel Gil de la Guardia, also a *Judeo-converso*, future Procurador de Causas de la Real Audiencia de Manila (Attorney of Judicial Causes of the Royal Audience of Manila of the Spanish East Indies (AGN, *Inquisición*, 1597, vol. 160, exp. 1: 74v)).

Díaz de Cáceres would advance the capital and labour as captain, on which he would charge a payment, and Los Cobos invested the capital and half of the merchandise. A third investor, Hernando de la Vega, invested the amount of 4000 pesos and the forth investor, Jorge de Almeida, brother-in-law of Díaz de Cáceres, 1040 pesos (AGI, *Inquisición*, 1596, vol. 159, exp. 1: 79).

In addition to these investments, the ship, with a crew of 45 sailors, also carried 25 passengers, and each of them had to pay 50 pesos to the captain. The ship would carry silver, wine, olive oil and olives. Arriving in the Philippines, in the port of Cavite, a secondary port, mainly used for smuggling, the vessel needed repairs in the order of 4000 pesos. An official report discovered that half of the goods transported by Díaz de Cáceres were not declared to customs in Acapulco, having been transported illegally. To avoid confiscation and imprisonment, de Cáceres bribed the authorities raising the value of the real damage of the vessel (Uchmany 1989: 164). In order to be able to meet the expenses and increase the profit margin, he decided to travel to Macau. Soon after his arrival in Macau (1590), he was arrested and accused of having entered the port without official permission, thus violating the ordinances of the city and of the Viceroy of Portuguese India prohibiting any commercial contact between Macau and the Philippines. Imprisoned and chained to the wall of a vessel destined for Goa, he prepared for a tragic end at the hands of the Goa Inquisition. Yet, before his departure, he managed to escape.

After Head Captain Aires Gonçalves de Miranda's inquisitorial attempt in 1583 and Captain João Gomes Fayo's second attempt in 1587, the third notable person to represent the Inquisition of Goa was Head Captain Roque de Melo. Having arrived in Macau in 1591 with the objective of capturing *Judeo-conversos* traders, Roque de Melo failed again to capture any Sephardic merchants settled in Macau or newcomers like António Díaz de Cáceres or the Perez family. In the case of the Perez family, Melo travelled to Nagasaki, where he tried to imprison them. Yet they managed to escape to Hirado with the assistance of the Society of Jesus and from this port they successfully fled to Manila with the help of the ambassador of the Philippines, Pedro González Carvajal, a Portuguese man and with no known Jewish background. The tenacity, adjustment and integration of the *Judeo-conversos* in Macau contributed to the growing opposition to any inquisitorial effort and, because of this, on 17 March 1597, King Philip II, through his representative Pedro Álvares Pereira, sought to intervene in Macau by issuing a new order for the expulsion of the *Judeo-conversos* settled in the city. The then Viceroy of India, Matias de Albuquerque (1591–1597), was unable to fulfil the order, probably due to pressure exerted by the local mercantile elite. Hence, no direct intervention in Macau occurred (Boyajian 2008: 80).

By the end of the sixteenth century, the Goa Inquisition had only captured three more individuals in Macau. The first victim would be Leonor da Fonseca, a widow, captured in 1594, Francisca Teixeira's sister (the first victim of the Portuguese Inquisition in Macau). Leonor Fonseca's scandalous life in Macau, conducting many love affairs including one with a local priest, would be the main reason for her capture. Alone, abandoned and without any allies, she would eventually die in prison in Goa a few years later (Lourenço 2008: 145–165; 2012).

Nuno Paredes, a merchant, was the second *Judeo-converso* to be sent to Goa (1595). Unfortunately, the content of his inquisitorial process was destroyed. Hence, I was not able to identify the charges made against him.

The merchant/mercenary Pêro Rodrigues, sent to Goa in 1599, was also accused of Judaizing and of murder. On the latter charge, despite the fact that the court records do not survive, we know that he was a friend of Leonor da Fonseca's family. Despite having been arrested by the Inquisition, he managed to free himself, settling in Japan in 1603 (IAN/TT, *Inquisição de Lisboa*, n. 4279: 46).

2.2 The General Pardon of 1605 and the Revolts of the Judeo-Conversos in Macau in 1611

In Europe, from 1600, the Treasury Council required new measures to be taken against *Judeo-conversos*. King Philip III (1578–1621), in an attempt to obtain quicker and secured financing, required the major *Judeo-conversos* of Lisbon, Oporto and Évora to purchase royal pepper at a price set by the crown. The pepper allotment was then sold at exorbitant prices (Boyajian 2008: 88). In 1601, the royal pepper was sold at a price of 52 *cruzados* per *quintal*, 20 *cruzados* above the market price, and the total transaction was 515,529 *cruzados* (Boyajian 2008: 90). In this process, the *Judeo-conversos* Jorge Rodrigues Solis and Rodrigo Andrade Évora were the representatives of the main mercantile families in the negotiations with the king (Costa 2008: 859–899). This period also coincided with the arrest of many descendants of Jews in Portugal and Portuguese India, as well as in Spanish and Portuguese America. These arrests had a major impact on the Sephardic commercial network, since many of these Iberian Jews and their descendants were in possession of extraordinary wealth at the time and their investments were vital to the stability of commercial circuits. However, at the same time, a period of new negotiations between representatives of the main Iberian *Judeo-converso* families and the Holy See started. In 1604, after many petitions and donations, the *Judeo-conversos* obtained the official pardon of the Pope (Codes 2010). Yet this pitfall for the Inquisition could only be successful if it was officially approved by the king, and for that it was necessary to convince the Iberian political elite to publish the papal pardon and bring it into force. Taking advantage of this situation, Francisco de Sandoval y Rojas, Duke of Lerma (1553–1625), using his authority over the king, negotiated the amount of 1.7 million *cruzados* for the publication of the General Pardon. In fact, the precise amount would be slightly higher, and if we take into account the additional expenses associated with it, it would have been 1.8 million *cruzados*. The *Judeo-conversos* of Portugal, Castile and their respective colonies in Asia and the Americas proposed to divide the required amount among themselves. At the head would be Lisbon's mercantile community with 718,377 *cruzados*, then the remaining communities in Portugal with 736,053 *cruzados*; the communities of Castile with 200,000 *cruzados*; New Spain and Brazil together would pay 87,035 *cruzados*; and finally the communities in Portuguese India and the Far East would pay 75,000 *cruzados*. The granting of the General Pardon ran from March 1605 until May 1615 (AGS, Secretarías Provinciales, Portugal, libro 1557: 167 fls.). During the period 1605–1610, the amount of capital gathered 72% (1120,866 *cruzados*) was invested in the India Run; 12% (187,798 *cruzados*) went to the royal family and the Duke of Lerma; 11% (169,085 cruzados) was spent on the Flemish War; and 5% (71,476 *cruzados*) on additional expenses. Between 1605 (the date of the General Pardon) and 1610 (the date of its withdrawal), the Iberian crown received from the *Judeo-conversos* a total of 1,549,225 *cruzados*. The amount of 150,775 *cruzados* was not collected. The Castilian community owed the monarch 74,225 *cruzados*, while the *Judeo-conversos* of Portuguese India and the Far East communities did not contribute any amount (75,000 *cruzados*).

It was following these events that the newly appointed Head Captain of Macau (1605–1606), Diogo de Vasconcelos (d. 1640), together with the judicial magistrate, was sent to China in order to conduct a survey of the *Judeo-conversos* living in the city and charge them a *finta*. The *finta* was an extraordinary monetary tax levied by the Portuguese monarchs to Jews and their descendants. These funds were used to sponsor the General Pardon that the *Judeo-conversos* merchants, although they had committed themselves to support in full, had not paid. This arrival brought significant changes in the community. This tax had been repealed in 1610 by the monarch because, in practical terms, this requirement was illegal. Yet, we should also remember that at the time, trade with Japan had been temporarily interrupted in 1609, only to be re-activated in 1611 by Nuno de Soto Maior (BA, *Jesuítas na Ásia*, Códice 49-V-3, Francisco Pires S.J., *Pontos do que me alembrar:* 14v; Charles Boxer 1959: 78–79). Hence, during these three years (1609–1611), the Macau *Judeo-conversos* had lost much of their main income.

When the most important private merchants of the city were menaced by the judicial magistrate, on behalf of the Head Captain, to pay the tax, amounting to 4000 *cruzados*, a considerable sum for the time, the householders of the city, offended by this extortion, organized a rebellion and in several bands pursued the judicial magistrate and Head Captain Diego de Vasconcelos. Immediately, the *Judeo-conversos* of Macau sent news of what had transpired to Europe. Simultaneously, the judicial magistrate of Macau also sent to Europe a report describing these events, which alas was eventually lost. As a response to this controversial episode, on 26 March 1612, the representative of the king, Bishop Pedro, sent a letter to the Viceroy Jerónimo de Azevedo reprimanding the judicial magistrate's behaviour and stating that the *finta* tax asked of the most honourable citizens 'do not serve me; and I recommend you, to strictly reprimand the judicial magistrate for the excesses he committed, and also that you order that similar *fintas* will not be executed without previous knowledge and consideration and whether who are the people of the nation' (Rivara 1875, vol. 6: 930). As for the 4000 *cruzados*, they were to be delivered and invested in copper and, upon their arrival in Goa, they were to be applied towards the manufacture of artillery pieces (Rivara 1875, vol. 6: 932). As for the judicial magistrate, he should be punished in accordance with his abuses of power (Rivara 1875, vol. 6: 931). Regarding the *Judeo-conversos* of Macau, they also should be investigated, but with the right to present their own defence, which would be compiled in a report and sent to the Court of Goa. (Rivara 1875, vol. 6: 930).

Despite these indications from the crown, the *Judeo-conversos* of Macau were never listed as such, their names were not sent to Goa, and in the following years the Inquisitions of Goa and Lisbon did not take any measures in order to identify, pursue, arrest or prosecute any *Judeo-conversos* traders hailing from this region.

In conclusion, this extortion attempt by the Portuguese administration of Goa also proves, once again, that the main private merchants of Macau, the *notable householders of the city*, as they were designated, were in fact a result of the complex phenomenon of the Iberian Jewish Diaspora in Europe and Asia. The constant influx of people of Jewish descent living, passing by and/or doing business in Macau, either for political or commercial reasons, shows a community active not only in terms of commerce but also in terms of diplomacy, able to disarm the Inquisitorial attempts of repression. Unfortunately, we do not have any demographic data from which we can infer their real social and economic contribution to Macau or their adjustment and assimilation processes to Macanese society.

3 THE SEPHARDIC PRESENCE IN JAPAN

3.1 *Judeo-Conversos and the Society of Jesus in China and Japan*

As for the acceptance of *Judeo-conversos* by the Society of Jesus, this process was initiated by Father Ignatius of Loyola (1491–1556), founder of the Society.[16] The mentality of this individual differed radically from the anti-Semitic policies enacted by different religious orders in the Iberian Peninsula during the sixteenth century.

In fact, the Society of Jesus was the only religious congregation where the *Judeo-conversos* could enter and the *Limpieza de sangre* (Spanish for 'purity of blood') statutes were not followed (Maryks 2010: 29–31, 76–90). The statutes of *Limpieza de sangre* were a means of legal discrimination against newly converted people to Christianity in the Iberian Peninsula, or against people suspected of secretly practising their old religions, especially the *Marranos* (or rather the *Anusim*), the *Conversos*, or the New-Christians, in the case of Jewish minorities, and Muslims and their descendants.

The statutes of *Limpieza de sangre* varied and could cover one or two generations, or generations even further down the genealogical line. Hence, before any individual had access to administrative positions, military orders and/or religious role in the Portuguese and Spanish Empires, he had to go through different tests proving that he was a Christian with no Jewish or Muslim blood (Rastoin 2007: 14–15).

This segregation policy would be rejected by Loyola, hence the discontent among some of its members, especially among Jesuits hailing from the Iberian Peninsula, a region where the anti-Jewish rhetoric was particularly strong. The first important personality who opposed Loyola was the Portuguese Simão Rodrigues (1510–1579), co-founder of the Society of Jesus and Jesuit Province of Portugal. In 1551, this individual clearly disobeyed his superior and ordered that no *Judeo-converso* should be admitted to the Jesuit missions in Asia. Francis Xavier (1506–1552) followed these directives for some time until Loyola, informed of the anti-Semitic policies introduced on his behalf by Simão Rodrigues, revoked the anti-Semitic regulations, again making it clear that the Society of Jesus indeed accepted the descendants of Jews. Unfortunately, this discriminatory attitude ran between 1548 and 1558 (Rastoin 2007: 10–11) until it was overturned by Loyola.

The *Judeo-converso* acceptance policy by the Society of Jesus began to be widely challenged only after the death of Loyola (1556) and his successor Diego Laínez (1512–1565), also a *Judeo-converso*.

In 1584, the *Congregação Provincial Portuguesa* (Portuguese Provincial Congregation) deliberated that the *Judeo-conversos* should not be accepted by the Society of Jesus. The final blow arrived in 1593, when the Fifth General Congregation of the Jesuits issued an official decree banning all *Judeo-conversos* from entering the Society of Jesus (Rastoin 2007: 13–15).

And what would then happen to the *Judeo-conversos* who had been previously admitted? Because of the deeply rooted prejudice against the Portuguese and Spanish *Judeo-conversos*, they were forced to work outside the Iberian Peninsula and outside Europe, in places like Central and South America, India, China or Japan.

In the case of Japan, the *Judeo-conversos* entering in the Society of Jesus tended to be from wealthy families and their level of education was also very high. As for this small group of *Judeo-conversos* that we know, we can divide them into two subgroups: the first subgroup includes individuals such as Pedro Gómez (in Japan) and Duarte de Sande (in Macau), who were admitted to the Society of Jesus in Europe, whereas the second group includes names such as Luís de Almeida and Aires Sanches, who were accepted by the Society in Asia. Both were affected by the same prejudice. They had difficulty in ascending the religious hierarchy of their order. If the *Judeo-converso* Pedro Gómez was appointed Vice-Provincial of Japan (1590–1600), generating animosities among his peers, the Jesuits Luís de Almeida e Aires Sanches had to face major challenges. Being received as brothers by the Society of Jesus, only at the end of their lives were they ordained priests as a reward for the work performed on behalf of the Japanese mission.

A few words highlighting their significant contributions to the Society of Jesus in Japan are necessary here. Pedro Gómez was born in Antequera, Spain in 1535; he had seven siblings. As he himself stated, 'my duty was to study until I joined the Society' (Ruiz-de-Medina 2005: 170). This objective was achieved on 21 December 1553, when Gómez officially joined the Society of Jesus in Alcalá de Henares. At this University, he acquired good training in grammar, the arts, philosophy and theology. His Portuguese experience started in 1555, when he travelled from Cuenca to Coimbra, where he taught until 1559. From 1560 onwards, he travelled between Plasencia, in the Extremadura (Western Spain) and Évora, capital of the Alentejo region in Portugal—roughly 270 km, via Badajoz, on the Spanish-Portuguese border—studying theology and special cases that were useful when converting and giving confession to the Gentiles (Ruiz-de-Medina 2005: 170).

Between 1567 and 1570, Gómez preached in the Portuguese cities of Coimbra and Évora before travelling in 1570 to Angra, on the Island of Terceira, the Azores. On 24 March 1579, Gómez travelled again, this time on the Portuguese Armada to India. This Armada was the first sent to India after the death of King Sebastian of Portugal (1578) (Maldonado 1985).

Gómez arrived in Goa on 9 October 1579 and travelled to Macau in April 1581. On 25 July 1583, he arrived at the port of Nagasaki and became the Superior of the Society of Jesus for the region of Bungo (present-day Oita). With the death of Vice-Provincial Gaspar Coelho (7 May 1590), Gómez was appointed by Father Alessandro Valignano (1539–1606) to succeed him in office, remaining in this post until his death (Ruiz-de-Medina 2005: 171–172).

In the last stage of his life, Gómez's educational background, along with his Jewish heritage, eventually influenced his writings on forced conversion to Christianity in Japan in the *Compendium Catholicae Veritatis, Pars I. Chap 68* (Gómez 1997). On the issue entitled 'quando infideles gentios possunt compelli ad fidem recipiendam. Chapter 68', Gómez explains the two opinions that existed in the Catholic Church: the first defended that it was legitimate to convert the Gentiles by force, but the second opinion stated that forced conversion was illegitimate. In Chapter 68, Gómez believed that conversion was to be performed without the use of force. Though coercion had been used in the Iberian Peninsula and in Japan through vertical conversion (i.e., the baptism of a Daimyo meant the immediate adherence to Christianity by their subordinates), Gómez was against this strategy. Undoubtedly, his thorough knowledge of the religious context of the *Judeo-conversos* contributed immensely to this opinion.

Luís de Almeida was born in Portugal in 1525, probably in Lisbon, the same city where on 30 March 1546, he was declared fit to practise medicine and surgery by the *Cirurgião-Mor* (Surgeon-Major, equivalent of today's Chief of Surgery) of the Kingdom of Portugal, Master Gil (de Carvalho 1994: 105–122). Almeida embarked for India on 17 March 1548, devoting himself to trade. The year 1552 marked his first visit to Japan and the year 1553 marked his meeting with the Jesuit Cosme Torres that would influence their decision to join the Society of Jesus and his official acceptance on 15 April 1556 at the port of Funai. His ordination as priest occurred 24 years later, in Macau (6 May 1580). At the end of his life, Almeida was appointed Superior of Amakusa (1581–1583). He died in Kawachinoura in October 1583 (Yuuki 1989).

This *Judeo-converso* devoted his life to the implementation of a European system of medicine in Japan (Heynick 2002: 162), building hospitals for the sick, those with then-incurable diseases like leprosy and for the socially deprived.

In addition to donating a large sum of money to the Society of Jesus in Japan, Almeida organized the Society of Jesus as a trading company. This monetary donation to the Society of Jesus is famous since it was considered by the Superior of the Jesuits in China and Japan, Francisco Cabral (1570–1581), and the Visitor of the Society of Jesus, Alessandro Valignano (1574–1606), as the beginning of the religious investment in the Macau-Japan trade (Valignano 1598). That money was invested by

Luís de Almeida, through his Portuguese trader friends (Schütte 1975: 465; Wicki 1977: 349; de Sousa 2015: 48). This strategy would continue untouched until 1563, the year in which new economic changes were introduced in the Society of Jesus in Japan. In this year, the Provincial Father António de Quadros (1559–1572) ordered that trade should not be made directly by the Jesuits, but rather through trusted merchants, allies of the Society of Jesus, which should invest the money on their behalf, and upon concluding their sales, they should leave in Japan the necessary amount of money for the support of priests and of the evangelization project. The remaining money should be invested in the trade of the following year (ARSI, Jap-Sin 9 II: 63v). For this purpose, the post of Procurador in Japan was created. The Procurador was the Society's commercial manager who supervised the merchants who invested the Society's funds, the accounting of the investments and profits in the trade between Macau and Japan, plus the amount that should be invested in the following year. In 1563, the first Procurador of Japan, Miguel Vaz, was elected. Vaz represented the financial interests of Portuguese traders and the Society of Jesus until 1582 (Koichirō 1977: 521–534). As a matter of fact, although there had not been any official designation, Almeida was the first Procurador, doing, precisely the same activities that Miguel Vaz later undertook. Even the position and characteristics of the Procurador were modelled on Almeida's experience.

Aires Sanches was probably born in 1527 in Lisbon.[17] He was admitted to the Society of Jesus in 1562. Like Luís de Almeida, Sanchez studied medicine, following the Jewish tradition. Yet it is not possible to indicate where he must have acquired the *licentia practicandi* to practise medicine. Most likely it was the *Hospital de Todos os Santos* (the Hospital of All Saints), the centre of Jewish medicine in Portugal. In addition to medical studies, Aires Sanches was particularly gifted at writing. This has led some authors to speculate that he must have started studying grammar and the humanities from an early age. Besides these talents, Sanches also excelled in musical training. Despite his Jewish ancestry, as a reward for the work done in the Society of Jesus, he was ordained as a priest in Macau in 1579–1580 (Wicki 1977: 349).

In Japan, Sanches was one of the few Jesuits to actually master the Japanese language. This made him particularly important for the Society of Jesus. He died in Omura in June 1590.

3.2 The Community of Sephardic Origin in Nagasaki

The suspicions of the existence of *Judeo-conversos* in the Far East appeared immediately after the arrival of the Portuguese in Japan, especially Francisco Zeimoto and Diogo Zeimoto. Francisco was named by the author António Galvão in the work *Treaty of Discovery* as one of a group of deserters from a Portuguese ship in Siam who sailed to Japan (Galvão 1563), and Diogo Zeimoto was named by the author Fernão Mendes Pinto in the book *Pilgrimage* as one of the first adventurers who arrived in Japan and in particular for having been the first European to introduce firearms in the region (Pinto 1614). Portuguese and Japanese historiography would give greater credibility to António Galvão's version of the arrival of the first Europeans to Japan; however, it is important to point out something that thus far has not been studied or mentioned. The Zeimoto family name can be traced belonging to *Judeo-conversos* of Spanish origin who arrived in Portugal after the 1492 expulsion.[18]

Another individual strong suspected of being a *Judeo-converso* was the most important merchant of Macau, Bartolomeu Landeiro (de Sousa 2010: 63–74; 2015: 49–56). In his autobiographical account, Landeiro reveals that he had helped a Christian Japanese daimyo in the battles against other daimyos who professed other religious beliefs. At the same time, he informs us that he brought a ship with more than 600 tons and that following his arrival and his diplomatic skills, he managed to bring peace to the region. He also points out having built sumptuous churches in Japan where Christian sacraments were administered (de Sousa 2010: 29). To this description we should add some additional information presented by Juan Román Baptista, treasurer of the city of Manila, and Diogo Ferreira, a Portuguese merchant living in Manila. Juan Baptista Román testified that many Portuguese, and particularly the Jesuits, claimed that Landeiro had the possibility of obtaining high profits on the sale of goods in a Japanese port ruled by a non-Christian daimyo. Yet, he obeyed the request of the Jesuits, moving his vessel to another port that belonged to a Christian daimyo, spending a lot of money there and re-establishing Christianity in that region. The merchant Diogo Ferreira adds that Landeiro had built many churches and spent a lot of money on conflicts he had had with enemies in Japan (de Sousa 2010: 23).

However, information about the existence of a small permanent *Judeo-converso* community in Nagasaki would only arise in the late sixteenth century, with the arrival of the Perez family in Japan. In 1591, the

Head Captain of the city of Macau, Roque Melo, pursued this family to Nagasaki, who escaped to Hirado and then to Manila. However, Roque de Melo did not dare to interfere with other more powerful *Judeo-conversos* merchants of Nagasaki (de Sousa 2015: 112).

Despite the intervention of the Portuguese Inquisition in Macau, in the case of Japan, until 1598, *Judeo-conversos* lived freely among the Portuguese and Japanese residents of the city. With the arrival of Bishop Luís Cerqueira in Nagasaki, this situation radically changed. As one of the first steps after his establishment in Nagasaki, the Bishop, upon discovering an *ajuntamento ruin* (bad group of people), imprisoned five *Judeo-conversos*, sending two directly to the Inquisition of Goa for trial and three to Macau. This unexpected intervention, according to the letter of the Visitor Alessandro Valignano, generated panic among the *Judeo-conversos* who remained in the city and feared that they too would turn into future victims of the jurisdiction of Bishop Cerqueira:

> It existed also a very bad group of some Portuguese in Japan, which gave [a] bad example to the Japanese, and sent two of them imprisoned to Goa, to the Holy Inquisition, which were New Christians of Jewish descent; and other three (New Christians) living well outrageously, were sent to Macau and with it he (the Bishop) put a strong brake and fear in some other married Portuguese who live here, who up until now did not fear anyone and were getting too much freedom, causing many problems and concerns to ours (the Company's members of Jesus in Japan. (ARSI, Jap-Sin 13-2, 1599-20-02: 213v)

This intervention by the Bishop seems to have been the last, since no further evidence of any *Judeo-conversos* being sent from Japan to Goa or Macau exists. Interestingly enough, the inquisitorial record of Goa do not make any reference to these prisoners and there is no reference to this episode in the documentation produced in Macau. Unfortunately, we do not know the names of the victims, the charges or the legal outcome. However, we can state that, with respect to the *Judeo-converso* community that remained in Nagasaki, most of its members established a good relationship with Bishop Cerqueira and with other Jesuits.

As for the *Judeo-converso* community in Nagasaki, among its finest was the merchant Francisco Rodrigues Pinto (b. 1551), resident of Nagasaki (AGN, *Inquisición*, 1601, vol. 263, exp. 1U: 139; ARSI, Jap-Sin 31: 209). His Jewish origins were publicly known within the European community, something which did not prevent him from testifying on behalf of the Society of Jesus against other *Judeo-conversos* or maintaining an important alliance with the Bishop of Japan, Luís de Cerqueira (1598–1614), who would characterize Francisco as being 'de mucho hablar, es hombre de bien y que no deixara de hablar verdade en negocio de juramento' ('a very talkative person, an honest man who will speak the truth after taking the oath') (AGN, Inquisición, 1601, vol. 263, exp. 1U: 136).

Even though the exact time when Rodrigues Pinto began living in Nagasaki is unknown, it is known that between 1588 and 1601, he lived in Nagasaki. We also know that he was involved in an important religious controversy in 1598. This controversy had its roots in the *San Felipe* galleon incident. Departing from Manila bound for Acapulco, the *San Felipe* galleon ultimately arrived in Japan on 14 October 1596. The diplomatic problem that it generated in the ensuing months between the various religious orders in Japan and with the government of Hideyoshi eventually had an unfortunate outcome: the commodities of the galleon were confiscated by the Japanese authorities and 26 people in Nagasaki were ultimately executed. The Society of Jesus, in order to prove their innocence and given that many books started circulating in Europe accusing them of being the main cause of this tragedy, some of which are dedicated to the highest dignitaries like Pope Clement VIII (*BNC*, Rome, 9-18-A-4; María 1599a) or Philip III (*BNC*, Rome: 14-33-B-56; María 1599b), eventually sent two reports to Father General Claudio Acquaviva (*Biblioteca Nazionale Centrale*, Rome, 41-6-D-13; Fróis 1607) their version of the events. The Jesuits also performed various inquiries in Japan to investigate what eventually happened with the *San Felipe* galleon with the intention of exonerating the Society of Jesus' intervention in this sad episode. At the same time, though, many rumours of alleged miracles that occurred at the place of execution of the 26 victims executed in Nagasaki started circulating. To placate this wave of superstition, the Bishop of Japan, Luís de Cerqueira, ordered a special investigation, initiated in September 1598 in Nagasaki, which tried to analyse the supernatural phenomena described.

It is in this context that Francisco Rodrigues Pinto appears as the main eyewitness of one of these miracles published by the Franciscans in the *Relacion del martirio de seus frayles descalços de San Francisco de la Santa Provincia de San Gregorio de las Philipinas que padecieron en el puerto de Nangasaqui (Report of the martyrdom of friars of St. Francis of the Holy Province of St. Gregory of the Philippines suffered at the port of Nangasaqui*).[19] The *Judeo-converso* Rodrigues Pinto was present before Bishop Cerqueira on 28 September 1598 to deny the miracle of seeing several columns of fire where the 26 martyrs were executed. This statement has the particularity of containing the signature of Francisco (ARSI, Jap-Sin 31: 209). In the same survey we also have the testimony of Japanese Moro João, which shows that Francisco Rodrigues Pinto's reputation in Nagasaki was not very positive, and *tenido en esta tierra asi entre los portugueses como entre los japones por hombre que finge algunas historias* (*seen on this land among the Portuguese and among the Japanese as a person who invented some stories*) (ARSI, Jap-Sin 31: 211). The above investigation on these miracles was completed on 3 February 1599, with the final verdict that no miracles had occurred, that the preservation of the bodies of 26 martyrs was due to the cold weather and that the Japanese guards protected the bodies of the martyrs from the carrion birds (Cooper 2003: 177–178).

Another important Sephardic merchant was Manuel Rodrigues/ Manuel Rodrigues Navarro (b. 1547), whom the Bishop said was 'judio de nación, pero hombre de bien y de verdad' ('from the Jewish Nation, but a good and honest man') (AGN, *Inquisición*, 1601, vol. 263, exp. 1U: 136*)*. Rodrigues, who was married, chose to live in Nagasaki (AGN, *Inquisición*, 1601, vol. 263, exp. 1U: 136), at least between 1588 and 1621. Navarro escaped the Mexican Inquisition, despite having been denounced by a Portuguese merchant named Gaspar Mendes. Through this denunciation, we know that Navarro was born in Beja, Portugal (AGN, *Inquisicion*, vol. 237: 218). Between 1588 and 1621, despite being settled in Nagasaki, he conducted numerous commercial journeys to Macau, the Philippines and New Spain. For example, in 1592 he departed to Acapulco with the *Judeo-converso* Antonio Diaz de Caceres (Uchamany 2003: 87) and then to Mexico City, a place where he established a friendship with the *Judeo-conversos* Manuel Gil de la Guardia and Luis Carvajal. Years later, Carvajal revealed to the Mexican Inquisition that Navarro had also lived in Macau and Manila for some time having unravelled in secret the daily life of the Sephardic community in China:

> Manuel Gil de la Guardia who also travelled to China, said that the abovementioned Manuel Rodriguez Navarro was a Jew; thus, he saw and visited him.

And there he confessed to him, and vice versa, that both were Jews and obeyed to the aforementioned religion. The said Manuel Rodriguez Navarro told him the things the Jews did in China and had no further conversation with the aforementioned Manuel Rodriguez Navarro. (AGN, Inquisicion, 1597, vol. 160, exp1: 1)

In 1594 (AGN, *Inquisicion*, 1597, vol. 160, exp. 1: 74v), Manuel Gil de la Guardia travelled to the Philippines onboard the same galleon used by Manuel Rodriguez Navarro on his return to the Americas (AGN, *Inquisicion*, 1597, vol. 160, exp. 1: 26). Unlike Navarro, Manuel Gil de la Guardia did not settle in Macau or Nagasaki; instead, he chose to live in Manila. Obviously, the information that Navarro had given him would be of great use to achieve prestige in the city. In Manila, la Guardia gradually ascended the hierarchy of power, reaching the pinnacle of his career when he was appointed *Procurador de Causas de la Real Audiencia de Manila* (Attorney of Judicial Causes of the Royal Audience of Manila of the Spanish East Indies). Soon after, he became attorney of the *sangleyes*, term used by the Spanish in the Philippines to classify the Chinese settled in this region, whose interests la Guardia protected by writing petitions against their enemies (AGN, *Inquisicion*, vol. 237: 176, 177). While la Guardia was captured by the Mexican Inquisition, Navarro managed to escape the inquisitorial persecutions and was never caught by the Portuguese or Spanish Inquisitions. This achievements must have been decisively assisted by the protection of the Bishop of Japan, Luís Cerqueira (AGN, *Inquisición*, 1610, vol. 903: 240–241v). After the expulsion of the Jesuits from Japan (1614), Navarro would continue to live in Nagasaki, making many commercial connections. For example, on 11 May 1620, he reached Cavite captaining the boat *Santo António* (*St. Anthony*), carrying 101 Japanese sailors (AGN, Indiferente Virreinal, caja-exp. 4154-001; *Inquisición*, 1620: 15). When questioned by the Inquisition, Navarro stated that he was a full Christian with no Jewish ancestry and that his place of origin was the region of St Thomas in India (AGN, *Indiferente Virreinal*, caja-exp. 4154-001, *Inquisición*, 1620: 15), when in fact he lived in Nagasaki on Hirado-Machi Street (Iwao Sei'ichi 1983: 235). His ship was carrying as main commodities flour and fabrics (AGN, *Indiferente Virreinal*, caja-exp. 4154-001, *Inquisición*, 1620: 15). A notebook in Japanese with information about Navarro has been preserved with details of another trip from the port of Nagasaki to Manila in 1621. This document reveals in detail the goods commercialized: flour, cookies, miso barrels, barrels of salted fish, beans, pork legs, oil pots, iron boxes (crafts) and cotton fabrics (Iwao Sei'ichi 1983: 291–293). From this date onwards, we lose track of Navarro.

There are also references to other *Judeo-conversos* traders who would live temporarily in Nagasaki and whose relationship with the Society of Jesus and Bishop Luis de Cerqueira was not so close. They were: Afonso Vaez, Francisco Vaez, Diogo Jorge, Vilela Vaz, Pero Nabo, Góis, Paulo Gonçalves and Pero Rodrigues.

The merchant Afonso Vaez was born in Portugal and with his son, Francisco Vaez, a child, fled to Nueva España, where he became very wealthy. Due to religious persecution triggered by the Mexican Inquisition, Afonso Vaez decided to flee to Asia. His departure coincided with the *auto-da-fé* of 8 December 1596, in which 69 people were victims of the Inquisition. On the eve of the event, in the port of Acapulco, Vaez and his son were recognized by a Portuguese trader who was surprised to see this rich merchant poorly dressed in servant's clothes (AGN, *Inquisicion*, 1594, vol. 223: 113).

Although he was discovered in Acapulco, Afonso and Francisco Vaez outmanoeuvred the colonial authorities, travelling to Asia and living in Manila for a few years (AGN, *Inquisicion*, 1594, vol. 223: 113). Religious persecution in the city led them to move on to Nagasaki (on an unknown date). Ironically, the same Portuguese merchant who found them in Acapulco also travelled to Japan and, living in Nagasaki, found and recognized them (AGN, *Inquisición*, 1594, vol. 223: 113). It is also in this city that that trader read the *Historical Account of the Funeral Obsequies of the Majesty King Philippe II* (*Relacion historiada de las exeqvias fvnerales de la Magestad del rey d. Philippo II*) (Flórez 1600)[20] and found a reference to Francisco Vaez, in a chapter devoted to fugitives *Relaxed in Statue*, which has the following passage: 'Francisco Vaez, Portugues, moço soltero por observante de la ley de Moysen ausente relaxado en estatua' ('Francisco Vaez, Portuguese, young unmarried observant of the Law of Moses absent relaxed in statue') (Flórez 1600: 137v). Realizing that this was the same person, the merchant secretly revealed all this information to the Bishop, Luís de Cerqueira. The Bishop started a secret inquiry on Vaez and discovered that, meanwhile, both father and son had decided to live in Macau and had then travelled to Goa. The Bishop then sent a letter to the Inquisition of Goa to inquire about Vaez and to report the event. On 27 April 1612, this letter was answered in Goa, and being received in July of the same year by the Bishop, the Inquisition asked for more information on the inquisitorial process of Vaez in Mexico before proceeding to arrest and confiscate the property of the family (AGN, *Inquisición*, 1594, vol. 223: 113). However, Francis' life changed dramatically with the disappearance of his father Afonso, who died suddenly during a new commercial journey from Macau to Goa. In Goa, Francisco paid his debts and received money of investments; he later decided to return to Macau and then to Japan, where he lived in 1613. In the same year, on 21 March, the Bishop sent the Inquisition of Mexico a new letter asking for more information on Francisco Vaez's trial and about his late father Afonso (AGN, *Inquisicion*, 1594, vol. 223: 113). On this person we have no further information, nor do we know if any correspondence from the Mexican Inquisition was ever sent to Japan. However, it is unlikely that this has happened due to the events of 1614 (the death of Bishop Luis de Cerqueira in Nagasaki and the Society of Jesus' expulsion from Japan). In this context, we lose track of the merchant Francisco Vaez.

As to the *Judeo-converso* Paulo Gonçalves, the only information available on the accounts is that he was a merchant and that he lived in Nagasaki (AGN, *Inquisición*, 1601, vol. 263, exp. 1U: 140v, 141). Is it quite probable that he was a blood relation of the merchant Manuel Gonçalves, also a Nagasaki resident. Gonçalves was involved in the trade between this city and Manila, Siam and Cochinchina, participating in the *shuisen* trade (Iwao Sei'ichi 1983: 291–293).

Another *Judeo-converso* merchant living in Japan was Diego Jorge. He was a Lisbon native (b. 1559) (AGN, *Inquisición*, vol. 237: 473v–474) and at a young age left Portugal for India, becoming part to the Sephardic community that lived in Macau in the early 1580 s. When in 1583 Head Captain Aires Gonçalves de Miranda travelled to Macau aiming to imprison and send all merchants of Jewish descent to Goa, he was one of the persons covered by this law. Even though the Head Captain's mission eventually failed, Diego Jorge became publicly well-known in Macau for being a *Judeo-converso* (AGN, *Inquisición*, vol. 237: 488). To escape from the inquisitorial attempts to capture him in Macau, he fled to Nagasaki. Ten years later, in 1593, he fled for the same reasons to Manila, where he again became a potential victim of the Inquisition (AGN, *Inquisición*, vol. 237: 488).[21] Before being captured, he escaped, and after 19 years, we can find Diego Jorge living again in Nagasaki. The merchants Manuel

Gonçalvez, Jorge Bastião, António da Silva and Francisco Martins together with Diego Jorge will write a Report in 1614 containing various informations in defense of the Society of Jesus in Japan. His Jewish identity is not revealed. This document has the peculiarity of including the signature of Diego Jorge (ARSI, Jap Sin 16I, fols. 134–135v).

As for the *Judeo-converso* merchant Vilela Vaz, the only known detail is that, like Diego Jorge, after having lived for some time in Nagasaki, he travelled to Manila. Although persecuted by the Inquisition, he also escaped, leaving no clues as to his destination. As for the *Judeo-converso* Pêro Rodriguez Nabo, we only know that he lived and died in Nagasaki (AGN, *Inquisición*, 1601, vol. 263, exp. 1U: 141) and that he was a close friend of the Perez family together with the *Judeo-conversos* Góis, a merchant who travelled to Siam after 1588 (AGN, *Inquisición*, 1601, vol. 237: 457), and with the merchant Paulo Gonçalves, who also disappeared from the records and who probably fled from Japan (AGN, *Inquisición*, 1601, vol. 263, exp. 1U: 140v–141).

The last identified *Judeo-converso* in Nagasaki was Pero Rodrigues, a friend of the *Judeo-converso* Fonseca family of Macau who, because of inquisitorial persecution, fled from Macau to Japan, where he lived as a merchant (IAN/TT, *Inquisição de Lisboa*, n. 4279: 46). There are also references to other *Judeo-conversos* who lived and socialized in Nagasaki; however, their names were not recorded for posterity (AGN, *Inquisición*, 1601, vol. 263, exp. 1U: 140v).

The presence of *Judeo-conversos* in Nagasaki remained during the period of religious persecution: e.g., the 20 September 1618, letter of the Jesuit Francisco Vieira seeking to exonerate another Jesuit, Mateus de Couros, of accusations and rumours of leading an immoral life in Nagasaki. Vieira's relevant testimony states that after 1614, de Couros remained in Nagasaki, hid in the house of a Japanese Christian, that this house served as a church for the city's Christians, and that it was frequented by many Japanese women. This house was situated in a residential area; according to him, it was 'rodeada de portugueses maliciosos e cristãos novos' ('surrounded by malicious Portuguese and New Christians [*Judeo-conversos*]'), and they would feed the rumours about de Couros disrespecting the vow of chastity. Later, both the Portuguese and the *Judeo-conversos* would state in a survey conducted by the Jesuit Francisco Vieira that the charges against de Couros were 'zombaria e que bem sabem ser tudo mentira' ('a mockery and it was well known to everyone that it was a lie') (ARSI, Jap-Sin 17: 156v).

This would be the last reference to the *Judeo-conversos* in Nagasaki. From this period onwards, the new challenges posed by the arrival of the Dutch and English in the Far East, the expulsion and persecution of the Japanese Christians, as well as the decline of the Portuguese State of India would weaken the presence of the Goa Inquisition in this region. At the same time, the interest of the Society of Jesus in this region was focused on the survival of the mission and of Christianity. Hence, for all these reasons, the Jewish presence was relegated to anonymity.

4 Cognitive Perceptions of *Judeo-Conversos* in China and Japan in the Early Modern Period: The Perez Family Case

Unfortunately, we do not have much information on the presence of *Judeo-conversos* in Macau and Japan to provide us with details on how a Jewish convert was identified in these communities. So far, the most important documentary source for this period is the inquisitorial trial that was carried out to verify the Perez family, whereby the Inquisition gathered numerous testimonies from Europeans and Japanese Christians, as well as *Judeo-conversos*. This collection of documents proves that the process of integration of newly arrived *Judeo-conversos* was not easy or quick; on the contrary, it provoked resistance from local Christian or *Judeo-converso* communities that had settled there. Throughout this trial, we can also identify and isolate how *Judeo-conversos* were categorized in China and the rest of the Far East.

Although they were formally considered as Portuguese citizens and were therefore subject to the Catholic Church, were educated in the same places as Christians, lived in the same places and possessed Christian names, the *Judeo-conversos* in Macau and Nagasaki continued to represent symbolically the ancient religion; hence, they became a target of discrimination. For example, in investigations against the Portuguese Rui Perez, the *Judeo-conversos* in Nagasaki were categorized by Bishop Luís de Cerqueira as 'hombre de la nación/homem da nação' ('man of the nation') or as 'judio[s] de nacion' ('Jew[s] of the nation'). On the other hand, the markers used by the witnesses of that investigation would be very different. They used the marker 'Cristãos-novos' ('New Christians') rarely. Instead, the markers 'Judeus' ('Jewish') and 'casta de judeus' ('caste of Jews') were mostly used by witnesses (AGN, *Inquisición*, 1601, vol. 263, exp. 1U: fls 136). Thus, we can conclude that there was no single marker to characterize the *Judeo-conversos* in China and in Japan; on the contrary, a set of terms were applied applied to them, which reveal a great ambiguity and flexibility.

Another symbol associated with the *Judeo-conversos* would be the devil. In Macau, the Perez family were regarded as Jewish and their arrival was seen as the devil's work:

> y en macan chicos e grandes lo tenian por judio y de casta de judios y dezian quien diablo los traxo a esta çiudad a este judio no basta los que aca estan (in Macau children and adults thought that he was a Jew and that he belonged to the caste of the Jews and they said: 'What the hell brought this Jew to this city, there are already enough of those living here!') (AGN, Inquisición, vol. 237: 461; de Sousa 2015: 71, 190)

The demonization of the Jew would be accentuated by the physical marker, i.e., the importance of the body also emerges as an important distinguishing factor between Christian and *Judeo-conversos* in China and Japan. In the case of Perez, skin colour was not used as a form of discrimination; however, other physical markers such as the nose or the feet were used for distinguishing between *Judeo-conversos* and Christians. For example, the patriarch Perez was identified as a Jew through his nose and big feet (AGN, *Inquisición*, vol. 237: 458). This racial stereotype had been prevalent in Europe since medieval times; in the case of the Perez family, it was transplanted successfully to the Far East.

Another aspect also used to distinguish between *Judeo-conversos* and Christians was the different forms of socialization. With the exception of a minority, which collaborates with the Church, the *Judeo-conversos* in Macau and Nagasaki were considered a distinct group of the remaining Portuguese. Ordinarily, they lived isolated, also communicating with individuals with Jewish ancestry and were subject to discrimination on the streets, being called publicly 'judeus' ('Jews') by Europeans and Japanese. Documents are unanimous in indicating that the Japanese also participated in this discrimination process in Nagasaki (AGN, *Inquisición*, vol. 237: 443–477):

> Todos los de la çiudad los llamavan de judios y tenian por tales assi Japones como portugueses y assi andaban solos que aun los portuguesses que en la dicha çiudad havia no los admitian en sus cassas (All of the city, called them Jews and they were seen as Jews both by the Portuguese and Japanese, and they lived isolated and the Portuguese in this city did not admit them in their homes). (AGN, Inquisición, vol. 237: 446; de Sousa 2015: 174)

Other distinguishing markers used for this discrimination were the various elements that constituted the Catholic ritual, which was allegedly tainted by ignorance or deliberately by *Judeo-conversos*. In the case of the Perez family, one of the points used in their public condemnation was that they ate behind closed doors without the company of slaves, thus avoiding the opportunity to observe Jewish rituals. In the case of the Perez patriarch, one of the charges against him was that he ate meat during Lent or, rather, during a time when abstaining from eating meat was mandatory (AGN, *Inquisición*, 1601, vol. 263, exp. 1U: 139), and the animals that were used for daily feeding were supposedly slaughtered according to Jewish tradition (AGN, *Inquisición*, vol. 237: 446v–447; de Sousa 2015: 132–133).

In sum, these religious and physical markers converge to show that the echoes of European anti-Semitism successfully travelled to Macau and Nagasaki.

5 Conclusion

During this research, I have found that the identified Sephardic members were usually itinerant merchants who for some reason (usually religious persecution) were forced to leave their original communities. Another aspect that stands out in the documents that I have analysed is that these *Judeo-conversos* were mostly foreign to the Sephardic communities of Macau and Nagasaki. There is little information on these communities and their members, and we do not know the veracity of the events that are extant. They are only referenced when there are drastic political and economic changes, such as dynastic succession (the fusion of the Portuguese and Spanish crowns, 1580–1640), the opening of trade routes with other Asian regions (the Macau-Philippines route) or the collection of taxes (the *finta* imposed on the *Judeo-conversos* of Macau).

Another important aspect to note is that this *Judeo-converso* community concentrated in Macau and Nagasaki organized their commercial networks using not just family members of Jewish origin as agents, but also commercial agents without Jewish ancestry. The arrest and confiscation of property (half for the Inquisition and the other half reverting to the accuser) shows that the Sephardic network required the participation of persons outside the community to prevent their decline. The communities mentioned herein also cannot be characterized as harmonious and cohesive. Cases like the Perez family show exactly the opposite to have been the case. The Sephardic communities of Macau and Nagasaki distanced themselves from the Perez family; hence, the ultimate aid came from Christians like the Head Captain of Macau or from the ambassador of the Philippines to Japan. Ironically, some elements of the Sephardic community of Nagasaki (Francisco Rodrigues Pinto and Manuel Rodrigues Navarro) assisted Bishop Luís de Cerqueira and the Inquisition of Mexico in the persecutions. These documents demonstrate that the idea of the Diaspora as an endogamous community, featuring commercial cooperation based on an idea of Jewishness, is not verifiable in Macau as well as in Nagasaki.

We can also conclude that in Macau there was a permanent *Judeo-converso* community, which established itself in the first decades of the city's foundation. This community, unachievable by the Inquisition in Goa, was gradually revealed by *Judeo-converso* fugitives seeking shelter in Macau to escape the Inquisition.

This permanent community can be verified through the example of the Manuel Teixeira family. The capture of Francisca Teixeira and, years later, Leonor da Fonseca reveal a Sephardic presence of several generations in Macau.

As for the nomadic community, essentially composed of fugitive merchants either from India or the Americas and the Philippines, this community established important temporary refuge places in Macau and in Nagasaki.

The Sephardic community of Nagasaki was composed of a nomadic community and, at least in the late sixteenth century, there was no fixed Sephardic community dating back several generations, but rather there was a community of merchants brought by the Indian and the Pacific Ocean commercial routes. They arrived at Nagasaki and lived there for short periods of time, only to be expelled when the Macau-Nagasaki trade was closed.

Unfortunately, because of the precariousness of this presence both in Macau and in Nagasaki, dependent on religious, social, economic and political considerations, secrecy was the way they found to ensure their survival. As a result, we are able to catch a glimpse of only a small part of the social and commercial reality of these communities in China and Japan.

NOTES

1. The first in-depth study of this community was prepared by Walter J. Fischel, subsequently expanded and surpassed by José Alberto da Silva Tavim (Fischel 1962: 33–59; Tavim 1994: 137–261; 1997: 108–117; 2003).
2. This movement is studied by Baião (1930–1949), Tavares (2004) and Lourenço (2007). The Portuguese Inquisition structure has been studied by many authors. I would like to point out here the most recent works by Franco and de Assunção (2004) and Bethencourt (2009).
3. On this topic, see the classic works by Ortiz (1978), Liebman (1970 and 1982) and Toro (1982).
4. On this topic, see Hordes (1980), Quiroz (1985) and Splendiani (1997).
5. The case of the merchant Diego/Diogo Jorge (AGN, Inquisición vol. 237: 488).
6. From the Reportório of João Delgado Figueira in Lourenço (2007: 216). BNL, Códice 203, Repertório....
7. Bribery.
8. IAN/TT, Inquisição de Lisboa, n.13360, document not paged, fourth session.
9. IAN/TT, Inquisição de Lisboa, n. 4279. Case of Manuel Fernandes de Araújo in Lourenço, 2012, I: 80.
10. BNP, Códice 203, Reportorio...: 312–312v.
11. BNP, Códice 203, Reportorio...: 502v.
12. João Gomes Fayo was Captain of Cranganor in 1607 (Pato 1880: 17, 77, 132).
13. Making a temporal estimate of a journey between Macau and Goa, the return of João Gomes Fayo to Goa occurred after 1588.
14. The Perez family was briefly studied by Eva Alexandra Uchmany. Lúcio de Sousa wrote two biographical works on Rui Perez and the Macau, Nagasaki and Manila *Judeo-converso* communities in the sixteenth and seventeenth centuries. See 1982: 85–104; de Sousa 2010: 69; 2013: 71–91; 2015; Lourenço 2016: 95–116.
15. Testimony of Francisco (21-10-1596) (AGN, Inquisición, vol. 237: 443v).
16. The first historian to study the presence of *Judeo-conversos* in the Society of Jesus was Josef Wicki, who wrote an important biographical study of some of these Iberians of Jewish descent. He also compiled an important list with the names of *Judeo-conversos* who belonged to the Society of Jesus (Wicki 1977: 342–361).
17. The *catalogue of Dimissi, defuncti, admissi* between 1587–1592 points to Viana as is place of birth. Yet, Wicki believes that he was born in Lisbon.

18. There is a reference to Zeimoto in the academic research of Maria José Ferro Tavares (Tavares 2010a, b: 185; 2014: 327). See: www.hum.huji.ac.il/upload/_FILE_1379400106.pdf; http://sefarad.revistas.csic.es/index.php/sefarad/article/viewFile/699/803.
19. Only parts of this book, now lost, are found in the ARSI in Rome (ARSI, Jap-Sin 3 1: 217).
20. http://nrs.harvard.edu/urn-3:FHCL.HOUGH:8140420.
21. Diego was recognized by the Dominican Francisco Sanches de Carvajal, who accused him of being a judeo-converso to the Commissioner of the Holy Office, Fray Diego.

References

Adler, Cyrus. 1896. Trial of Jorge de Almeida by the Inquisition in Mexico. *Publications of the American Jewish Society* 4: 29–79.
Baião, António. 1930–1949. *A Inquisição de Goa: tentativa de história da sua origem, estabelecimento, evolução e extinção*. Lisboa: Academia das Ciências.
Baião, António. 1930b. *A Inquisição de Goa, Correspondência dos Inquisidores da Índia (1569–1630)*, vol. II. Coimbra: Imprensa da Universidade.
Bethencourt, Francisco. 2009. *The Inquisition: A Global History 1478–1834*. Cambridge: Cambridge University Press.
Boxer, Charles. 1959. *The Great Ship from Amacon. Annals of Macao and the Old Japan Trade, 1555–1640*. Lisbon.
Boyajian, James. 2008/1993. *Portuguese Trade in Asia under the Habsburgs, 1580–1640*. Baltimore: The Johns Hopkins University Press.
Braga, José Maria. 1998. *Jesuitas na Asia*. Fundação de Macau: Macau.
Carvalho, José Vaz de. 1994. Luís de Almeida, médico, mercador e missionário no Japão, 1525–1583. In *O Século Cristão do Japão. Actas do Colóquio Comemorativo dos 450 anos de Amizade Portugal-Japão*, ed. Roberto Carneiro e Artur Teodoro de Matos, 105–122. Lisboa: CEPCEP-IHAM.
Cerqueira, Luís de. 1607. *Relatione della Gloriosa Morte fattada sei christiani Christiani Giapponesi per la Fede di Christo, Alli XXV di Genaro M.DC.IV. Madata da Monsignor D. Lodovico Cerquera Vescovo di Giapone. Al Rever. Padre Cláudio Acquaviva Generale della Compagnia di GIESV*. Bologna: Per Gio Battista Bellagamba.
Codes, Ana Isabel López-Salazar. 2010. *Inquisición Portuguesa y Monarquía Hispánica en tiempos del perdón general de 1605*. Lisboa: Edições Colibri.
Cohen, Martin A. 1970. Antonio Díaz de Cáceres: Marrano Adventurer in Colonial Mexico. *American Jewish Historical Quarterly* 60 (2): 172–175.
Cohen, Martin A. 2001. *The martyr Luís de Carvajal*. University of New Mexico Press.
Cooper, Michael S.J. 2003. *Rodrigues, o Intérprete*. Lisbon: Quetzal Editores.

Costa, Leonor Freire. 2008. El imperio portugués: estamentos y grupos mercantiles. In *La monarquía de Felipe III*, ed. José Martínez Millán and Maria Antonietta Visceglia, 859–899. Madrid: Mapfre.
De Sousa, Lúcio. 2010. *The Early European Presence in China, Japan, the Philippines and Southeast Asia (1555–1590)*. Macau: Macau Foundation.
De Sousa, Lucio. 2013. A presença Judaica em Macau, Nagasáqui e Manila no século XVI: O caso Ruy Perez. In *Revista de Cultura* 43.III: 71–91.
De Sousa, Lúcio. 2015. *The Jewish Diaspora and the Perez Family Case in China, Japan, the Philippines, and the Americas (16th Century)*. Macau: Macau Foundation.
Fischel, Walter. 1962. Portuguese Documentation—Cochin in Jewish History: Prolegomena to a History of the Jews in India. *Proceedings of the American Academy for Jewish Research* 30: 33–59.
Flórez, Dionysio de Ribera. 1600. *Relacion historiada de las exeqvias fvnerales de la Magestad del rey d. Philippo II. nvestro senor hechas por el tribvnal del sancto Officio de la inquisicion desta Nueua España y sus prouincias, y ystas Philippinas : asistiendo solo el licenciado don Alonso de Peralta inquisidor appostolico, y dirigida a su persona por el doctor Dionysio de Ribera Florez, canonigo de la metropolitiana desta ciudad, y consultor del sancto Officio de inquisicion de Mexico. Donde trata de las virtvdes esclarecidas de su Magestad, y transito felicissimo: declarando las figuras, letras, hierogliphicos, empresas, y diuisas, que en el tumulo se pusieron, como persona que lo adorno y compuso, con la inuencio[n] y traça del apparato sumptuoso con que se vistio desde su planta hasta su senecimie[n]to*. Mexico: Pedro Balli.
Franco, José Eduardo, and Paulo de Assunção. 2004. *Metamorfoses de um polvo: religião e política nos regimentos da Inquisição Portuguesa (séculos XVI–XIX)*. Lisboa: Prefácio.
Fróis, Luís. 1599. *Relatione della Gloriosa morte di XXVI. Posto in Croce per comandamento del Re di Giappone, alli 5. di Febraio 1597, de quali sei furno Religiosi di San Francesco, tre della Compagnia di Giesù, & dicesette Christiani Giaponesi. Mandata dal P. Luigi Frois alli 15. di Marzo, al R. P. Claudio Acquaviva Generali di detta Compagnia. Et fatta in Italiano dal P. Gasparo Stitilli di Campli della medesima Compagnia*. Roma: Apresso Luigi Zannetti.
Galvão, António. 1563. *Tratado dos Descobrimentos...* Lisboa: Casa de João da Barreira.
George Bryan Souza. 1986. *The Survival of Empire: Portuguese Trade and Society in China and the South China Sea 1630–1754*. Cambridge: Cambridge University Press.
Gitlitz, David Martin. 2002. *Secrecy and Deceit*. University of New Mexico Press.
Gómez, Pedro. 1997. *Compendium catholicae veritatis: Compendia*. Kirishitan Bunko Library: Sophia University.
Heynick, Frank. 2002. *Jews and Medicine*. KTAV Publishing House.

Hordes, Stanley. 1980. *The Crypto-Jewish Community of New Spain, 1620–1690. A Collective Biography*. Unpublished Ph.D. Thesis. http://nrs.harvard.edu/urn-3:FHCL.HOUGH:8140420.
Koichirō, Takase. 1976. Unauthorized Commercial Activities by Jesuits. *Acta Asiática-Bulletin of the Institute of Eastern Culture* 30: 19–33.
Koichirō, Takase. 1977. *Kirishitan Jidai no Genkyu*. Tokyo: Iwanamishoten.
Liebman, Seymour B. 1970. *The Jews in New Spain: Faith, Flame, and the Inquisition*. Florida: University of Miami Press.
Liebman, Seymour B. 1982. *New World Jewry: 1493–1825*. Requiem for the Forgotten: Ktav Pub Inc.
Loureiro, Rui. 1996. *Em busca das origens de Macau: antologia documental*. Lisboa: Ministério da Educação.
Lourenço, Miguel José Rodrigues. 2007. O Comissariado do Santo Ofício em Macau (1582-1644) A Cidade do Nome de Deus na China e a articulação no distrito da Inquisição de Goa. M.A. Thesis, Universidade de Lisboa.
Lourenço, Miguel José Rodrigues. 2008. Attitudes and Practices of Sociability in Macao at the End of the 16th Century: The Case Against Leonor da Fonseca at the Goa Inquisition (1594). In *Bulletin of Portuguese-Japanese Studies* 17:145–165.
Lourenço, Miguel Rodrigues. 2012a. Macau, porto seguro para os cristãos-novos? Problemas e métodos sobre a periferia da Inquisição de Goa. *Cadernos de Estudos Sefarditas* 10–11: 452–499.
Lourenço, Miguel Rodrigues. 2012. *Macau e a Inquisição nos séculos XVI e XVII Documentos*. 2 vols. Lisboa: ICCM.
Lourenço, Miguel Rodrigues. 2016. Injurious Lexicons: Inquisitorial Testemonies regarding New Christians in Macau, Manila and Nagasaki in the Late Sixteenth Century. In: *The Conversos and Moriscos in late medieval Spain and beyond*, ed. Kevin Ingram; Juan Ignacio Pulido Serrano, 95–116. Leiden: Brill.
Maldonado, Maria Hermínia (ed.). 1985. *Relação das Náos e Armadas da Índia, com os sucessos dellas que se puderam saber, para noticia e instrucção dos curiozos, e amantes da Historia da Índia*. Coimbra: Biblioteca Geral da Universidade de Coimbra.
María, Juan de Santa. 1599a. *Relatione del Martirio che sei Padri Scalzi di San Francesco, et venti Giaponesi Christiani patirono nel Giapone l'anno 1597. Scritta dal R.P. Fra Gio. Di Danta Maria Provinciale della Província de S. Gioseppe degli Scalzi, & tradotta dalla lingua Spagnola nella Italiana, per ordine del R. P. Fra Gioseppe di Santa Maria Custode di detta Província per il Capitolo Generale. Et dedicata alla S.ta di N. S. Clemente VIII*. Roma: apresso Nicolò Mutij.
María, Juan de Santa. 1599b. *Relacion del Martírio que seys Padres Descalços Franciscos, y veynte Iapones Christianos padecieron en Iapon. Hecha por Fr.*

Juan de Santa Maria, Provincial de la provincia de S. Joseph de los Descalços. Dirigida al –Rey nuestro Señor don Felipe III. Con Privilegio. Madrid: Imprenta del Lic. Varez de Castro.
Ortiz, Antonio Domínguez. 1978. *Los judeoconversos en España y América*. Madrid: Istmo.
Pato, Raymundo Bulhão. 1884. *Documentos remettidos da India ou Livro das Monções, Tomo II*. Lisboa: Academica Real das Sciencias de Lisboa.
Pinto, Fernão Mendes. 1614. *Peregrinaçam...*. Lisboa: Pedro Craesbeeck.
Quiroz, Alonso W. 1985. The Expropriation of Portuguese New Christians in Spanish America, 1635–1649. In *Ibero-Amerikanisches Archiv*, 11:1.
Rastoin, Marc S.J. 2007. "The 'Conversos' in the Society of Jesus or From Windfall to Fall". In *Friends on the Way: Jesuits Encounter Contemporary Judaism*, ed. S.J. Thomas Michel, 8–27, New York: Fordham University Press.
Rivara, J.H. da Cunha. 1875. *Archivo Português Oriental*. Goa: Nova-Goa.
Rodrigues, Maria José Tavares.1979. *Os Judeus em Portugal no Século XIV*. Lisboa: Guimarães.
Ruiz-de-Medina, Juan. 2005. Gómez, Pedro. In *Missionação e Missionários na História de Macau*, ed. Maria Antónia Espadinha and Leonor Diaz Seabra. Macau: Universidade de Macau.
Schütte, José Franz. 1975. *Monumenta Missionum Societatis IESU – Monumenta Historica Japoniae I – Textus Catalogorum Japoniae 1553–1654*. Romae: Monumenta Histórica Societatis IESU a Patribus Eiusdem Societatis Edita.
Sei'ichi, Iwao. 1983. *Shinhan Shuinsen Bōekishi no Kenkyu* [New Edition A Study on the Red Seal Ship Trade] 朱印船貿易史の研究. Yoshikawa Kōbunkan.
Splendiani, Ana María et al. (eds). 1997. *Cinquenta años de Inquisición en el Tribunal de Cartagena de Indias*, 3 vols. Bogota: Centro Editorial Javeriano.
Tavares, Célia Cristina da Silva. 2004. *Jesuítas e Inquisidores em Goa: a cristandade insular (1540–1682)*. Lisboa: Roma Editora.
Tavares, Maria José Ferro. 2010a. Judeus de Castela em Portugal no final da Idade Média: onomástica e fontes documentais. In *Sefarad* 74 (2). http://sefarad.revistas.csic.es/index.php/sefarad/article/viewFile/699/803.
Tavares, Maria José Ferro. 2010b. The Castilian Jews in Portugal: Na Approach to their History. In *Hispania Judaica Bulletin* 7. www.hum.huji.ac.il/upload/_FILE_1379400106.pdf.
Tavares, Maria José Ferro. 2014. Judeus de Castela em Portugal no final da Idade Média: onomástica familiar e mobilidade. *Sefarad*, 74 (1), 89–144, Madrid.
Tavim, José Alberto da Silva. 1994. Os judeus e a expansão portuguesa na Índia durante o séc. XVI. In: *Arquivos do Centro Cultural Calouste Gulbenkian*, 137–261. Lisboa-Paris: Fundação Calouste Gulbenkian.
Tavim, José Alberto da Silva. 1997. Uma presença portuguesa em torno da "sinagoga nova" de Cochim. In *Oceanos*, 29: 108–117.

Tavim, José Alberto da Silva. 2003. *Judeus e cristãos-novos de Cochim. História e Memória (1500–1662)*. Braga: Edições APPACDM Distrital de Braga.

Toro, Alfonso. 1982. *Los judios en la Nueva Espana: documentos del siglo XVI, correspondientes al ramo de Inquisicion, Mexico*. Archivo General de la Nacion: Fondo de Cultura Economica.

Uchamany, Eva Alexandra. 2003. Encounters between New Spain and the Indian Subcontinent during the colonial Period. In *India-Mexico Similarities and Encounters Throughout History*, ed. Eva Alexandra Uchamany. New Delhi: Macmillan India.

Uchmany, Eva Alexandra. 1982. Criptojudíos y cristianos nuevos en las Filipinas durante el siglo XVI. In: *The Sepharadi and Oriental Jewish Heritage Studies*, ed. Issachar Ben'Amid, 85–104. Jerusalem.

Uchmany, Eva Alexandra. 1989. Entre la Nueva Espana y las Filipinas. Experiencia de algunos cristianos nuevos. In: *Homenaje a Isabel Kelly*, 161–174. México, D.F.: Instituto Nacional de Antropología e Historia.

Valignano, Alessandro. No Date. *Adiciones del sumario de Japon*. ed. José Luiz Álvarez-Taladriz.

Wicki, Josef. 1977. Die "Cristãos-Novos" in der Indischen Provinz der Gesellschaft Jesu von Ignatius bis Acquaviva. *Archivum Historicum Societatis Iesu* 46: 342–361.

Yuuki, Diego. 1989. *Luís de Almeida, 1525–1583. Médico, caminhante, apóstolo*. Macau: Instituto Cultural de Macau.

Open Access This chapter is licensed under the terms of the Creative Commons Attribution 4.0 International License (http://creativecommons.org/licenses/by/4.0/), which permits use, sharing, adaptation, distribution and reproduction in any medium or format, as long as you give appropriate credit to the original author(s) and the source, provide a link to the Creative Commons license and indicate if changes were made.

The images or other third party material in this chapter are included in the chapter's Creative Commons license, unless indicated otherwise in a credit line to the material. If material is not included in the chapter's Creative Commons license and your intended use is not permitted by statutory regulation or exceeds the permitted use, you will need to obtain permission directly from the copyright holder.

Quantifying Ocean Currents as Story Models: Global Oceanic Currents and Their Introduction to Global Navigation

Agnes Kneitz

1   THE CHARTS OF THE CURRENTS, OR WHAT THIS WORK IS DESIGNED TO ILLUSTRATE AS FOLLOWS

'They were toys destined only to bob up and down in nothing bigger than a child's bath—but so far they have floated halfway around the world', rhapsodized the *Daily Mail* in June 2007 when an armada of yellow rubber ducks was to reach the shores of Cornwall and southwest Wales (Clerkin 2007). Since their containers had fallen off a container vessel in the Eastern Pacific in 1992, the little floaters had gone on an incredible journey that certainly inspired lots of sailor's yarn, but actually revolutionized ocean science. They enabled researchers to track global ocean currents, and learn about the interplay of currents and gyres on a global scale, and are thus a colourful example of happenstance

---

A. Kneitz (✉)
Renmin University of China, Beijing, China

A. Kneitz
Rachel Carson Center for Environment and Society, Munich, Germany

turning into scientific evidence (Hohn 2007). In this case, it was oceanographer Curt Ebbesmeyer's curiosity that inspired him to follow in the footsteps of early researchers such as Admiral Alexander Becher, who used strategically placed bottle messages to gather information about gyres in the early 1800s. Apparently, Becher himself was inspired by two maps of sub-tropical gyres published by the British geographer James Rennell in 1822 (Ebbesmeyer 2009: 156).

Early ocean navigators relied on observation based on knowledge about global currents and wind patterns. Balancing on the shoulders of Galileo or Bacon, sailors and mariners later measured, experimented, calculated, and initiated more measuring, experimenting and calculation (Petterson et al. 1996). A unique scientific culture developed from increasing communication between naval professionals and lay scientists, based on seventeenth-century experimental work in European natural philosophy. But influenced by global commerce, currents needed to be mapped and understood more accurately, as they influenced the safety and outcome of (trade) expeditions. Such a largescale undertaking required the study of multiple widespread but interconnected phenomena, a practice that would become known as Humboldtian science (Dettelbach 1996). Previously, such data existed merely as eclectic pieces and without systematic framework in both the Western and Eastern hemispheres. Only the publication in 1832 of James Rennell's *Investigations of the Currents of the Atlantic Ocean* argued for a systematic approach based on modern scientific methods. This included the first comprehensive model of global ocean currents, but still advocated for floating body experiments (Rennell 1832: 35). However, the subsequent physical scientific understanding of the oceans as a complex system (Reidy 2008) has no equivalent in Chinese science (Needham 1971: 560).

From the Qin dynasty onwards, Chinese geographers produced accurate maps of terrestrial waters that find no equivalent in Western natural history (Needham 1959: 514ff); however, ocean waters seem to have been of no importance to them. And despite astrological explanations for water movement in rivers, they mostly displayed an animistic worldview (Needham 1959: 488). Influenced by the mechanistic worldview of the Enlightenment, Benjamin Franklin mapped the Gulf Stream in 1768 (Chaplin 2007), and Jean-Baptiste Lamarck published a *Hydrogéologie* in 1802 arguing that global ocean currents flowed from east to west, thereby moving the continents (Carozzi 1964), obviously reminiscent of Anastasius Kirchner's *Mundis Subterranaeus* (1665) that described underground channels to keep the earth's waters circulating around the globe.

Rennell proceeded to explain links between individual currents in relation to wind and weather systems as well as land masses and sea beds. Available observational data and his insightful knowledge then began to constitute a predicative system. However, his desired comprehension required stories or pictures—something equivalent to a model—as such data would make a better impression as 'a part of system, which operates like a band to keep the parts together in their proper places' (Rennell 1832: 17).

Although Rennell's *Investigations* presented a global model of the ocean currents, it relies on maps and data of the Atlantic and the Indian Ocean. He then extrapolated his observations onto a global scale. His main sources were his own travel accounts, supported by information from British sailors and navy officials (1832: 286). There is little data from the Arctic region that was sailed primarily by Russians (Williams 2013: 132f). Another grey area is the Pacific Ocean, for which most data would be held by Portuguese, Spanish, and Dutch sailors. Even after James Cook's voyages, data from that area remained less diverse. Following the end of the Napoleonic Wars, geographical eurocentrism was then re-defined by re-evaluating Europe and thus the Atlantic as the great theatre of world traffic and world history (Rupke 2001: 112f). Geographically, the Pacific itself supported the common perception of the Atlantic as 'Cultural Mediterranean': a wide body of water provided navigational obstacles. In early Chinese sources, this is attested to by describing the oceans—as compared to the navigated 'China Seas'—as frontier and mythical places alike (Schottenhammer 2012: 67). However, access to data about the 'China Seas' became limited by the seventeenth century. It is thus no surprise that there is no mention of China in Rennell's *Investigations*.

Yet Chinese and early modern European sources both apply bodily metaphors to describe larger systemic connections (Needham 1959: 487). Rennell presents complex patterns of flow, including swirls and eddies and side-streams on a global scale. But he translates his findings into a comprehensive account of accessible lay experiences rather than scientific jargon. This chapter is interested in how his model differs from earlier natural historical descriptions of the oceans, and why there might be no Chinese equivalent to his work. What role does the linguistic shift play in natural sciences that separated laymen and scientists as well as Eastern and Western professionals? How is it related to the development of scientific culture and practices? His way of arguing foreshadows modern issues of public trust in science—especially those studies with a global approach and impact. Is his work an example of broadening traditions?

Does it advocate a natural scientific 'motivation' for ocean research or is it a medium of communication? The *Investigations* accounts for China's absenteeism in global scientific development that was reinforced over the course of the nineteenth century. Can Rennell's work stand as a symbol of a partition of the world in two or more spheres on the basis of its oceans (Reinhard 2014: 66) that would only be overcome by the mid-twentieth century?

2 Embarking from Qualitative to Quantitative Sciences

James Rennell researched the geography of India and Africa, acting as an 'independent expert' on behalf of the British Navy, before he settled on hydrograpy. His affiliation flags the intimate connection between ocean science and economics, while accounting for the Atlantic-centrism of his global model. Both are a result of the imagination of inexhaustible natural wealth that originated from the discovery of a Second Earth in 1492 and what would ultimately result in an economic division of the world with the Atlantic at the centre (Worster 2016). China, which had been ahead of Europe in many areas—including nautical sciences—only tasted the benefits of the new world's resources through trade expeditions via the Indian Ocean, until the gap between Eastern and Western hemisphere had become almost insurmountable (Pomeranz 2000). Dividing the world into spheres of economic dominance and broadening their differences into metaphorical faults devalued transient waters like the Indian Ocean that had connected East and West as part of the maritime silk road for centuries (Ptak 2007: 78f). This applies to nautical scientific development and global ocean exploration at the same time. And the Indian Ocean had become gradually linked to the China Seas since the Sui dynasty (Ptak 2007: 54).

While studying the currents of the Atlantic, monsoons, trade winds, gyres and their influence on the drift of the ocean, Rennell developed his own practices of analysis and observation (Griffiths 1993), as well as an iconography for 'streams of currents'. Borrowing from Protolan maps that bore a close resemblance to Chinese coastal maps (Needham 1959: 560), he depicted currents as bodied entities of water. On each side, bounded by parallel lines of split arrows, this credits to how he had recorded his surveying on the rivers of India (Bravo 1993: 45; Rennell 1781). His 1778 *Chart of the Bank and Current of Cape Lagullas* is based on data he collected travelling back from Bengal (Pollard 1993: 25) and provides insights into shifting practices of proto-scientific data collection that would unfold in the mid-1830 s in tideology (Reidy 2008: 157). As Charles Batten suggested in 1990, the systematic coordination of Rennell's studies of winds and currents had at this point of time just created the need to establish the field of oceanography (150).

With the absence of technological precision equipment, Rennell's friends, like Admiral Beaufort, William Bligh or Tremayne Rodd and their logbooks were his main source of data (see Rennell 1832). They provided a basis for analysis, and with their reputations added credibility to his work. *An Investigation of the Currents of the Atlantic Ocean, and those which prevail between the Indian Ocean and the Atlantic* consists of seven annotated charts of winds and currents, based on an immense store of material, which was systematized by 1810 and continually revised for more than 20 years. Claudine Salomon mentions a deviationist of Chinese map-makers, Chen Lunjiong, who used the same method to collect data compiling a coastal map that would contain tidal times and wind directions in the late eighteenth century (Salomon 2006: 182). In their general appearance, Rennell's maps resemble Alexander von Humboldt's 1817 isoline technique for spatial distribution maps that were crucial to initiating the spacial turn in geography. These maps evolved with a significant epistemic shift (Rupke 2001: 115), signifying a harmonious unison of quantitative and mathematical cartography. In developing their work, both Humboldt and his cartographer mainly subscribed to the Rennellian concept of ocean circulation (Peterson et al. 1996: 64) and both parties employed British Navy data (Reidy 2008: 196). After a visit to London in 1827 and the acquisition of Rennell's papers, Humboldt encouraged Berghaus to prepare illustrations for his *Kosmos* that resemble the former's ocean currents (Rupke 2001: 95). As Kortum (2001: 94f) has laid out, Humboldt cites Rennell several times in his opus thereby attesting for the fruitful correspondende of the two researchers.

Rennell considered information from trustworthy sources only, treated it as a statistical average and most importantly reflected on sources of error, while spending much time discussing them (Rennell 1832, 162). Therefore, his acquisition of data reveals a modern understanding of scientific methods, and one that was mirrored by other emerging field sciences, such as meterology (Anderson 2007). In his book on the inclusion of intuition and induction in scientific thought, Paul Merderwar echoes Rennell, arguing that science 'comes not from the apprehension of facts, but from an imaginative preconception of what might be true' (Cornell 2013: 442). This kind of imaginative rending is true in the sense of being consistent with available observations. Models by themselves are just stories, just as data without models is mere numbers. Rennell, however, was both observer and modeller, which allowed him to self-validate the consistency of its idealized global ocean model. To solve persisting problems with scientific accuracy, he continuously acquired and revised data, and referenced his sources. Technological progress enabled him to integrate even more data (i.e., measured with chronometers) and to juxtapose it with previously collected traditional data (Bravo 1993: 46).

The influence and value of his work is reflected in its attribution by Humbold or Berghaus, and its relative validity for more than a century (Gould 1993: 28), the accuracy of his data adds credibility from a modern point of view (Schrier and Weber 2006: 10f). As he stated himself, 'the work at large will meet the appropriation of those who are competent judges of it' (Rennell 1832: 15). This further reflects awareness of a possible rejection by a scientific community that was entangled in internal struggles of hegemony at the time (Cawood 1979). Doubtless, his work was important, but the increasing emphasis on exploring the Arctic required differently precise data to secure of ships and crews (Millar 2013: 78). Rennell's prose reveals strong responsibility for the safety of his fellow seamen, and he saw potential in combining old and new practices to enhance it. In discourses within the Royal Society, he especially advanced the argument of mechanical perfection: the compass was the 'heavenly gift' on which 'the lives of so many brave and useful men often depend'.[1] But research and publishing opportunities for naval officers were few, and hydrography (like meteorology) was not considered a formal science.

Considering this period a scientific 'Sattelzeit' in Kosellek's understanding, it technologically materialized in iron ships and their material qualities challenging the security of both expeditions and data. In a trend of standardization, lay practitioners then replaced their south-pointing compass needles from the Chinese tradition (Needham 1962: 330ff) with the mariner's north-pointing ones. By aligning Western techniques, errors in data acquisition deriving from heterogeneous practices were slowly being obviated. However, this homogenization reinforced a scientific Western-centrism and resembled a technological enforcement of Eastern and Western spheres of knowledge. But in both of them, the ocean stood for uncounted mysteries and Rennell sensed that his work was still fragmentary. Concerning his model of the North Atlantic current, he wrote that: 'Materials are wanting for the filling up of one large proportion of this great extent of the course; nor is it surprising considering the vastness of the whole' (Rennell 1832: 406), which also attests to his awareness towards limited accuracy in his scientific method.

As Sarah Cornell points out in her commentary on the *Investigations*, good model-making requires intuition and imagination, which Rennell demonstrates when imagining for his reader 'a globe *covered with water*' that would be affected by opposing trade winds and currents, merging into a broad stream 'along both sides of the Equator, round and round the globe for ever' (Rennell 1832: 127). But as the actual globe is broken up into pieces with landmass predispositions, obstacles and other irregularities, these would necessarily be taken into account allow for the real-life applicability of his model. The already emerging nineteenth century saw increasing motivation to quantify and model nature for modern natural scientific purposes. At this epistemological turning point, Rennell's model seems a hybrid: still representing geopolitical hopes for sea power (Baugh 1990: 42), while combining antiquarian and modern practices of data collection (Bravo 1993: 41).

3   Practices of Data Collection and Knowledge Production

As much as Rennell witnessed radical changes in politics and ideology, he witnessed shifts in scientific philosophy and practice. While the 'scientist' emerged as a new being (Reidy 2008: 236), but was abstracted from his discoveries (Schaffer 1986: 412), isochronal focus on mathematics and physics entailed precise language for expert communication, and technological advancement led to accurate instruments (Miller 1986: 119). These possibilities manifested themselves during the aftermath of experimental philosophy's 'cornucopia' after the Renaissance, which marks the transition from quantitative to mathematical ways of investigation, but which does not find an equivalent in Chinese science (Needham 1971: 559). Considering the broad scope of scientific change during the Sattelzeit, the accumulative power and creative force unleashed with the end of absolutism was forceful. Since the mid-seventeenth century, the notion of doing something 'carefully' had already broadened the meaning of doing something 'accurate' to that of 'being exact'. Concurrently, the (mental) abstraction of 'precision' became part of scientific language. Due to these linguistic shifts, studies and analysis from the mid-eighteenth and nineteenth centuries seem worlds apart. Rennell translates between these practical and scientific worlds from which nautical data was drawn.

Translating between practical and scientific sources, the hydrographer acknowledged the possibility of errors in this new discourse, considering that new instruments could also be inaccurate. This is notable, as this meant it was Rennell as a representative of what had become considered the 'faulty human element' during the Enlighthement's sparking techno-optimism, who still provided balance between the differenent practices of data acquisiton. Considering this source criticism a sign of quality management, his work reflects high standards also in his awareness of the limited accuracy of his own method and the grey areas for missing data. Both problems would be addressed carefully by the following generations of scientists, especially by filling knowledge gaps with data available through international research cooperation and precision instruments. Unlike during medieval times, when the concept of the magnetic compass was passed on from China to Europe via the Indian Ocean, the knowledge of the Eastern hemisphere was not tapped into at this point (Needham 1962: 330).

Matthew Fontaine Maury wrote on winds and currents in the North Atlantic, where his predecessor simply lacked data due to technical and polito-lingusitic obstacles (Gould 1993: 29; Williams 2013: 132f). In comparison, the situation in the 'China Seas' differed not as significantly as the 19th century believed: The 'Asian Mediterranean' was a place of vibrant economic and cultural exchange (Zurndorfer 2016: 66). But climatically, it was influenced by seasonal monsoon winds, whose existence had been reported since the Han dynasty (Schottenhammer 2012: 67); but no systematic description would have been accessible to Rennell. Similarly, integrating foreign language data on the 'Silent Ocean' seemed unlikely in the context of European domination. Supporting the recovery of a sea-wrecked steamer in 1852, Maury introduced knowledge about ocean circulation into the ocean of circulating knowledge on ocean circulation, as Julia Heunemann phrases it (2014: 150). Chinese navigation still relied on junks that would only slowly become replaced after the Opium War (Granados 2012: 95). Both Maury's and Rennell's work became possible with the invention and availability of chronometers that made it possible to measure weaker currents from around 1800 (Charnock and Deacon 2001: 155). As Rennell stated himself, this fostered the systematic collection and analysis of data (1832: 10). Previously, the Chinese physical sciences had provided comparably prescient measurement techniques. But with their stagnation after the Kangxi emperor (Needham 1971: 555), these practices seemed outmoded compared to Western precision instruments, despite their accuracy.

The next oceanographic model, featuring the relationship between the distribution of marine organisms and deep-sea temperature, originated from William B. Carpenter's curiosity to further investigate Rennell's groundwork. Instrumental in organizing the 1868 Challenger Expedition, Carpenter is an example of a late naturalist engaging in debates around physical science exploration, trying to align and finally standardize the skills and ambitions of mixed research groups along shared research programmes (Miller 1986: 107). He developed a theory of ocean currents being driven by differences in water density, but it was considered insufficient, neglecting the importance of wind patterns (Heunemann 2014: 156). Within a few decades, technological process enabled more 'precise and accurate' observations of ocean temperature and water density. From the *Challenger* Expedition onwards, the depth of the ocean was recognized to influence cold weather originating from the surface in the polar regions (Deacon 1997: 310–348). Although these studies built on the *Investigations*, there is no evidence that Rennell considered the layers of oceanic waters beyond the common understanding of a cover stratum over a deep unknown (Schlee 1973).

Later observations depended on the quick advancement of technology, increasing international exchange and oceanography becoming a truly global field of inquiry. The German *Meteor* Expedition to the South Pacific (1925–1927), for example, used early sonar to identify a broad meridian convective cell as forging sinking polar water towards the equator. But it took American Henry Stommel until 1948 to rectify their errors. At the same time, virtually no direct measurements of currents below the surface were taken until 1950 (Heunemann 2014: 157). This again showcases the connection between the advancement of technology, pushing the frontiers of knowledge and the wider expedition radius. Rennell had already acknowledged this mutual dependency and the resulting limitations for his work. In his first hydrographic study, he had analysed the Agulhas Current around South Africa separately, but never touched upon areas further south, which he identified as 'imperfectly known; so that generally, between 30 and 40 degrees of latitude, and longitudes 25° and 40° W is nearly a blank on the chart' (Rennell 1832: 280). His later index map visualized how that gap of knowledge south of the Southern Connecting Current had not been closed during his lifetime.

Conducting seminal research on individual currents, questions of water quality or other local (less global) qualitative and quantitative aspects, Rennell furthered germinating oceanography (Rodd 1930: 296). His model of a global oceanic body of water allowed for a new systematic approach, making it possible to integrate local data into global charts while deducting generalized statements. It also highlights the uses and benefits of scientific models, while identifying levelled scientific development as a precondition to accurately designing and calculating them. Great advancements had been made over the seventeenth century, even without modern precision standards for scientific equipment (Howse 1990: 183). However, chronometer and improved methods to measure longitude at sea allowed Rennell and his epigones to collect accurate, if not reliable data (ibid., 1f). But most importantly he visualized logbook data and annotated this new source of information, making it accessible to both marine practitioners and landborne scientists.

4 Changes in Scientific Values and the Perception of Nature

During the Sattelzeit, the meaning of the term 'precision' depended on its application in scientific language. Different meanings invited for comparison and—arguably—licensed multiple terms of reference. Since James Cook's pacific encounters, when (lay) scientists and even artists became a permanent feature of British naval explorations, the terms 'precision' and 'accuracy' could refer to a person's habits of observation, their care and trustworthiness. Alternatively, if a traveller corrected a natural philosopher's previously made descriptions, this assessment was regarded as more 'precise'. This indicates a qualitative increase through multiple opinions, but more importantly through data collected with state-of-the-art technology and methods. In the Chinese tradition, geographers and travellers had played a similar role for knowledge acquisition since the fourteenth century. And like 'travel books' and 'natural histories' compiled by Western travellers, their accounts eventually resulted in a specific genre of 'maritime travel literature', shaping perceptions of the oceans (Ptak 2007: 211). Despite advanced knowledge in astronomy and physics, they were greatly infused by cosmological and mystical elements (Needham 1971: 563), which finds its equivalent in fantastic creatures decorating Western maps or fictional descriptions of alien environments.

Even more so, the Western authority of 'precise knowing' owed much to the design and construction of quadrants, sextants, chronometers and other technical equipment (Baugh 1990). And this authority grew and strengthened quickly over the nineteenth century, when materials were more finely harnessed towards perfection in their geometric division and measurement. While Chinese sciences were 'sabotaged' by political and social instability, the West began to think in larger volumes of data and even more dimensional layers (Corbin 1994: 106). The capacity of the term 'precision' to sanction authority in these multiple contexts gained considerable rhetorical force, as 'the gentlemen [scientists] clothed themselves in the language of precision' (Bravo 1993: 164) and the elasticity of the term lent itself to extensive usage. Yet it retained specific, tangible meanings, which for the scientific traveller continued to rest on reliable work habits (Williams 2013: 124). Retrospectively, the terms had substantially different social origins (Bravo 1999: 163), and when oceanography became fully fledged in the 1880s and 1890s, it 'was hardly a discipline that shared a common set of intellectual questions, nor is it today. Rather, it was (and remains) a science that focuses the attention of many physical, chemical and biological fields on the project of understanding a geographic place' (Rozwadowski 1996: 409).

In order to combine these areas into a common knowledge space, practitioners required literacy in more than one discipline, but as a group they were even more defined by the act of going to the sea (Rozwadowski 2008). This shift in practices and attitude as a response to the transition from quantitative to mathematical observation and cartography is not attested to in the Chinese sciences. Like the Western seamen, the Chinese also required steady conditions to conduct astronomical measurements, although their early reliance on the magnetic compass had made them independent from most weather conditions. The importance of this object features in the traditional name for the navigation officer, which translates as 'person in charge of the light' (Gang 1997: 40). Being unaffected by the Western scientific revolution, Eastern seafaring still relied on time—and field-tested practices that also did not require changes in map-making. However, the seventeenth-century Western-inspired geographical representations on Chinese maps represent the intellectual dilemma of incorporating humanist ideas from the 'Far West' (Ptak 2006, 2007).

Only with the beginning of the nineteenth century were gradual shifts towards accuracy in a Western sense recorded in both cartography and maritime technology. These were connected to the defensive strategy of securing Chinese borders and waters against increasing piracy, smuggling and foreign intrusion along the south coast. Before such threats in the 'maritime frontier area' (Salomon 2006: 178), Protolan-style maps had been sufficient tools for navigation as ocean exploration had been abandoned after Zheng He's travels and Chinese maritime involvement focused on coastal waters. But even for overseas trade with Asian partners, a refined method of compass use made technological and cartographical innovation obsolete. Only the adaption to Western-style ships finally required or inspired changes in navigational practices that became visualized in the commonly used coastal maps.

Mechanized instruments and heavier more stable ships gradually counterbalanced the 'faulty human element' that became free to engage in evaluating and interpreting data, from which it was actually practically and cognitively separated (Schaffer 1986). For Rennell and his peers, the new relationship with seemingly homogenous information on different scales and different places was still to be revealed. But according to Bravo, a delay in changing practices and habits was the actual problem for natural science to remain in its pre-stage (1993: 166). Similar circumstances may have applied to Chinese maritime navigation, as it only deferred to struggle for technological competitiveness in view of foreign ship building that forced to alter military and economic considerations (Granados 2012: 104). This left little room for scientific ambitions. Linking the Pacific Theatre to Asia and Africa, the further influenced the relationship between the concepts of curiosity and precision in scientific research. Fundamental linguistic and related changes in methodology during the eighteenth century are crucial to understanding those in the nineteenth century, as they concern both the motivation to collect marine data as well as associated social and scientific practices.

Francis Bacon's essay on travel, for example, emphasizes procedures like keeping a journal and making topographical sketches as antecedents for the later European expansion in the Pacific (Deacon 1997: 15). When Europeans began to venture into the waters between Asia and the Americas, they gradually took over the roles formerly operated by Asian traders and with this opened up the 'China Seas' (Schottenhammer 2012: 83ff). Cartographers in the East, on the other hand, had begun to integrate Western standards since Matteo Ricci (Ptak 2006: 206). Maps were predominantly individual, safely kept possessions, but although maps were predominantly individual, safely kept possessions, Rennell's new annotated compilation resembles the eighteenth-century *Nautical*

Almanach (Miller 1983: 18ff). For him, logs were artifacts of similar quality, and each navigational chart was accompanied by a memoir to enhance its accessibility. The only Eastern Empire that had comparably reliable scientific information on global navigation had destroyed it after the expeditions of Zheng He (Schottenhammer 2012: 65).

Reflecting both political consciousness and research skills, this understanding was Rennell's keystone for putting his ideas about precision into practice. Methodologically, his *Investigations* were designed to make information processing accountable and transparent, and therefore adopted high-quality cartographic conventions of toponym and source citation. In the process of integrating and showcasing new techniques, practices of knowledge acquisition and distribution, he kept his model close enough to traditional standards to secure its acceptance among professionals. In juxtaposition, these practices minimized errors, as 'the differences in northing and southing, between the dead-reckonings and observations', for example, 'might be pointed out by the observations of latitude, yet the error of longitude, of easting and westing, would, of course, escape detection altogether' (Rennell 1832: 10f). With his dual expertise, he carefully synthesized the material and provided general assumptions.

A subjective notion of 'trustworthiness', based on curiosity and precision can be interpreted as characteristic of modern science. With technological advancement and disciplinary specialization, however, the means of generating credibility were altered in response to the changing attitudes of lay and professional audiences (Reidy 2008: 247). Progressing change in Western scientific values therefore focused on mathematical calculation and scientific modelling (Miller 1983: 14f). At the turn of the eighteenth century, it lay within reach to measure the world as a whole, which Humboldt attempted to in his *Kosmos*. Mathematics had just entered the field, providing a new language for its representation (Reidy 2008: 55). However, for Rennell's model of global ocean currents, the growing influence of Newton and Bernoulli was ambivalent, as they perceived the oceans as an equilibrium, leaving no space for their flows.

5   Models Are Stories: Shifts in Narratives

Rennell's currents visualized cartographers' 'rough work' and demanded they disclose their sources. They emphasize the necessity of explaining rationales while distinguishing between those areas of a map that are demonstrably 'true' and those interstitial spaces that are merely coincidental and empirically unsubstantiated. This communication process required learned travellers, armchair geographers and reviewers to incorporate cartographic conventions in their repertoires (Rupke 2001: 93f). Here, Rennell's work fostered information exchanges between laymen and savants, otherwise, ignorance of accuracy conventions invited censure from fellow travellers, editors, mariners, etc. The *Investigations* further provided a new vocabulary and methodology that helped to produce more credible and precise accounts, again improving popular scientific communication.

In terms of offering modelled insights on a globe covered with water, Rennell explained the difficulties for contemporaneous oceanographic science as follows: 'one might expect, that the opposite trade-winds would impel the surface waters, subject to their operation ... But as our globe is terraqueous, and the land broken into an endless variety of forma [sic!] and positions, those gently moving surfaces, which would, in the other case have flowed so smoothly and uninterruptedly, are here interrupted in various ways; and, accumulating into different streams, are projected in such directions, as the positions of the several obstacles necessarily produce' (1832: 127). There was yet no satisfying solution to analysing an object that was so strongly influenced by different kinds of physical materiality. In naturalist tradition, Rennell treated the river systems of India as special cases of mapping continental coastlines in order to add them to the British network of navigable sea routes that closely resembled Chinese sources (Needham 1959: 487). Yet he immersed himself in natural science over the years, a professional act of adaptation to changing practices and scientific requirements, but supported by his personal method, and interest in physics and experimental equipment (Griffiths 1993: 37).

Precision and accuracy were important for Rennell. His frequent referencing a variety of oral sources features the *Investigations* as a historical text filled with social energy (Greenblatt 1988). By contrast, it exposes how today's scientific writing (that pursues the ideal of 'objectivity') risks to become dehumanized to an almost problematic extent. Rennell thus not only explicitly names his informants, but also refers to his own professional and personal experience, almost foreshadowing the attention modern scientists ascribe to 'contributory' expertise. His background not only equipped him with the availability to see beyond 'naked standing facts' (Rennell 1832: 5) and integrate them into a larger picture, but assigned credibility in front of his increasingly diverging target audience, almost like a collective travel-log, from which scientific data is retrieved, and which is framed with more or less personal experience as visual aids (Rennell 1832: 262).

Scientific writers, beginning with Franklin, employed organic and bodily metaphors increasingly through the nineteenth century. Like Rennell, considering the causes and effects of different currents to describe the ocean as a body is moved by different forces (Rennell 1832: 57). 'A great enlightened [organic] machine, whose prime movers were some main currents by the aid of adjunct waters [and winds]' (Rennell 1832: 48)—a narrative that accounts for the still-dominant mechanist view of nature. But in his methodological borrowing from geography, as in modelling oceans after continental rivers, he contemplates how 'a *sea current* is not like the *stream of a river*, which *passes on* its way to the sea, but rather like one that should finally spread its waters over a level of a country, in [the] form of a lake' (Rennell 1832: 530). This seems to be an allusion to more holistic understanding of nature. But while striving towards accuracy and precision, scientists admittedly romanticized the sea and seafarers: steamships replaced sailing ships and this transition was reflected in popular narratives about the world's oceans (Rozwadowski 2008: 216).

6   Enlarged Descriptions and Details of Several Conclusions

The 'Sattelzeit' natural sciences saw changes in technology, motivation, culture and politics of marine knowledge production, like oceanic swirls and eddies and side-streams that can almost be read as tropical for the various twists and turns within the scientific community. Here, Rennell embodies a community of naval officers and marine laymen in personal union with natural scientists. And to a certain extent, he challenged or at least restructured the existing traditional order from which a new scientific maritime culture emerged. Yet he represents the Eurocentric perspective on the world's oceans that had established itself with Western dominance in world economic relations since the discovery of a Second Earth. The congruent (self-)perception of European scientific superiority seems to reinforce itself by abandoning Eastern-inspired practices of navigation, like the reintroduction of the dry pivoted compass to China by Portuguese and Dutch merchants via Japan from the sixteenth century onwards (Needham 1964: 334).

The *Investigations* exhibits the power of quantification and systematization, providing both a rich description of the ocean's large-scale behaviour and weighing its exhortation to apply its compiled knowledge 'to avoid or delay danger' (Rennell 1832: 12). Its predictions of maritime currents and their hazards were valued and taken seriously by navigators and scholars alike. However, by today's standards, the evidence base relies on too few numbers and even precarious ones: the record of ship's logs is incoherent and is supplemented by occasional records of bottle landings and bits of shipwrecks washing up on beaches. It is also noted how the assumed correctness of the chronometer was ascertained by lunar observations. The technology Rennell used corresponds with Western standards that had long forgotten their Chinese origins, and his quantification and systematization produced a robust conceptual representation of the ocean circulation system.

At the same time, modern trust in science has not merely been conjured by its data-intensive technologically sophisticated nature, as curiosity about floating ducks can also serve this function. But quantification and systematization have a predictive power, their application often entails other kinds of power, much of which provides cognitive (perceived) security. In the long term, this would become conceptually adopted by the Chinese and translated into maritime practice (Xiang 2010). Continental geopolitics, scientific advancement and different levels of global exploration required comprehensive approaches that were infused by recognizing an increasing importance of in-depth studies forged by unknown amounts of data.

Today, much global change research takes place with a supposed detachment from values and policies, even as it is channelled into contributing to politics of global change. Quantitative trajectories of future socio-environmental pathways—leading to utopias and dystopias alike—are described as model outputs. These values are merely occluded, and the relationship between hidden agendas and power is often complex. Unsurprisingly, global change research occasionally faces issues relating to public trust in Western-style mathematics-based science. But as its output increasingly informs policy making, the need to probe, illuminate and (self-)critique grows rather than vanishes. As society today faces many new scale global challenges, it might be useful to remember that scientific measurement and prediction are just part of the process. Just as global change during the Sattelzeit equally demanded changes fostering change in science, today's science might profit from self-reflecting on facing a similar threshold: by reversely integrating broad general knowledge and understanding beyond the personal level, while granting a meaningful use of numbers and data deeply connected with the present and past lived experience as well as basic personal observation. Maybe a few rubber ducks are all that is needed.

Note

1. Quoted in Bravo (1999), 182, FN 36.

References

Anderson, Katherine. 2007. *Predicting the Weather: Victorians and the Science of Meteorology*. Chicago: University of Chicago Press.

Batten, Charles. 1990. Literary Responses to the Eighteen Century Voyages. In *Background to Discovery: Pacific Exploration from Dampier to Cook*, ed. Derek Howse, 128–159. Berkeley: University of California Press.

Baugh, Daniel. 1990. Seapower and Science: The Motives for Pacific Exploration. In *Background to Discovery: Pacific Exploration from Dampier to Cook*, ed. Derek Howse, 1–55. Berkeley: University of California Press.

———. 1993. James Rennell. Antiquarian of Ocean Currents. *Ocean Challenge* 4: 41–52.

———. 1999. Precision and Curiosity in Scientific Travel: James Rennell and the Orientalist Geography of the New Imperial Age (1760–1830). In *Voyages and Visions: Towards a Cultural History of Travel*, ed. Jas Elsner, 162–183. London: Reaction Books.

Carozzi, Albert. 1964. Lamarck's Theory of the Earth. Hydrogeologie. *Isis* 55 (3): 293–330.

Cawood, John. 1979. The Magnetic Crusade. *Isis* 70: 493–518.

Chaplin, Joyce. 2007. *The First Scientific American: Benjamin Franklin and the Pursuit of Genius*. New York: Perseus.

Clerkin, Ben. Thousands of Rubber Ducks to Land on British Shores After 15 year Journey. *Daily Mail Online*, 27 June, 2007. http://www.dailymail.co.uk/news/article-464768/Thousands-rubber-ducks-land-British-shores-15-year-journey.html. Accessed 12 Aug 2015.

Charnock, Henry, and M. Deacon. 2001. Introduction. Ocean Circulation. In *Understanding the Oceans: A Century of Ocean Exploration*, ed. Henry Charnock and Margaret Deacon, 155–157. London: Routledge.

Corbin, Alain. 1994. *The Lure of the Sea: The Discovery of the Seaside in the Western World, 1750–1850*. Cambridge: Polity.

Cornell, Sarah. 2013. Commentary. In *The Future of Nature. Documents of Global Change*, ed. Libby Robin et al., 442–444. New Haven: Yale University Press.

Deacon, Margaret. 1985. An Early Theory of Ocean Circulation. J.S. Von Waitz and his Explanation of the Currents in the Street of Gibraltar. *Progress in Oceanography* 14: 89–101.

———. 1997. *Scientists and the Sea*. London: Ashgate.

Dettelbach, Michael. 1996. Humboldtian Science. In *Cultures of Natural History*, ed. Nicolas Jardine, 287–304. Cambridge: Cambridge University Press.

Deng, Gang. 1997. *Chinese Maritime Activities and Socioeconomic Development, c. 2100 B.C.–1900 A.D.* Westport: Greenwood Press.

Ebbesmeyer, Carl. 2009. *Flotsametrics and the Floating World: How One Man's Obsession with Runaway Sneakers and Rubber Ducks Revolutionized Ocean Science.* New York: Harper Collins.

Gould, James. 1993. James Rennell's View of the Arctic Circulation. A Comparison with our Present Knowledge. *Ocean Challenge* 4: 26–33.

Granados, Ulises. 2012. Modernization and Regionalism in South China: Notes on Costal Navigation in Guangdong Province During the Late Nineteenth and Early Twentieth Century. *International Journal of Maritime History* 24 (1): 89–114.

Greenblatt, Stephen. 1988. S*hakespearian Negotiations: The Circulation of Social Energy in Renaissance England.* Berkeley: University of California Press.

Griffiths, Gwyn. 1993. James Rennell and William Scoresby. Their Separate Quest for Accurate Current Data. *Ocean Challenge* 4: 34–40.

Heunemann, Julia. 2014. No Straight Lines. Zur Kartographie des Meeres bei Matthew Fontaine Maury. In *Weltmeere. Wissen und Wahrnehmung im langen 19. Jahrhundert*, ed. Alexander Kraus and Martina Winkler, 149–168. Göttingen: Vandenhoeck & Ruprecht.

Hohn, Donovan. 2007. Moby-Duck. Or, the Synthetic Wilderness of Childhood. *Harpers Magazine*, January 2007. http://harpers.org/archive/2007/01/moby-duck/. Accessed 12 Aug 2015.

Howse, Derek. 1990. Navigation and Astronomy in the Voyages. In *Background to Discovery: Pacific Exploration from Dampier to Cook*, ed. Derek Howse, 160–184. Berkeley: University of California Press.

Kortum, Gerhard. 2001. Humboldt und das Meer: Eine Ozeanographiegeschichtliche Bestandsaufnahme. *Northeastern Naturalist* 8 (1): 91–108.

Markham, Clements. Rennell, James. *Dictionary of National Biography* (1885–1900): 14–15.

Millar, Sarah Louise. 2013. Science at sea: Soundings and instrumental knowledge in British Polar expedition narratives, c. 1818–1848. *Journal of Historical Geography* 42 (3): 77–87.

Miller, David. 1983. Between Hostile Camps: Sir Humphry Davy's Presidency, 1820–1827. *British Journal for the History of Science* 16: 1–47.

———. 1986. The Revival of the Physical Sciences in Britain, 1815–1840. *Osiris* 2: 107–134.

Needham, Joseph. 1959. *Science and Civilization in China. Vol. 3: Mathematics and the Sciences of the Heavens and the Earth.* Cambridge: Cambridge University Press.

———. 1962. *Science and Civilization in China. Vol 4: Physics and Physical Technology. Part 1: Physics.* Cambridge: Cambridge University Press.

———. 1971. *Science and Civilization in China. Vol 4: Physics and Physical Technology. Part 3: Civil Engineering and Nautics*. Cambridge: Cambridge University Press.

Petterson, R.G., L. Stramma, and G. Kortum. 1996. Early Concepts and Charts of Ocean Circulation. *Progress in Oceanography* 37: 1–133.

Pollard, R. 1993. James Rennell. Father of Oceanography. *Ocean Challenge* 4: 24–25.

Pomeranz, Kenneth. 2000. *The Great Divergence: China, Europe, and the Making of the Modern World Economy*. Princeton: Princeton University Press.

Ptak, Rudolf. 2006. The Sino-European Map (Shanhai yudi quantu) in the Encyclopaedia Sancai tuhui. In *The Perception of Maritime Space in Traditional Chinese Sources*, ed. Angela Schottenhammer and Rudolf Ptak, 191–207. Wiesbaden: Harrassowitz.

———. 2007. *Die maritime Seidenstraße. Küstenräume, Seefahrt und Handel in vorkolonialer Zeit*. Munich: C.H. Beck.

Reidy, Michael. 2008. *Tides of History. Ocean Science and Her Majesty's Navy*. Chicago: University of Chicago Press.

Reinhard, Wolfgang. 2014. *Die Geschichte der Welt 1350–1750: Weltreiche und Weltmeere*. Munich: C.H. Beck.

Rennell, James. 1781. *A Bengal Atlas: Containing Maps of the Theatre of War and Commerce on that Side of Hindoostan*. London.

———. 1832. *An Investigation of the Currents of the Atlantic Ocean, and Those Who Prevail Between the Indian Ocean and the Atlantic Ocean*, ed. J. Purdy. London. Digital file [ibooks reader 4.3, 751p]. Retrieved from http://www.en.bookfi.org.

Rodd, Rennell. 1930. Major James Rennell. Born 3 December 1742. Died 20 March 1830. *The Geographical Journal* 75 (4): 289–299.

Rozwadowski, Helen. 1996. Small World: Forging a Scientific Maritime Culture for Oceanography. *Isis* 87 (1): 409–429.

———. 2008. *Fathoming the Ocean. The Discovery and Exploration of the Deep Sea*. Cambridge: Belknap.

Rupke, Nicholas. 2001. Humboldtian Distribution Maps: The Spatial Ordering of Scientific Knowledge. In *The Structure of Knowledge: Classification of Science and Learning Since the Renaissance*, ed. Tore Frängsmyr, 93–116. Berkeley: Office for History of Science and Technology.

Salomon, Claudine. 2006. Coastal Maps from the Beginning of the Qing Dynasty, With Special Reference to the *Qingchu haijiang tushuo*. In *The Perception of Maritime Space in Traditional Chinese Sources*, ed. Angela Schottenhammer and Rudolf Ptak, 177–189. Wiesbaden: Harrassowitz.

Schaffer, Simon. 1986. Scientific Discoveries and the End of Natural Philosophy. *Social Studies of Science* 16 (3): 387–420.

Schlee, Susan. 1973. *On the Edge of an Unfamiliar World: A History of Oceanography*. New York: Duttoon.

Schottenhammer, Angela. 2012. The 'China Seas' in World History. A General Outline of the Role of Chinese and East Asian Maritime Space from its Origins to c. 1800. *Journal for Marine and Island Cultures* 1: 63–86. doi:10.1016/j.imic.2012.11.002.

Van der Schrier, G., and S.L. Weber. 2006. *The Gulf Stream and Atlantic Sea-Surface Temperatures in AD 1790–1825*, 1–28. De Bilt: Royal Netherlands Meteorological Institute (KNMI).

Williams, Glyn. 2013. *Naturalists at Sea. Scientific Travellers from Dampier to Darwin*. New Haven: Yale University Press.

Worster, Donald. 2016. *Shrinking the Earth: The Rise and Decline of American Abundance*. New York: Oxford University Press.

Xiang, Jianhai. 2010. *Marine Science and Technology in China: A Roadmap to 2050*. Berlin: Springer.

Zurndorfer, Harriet. 2016. Oceans of History, Seas of Change: Recent Revisionist Writing in Western Languages About China and East Asian Maritime History During the Period 1500–1630. *International Journal of Asian Studies* 13 (1): 61–94. doi:10.1017/S1479591415000194.

Open Access This chapter is licensed under the terms of the Creative Commons Attribution 4.0 International License (http://creativecommons.org/licenses/by/4.0/), which permits use, sharing, adaptation, distribution and reproduction in any medium or format, as long as you give appropriate credit to the original author(s) and the source, provide a link to the Creative Commons license and indicate if changes were made.

The images or other third party material in this chapter are included in the chapter's Creative Commons license, unless indicated otherwise in a credit line to the material. If material is not included in the chapter's Creative Commons license and your intended use is not permitted by statutory regulation or exceeds the permitted use, you will need to obtain permission directly from the copyright holder.

PART III

Circulation of Technology and Commodities in the Atlantic and Pacific

This part serves as a main node to link the economic performance of China and Japan economies and commerce in the South China Sea and South-East Asia, as well as the trans-Pacific trade, mainly through the route that followed the Manila-Acapulco galleons connecting East Asian markets with those from the Atlantic reaching European regions. Special attention is paid to changes in consumer behaviour, which definitively, as an important sub-field in global history, played a crucial role in last decades. The circulation of technologies, raw materials and ready-made products, as well as different forms of knowledge fostered market integration between East Asian zones and those from the Americas and Europe. Under the framework of a big administration system of the Spanish Empire, the control of institutions and forms of knowledge, such as books, prints, engravings, etc., through political elites, was crucial to efficiently apply such knowledge to develop new technologies and therefore a sustainable model of economic growth at the dawn of the era of European industrialization.

Global History and the History of Consumption: Congruence and Divergence

Anne E.C. McCants

Something very interesting has been happening at the edges of economic history for the past quarter of a century or so. This is the emergence of a new sub-discipline in academic history departments known as 'world history' (or sometimes in what is a more or less contested historiographical space as 'global history').[1] Now obviously in some banal way, all history as it has ever been practised, whether professionally or otherwise, contributes to a history of the world. So if it were to be truly new, the object of this line of inquiry had to go well beyond the mere illumination of additional individual pieces to the larger puzzle of human experience. Indeed, as the Mission Statement of the North American-based World History Association (established in 1982, hereinafter WHA) notes, the goal of world history is 'to advance scholarship and teaching within a transnational, trans-regional, and trans-cultural perspective. Through the researchers, teachers, students, independent scholars, and authors who are its members, the WHA fosters historical

A.E.C. McCants (✉)
Massachusetts Institute of Technology, Cambridge, USA

analysis undertaken not from the viewpoint of nation states, discrete regions, or particular cultures, but from that of the human community'.[2] In other words, world history is characterized by its methodology rather than by its specific object of study. It calls for both the tools of comparative analysis and a shifting of one's frame of reference away from the traditional (that is, at least, since the nineteenth century) objects of historical study, most especially the nation state and its projects. While the whole world—at all times and in all places—is obviously too much for any one mind to grasp in terms of all of its particulars, the call here was to think about any given historical problem in terms of its connections to other places, and perhaps also to other times, although how chronology will ultimately fit into the world history methodology still seems to be an open question to this historian.

But why begin this chapter with the claim that the rise of world history took place at the edges of economic history? To anyone working in the Anglo-American academic context, this may seem especially odd, as economic history as a formal sub-discipline has all but disappeared from many history departments. Instead, it is mostly studied in economics departments, certainly if the institutional affiliations of the membership of the Economic History Association are any guide. Nonetheless, as our colleagues have lamented recently in various forums, economic history faces a relatively grim prospect within economics departments as well.[3] Yet despite these setbacks, one research agenda of economic history is clearly flourishing and even garnering well-deserved public attention. This is the comparative history of long-term economic development and its alter-ego economic inequality. This is a research agenda that lies precisely at the intersection between the concerns of economic history and the methodologies of world history. The 2014 runaway bestseller by Thomas Piketty, *Capital in the Twenty-First Century*, is far from the only example of recent successes. Major books with wide readerships that address one or both of the twin questions of economic growth and distribution have been written by Robert Allan, Philip Hoffman, Deirdre McCloskey, Joel Mokyr, Ian Morris, Jean-Laurent Rosenthal, Bin Wong and Anthony Wrigley, most of whom self-identify as economic historians.[4] Most notably, Kenneth Pomeranz's *The Great Divergence* (2000) spawned an entire cottage industry of 'divergence' research published in an ever-expanding output of articles and books. Pomeranz himself recently served a term as President of the American Historical Association, and conference sessions with 'divergence' in the title continue to draw reliably large audiences. Historians are genuinely interested in understanding how the economic world came to look as it does today, and while they may have turned their backs resoundingly on the 'cliometric' history on offer from the economics department from the 1970s onwards, they cannot seem to get enough of a 'big history' in search of answers to fundamentally economic questions.[5]

Not only does the new world history find common ground with economics, especially in the particular areas noted above, it also shares a methodological imperative and some basic questions with the political science sub-discipline known as the 'international political economy' (IPE). As another relatively newer sub-discipline (dating from the late 1970s), IPE also faces contested boundaries, but its well-established core mission is to understand the influence of political factors on the shaping of the international economy. As such, it must draw from the historical record if it is to be at all effective in explaining change over time. Moreover, like world history, IPE scholars have rejected nation-focused explanations of economic developments in favour of those that demonstrate a full accounting for an integrated and interconnected global system. Not surprisingly, then, an increasingly recognized name for this field is 'global political economy' (GPE). But whether the modifier employed is global, international or world (and serious disagreement about the use of these terms persists),[6] the point of overlap in the research agendas of world historians, economic history and the IPE/GPE wing of political science has opened up some of the strongest connections between the historical profession and other social science disciplines in many a year.

A key element of the shared research agenda I have suggested above has been first and foremost to understand the timing, direction and volume of commodity flows, of both raw materials and manufactured goods around the globe. Other queries have been focused on the multifaceted characteristics of labour migration(s),[7] the diffusion of new technologies, the coordination of prices across expanding zones of commerce and, of course, the coordination and exchange of monetary units. While cultural exchanges are likewise of interest to world historians, much of the intellectual energy behind the new journal offerings and scholarly associations that explicitly claim the mantle of world (or global) history came from those whose work was primarily focused on commercial exchange and the macro-economic processes surrounding it. These phenomena are all closely associated with popular notions of globalization, a process that the public widely ascribes to the very recent past. But world historians have found equal or even more resonance for their agenda in periods that pre-date the twentieth century. Indeed, one early focus for this new kind of history was the increasingly well-documented rise of a 'consumer society'. The first historians of the nineteenth century highlighted the possibilities for a new kind of consumption with the rise of department stores and other mass public spaces. The eighteenth-century historians were not far behind in demonstrating the veritable explosion of new consumer goods to be found in their period, a phenomenon that Michael Kwass has called 'a buying spree of historic dimensions'[8]. Yet further research has even pushed the site of the consumer revolution earlier into the seventeenth century, especially for precocious locations such as parts of Flanders and the Dutch Republic. In every case the early work of documentation was centred squarely in either Europe or America (in terms of both the location of the historians themselves and also the objects of their study). Yet it was impossible to go very far in this pursuit without having to engage with the flood of exotic commodities coming into Europe and America from other parts of the world, which were moreover themselves such a strong catalyst for the new kinds of consumer desire being described by historians.

1 THE EARLY MODERN CONSUMER REVOLUTION

It is this specific connection between the rise of world history as a subdiscipline and the discovery of a 'consumer revolution' by early modernists that I want to pursue here. Indeed, this chapter began with a hunch: that the burgeoning historiography of consumption, the discovery of one or possibly several 'consumer revolution(s)' and a new interest in the history of commodities themselves were all in some way critically linked to what seemed like the almost simultaneous take-off of world history as a recognized field worthy of its own associations, journals and graduate training programmes. To probe this hunch empirically, I first checked the English-language corpus of books available for review using the Google Ngram Viewer. Running a search across the twentieth century and into the current one (1900–2008) on the phrases 'world history', 'global trade', 'global history' and 'consumer revolution' yields the graph reproduced in Fig. 1. 'World history' is by far the most common of these phrases, rising steadily from even before the Great Depression

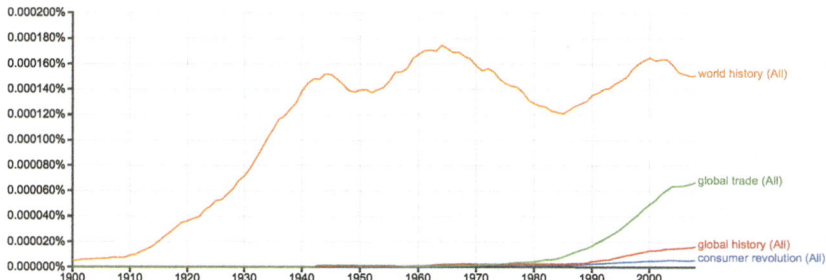

Fig. 1 World History' as a subject in 20th c. English language books. *Source* Google Books Ngram Viewer, https://books.google.com/ngrams (accessed 8 July 2016)

and peaking twice, first in the context of the Second World War and then again in the mid-1960s. 'Global trade', 'global history' and 'consumer revolution' by contrast all only make a first barely noticeable appearance as phrases in the 1940s. It is not until the 1980s that each of them gains some real traction. However, what becomes clear when we refine this exercise further is that they gain that traction together. If we remove 'world history' and 'global trade' from the search, and limit the chronology to 1940–2008, it is possible to get a more nuanced reading of the remaining two terms. The results of this exercise are shown in Fig. 2. Clearly, at least in the English-speaking world, interest in global history (likely a more accurate reflection of the scholarly agenda outlined above than the more generic phrase 'world history') and in the consumer revolution moved in tandem with each other, both really taking off in the 1980s, exactly as we would expect given the chronology of major publications in both fields.[9]

A similar spike of interest in the history of consumption is also evident in French-language books as tracked by the Google Books database. Using the search terms 'société de consommation', 'histoire mondiale' and 'histoire du monde' for the French corpus gives the graph in Fig. 3. Several things are noteworthy about the comparison with the similar (acknowledging the different nuances, of course) English phrases. First, the tight link between the rise in usage of global history and the consumer revolution is not present in French; indeed, there is no link at all. Second, the remarkably sudden emergence of writing about a 'société de consommation' pre-dates the English discovery of a consumer revolution by at least a decade. Here the rise already begins in the 1960s, peaks

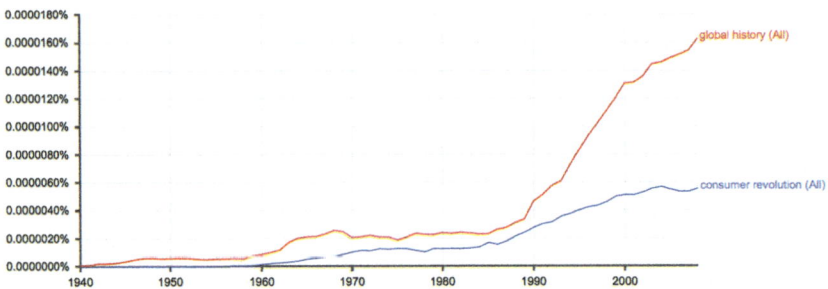

Fig. 2 The rise of 'Global History' since 1940. *Source* Google Books Ngram Viewer, https://books.google.com/ngrams (accessed 8 July 2016)

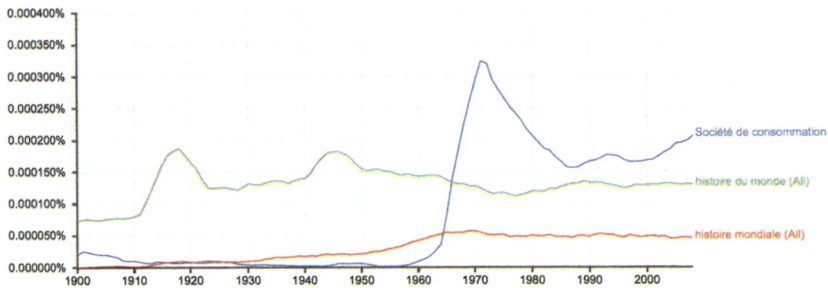

Fig. 3 World history as a subject in 20th c. French language books. *Source* Google Books Ngram Viewer, https://books.google.com/ngrams (accessed 8 July 2016)

in the early 1970s and diminishes thereafter. In fairness, if one searches using the more directly translated English term 'consumer society', the rise also begins in the 1960s (with a peak in the late 1990s). But this latter term also captures a good deal of writing about contemporary consumer culture (for both the French and Anglo-American cases), whereas the specifically English usage of consumer revolution is predominantly an historical phenomenon. So while the French-speaking world took notice of consumption and its connection to society at about the same time that the English-speaking world did, it did not then go on to develop a special fascination with an historical episode labelled as a consumer revolution. Nor did it see any particular simultaneous rise of interest in world (or global) history.[10]

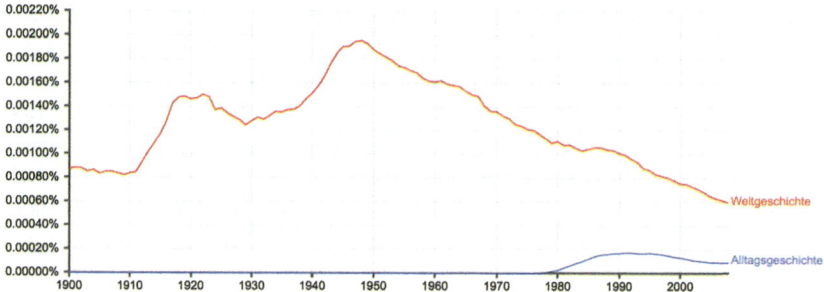

Fig. 4 World history as a subject in 20th c. German language books. *Source* Google Books Ngram Viewer, https://books.google.com/ngrams (accessed 8 July 2016)

What this exercise suggests is that the rise of global/world history as a distinct sub-field of history and the simultaneous move by historians to see the origins of modern consumer society in an early modern consumer revolution were indeed linked very strongly, particularly in the English-speaking world. Which interest may have sparked the other is of course impossible to say. Nonetheless, it is hard to even think about the broad concerns of global history in any context that does not include globally traded consumer goods as an object of particular interest. We might even wonder then if consumption history is a *sine qua non* for global history. Or was it our increasing awareness of extensive global connections in the period before the nineteenth and twentieth centuries that made us start paying attention to the history of consumption in the first place? The remainder of this chapter explores the larger themes of these two sub-fields of history by posing some questions that arise from my own research on eighteenth-century consumption of new goods in the Old World.

2 The Objects of Consumption

Presumably there are many other ways of understanding global interconnectedness than just via the exchange of consumer goods. As already argued above, labour and technology circulate, as do ideas, art, literature, modes of political organization, and religious values and practices. And to our collective sorrow, there always seem to be armies on the move. Still, we might wonder whether it is possible to be a global person if not via consumption. All of these other facets of the human experience are inextricably linked to the material goods with which they are instantiated. Art requires artifacts, literature insists on books and implements of writing, and new processes depend on the gadgets that make them effective. Even religious ideas are more often than not inseparable from their objects of devotion, instruction or ritual. Without goods, whether as raw materials or as highly finished products, or anything in between, very little could be communicated across a distance. Causality runs in the other direction as well, as Michael North has argued persuasively. The cumulative research amassed on this subject for Western Europe in the eighteenth century 'has shown that consumption – including cultural consumption – also created identities.'[11] Europeans increasingly came to define their regional and even local identities by the periodicals they read, the music they listened to or performed, the foods they ate, the clothes they wore and the objects on display in their homes, even when a good many of those items in fact came from somewhere else, often for that matter the other side of the world. It is certainly consistent with the evidence to say that it would be difficult to imagine a consumer revolution taking place without the availability of consumables from the whole world, just as it seems impossible to have a global history without globally traded consumer goods.

My own research on a collection of nearly 1000 after-death household inventories drawn up by the Regents of the Amsterdam Municipal Orphanage (the *Burgerweeshuis* or BWH) between 1740 and 1782 has been especially productive for thinking about the link between cultural identity formation and new kinds of consumption. To be eligible for admittance into the Municipal Orphanage, a child had to have lost both of his or her natural parents, both of whom also had to have been citizens of the city for a period of at least seven years. Citizenship could be inherited, but also purchased. Thus, the BWH archives contain inventories on a remarkably diverse collection of households, displaying much more heterogeneity than the typical range of households captured by notarial records. Decedents whose estates were surveyed by the orphanage included married as well as widowed men and women—the married ones having remarried with a second or higher spouse after the death of their first. There are also single men and women who had been formerly orphans themselves and by virtue of dying without heirs of their own, the BWH could claim their estate. Many of the households surveyed by the BWH were also exceedingly poor, a group that rarely finds its way into the documentary records of inheritance or probate. Finally, the data sample also includes both native-born Amsterdamers and those who were successful migrants to the city such that they could afford to pay the fairly steep fee for citizenship status.

It is this diversity of sample population, especially into the ranks of the extremely poor, that makes the surprisingly wide diffusion of Asiatic textiles (or Asian-inspired European imitations) as well as housewares associated with the consumption of colonial groceries of such interest to historians of consumption. Nearly 60% of the households (533 out of 912 complete inventories) owned at least one item for the making or serving of tea or coffee. A total of 54% (492 households) owned delftware and a remarkable 38% (341 households) owned real porcelain, even if some of it was described as old, chipped or otherwise in poor condition. Asiatic textiles seem not to have as yet penetrated the BWH population as fully as had exotic tablewares, but nonetheless 23% of households owned something identified as made of cotton and more or less the same percentage owned items made of silk (213 households for cotton and 207 for silk). Even highly prized Indian chintz was present in 134 of the homes of BWH affiliates (that is 14.6% of the BWH population). Of course, a sizeable quantity of the clothing listed in these inventories was also in poor condition and thus was not described in any detail at all. While it seems likely that identification would be more forthcoming from the bookkeeper tasked with making the inventory if the materials used were of exotic origin, nevertheless it is safe to assume that these percentages represent the absolutely lower bounds for the presence of cotton and silk in the homes of poor to middle-income eighteenth-century Amsterdamers.[12]

The factors that allow (or even encourage) some individuals to purchase new goods, acquire new tastes and take on new habits are much debated. It seems obvious (even if somewhat circular in its reasoning) to suggest that it was rapidly increasing wealth that allowed early modern Europeans to assume new consumer behaviours with such enthusiasm. But at the same time, it has been the documentation of the ownership of these goods that has been instrumental in supporting the claim that Europeans were growing richer. This logical problem notwithstanding, social and cultural historians have argued more recently that it is not enough just to be able to afford new consumer practices regardless of how that economic capacity might be identified; it is also necessary for there to be both flows of information and community norms of behaviour to facilitate the diffusion of new commodities across the landscape, whether this is understood in physical, sociological or economic terms.

The BWH population offers a remarkably clear test of the relative importance of wealth versus social learning because of the different wealth profiles of those born in the city of Amsterdam versus those who immigrated to it later in life (but nonetheless became citizens by paying the required entry fee). BWH immigrant parents were almost twice as wealthy (as measured by the asset valuations of the inventories themselves) as their native-born peers. The median household wealth of the latter was only 40.5 guilders, while the former enjoyed a median household wealth of 78.8 guilders. Other measures of wealth, such as the number of rooms in their dwelling and the size of the debts left unpaid at death (higher debts are a sign of greater wealth and economic activity in a society where so much ordinary business was conducted using credit and assets were necessary to getting credit), also favour the immigrants over the native-born[13]. As my work has shown, despite the economic advantage held by the immigrants, their enthusiasm for the eighteenth-century craze for *chinoiserie* nonetheless paled in comparison to that of their relatively less prosperous native-born neighbours, for the latter consistently reveal themselves to have been eager participants in the new consumption practices. They adopted new products sometimes to an even greater extent than their much wealthier peers, but always just as soon as they could possibly afford them, even if it meant the acquisition of only one item and in a context of very few other material possessions. The immigrants, on the other hand despite their wealth, seem to have added exotic tablewares and fabrics only once they were first relatively well supplied with more traditional goods.

In short, people have to learn how to become consumers of new things. It is this learning process that makes for especially rich fodder for the new world/global history. We overlook at our peril the importance of information flows and social learning (sometimes location-specific as in the global emporium that was seventeenth and eighteenth-century Amsterdam) to informing consumer choices. Living in a port city overflowing with products from the entire world such as one found in Amsterdam towards the end of her 'golden age', must have complicated those choices considerably. But growing up in that environment also seems to have equipped people, even those who were desperately poor by our reckoning, to make such choices with a surer hand than their economic fortunes alone might have suggested possible.

3 Conclusion

This essay began with a hunch, that the veritable explosion of research beginning in the late 1980s on the history of consumption among both economic and cultural historians, along with the concomitant discovery of one, or more likely several, "consumer revolutions," was part and parcel of the broader phenomenon of the takeoff of world history as a distinct field complete with professional associations, dedicated journals and doctoral research programs. There are of course a good many paths towards global interconnectedness beyond just via the long-distance exchange of consumer goods. Appropriately, historians have not neglected the circulation inherent in labor migrations and technological diffusion, nor the rapid speed-up in the spread of other kinds of ideas via art, literature, political organizations, and religious institutions. Nonetheless, the emergence of the global citizen seems to have been most fully captured as an historical phenomenon through an examination of these citizens' new patterns of consumption. What remains to be done by historians of consumer culture, and likewise by global historians more generally, is to more completely document the mechanisms by which this thoroughgoing transformation took place. How did formerly locally focused communities become educated to both a desire for, and useful knowledge of, goods from the entire world? That is to say, how did the global citizen-consumer come into being? The consumer habits of poor and lower middling citizens of Amsterdam in the middle decades of the 18th century offer one very good place for historians to begin their quest.

Notes

1. That the emergence of the sub-discipline of world history is a relatively recent development as well as a real growth area for history departments is easily attested to by a few basic facts. When I began graduate school in the mid-1980s none of us would have identified ourselves as interested in world history, even though there was already then a growing desire to study more of the world than just Europe and the USA. Now the WHA lists 116 PhD programmes in the USA alone that offer a specific field option in world history. While the rest of the world has been somewhat slower to join this movement there are also 16 such programmes outside of the USA, including nine in Canada, two each in Germany and the UK, and one apiece in Australia, Hungry and the Netherlands. At the secondary level, the College Board introduced a World History Advanced Placement exam in 2002. There are also three referred scholarly journals dedicated to the field: the *Journal of World History* (begun in 1990), the *Journal of Global History* (begun in 2006) and the *New Global Studies Journal* (begun in 2007).
2. http://www.thewha.org/about-wha/history-mission-and-vision-of-the-wha (accessed 3 July 2017).
3. See, for example, Temin 2014.

4. Indeed, in the first issue of the *Journal of Global History*, four of the total of six articles were by economic historians, along with one article by an historian of technology and one early modernist.
5. The WHA lists the following areas of specialization on its website under the rubric of 'Economic Themes of World History': commodities; economy; globalization; industrialization; maritime trade; mono-cultural economies; nomadic and pastoral peoples, impact on trade; overland trade; plantation economies; southernization; trade diasporas; and transoceanic voyaging. See http://www.thewha.org/about-wha/areas-of-specialization-in-world-history (accessed 3 July 2017).
6. See, for example, Mazlish and Buultjens 1993; and, more recently, Olstein 2014.
7. A good example of this can be seen in the major research endeavour at the Humboldt University of Berlin called 'Arbeit und Lebenslauf in globalgeschichlichter Perspektive' ('Work and Human Life Cycle in a Global Perspective').
8. Kwass 2003: 87.
9. For the consumer revolution, two critical publications both appeared in the early 1980s: McKendrick et al. 1982; Williams 1982.
10. A similar exercise can be conducted for the German-language literature stored in Google Books, but once again the specific terms of interest do not translate particularly well. In the German case, I searched on the terms 'Alltagsgeschichte' and 'Weltsgeschichte'. The latter shows a steep decline beginning in the late 1940s, perhaps not surprisingly given the traumatic aftermath of the Second World War. The former, 'the history of everyday life', made its appearance in the 1980s at more or less the same time that the consumer revolution was being explored for the first time by English historians, but the use of this term had diminished greatly by 2000, unlike for the consumer revolution, which lives on strong into the present. See Fig. 4.
11. North 2008, p. 171.
12. For details of the data cited here see, McCants 2015 and 2016.
13. McCants 2015, Table 2; and Muldrew 1998.

References

Kwass, Michael. 2003. Ordering the World of Goods: Consumer Revolution and the Classification of Objects in Eighteenth-Century France. *Representations* 82 (1): 87–116.

Mazlish, Bruce and Ralph Buultjens, co-eds. 1993. *Conceptualizing Global History*. Boulder, CO: Westview Press.

McCants, Anne. 2015. Becoming Consumers: Asiatic Goods in Migrant and Native-born Middling Households in 18th Century Amsterdam. In: *Goods from the East: Trading Eurasia 1600–1830*, ed. Maxine Berg, 197–215. New York: Palgrave Macmillan.

———. 2016. Textile Meanings in a Global Capital: Fabric and Fashion in 18th c. Amsterdam. In: *Linking Cloth-Clothing Globally*, ed. Miki Sugiura. Tokyo: Ochanomizu Publishing (Forthcoming).

McKendrick, Neil, John Brewer, and J.H. Plumb. 1982. *The Birth of a Consumer Society: Commercialization of Eighteenth Century England*. Bloomington: Indiana University Press.

Muldrew, Craig. 1998. *The Economy of Obligation: The Culture of Credit and Social Relations in Early Modern England*. London: Palgrave.

North, Michael. 2008. *Material Delight and the Joy of Living: Cultural Consumption in the Age of the Enlightenment in Germany*. London: Routledge.

Olstein, Diego. 2014. *Thinking History Globally*. London: Palgrave-Macmillian.

Temin, Peter. 2014. The Rise and Fall of Economic History at MIT. *History of Political Economy* 46 (suppl 1): 337–350.

Williams, Rosalind. 1982. *Dream Worlds: Mass Consumption in Late Nineteenth Century France*. Berkeley: University of California Press.

Open Access This chapter is licensed under the terms of the Creative Commons Attribution 4.0 International License (http://creativecommons.org/licenses/by/4.0/), which permits use, sharing, adaptation, distribution and reproduction in any medium or format, as long as you give appropriate credit to the original author(s) and the source, provide a link to the Creative Commons license and indicate if changes were made.

The images or other third party material in this chapter are included in the chapter's Creative Commons license, unless indicated otherwise in a credit line to the material. If material is not included in the chapter's Creative Commons license and your intended use is not permitted by statutory regulation or exceeds the permitted use, you will need to obtain permission directly from the copyright holder.

Mexican Cochineal, Local Technologies and the Rise of Global Trade from the Sixteenth to the Nineteenth Centuries

Carlos Marichal Salinas

The history of Mexican cochineal over several centuries represents a key chapter in the origins of early modern globalization, both cultural and economic, since this dye was the most expensive in the world as a result of the consistent demand for luxury textiles—dyed with bright crimson, scarlet or purple colours—by monarchs, the hierarchy of the Catholic Church and aristocrats in Europe, as well among the very rich almost everywhere. Indeed, since the time of the Roman Empire, red and purple had been widely identified with power and wealth. For a long time, European and Asian red dyes were used for this purpose, in particular the Mediterranean kermes dye and the dyes known as Polish and Armenian cochineal. But the special attractions of Mexican cochineal dyes, which arrived in Europe from the early sixteenth century onwards, were that they fixed a more brilliant and deep red colour into woollen or silk cloth, and that they could last unblemished for years and, indeed, as was later learned, continued to do so for centuries. A recent and very attractive

C.M. Salinas (✉)
El Colegio de Mexico, Mexico City, Mexico

museum exhibition has demonstrated that Mexican (and to a lesser degree Peruvian) cochineal was sold and applied in luxury textile manufacturing and commercial centres not only in Europe but also throughout the Ottoman Empire, South India the Spice Islands, China and Japan from the mid-sixteenth to the mid-nineteenth centuries.[1]

The first news of cochineal arriving in Europe came shortly after the conquest of the Aztec Empire by the Spanish conquistador Hernan Cortes in 1521. In fact, it was the Emperor Charles V who as early as 1523 wrote to Cortes, indicating that he had received reports of the existence in Mexico of a red dyestuff—referred to as 'grana'—and urging him to send cargoes to Spain since it could be of importance for the royal treasury. The new conquerors and rulers of Mexico were actually more interested in the gold and silver of New Spain, but gradually came to appreciate the high value of the little bags of cochineal dye known as 'grana cochinilla', which were then sent on ships of the Spanish fleets to Seville on their return journey. Cortes had no problem in collecting the red dye as it was a frequent component of the tribute paid by many of the peoples formerly subject to the Aztecs. The administration of Cortes adopted the practice of collecting tribute on the basis of the *Matrícula de tributos*, an early sixteenth-century Mexican codex, which detailed lists of products paid by thousands of peasant communities to the Emperor Moctecuhzoma II before his death in 1520. An indication of their importance was the fact that the Zapotec peoples of the central Oaxaca valley had traditionally been obliged to contribute 20 bags of grana cochinilla every three months, as well as 400 *huipiles* (artistically woven covers), 800 plain tunics and 20 gold discs, all destined for the court of the Aztec Empire.[2]

Cochineal had long been cultivated in Tlaxcala and several other regions of New Spain, but by the late sixteenth century, the bulk of cochineal of the finer quality came to be concentrated in the region of Oaxaca as a result of the strategy adopted by the Spanish administration to establish monopolistic control over the production of 'grana fina', which produced a much higher quality of dye than the more common variety of 'grana silvestre'. This superior type of cochineal was the result of the careful cultivation of the most productive cochineal insects on small plots of nopal, the thick, juicy leaf of a certain variety of cactus that was tended by peasant families. The considerable population density of peasant communities in the mountainous territory of Oaxaca was an important precondition for the highly labour-intensive cultivation of the nopal plants on which the cochineal insect thrived.

Contemporary descriptions of the cultivation of cochineal evoke the enormous amount of meticulous peasant labour required, which was similar to that of the production of silk worms in rural China in the same era. These parallel and very long commodity chains with peasant origins—silk from China and cochineal from Mexico—met and meshed in Europe in the leading luxury textile centres from the mid-sixteenth century onwards, a fact that indicates the complex nature of early modern globalization and its economic importance to the peoples of three continents. In other words, this chapter suggests the importance and need for future detailed studies on the interaction of the silk commodity chains that originated in China and crossed Asia to Europe, with the cochineal commodity chains that had their origins in colonial Mexico and, for centuries, crossed the Atlantic to the textile centres of Europe and also travelled across the Pacific to Asia via the famous Manila galleons.

In this chapter, emphasis is placed on a series of elements which examine the question of how some special commodities—in this case cochineal—produced in the early modern era by peasants in non-European regions came to play a major role in stimulating global trade and contributed to textile *protoindustrialization* in other continents. We argue that it is essential to understand the relatively simple but also sophisticated technological adaptation carried out by peasants over centuries of an available but highly specialized natural resource that actually led to the creation of a product which quickly generated a global demand. The case of cochineal is our subject here, but other products such as indigo, silk, pepper, cloves, coffee, tea and tobacco provide notable parallels for understanding the peasant and extra-European origins of early economic globalization.[3]

These stories can also serve as a counterpoint to the narratives of tropical commodities in early globalization that traditionally focus more on the role of slavery in plantation economies and particularly on the sugar colonies. In this sense, we suggest that it is also of major importance to analyse the way in which peasant communities in different parts of the world engaged in a series of commercial commodity chains that were essential to the building of global trade in the early modern period. At the same time, it is necessary to analyse the interface between peasants and other actors, whether mercantile or political, who played a key role in the management of the production, taxation and trade of the commodities mentioned. In this chapter, for reasons of space, the second part of our text focuses on the regional as well as international merchants who took control of the longer and most lucrative parts of the cochineal commercial chains that literally spanned the globe for three centuries.

1 THE OAXACA INDIAN COMMUNITIES, RURAL TECHNOLOGY AND THE SECULAR PRODUCTION OF COCHINEAL

The name of the most expensive American dye of the *ancien régime*, 'grana cochinilla', was imported directly from Europe, being derived originally from the old Latin term of *coccina* (in Spanish *cochinilla*), which had been used since ancient times to refer to the rich, red colours produced by insects which, when desiccated, were described as *grana* (little grains). The modern scientific name of the little Mexican insect that produces the famous dye is 'Coccus cacti', which refers to the fact that it thrives upon the cactus known as *nopal*, which is abundant in central and southern Mexico.

In the colonial era, the historian Manuel Miño noted that it was also known as 'Nopalae coccininelifera', an insect living on the leaves (nopal) of a native cactus (Miño 1993: 74). According to Richard Donkin, who carried out an exhaustive historical study on cochineal:

> Cochineal insects are parasites of cacti belonging to two closely related genera, *Opuntia* and *Nopalea*; the latter includes eight or nine species, the former over two hundred ... The early Spanish historians, commencing with Oviedo y Valdes (1526), compared the fruit (tuna) to large figs, hence the subsequent description 'Indian fig'(higuera de las Indias) ... The species most commonly used in rearing cocínela was Opufntia Ficus-indica, found today only in cultivation. (Donkin 1977: 12)

As to the cochineal insect, which is the parasite of the nopal, Donkin offered the following precise commentary:

> Cochineal insects belong to the family Coccidae and to the genus Dactylopius...From the time of our earliest knowledge of the New World, two main kinds of cochineal insect have been recognized: a domestic form, source of *grana fina* (nocheztli), and a wild form, from which *grana silvestre* (xalnocheztli, ixquimliliuhqi) was obtained. *Dactylopius coccus* is double the size of other species and takes about twice as long to complete its life cycle. Father Bernabe Cobo (1653) compared the full-grown insect (4 to 6 mm in length) to a chickpea or kidney bean. (Donkin 1977: 12)

During the colonial era, a natural, wild variety of cochineal, called *Grana silvestre*, was found and cultivated in relatively small quantities not only in Mexico but also in Guatemala and in South America (in Peru and Tucumán, and northwest Argentina) with up to six annual harvests per year, but producing a relatively low-grade dyestuff. The most valuable and important variety of cochineal was the domesticated type grown in Mexico known as *Grana fina*, being twice the size and producing a much richer dye. However, it could only yield three harvests (May, July and October) with production levels of about 250 kilos of these insects per hectare of planted nopals. The enormous amount of peasant labour expended can be indicated by the fact that one pound of the final dye known as 'grana cochinilla' required the desiccation of 70,000 tiny insects.[4]

The cochineal insects were cultivated with extraordinary care by Mexican Indian peasants on the nopal plants. According to both the Spanish chronicles of the sixteenth century and later documents, the Mexican peasants developed a complex pattern of cultivation of the nopal cactus which provided the essential sustenance to the valuable dye-producing insect. In the early chronicle written by Friar Bernardo de Sahagún (the greatest ethnographer of sixteenth-century Mexico), there appear various detailed drawings which illustrate the Nopal plant, the process of harvest and cleaning of the cochineal insects, the use of cochineal for painting and the fabrication of the small loaves of cochineal and their sale at market. These engravings clearly point to a widespread cultivation of cochineal as well as production and trade of the red dye from prehispanic times (see Sahagún 1577).

In short, the technology for development of the red dye was the result of centuries of experimentation by peasant communities who soon found substantial local demand for the product. It is now well-known that Aztec women used cochineal for painting their lips and bodies, that local painters used it for artwork and that it was used for dyeing the leather garments, furs and feathers used by the Aztec nobility. When this consumption largely disappeared after the conquest, it was immediately replaced by the burgeoning demand of European markets for this rare and valuable red dye, the price of which soon rose to great heights.

According to the most detailed reports on the cultivation of the nopal and 'grana cochinilla', most of which date from the eighteenth century, in order to be able to maintain regular harvests of fresh cochineal, the peasants of Oaxaca and some other regions would habitually open up new fields near their villages by using slash and burn methods, later proceeding to open holes along long lines, using the traditional wood instrument of 'coa' with its sharp point that allowed the user to delve into the earth. Subsequently the peasants would take two or three of the big nopal leaves (each larger than a man's hand) and would insert them into the holes. This process of seeding would normally take place in the months of May or June or alternatively in November or December after the end of the rainy season. In two or three years, the cactus plant acquired maturity and would have many nopal leaves.

Later, there followed a laborious sequence of tasks that included seeding each of the nopal leaves with some 50 baby cochineal insects previously prepared with great care. Throughout this process, the peasants would have to weed with care and be very vigilant in order to eliminate the numerous natural predators that might eat the cochineal insects, as well as to protect the plants from excess rain or cold frosts.

Once the cochineal had matured, the peasants had several ways of killing them in order to extract the valuable red dye. They could do so by boiling thousands of insects directly in hot water and then drying them until they became a red-brown colour. Alternatively, they were baked slowly in the hot sun, making them a silver colour, or they were baked in hot pans or ovens which made the final colour of the 'grains' (grana) black. Subsequently the grains were packed together using diverse procedures, until finally the valuable 'bricks' (*zurrones*) of dried dyestuff were ready for shipment, mainly to Europe.

Originally cultivated in Tlaxcala and several other regions of New Spain, production came to be concentrated in Oaxaca by the late sixteenth century. We have already mentioned the importance of the high population density of peasant communities in this mountainous territory for cochineal production, but, in addition, a complex incentive structure was gradually put in place by the Spanish colonial regime, which made it attractive for Oaxaca peasants to specialize in the production of this natural dye. Local agriculture was mainly subsistence as the production and sale of any agrarian surplus was limited due to poor soils, small regional markets and high transport costs. The high prices of cochineal, in contrast, allowed Indian peasant families to obtain a modest but welcome income from the dyestuffs. In many Oaxaca towns the peasant families also obtained income from the sale of cotton produced in the valleys and from the manufacture of richly coloured textiles.

For the Spanish crown, there were clear fiscal advantages that favoured incentives for the increased production of cochineal. Since the Indian communities (called 'repúblicas de indios') were obliged from the sixteenth century onwards to pay tribute to tax collectors of the colonial administration, it was soon stipulated that in Oaxaca they should preferably do so in cochineal. The reasons were transparent: royal functionaries made substantial profits by selling the dyestuffs to merchants for silver or gold, whereas they had more difficulty in selling other commodities produced by the local, Indian peasant communities.

But the mechanisms of the colonial administration also included a complex dynamic of mercantile control of the cochineal production and trade, which operated on the basis of a close alliance between merchants and local bureaucrats who exploited the Indian communities as far as they could. Two researchers, Brian Hamnett and Carlos Sánchez Silva, have underlined the coactive methods that were employed to force Oaxaca peasants to produce cochineal from the sixteenth century through to the end of the colonial regime (Hamnet 1971; Sánchez 1998). However, coaction was not the only factor involved. The historian Jeremy Baskes has carried out innovative and detailed studies on the cochineal trade in eighteenth-century Oaxaca, arguing that incentives (provided by both merchants and the vice-regal administration) help explain the continued specialization of Oaxaca peasants in the cultivation of the cochineal insects and the production of the dyestuff (Baskes 2001).

Certainly, it would appear that the *repartimiento* system (which lasted until 1787) proved quite successful in ensuring a consistently large cochineal harvest each year. In very basic terms, *repartimiento* functioned as follows: leading Mexico City merchants advanced funds to Oaxaca merchants, who, in turn, provided funds to local bureaucrats (*alcaldes mayores*) in the cochineal-producing towns and villages. The functionaries would lend the monies to the peasants so that they could plant nopal plants or pay for sustenance until the cochineal insects were harvested and sold. Alternatively, the royal functionaries (who actually also operated as merchants) could advance livestock, mainly mules, oxen and bulls, to the farmers who were thus obliged to pay back in an equivalent amount of silver or cochineal at a given date. Therefore, in exchange for the funds or livestock advanced, the peasants agreed to return payment to the *alcaldes mayores* with cochineal at a fixed price (lower than the current international price). The profits made by the royal bureaucrats was largely based on the difference between the almost fixed price at which they valued the cochineal provided by the peasants (usually 12 silver reales per pound of good cochineal) and the price they received from merchants. This difference varied over time and was very much a function of the complex relations between the Mexican merchant bankers and the local 'alcalde mayores'.

The most abundant statistical information on the Mexican cochineal trade that exists covers the second half of the eighteenth century and the first half of the nineteenth century. It provides an overview of cochineal production in Mexico and its relation to the fluctuations of international prices of this precious red dye. The most complete series are based on data registered at the local treasury of Oaxaca on annual production by weight and value, as well as on annual price trends. The long-term tendencies indicate that physical production declined from the end of the eighteenth century, but that there was a notable price increase during the age of the Napoleonic Wars and later during the wars of independence in Mexico (Fig. 1).

The review of the data suggests a need for a further breakdown from the century-long trend to shorter time periods. Analysis of a first quarter century spanning the years 1758 to 1783 demonstrates that this was an age of prosperity as far as cochineal was concerned: annual production averaged 922,600 lb, which, at a price of almost 20 silver reales (two-and-a-half silver pesos = 10 shillings) per pound, produced over two million silver pesos per year for local producers and merchants in Mexico (the peso was worth exactly one dollar). However, a marked drop in production levels took place from 1784 and took production of cochineal to slightly less than half a million pounds per year until 1803. At the same time, prices declined slightly, hovering at an annual average of some 10 silver reales per pound until the turn of the century, when they began to recover and climb.

That production should have fallen so abruptly after 1784 and continued to remain depressed despite the continuing Oaxaca monopoly of cochineal would seem to suggest that it was the disruption of this complex credit-mercantile mechanism which contributed to the decline of cochineal. Baskes demonstrates the remarkable fall in production after the abolition of the 'repartimiento' schemes and argues that peasants depended heavily on the old credit mechanisms. Other authors have also insisted that additional factors were involved, such as increasing taxation in the final decades of the eighteenth century, but the arguments

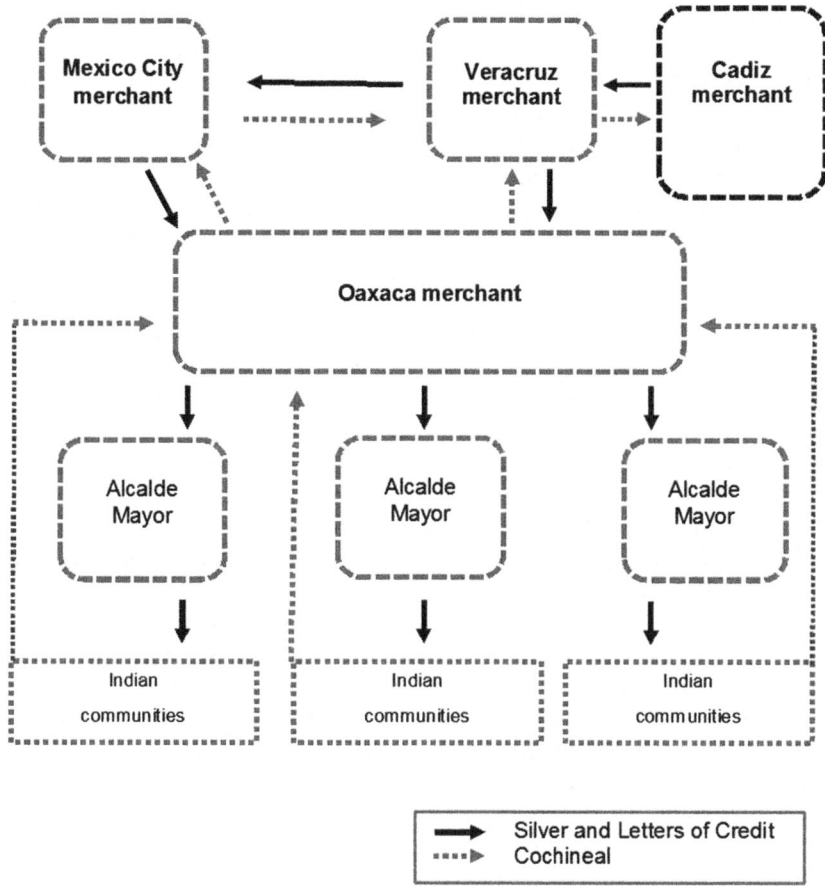

Fig. 1 The cochineal trade: Mercantile networks in Mexico

of Baskes are convincing. At any rate, the subject would appear to merit future investigation.

It is also likely that these trends reflected shifts in the demand for cochineal in Europe, which may been caused by the multiplication of international wars at end of the eighteenth century and first years of the nineteenth century that certainly affected global trade; the recovery of prices was probably related to the decline in Atlantic maritime trade, particularly after the Battle of Trafalgar. In any case, it may be speculated that expensive scarlet cloth probably lost some favour at the close of the *ancien régime* with the decline in the pre-eminence of both the aristocracy and the Church at the time when the emerging middle classes gained strength as a result of the Industrial Revolution and of democratic revolutions in the USA and parts of Europe, all of which had extensive impacts on consumer patterns.

There were also domestic reasons for the steep reduction in the production of Oaxaca cochineal which were apparently not related to the rather modest price decline, but rather have been ascribed by historians to two causes: (1) the terrible impact of the plagues and demographic crisis of 1784–1785 (during which over 300,000 people died in New Spain), which is believed to have deeply affected the Oaxaca peasant communities and disrupted production; and (2) the impact of fiscal and administrative reforms which restructured traditional forms of commercialization of cochineal locally and, at the same time, implied higher taxes on this commodity (Baskes 2001; Hamnett 1971; Contreras 1996; Sánchez 1998). In sum, a complex series of new conditions—demographic, fiscal, administrative and mercantile—disrupted traditional levels of local production of cochineal in Oaxaca and initiated a phase of relative decadence.

During the following fifteen years, (1804–1819), production of Oaxaca cochineal continued to decline, but was compensated for by the rise in the international price of the dyestuff, which rose to an average of 26 silver reales per pound during these years of war and intermittent interruption of navigation between Mexico and Europe. After the independence of Mexico in 1821, the international price of cochineal dropped steadily mainly because of the end to the Mexican monopoly on cochineal and the emergence of competing production in other regions of the world, in particular Guatemala and the Canary Islands. Despite the fall in prices, it should be noted that the annual production of Oaxaca grana (as measured in pounds) increased, a fact which would appear to suggest that peasant producers sought to maintain income levels by intensifying their labours in spite of the drop in profitability, and they continued to do so for decades (Fig. 3).

2   AMERICAN DYES AND THEIR ROLE IN TEXTILE PROTOGLOBALIZATION

The international trade in cochineal was highly complex. Its axis originated in Mexico because the Spanish crown made it policy to foster a virtual production monopoly of *Grana fina* in the region of Oaxaca. But it should also be noted that New Spain (colonial Mexico) was also important as an intermediary for other American dyes, in particular indigo (some produced in Mexico but mostly in neighbouring Guatemala) and dyes from Campeche wood (palo de Campeche).[5] Indigo was in high demand in Europe for the making of blue cloths, while Campeche dyes were used for deep blacks, which were in high demand for religious reasons in both Catholic and Protestant countries as well as because of fashion, as can be seen in the contemporary paintings of the Spanish court of Philip II of Spain.

The importance of cochineal was reflected in its price, being the most expensive of all dyes. As a result, it often represented a higher proportion of the final costs of fine cloth than other materials essential to their manufacture, including raw or processed fibres, whether wool, silk or linens. But why was this so? Scarcity of high-quality dyestuffs, of course, played a major role in this, but it is also worthwhile underlining that certain colours had great socioeconomic significance in traditional society for the maintenance of hierarchies. In this regard, it is worthwhile recalling that from the medieval era, one of the colours most prized by the crown, church and nobility in Europe for their finest fabrics was that of carmine or deep crimson. It is well-known that from the fourteenth century onwards, the leading luxury textile centres of Europe—particularly Florence and Flanders—produced crimson cloth (in various shades and tones) by using a variety of red dyestuffs. According to the historian John Munro, the 'medieval scarlets' owed their 'splendor, fame and high cost to the dyeing process' (Munro 1983: 39). This was so largely due to the fact that such dyestuffs (particularly derived from insects, such as the *kermes* from the Mediterranean) were quite rare and because the dyeing processes were complex and required considerable technical skill. The expensive scarlet or crimson fabrics could only be acquired by the wealthiest members of late medieval society, but despite their high price, from the early sixteenth century onwards, the demand for luxury crimson and scarlet cloth continued to climb all over Europe, although perhaps most noticeably in England, Flanders, France and Italy. Inevitably, the demand for high-quality and long-lasting red dyestuffs also rose.

From the late 1520s, Mexican cochineal had begun to appear on European markets in small quantities, but soon gained wide acceptance as the finest and most durable crimson dyestuff for textiles, particularly woollens and silks. According to one historical study: 'Cochineal possessed from ten to twelve times the dyeing properties of kermes; it also produced colors far superior in brilliancy and fastness' (Lee 1951: 61). This dyestuff thus quickly won growing markets in the leading luxury textile manufacturing centres of Europe, including Segovia in Spain, Suffolk in England, Florence, Milan and Venice in Italy, Rouen, and Lyon in France and various centres in Flanders. Interdisciplinary scientific studies provide concrete evidence on the rapid expansion of European demand for cochineal. A laborious chemical research programme on hundreds of samples of medieval and early modern dyed textiles has provided 'concrete evidence to substantiate the historical assertion that Mexican cochineal within fifty years of its introduction into Europe (c. 1520–30) fully displaced kermes in scarlet textile dyeing' (Hofenk-De Graaff 1983: 75).

The luxury textile industries of Italy were among the most important of sixteenth-century Europe and hence were among the major markets for expensive dyes. Substantial quantities of the 'grana cochinilla' sent from Veracruz to Seville and Cadiz made their way to the port of Livorno. The Spanish economic historian Felipe Ruiz Martín used the correspondence of contemporary Spanish merchant bankers to trace the exports to Florence where a booming luxury textile industry consumed large quantities of dyes (Ruiz 1965). But he also noted that a substantial volume of cochineal was trans-shipped from Livorno to Venice, where it was used to dye the cheaper textiles—'pannina'—sent to Constantinople as well as for the famous Venetian 'fez', the religious caps used throughout the Muslim world. According to both Spanish and Genoese merchants involved in this trade, the crimson dyestuff was always profitable and in fact its price quadrupled over the sixteenth century, even as the volume of trade rose rapidly.

The high prices and specialized demand for cochineal probably explain why it appears prominently in the correspondence of international merchants from the sixteenth to the early nineteenth centuries. Moreover, the possibility of cornering the market in cochineal was apparently greater than in the case of the other dyestuffs and hence was generally seen as offering more potential for profit-taking by those in a position to invest large sums in such speculations.

From the mid-sixteenth century onwards, leading European merchants and merchant bankers became interested in cochineal because it was a high-value commodity with low weight; in this regard, it was similar to other leading global commodities of the era such as silks, pepper and spices, as well as precious metals which were easily transportable by sea or land and allowed for great profits because of their high but fluctuating prices. As a result, it was not strange that cochineal should have become the object of much financial speculation.

Examples abound from the late sixteenth century of attempts to corner the cochineal markets in Europe, including the manipulation of the cochineal trade by groups of leading Spanish and Italian merchant bankers, a number of them closely linked to the finances of the Habsburg monarchy. The historian Ruiz Martín edited a selection of the abundant correspondence of the Spanish merchant Simon Ruiz with Italian merchants, which includes extremely frequent references to cochineal (the mercantile correspondence of Simón Ruiz is among the richest in that of contemporary Europe, including over 6000 letters, now in deposit at the University of Valladolid: Ruiz 1965). Such merchant bankers were engaged in the trade circuits linking Seville/Cadiz, Genoa, Livorno and Florence. Cochineal arrived from Mexico to Seville and Cadiz and from there was redistributed to the rest of Europe. Most of the cochineal which went to Italy went to Livorno (Leghorn) and was transported in the same ships that brought the famous merino wool that was also a commodity much in demand in the Florentine luxury textile manufacturing sector.

The most spectacular speculative operation in the late sixteenth century related to cochineal was that carried out by the Florentine merchant banking family known as the Capponi, who, in alliance with the powerful Maluenda merchant bankers of Burgos, Spain, attempted to corner the entire shipment of cochineal from Mexico arriving at Seville in 1585. They also bought up the bulk of stocks in other European ports in order to reinforce a strategy aimed at gaining a virtual monopoly of the valuable dyestuff. The ambitious plans of the speculators were quite successful and allowed them to push prices upwards, although there was stiff resistance by the artisans in the leading textile centres of Europe. Ruíz Martín notes that in some cases the decline in demand obliged the merchants to offer extended time spans for payment of the cochineal (Ruiz 1965).

The published data and information on the cochineal trade is relatively scarce and scattered for the seventeenth century, but the historian Louisa Hoberman has provided important information with regard to the cochineal trade at this time in her excellent study on the merchants of New Spain. According to her research, on average, it can be estimated that one pound of cochineal would cost anywhere between four and six

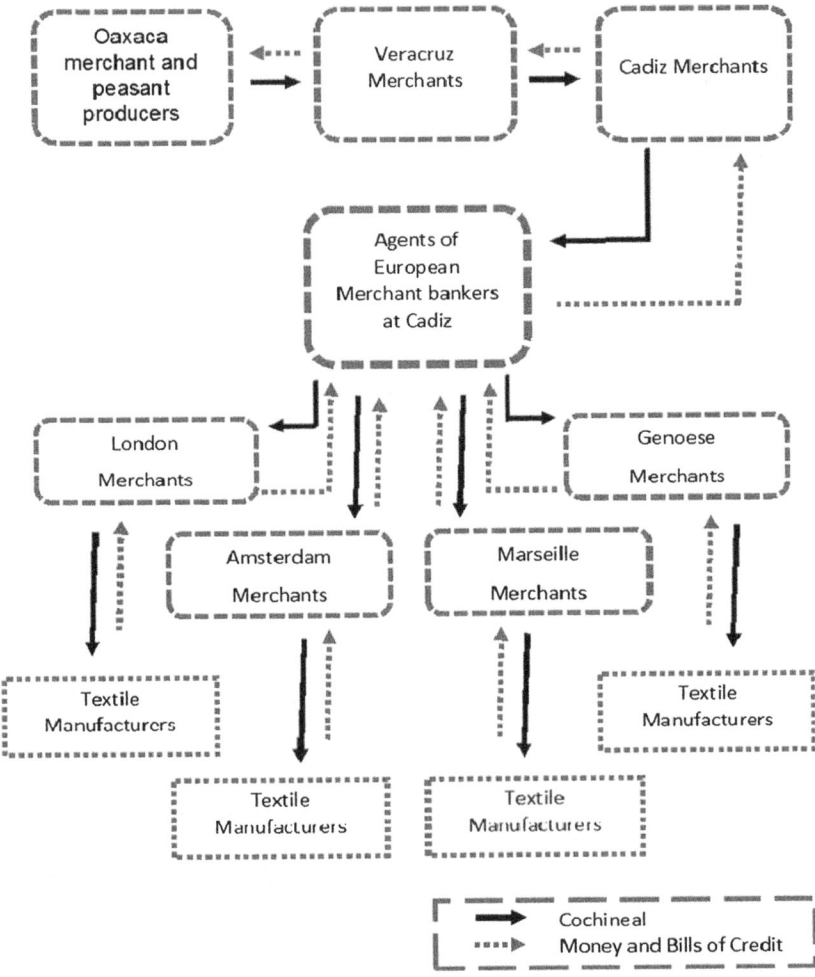

Fig. 2 The Commodity Chain of Cochineal from Oaxaca and Veracruz to Europe, circa 1780

silver pesos in the early seventeenth century. Hoberman adds that the high unit value of cochineal can perhaps be best judged by comparing it to other commodities. In the decade of 1610–1620, for instance, 25 lb of cochineal cost 60 times more than an equivalent weight of sugar; in the 1630 s, cochineal was worth 30 times the value of an equivalent weight of sugar (Schell 1991: 121–122).

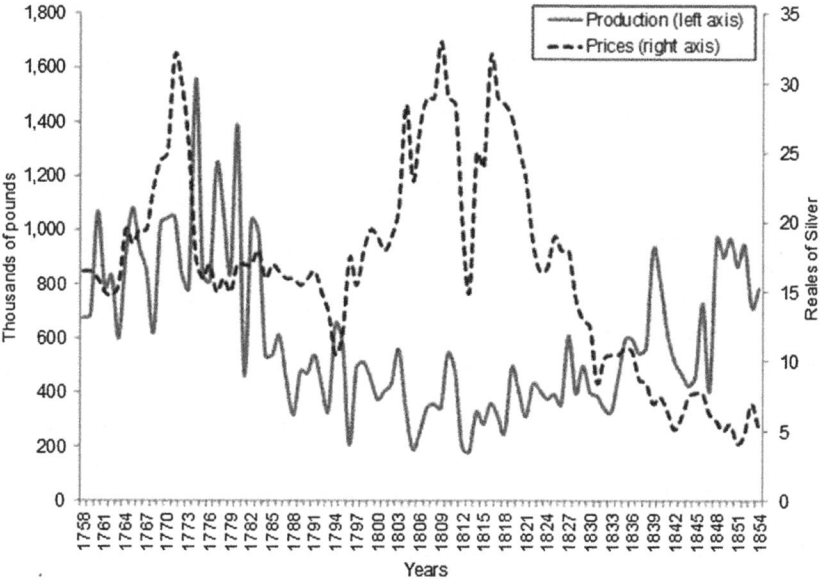

Fig. 3 Annual Production and Prices of Cochinilla Registered at the Oficina del Registro y la Administración Principal de Rentas, Oaxaca, 1758–1854. *Source* Barbro Dahlgren, *La grana cochinilla*, México, UNAM-Instituto de Investigaciones Antropológicas, 1990, pp. 331–332

*There are no values for 1820. It has been averaged using the values of 1819 and 1821

The international trade in cochineal hence became ever more important, but as it remained a Spanish commercial monopoly, practically all of the valuable dye from Oaxaca was channelled via the Spanish port of Cadiz to the multi-faceted European mercantile community, as can be seen in Fig. 3.

A review of the trade in cochineal indicates that speculation continued to be a common feature of the international trade in this dyestuff from the sixteenth century to the late eighteenth century. For example, financial historians have identified the huge cochineal speculation by two of the leading merchant banks of Europe, Hope and Company of Amsterdam and Baring Brothers of London, in 1788. The operation involved buying up most of the stock of cochineal in all the principal European ports—Cádiz, Marseilles, Rouen, Genoa, Amsterdam, London and even Saint Petersburg—with the object of obtaining a virtual monopoly. The transactions required particular attention to acquiring practically all the dyestuffs received from Mexico in Cádiz, since failure there would condemn the whole, vast transaction. The agent of the bankers at Cádiz was not entirely successful in this part of the project and rival merchants in other ports were also able to buy up substantial stocks of cochineal, probably because they had gotten wind of the aims of the Hope/Baring alliance. As a result, the monopoly was nowhere complete and attempts to rig prices failed, causing substantial financial losses to the main partners in the speculation (Buist 1974).

But European merchants were not alone in the international cochineal business. Some of the great eighteenth-century mercantile firms of Mexico City and Veracruz were also heavily involved in the management of this complex commodity chain on the American side and in its connections to both Europe and Asia. Studies by various historians on the operations of the wealthy house of the Iraeta merchant family of Mexico City reveal the complexity of the control of the cochineal trade inside New Spain, the complex connections to Cadiz merchants those with Asian markets where there was considerable demand for the cochineal which was shipped via the Manila galleon across the Pacific in its long, annual journey, from Manila to Acapulco.

3   Conclusions

It was indeed remarkable that the Spanish crown could have successfully maintained a virtual Mexican monopoly of cochineal production from the sixteenth century up to 1820. Such exclusive control was essential for two aspects of the cochineal business: to guarantee the high quality of the product and to maintain its high price. Precisely for these reasons, the rivals of the Spanish crown expressed great interest in the singular insect and its capacity to produce the valuable carmine dye. It is known that already by the late eighteenth century, the French botanist Thierry de Menonville smuggled some cochineal insects out of New Spain and took them to Saint Domingue (Haiti), where he attempted to promote their cultivation, but without success (Sarabia 1994: 35–36). Less well known is the fact that from the mid-1820 s, cochineal began to be cultivated successfully and on a large scale in nearby Guatemala and in the Canary Islands, and cochineal actually became their leading export for almost half a century. The results of the increase in cultivation and production of the dyestuff were dramatic, causing a steady price decline per pound. Despite this turn of events, Oaxaca peasants responded by increasing production after 1824, although profitability was falling, year by year, as can be seen in Fig. 1 in relation to price trends. Their strategy to intensify the cultivation of nopal, and cochineal was actually fairly successful in maintaining this export trade in what became an increasingly cheaper crimson dyestuff decades after Mexican independence.

Nonetheless, the Oaxaca peasant communities faced increasing difficulties in the first half of the nineteenth century, for by 1870 the peasants of Canary Islands eventually became the world leaders in the cultivation and harvest of cochineal, producing up to five million pounds a year itself, much more than either Guatemala or Mexico (Butler Greenfield 2005). Yet suddenly, at this time major advances were made in the chemical dye industries in Germany and Britain, and natural dyes were quickly substituted by synthetic ones, leading to a steep drop in prices and demand for natural dyes such as cochineal. Indeed, the steep and abrupt decline of the cochineal trade marked the end of early globalization, as it gave way to a different kind of economic process which we know today as modern globalization, which had strikingly new characteristics.

In summary, the fortunes of these dyes from the New World followed the trajectory of the labour-intensive textile production of the *ancien régime*, which was later supplanted by the age of factory production of textiles. Hence, this is a story of how specialized peasant production in the Americas influenced proto-industrialization and early industrialization in Europe with the expansion of the supply of natural dyes, although later they were replaced by artificial dyes as a result of the triumph of the Industrial Revolution and its new technologies.

Notes

1. The exhibition curators contracted more than a dozen museum experts in chemical analysis of dyes to carry out detailed studies on presence of cochineal in textiles and arts of the early modern period in various countries. See Anderson and Padilla (2015).
2. Much additional information on tributes from different towns of New Spain can be found in Lee (1948: 452).

3. For a recent interpretation of the importance of these commodities on early globalization, which focuses mainly on changes in European consumption and on ideological factors, see Carmagnani (2012).
4. Valuable information can be found on the subject in Lee (1948), 449–473.
5. Some of the material included in this section is derived from a previous essay: Marichal (2013): 197–215.

References

Anderson and Padilla. 2015. *A Red Like No other: How Cochineal Colored the World: An Epica Story of Art, Culture, Science and Trade*, 1st ed. New York: Museum of International Folk Art and Skira Rizzoli.

Baskes. 2001. *Indians, Merchants and Markets: A Reinterpretation of the Repartimiento and Spanish-Indian Economic Relations in Colonial Oaxaca, 1750–1821*. Stanford: Stanford University Press.

Buist, Marten G. 1974. At Spes Non Fracta: Hope and Company, 1770–1815, Merchant Bankers and Diplomats at Work, (The Hague, Martinus Nijhoff).

Butler. 2005. *A Perfect Red: Empire, Espionage and the Quest for the Color of Desire*. New York: Harper Collins.

Carmagnani, M. 2012. *Las islas de lujo: productos exóticos, nuevos consumes y cultura económica europea, 1650–1800*. Madrid: Marcial Pons.

Contreras. 1996. *Capital comercial y colorantes en la Nueva España en la segunda mitad del siglo XVIII*. Zamora: El Colegio de Michoacán/ Universidad Autónoma de Yucatán.

Donkin. 1977. Spanish Red: An Ethnogeographical Study of Cochineal and the Opuntia Cactus. *Transactions of the American Philosophical Society*, vol. 67, part 5, pp. 1–83.

Lee, R.L. 1948. Cochineal Production and Trade in New Spain to 1600. *The Americas* 4 (4): 449–473.

Lee, R.L. 1951. American Cochineal in European Commerce, 1526–1625. *Journal of Modern History* 23 (3): 205–224.

Hamnett. 1971. *Politics and trade in Southern Mexico; 1750–1821*. Cambridge: Cambridge University Press.

Hofenk-De Graaff. 1983. The Chemistry of Red Dyestuffs in Medieval and early Modern Europe. In: *Cloth and Clothing in Medieval Europe*, eds. Harte and Ponting. London: Heinemann. pp. 71–79.

Marichal, C. 2013. Mexican Cochineal and European Demand for a Luxury Dye, 1550–1850. In: *American Products in the Spanish Empire. Globalization, Resistance, and Diversity, 1492–1824*, eds. B. Aram and B. Yun-Casalilla, 197–215. New York: Palgraves Macmillan.

Marten, G. 1974. *Buist At Spes Non Fracta: Hope and Company, 1770–1815, Merchant Bankers and Diplomats at Work*. The Hague: Martinus Nijhoff.

Miño, M. 1993. *La protoindustrial colonial hispanoamericana*. *El Colegio de México*. Mexico City: Fondo de Cultura Económica.
Munro, John. 1983. "The Medieval Scarlet and the Economics of Sartorial Splendour". In: eds. N.B. Harte and K.G. Pointing. Cloth and Clothing in Medieval Europe, London, Heineman, pp. 13–70.
Ruiz, F. 1965. *Lettres marchandes échangées entre Florence et Medina del Campo*. Paris: Ecole Practique des Hautes Etudes.
Sahagún, B. 1577. *Historia general de las cosas de Nueva España*. Avaiable at: https://www.wdl.org/en/item/10096/view/1/1/.
Sánchez. 1998. *Indios, comerciantes y burocracia en la Oaxaca poscolonial, 1786–1860*. Oaxaca: Instituto Oaxaqueño de las Culturas.
Sarabia. 1994. *La grana y el añil: técnicas tintóreas en México y América Central*. Seville: Escuela de Estudios Hispanoamericanos/Fundación del Monte.
Schell. 1991. *Mexico's Merchant Elite, 1590–1660: Silver State and Society*. Durham, North Carolina: Duke University Press.

Open Access This chapter is licensed under the terms of the Creative Commons Attribution 4.0 International License (http://creativecommons.org/licenses/by/4.0/), which permits use, sharing, adaptation, distribution and reproduction in any medium or format, as long as you give appropriate credit to the original author(s) and the source, provide a link to the Creative Commons license and indicate if changes were made.

The images or other third party material in this chapter are included in the chapter's Creative Commons license, unless indicated otherwise in a credit line to the material. If material is not included in the chapter's Creative Commons license and your intended use is not permitted by statutory regulation or exceeds the permitted use, you will need to obtain permission directly from the copyright holder.

Social Networks and the Circulation of Technology and Knowledge in the Global Spanish Empire

Bartolomé Yun-Casalilla

Is it possible to think of a global empire where there is not a substantial circulation of technology and technological knowledge? Can we imagine the sixteenth and seventeenth-century scientific revolution without the circulation of knowledge and objects which made it possible and without the most important space for such circulation? This is what Masson de Morvillers did when, referring to scientific development in a famous

---

This work has been carried out within the framework of the activities of the research group 'Globalización Ibérica: Redes entre Asia y Europa y los cambios en las pautas de consumo en Latinoamerica. HAR2014-53797-P', as well as of GECEM ('Global Encounters between China and Europe: Trade Networks, Consumption and Cultural Exchanges in Macau and Marseille, 1680–1840') project hosted by the Pablo de Olavide University, UPO (Seville, Spain). The GECEM project is funded by the ERC (European Research Council)-Starting Grant, under the European Union's Horizon 2020 Research and Innovation Programme, ref. 679371, www.gecem.eu. The P.I. (Principal Investigator) is Professor Manuel Perez Garcia (Distinguished Researcher at UPO).

B. Yun-Casalilla (✉)
Pablo de Olavide University, Seville, Spain

article in *L'Encyclopédie Méthodique*, he wrote 'in two centuries, in four, or even in six, what has Spain done for Europe?' Spain, he added, is a country where it is necessary 'to ask priests for permission to read and think' (Masson de Movillers 1782: 575).

This chapter aims at drawing attention to the role of the Spanish Empire in the circulation of technology and technological knowledge during this epoch. It focuses on the role of informal institutions and social networks regulating such circulation and examines the relationship between political power and the control of technological knowledge, as well as the often-simplified interplay between globalization and empire.

1   Iberia and the Empire: Channels of Knowledge

A new image of the technological development in the Spanish Golden Age has emerged since 1988, when David Goodman published his influential *Power and Penury* (Goodman 1988). This book made clear the interest of Philip II (1527–1598) in mining technology, metallurgy, navigation, mathematics, medicine and many other sciences. Goodman's research aimed at defending the image of the king as a patron of science and technological development. But the book also wanted to change the stereotype of the 'Castilians as uninterested in technology and science' (Goodman 1988: 264). Three decades of further research has corroborated the idea of significant scientific development in Spain and has also stressed the importance of fields not directly linked to the king's action. In an attack against the traditional view, Eamon (2009) has summarized this new view and has shown the Black Legend's Prejudices that underlay previous and negative stereotypes. This contrasts with a recent and simplistic vision that still emphasizes the idea of Spain as an absolutist state and of its monarchy as able to abort the rise of positive institutions (Acemoglu, Jonson and Robinson 2005).

This new less biased image has still neglected the study of the role of the circulation of goods and, more importantly for us, that of technological awareness as the base for technological progress. Regarding to this aspect I propose to start by taking into account also the role of informal institutions, based on personal relationship, in such a circulation.

One has to consider that the Iberian Peninsula was from the tenth century onwards a privileged area of intercultural exchange. Inventions or the use of inventions such as the compass and gunpowder, and scientific developments in fields like trigonometry, cartography or mathematics provided the base for overseas expansion in the fifteenth century. We also need to remember that this was the outcome of a cross-fertilizing convergence in this area of Hebrew, Islamic and Christian webs of knowledge that can be followed into Asia. These were already the product of a globalizing process. Even the caravel, apparently a genuine Iberian product, was the result of the confluence in Iberia of navigation techniques from Northern and Southern Europe.[1]

This crossroads character of the Iberian Peninsula did not disappear; on the contrary, it intensified during the sixteenth century. Some scholars have rightly underlined the negative effects for scientific and technological development of the Jews' expulsion in 1492 and the prosecution and final deportation in 1608–1609 of the *moriscos*. It is also impossible to forget the negative effects of the Inquisition on creative thinking. But it is also true that by the sixteenth century, Iberia had become the core of a dispersed European composite monarchy. This implied the strengthening of the previous social and intellectual networks on which knowledge, goods inspiring provocative thinking, technology and technicians, architects and engineers, pilots and seamen, soldiers familiar with warfare technology, geometry, mathematics and medical practitioners fluidly circulated. It is even possible that this created different and complementary types of networks from those studied by L. Epstein and others when putting the accent on the role of guilds and artisans for the diffusion of technological knowledge and know-how, of which an important precondition is religious tolerance. Of course, this type of network was not entirely absent from the Iberian Peninsula, at least until the beginning of the seventeenth century. We need to consider that communications with Italy, a Catholic country and maybe the core of technological developments until c. 1600, were very intense. Furthermore, the deportation of hundreds of *moriscos* within the Iberian Peninsula after the war of the Alpujarras (1568–71) contributed to the spread of technologies in the textile and the building sectors. But more importantly, this dispersed composite monarchy used patronage to form a web of aristocrats and elites from Iberia to Austria, Italy and the Low Countries, which facilitated the circulation of ideas, technicians, engineers, architects, medical practitioners and others. Maybe the most prominent example is Juanello Turriano, the architect, engineer and technician (including the art of clock-making) who would seek Charles V's protection (Zanetti 2017).[2] We know today that, in spite of the identification between book culture and the Protestant

Reform, these networks were crucial for the circulation of books (and not only on theology or religion), imprints, engravings and maps, which were agents for the circulation of knowledge. The aristocrats, the non-noble *letrados* and all types of literate people circulated books on geometry and mathematics (essential for the art of war), geography and history (also in many cases linked to war), engineering, pharmacopoeia, natural history and many other disciplines that were the basis for the diffusion of new technological knowledge, as well as for intellectual creativity in many different fields. These networks were interlinked by embassies, through consular agents, many of them traders, priests, or members of religious orders, and were also webs for the circulation of exotica, news, tools and cultural goods of great importance in the development of technological curiosity and information (Aram and Yun-Casalilla 2014).

These networks were increasingly dense as Castile became the centre of a global empire in need of new knowledge. We have considerable evidence that it is just the tip of the iceberg of something that deserves more systematic research. For example, it should be noted that many of the proponents of inventions to the king were non-Spanish and non-peninsular subjects of the Habsburgs (Tapia 1990). They were often Italians, which confirms the existence of a still-vivid Catholic technological world. But one can also find Germans, Flemish, Dutch and Europeans from many other regions. Crucial sectors, such as mining, were very active in attracting German experts, whose knowledge was productively absorbed (Sánchez Gómez 1989). But mining is even more meaningful in relation to these transnational and global connections if we consider that the Welser and the Fugger obtained the monopoly concession to exploit the mines of Almaden, thus promoting the migration of technicians from Central Europe to Spain (Kellenbenz 1999).

These transnational webs readily acquired a transatlantic dimension. Of the inventions for which permission to be introduced in America was sought between c. 1550 and 1600, some were promoted by non-Spanish, which is very revealing.[3] For obvious reasons, mining, and silver mining in particular, was a privileged sector for the diffusion of European technology to America (Bakewell 1976, 1989). Again, the examples of the Fugger and Welser are very pertinent (Sánchez Gómez 1989). Although the initial conquest of America was based on unsophisticated military technology, crucial knowledge generated by the European military revolution was also transferred to the New World (Headrick 2010: chapter II). Though it is a subject for further research, there are many sings of the diffusion of artisanal techniques in fields like building, the textile sector, metallurgy, woodwork, paper production and many others. The very sociology of the (legal) emigrants to Spanish America, many of them artisans, shows the importance of technological and know-how transferences. The demographic boom of villages such as Puebla in Mexico was brought about by the arrival of textile workers from Brihuega, a very important textile centre in Castile (Altman 2000). Strategically important techniques in Europe, such as the production of hemp for transport and shipbuilding, were introduced in the New World where ecological constrictions permitted. The development of the plantation economy obliged to export to the New World inventions and machines, such as the *ingenio* or *trapiche* for sugar production. And we need to stop here to abbreviate a long list.

America and Ibero-America in particular were the epicentre for the diffusion of knowledge which revolutionized the world of technology and sciences on a global scale. The knowledge of new crops and their cultivation techniques, like corn, tobacco, yucca (cassava or manioc) or the potato, had an impressive global and sometimes immediate impact in Europe, Asia and Africa (Russell-Wood 1998). Sectors such as dyeing were dramatically changed by the use of new dyes and techniques such as palo campeche, indigo or cochineal. Botany seems to have changed in Europe thanks to people like Nicolás Monardes and García de Orta. The collections of European aristocrats and princes incorporated much American exotica destined to become the bases for new ways of classifying and understanding nature and the possible human action upon it. Medical practitioners such as Francisco Hernández, *protomédico* of Philip II, were sent by the king in search of health remedies, which gives an idea of a top-down development of knowledge in which official formal institutions were very interested. But others, such as Monardes, undertook such studies *proprio motu* and thanks to personal networks, in this case strongly articulated through informal merchant and family connections (Yun-Casalilla 2014). All of this provided the foundations for more empirical knowledge, which paved the way for Baconian approaches to nature (Osorio 2006).[4] The influence not only on scientific knowledge but also on the relationship between basic and applied knowledge was really notable.

The circulation of techniques, knowledge and know-how flowed in many different and opposite directions and not only between Europe and America. The Spanish enhanced and created circuits for such diffusion in America. The Spanish conquerors extended the production techniques for yucca from the Caribbean to the Magdalena valley, while also spreading the mate herb and the techniques for its production. Many other examples could be added (Saldarriaga 2011).

This process had a twofold effect.

First, the Habsburg composite monarchy enhanced the most efficient corridors ever known before for the transnational and global ciculation of knowledge and technology. This was possible thanks to the ramifications of the monarchy in America and then, after the incorporation of Portugal and its empire in 1580, also in Africa and Asia. Although some of these facts are well known, considering them together gives us a richer image of what was happening. Many of these corridors already existed. They were very active in the Indian Ocean, in the Sea of China and even within the Americas. The connections between the Spanish and the Portuguese were also strong even before 1580. But the impulse given by the political connections interlinked previous spheres of exchange and even extended beyond the political frontiers of the Empire. Technological globalization was in part a consequence of the rise of empire building, yet went beyond it.

Second, we need to bear in mind that the circulation of knowledge provides a basis for the production of new knowledge. Medicine is a good example. Texts such as the *Discursos medicinales* written by the Spanish doctor Juan Méndez Nieto show the possibilities of cross-fertilization between American medicine and the use of local herbs in European medical practices. Even more importantly, these contacts facilitated synergies among apparently different fields of knowledge. The works of Juan de Cárdenas, who studied at the University of Mexico, for example, prove the potentialities of the dialogue between theoretical knowledge, natural history and mining, and reveal the many possibilities during the epoch for the conjunction between theory and practice (Osorio 2006: 75–79). In the mining sector, Julio Sánchez Gómez has shown how the 'contact of Central European and American experiences' produced improvements in Spain that would remain 'unknown in Central Europe until two hundred years later' (Sánchez Gómez 1989: 728).

We do not know to what extent this was the case in other sectors. But it is tempting to think that this circulation of knowledge in the Iberian Peninsula, which as noted above had been very active since the medieval period, is one of the reasons for heretofore disregarded pieces of European history that could change our image of Spanish technological development in the sixteenth century. To my knowledge, no historian has ever noted that a good deal of the projects presented to the English crown as inventions, were based on the introduction of techniques imported from Spain. This is the case of techniques for the production of leather, felt hats, needles, earthen pots and portable ovens, soap, silk stockings and others, which reveal the importance of Spain in industrial technology, one of the most neglected sectors and on which the legend of the Spanish industrial incapability has been built (Thirsk 1978).

2   Agents and Networks

What was the character of these networks and how did they function? It is impossible not to relate all of these technological developments to the commercial expansion taking place in this epoch. Trade networks were essential in that they created or accompanied the need for the introduction of new technologies. As it is well known, commerce activated the desire for foreign goods and then, in a second phase, processes of import substitution or the flow of inventions and know-how due to the emigration of artisans. But this is only a part of more complex mechanisms, and on many occasions, commercial webs were embedded in more multifaceted processes.

The case of Monardes and the way he gave Europe knowledge of many American plants through his publications is very meaningful. This Seville-based doctor obtained most of these plants—which were the sources for the diffusion of new products, such as tobacco, cocoa and others, as well as their cultivation techniques—thanks to the commercial networks created by his family and the possibilities to travel to America or to acquire its products that they facilitated. But this case is also an example of the strong intertwining between merchants and more general and diffuse social and intellectual webs, in this case with a scientific component.

The *guaranies* that the Jesuits used to defend their territory against invasion and disorder became familiar with Western military technology not through arms trafficking, but because of the direct actions of the members of this religious order, who provided them with such technology and even obliged them to use it (Svriz 2016). As in the case of Monardes, the commercial interests and the financial networks—of the Fugger and Welser in this case—were of great importance for the introduction of new inventions in American mining (Kellenbenz 1999). But Crown action, rather than the purchase of technology, was the key for such a process. The artisans of Brihuega did not sell their expertise to be transported to Puebla (Altman 2000). But the way they transferred their technology was partially provoked by migrations which were linked to an incipient labour market.

The circulation and diffusion of technology took place through many different types of agents. The pleas of a Sevillian priest as he offered military inventions to the king are very indicative of something that was in fact more common than he himself might have thought (Pérez-Mallaína Bueno 1983). Medical practitioners, soldiers, priests, traders, nobles and bureaucrats could play a crucial role in the transmission of technological knowledge and, hence, it would be a mistake to focus only on artisans or technicians to understand the process. The Hieronymites were responsible for introducing the techniques for sugar production to the Antilles by bringing inventions already proven in the Canary Islands, the Azores and Madeira. The Jesuits were crucial for the diffusion of cultivation techniques for yerba mate in some areas of South America.

It is also important to consider that the spread of new technology was the consequence of the interaction between these informal networks and the more formal institutions created by the crown. The Supreme Council of the Indies belonged to the latter and derived from it its competencies in the production of scientific and technological knowledge and the control of its diffusion into America (Schafer 2003: 351–379). But this institution was embedded in the networks that pilots, cosmographers and seamen created among themselves, which had some degree of autonomy from the king's institutions. The American universities which have been seen as nodal points in the intertwining among theoretical knowledge and natural history on the one hand and more empirical knowledge and technological practices on the other hand (Osorio 2006) depended on very informal social and intellectual webs of knowledge, in spite of their character as very formalized institutions.

We could continue, but that would only be useful to show something that is already known: the network approach is more useful when it focuses on the actions of mediators than when it aims at classification of the character of the web. As it has been noted, 'the agency operating in networks cannot be defined as a profession but as a function' (Cools et al. 2006: 9). This is important since there is a temptation among technology historians to define a priori the types of mediators to analyse.

This is, at best, an anachronism. It is grounded in the analysis of societies where technology constitutes very restrictive knowledge and the inventions' property right system strongly conditions circulations of knowledge that are very much based on the commercialization of technology. But, in the epoch that we are studying, much of the technological knowledge circulated through 'weak ties' and multifaceted networks (Granoveter 1973). These were very informal webs characterized by their low efficiency in implementing coercion and their high efficiency in circulating information.

3   Empire, Control of Knowledge and Globalization

This last feature of the social network through which technological information circulated facilitates a better understanding of the relations between technology and power as well as between globalization and empire. Although those relations can be studied from different perspectives, let me discuss only some of the possibilities.

As Goodman states, it is not clear whether the Inquisition was interested in the control of technological innovations. The many available studies on the Holy Office, as it was called in this era, do not show a clear interest in it. It is also interesting to note that the period of most intense activity of the Inquisition—between 1500 and the 1560s—coincides with the most dynamic epoch of inventions and technological improvements. But the fact remains that micro-history studies do show something substantial: the obviously negative effects of the Holy Office's actions in limiting individual creative thinking. Carlo Ginsburg's study (1980) on the case of Menocchio is very significant in this respect. These effects must have been even worse given the interrelationship between theoretical developments, which were very much exposed to the Inquisition actions, and empirical thinking, which was crucial for scientific progress. We also need to ask to what extent the 'pedagogy of fear' promoted until the 1560s was more effective in the following decades, when a very negative atmosphere was created that thwarted possible initiatives in the decades to come.

The enormous interest of the Spanish crown in controlling the circulation of technological knowledge is also well known. It has a parallel in the attempt to establish a commercial monopoly. But it is also a reflection of the fact that Philip II, like all princes of the epoch—any maybe beyond this—was aware of information's huge possibilities. He knew the importance of controlling, stocking, classifying and using [information or data perhaps?] for the ruling of his vast empire. The foundation of the Simancas Archive or of the Library of the Escorial may be the best proof of this awareness. For America, all this coincided with Ovando's reforms in the Supreme Council of the Indies based on the idea of ruling after considering all the information ('entera noticia') on all events (Brendecke 2009).

This perception of the relationship between power and technology explains why the Council of the Indies was immediately endowed with the supervision of the inventions transferred to America (Pérez-Mallaína Bueno 1983: 36–54). A system close to a patents register was soon implemented by the Council. The procedure was little more than a transposition to the American regions of the *arbitrismo*'s practices (Yun-Casalilla 2016). Very similar to the English projectors of monopolies, the method consisted of the registration of an invention in exchange for a royal privilege to implement it for a period of time.

This was a mechanism by which royal policy conditioned—it is difficult to say to what extent—the lines of technological development. Innovations in fields like cartography, navigation, mining and even medicine (an instrument to avoid demographic decline) were prioritized over other possible paths for progress (Schafer 2003: 351–379). Within these fields, some priorities also existed. The advancement in silver mining had stronger support than sectors such as iron mining and others. One of the leading specialists on the subject has even written that this explains 'the failure of the very wide interest in mining that existed in Spain during the 1560s' (Gómez 1989: 727). We should not be too rigorist when judging this aspect. These criteria can be explained by the epoch's bullionist perception of wealth, according to which prosperity was narrowly associated with the abundance of gold and silver. It has to be noted that we are considering a monarchy whose main and most urgent problem was fiscal and financial, and for which getting hold of easy money in the short run was more important than fomenting national wealth like the classical economists would prefer two centuries later. But the development of these fields of knowledge created synergies with many others. The foundation of the Academy of Mathematics by Philip II, for example, was most probably a consequence of his immediate needs, yet it must have had an impact beyond such short-term purposes. However, it is no less true that this emphasis on some fields filtered the allocation of talent and the opportunities of recognition for creative people.

It is equally interesting to come back to the way in which the control of knowledge was implemented through 'patents', which were in fact privileges for the use of inventions. As we have tried to prove in previous work, there was no significant difference between the so-called first patents and the way in which hundreds of *arbitristas* negotiated their advice, opinions (*pareceres*), news and *arbitrios*, some of them really excentric, with the king (Yun-Casalilla 2016). A well-known case of an *arbitrio* such as that of the credit institutions promoted by Luis Valle de la Cerda and the Dutch Peter Oudegherste shows how patronage networks in the court could be more decisive for its success than the quality of the project (Dubet 2000: 11–31; 2003). The dynamics of rivalry, patronage, interest groups and clientelism could be more important than the actual quality of the project or invention. As a result, the problems of obtaining the necessary support by the promoters of inventions must have increased by the end of the century, when the courtly patronage system became heavier and even more corrupt than before. Moreover, the extreme obsession of the 'inventors' with secrecy shows that they operated in a context of great uncertainty in which avoiding intellectual piracy and gaining some benefit from their own work and inventiveness was extremely difficult (García Tapia 1990). This fact becomes clearer if we consider that the privilege of monopoly, after being so arduously achieved, guaranteed the inventor's ability to implement his discovery, but did not recognize the benefits of further sale after that privilege expired. All these were disincentives for technological development that most likely increased during the seventeenth century. It is true that some of these problems were present in other countries and that the models might differ. The Dutch system was likely to have been more capable of guaranteeing inventors' rights and consequently more efficient in allowing technological development in many possible directions (Buning 2014; Davids 2000: 263–283). But the Spanish scheme does not differ much from the English projectors' system, which was also criticized at home. Consequently, the Spanish system cannot be considered an anomaly, but rather an example of behaviours that spread throughout Europe. The procedure for registering technological novelties was far from a system of creating a genuine patent market that guaranteed the inventors' property rights. What we could call the political economy of technology was becoming less and less competitive in terms of reinforcing creativity and progress to the degree that was necessary in a global empire.

All this goes against the image of an absolute and parasite monarchy aborting the development of society, in this case by controlling technological practices. More than a parasite, Philip II has been rightly presented as a promoter of technology (Goodman, 1988). Though within his own interests and schemes, like most rulers in history, he really tried to develop some specific fields of knowledge. This is very meaningful also on the relationship between power and technology in the Hapsburg monarchy. Many historians disagree with the idea of Acemoglu, Johnson and Robinson that the king's tyranny elevated the uncertainty and transaction costs of economic activities in creating insecure property rights. I would even argue that a very high degree of negotiation led to the maintenance of local and corporatist privileges (Yun-Casalilla, 2012) and that this was the reason for high transaction costs within the Iberian peninsula. The same could be said about the property rights and uncertainty associated with technological development: they were threatened not by royal tyranny but, rather, by the clientele's dynamics and the fragmentation of power inherent to the court system.

What has been said here is important to explain the relationship between empire and globalization from the history of technology's perspective. As we have noted above, the Iberian empires were powerful agents of globalization. This was the case in part due to their ability to recycle knowledge, which is a way of generating it. But it is also obvious that technological globalization itself weakened these empires. The networks of weak ties through which the ideas circulated created great difficulties to control knowledge and technology. Today we know that the commercial monopoly of the Indies was a chimera, an impossible wish. The same could be said of the attempts to control technological knowledge as a means to maintain power or leadership. Science and technological expertise flowed in circuits which were impossible to control. Indeed, they travelled beyond the empire, thus providing the king's enemies with the resources to confront him. We have referred to the little-studied transfer of knowledge from Castile to England, but we still need to add that those industrial technologies that travelled to England contributed to the increasing competitiveness of English products in Spain and the British capacity to take over the Mediterranean markets. More examples could be added. Many years ago, Herman Van der Wee (1967) illustrated the importance of sophisticated financial techniques originally developed in Castile for Northern Europe's business success. Two of the most knowledgeable specialists in the history of the Netherlands have made it clear that the great advances in the Dutch shipbuilding industry were made possible thanks to techniques imported from Spain (De Vries and A. Van der Woude 1997).

The same would apply to the imperial territories. Technological advances introduced in the colonies facilitated conquest and domination, as well as their systematic exploitation, but they also expanded the possibilities of autonomy from the crown and of political negotiation with it. The crucial role of Asian objects—a typical result of this first wave of globalization—in creating a Creole identity, neither Spanish nor American, has been recently stressed by José Luis Gasch (2012), which would be the basis for political and social negotiation of the Mexican elite with Madrid. Something similar could be said of the extraordinary capacity of introducing new technologies shown by the American elites in sectors such as the production of sugar or silver mining, thanks to which they reinforced their power and their capability to negotiate with the centre of the empire. If trying to control trade was a chimera, aspiring to a monopoly of technological knowledge was like attempting to restrain the ocean's water with one's hands. That is also why one needs to take a step back from these views of the relations between empire and technology that underline only the latter as a mechanism for imperial domination. Furthermore, the globalization of technology associated with imperial exploitation has also contributed to weaken those empires. Globalization and empires are two interlinked realities, but they do not always work in the same direction.

***

Assertions about Spain's total disregard and incapacity for technological development closely resemble the Black Legend and it does not make sense to return to them. Furthermore, we need to underline the very positive achievements of this country in the sixteenth century. But we also need to reflect on the limits of this model's capacity to generate technical development because of its biases, filters and methods. On the other hand, the emphasis on the role of Philip II as a promoter of technology in some particular fields, though has to be nuanced, is correct. However, in order to understand the complex reality of the epoch, it is also necessary to look not only at formal institutions created by the crown, but also at informal social and intellectual networks which were behind the transference of knowledge and technological improvement.

I would like to end by coming back to Masson's ideas. I think that contemporary research has render them outdated, as they belong to an old-fashioned and nationalistic view which concives scientific and technological progress within narrow national frameworks and forgets the transnational arena in which, then as today, knowledge evolves. There have been—and still are—countries able to create formal institutions capable of producing technological advances. Some of them, if not all, have also aimed to use technology as an instrument for political, economic and social dominion over others. But it is no less true that science and technology have also advanced thanks to transnational and very informal contacts. Sometimes those contacts and the transfers among the different agents have been almost imperceptible, as it is shown by the history of plagiarism and imitation. From this perspective, the contribution to the scientific revolution of the webs of knowledge that crossed the Iberian world is evident and has to be better identified. It is in any case palpable that there are many reasons to approach the problem in a way that substantially differs from that of the Black Legend's tradition.

Notes

1. See among many others, Mauro 1960.
2. I am grateful to the author for letting me use his work.
3. On this from a more general perspective, see Kamen (2003).
4. For some nuances on these ideas, see Portuondo (2014).

References

Acemoglu, D., S. Johnson, J. Robinson. 2005. "The Rise of Europe: Atlantic Trade, Institutional Change and Economic Growth." *American Economic Review* 95: 546–579.

Altman, I. 2000. *Transatlantic Ties in the Spanish Empire: Brihuega, Spain & Puebla, Mexico, 1560–1620*. Standford: Standford University Press.

Aram, B. and Yun-Casalilla, B. (eds.). *Global Goods and the Spanish Empire, 1492–1824*. Basingstoke: Palgrave.

Bakewell, P.J. 1976. *Minería y sociedad en el México colonial. Zacatecas 1546–1700*. Mexico: Fondo de Cultura Económica.

———. 1989. *Mineros de la Montaña Roja*. Madrid: Alianza.

Brendecke, A. 2009. *Imperium und Empirie: Funktionen des Wissens in der spanischen Kolonialherrschaft*. Köln: Böhlau.

Buning, M. 2014. *Privileged Knowledge: Inventions and the legitimization of knowledge in the early Dutch Republic* (ca. 1581–1621). Florence: PhD diss. European University Institute of Florence.

Cools, H. M. Keblusek and Noldus B. 2006. "Introduction. Profiling the early modern Agent." In *Your Humble Servant. Agents in early Modern Europe*, eds. Hans Cools, Marika Keblusek and Badeloch Noldus, Hilversum: Uitgeverij Verloren.
Davids, K. 2000. "Patents and patentees in the Dutch Republic." *History and Technology, no.* 16: 263–283.
de Vries, J. and A. Van der Woude. 1997. *The First Modern Economy: Success, Failure, and Perseverance of the Dutch Economy, 1500–1815*. Cambridge: Cambridge University Press.
Dubet, A. 2000. "El arbitrismo como práctica política: el caso de Luis Valle de la la Cerda (¿1552?–1606)." *Cuadernos de Historia Moderna* 24: 11–31.
———. 2003. *Hacienda, arbitrismo y negociación política. Los proyectos de erarios públicos y montes de piedad en los siglos XVI y XVII*. Valladolid: Servicio de Publicaciones de la Universidad de Valladolid.
Eamon, W. 2009. "Nuestros males no son constitucionales, sino circunstanciales: The Black Legend and the History of Early Modern Spanish Science." *The Colorado Review of Hispanic Studies* 7: 13–30.
García Tapia, N. 1990. *Patentes de inversión española en el Siglo de Oro*. Madrid.
Gasch, J. L. 2012. *Global trade, circulation and consumption of Asian goods in the Atlantic World: The Manila galleons and the social elites of Mexico and Seville (1580–1640)*. Ph.D. Thesis, European University Institute : Florence.
Ginzburg, C. 1980. *The Cheese and the Worms : The Cosmos of a Sixteenth-century Miller*. London : Routledge & Kegan Paul.
Goodman, D. C. 1988. *Power and Penury. Government, technology and science in Philip II 's Spain*. Cambridge: Cambridge University Press.
Headrick, D. R. 2010. *Chapter II. Power over peoples*. Cambridge: Cambridge University Press.
Kamen, H. 2003. *Empire: How Spain Became a World Power, 1492–1763*. New York: Harper Collins.
Kellenbenz, H. 1999. *Los Fugger en España y Portugal hasta 1650*. Salamanca: Junta de Castilla y León.
Masson de Morvilliers, Nicolas, 1782. Espagne. *Encyclopédie méthodique ou par ordre des matières. Géographie moderne*, vol. I, París: Panckoucke.
Mauro F. 1960. *Le Portugal et l'Atlantique au XVIIe siècle. Étude économique*. Paris: SEVPEN.
Pérez-Mallaína Bueno, P.E. 1983. "Los inventos llevados de España a las Indias en la segunda mitad del siglo XVI." *Cuadernos de Investigación Histórica* 7: 36–54.
Portuondo, M. 2014. "America and the Hermeneutics of Nature in Renaissance Europe." In *Global Goods and The Spanish Empire, 1492–1824*, eds. B. Aram & B. Yun Casalilla, 78–99. New York: Palgrave-Macmillan.

Osorio, A. B. 2006. *Experiencing Nature: The Spanish American Empire and the Early Scientific Revolution.* Austin: University of Texas Press.

Russell-Wood, A.J.R. 1998. *The Portuguese Empire, 1415–1808. A World on the Move.* Baltimore: John Hopkins University Press.

Saldarriaga, G. 2011. *Alimentación e identidades en el Nuevo Reino de Granada, siglos XVI y XVII.* Bogotá: Editorial Universidad del Rosario.

Sánchez Gómez, J. 1989. *De Minería, metalúrgica y comercio de metales. La mine ría no férrica en el Reino de Castilla, 1450–1610.* Salamanca: Universidad de Salamanca.

Schafer, E. 2003. *El Consejo Real y Supremo de las Indias. La labor del Consejo de Indias en la administración colonial,* vol. II, 297–298. Salamanca: Junta de Castilla y León y Marcial Pons.

Svriz, P. M. O. 2016. "La introducción de armas de fuego en las reducciones jesuíticas del Paraguay (s.XVII)." en *América en la Primera Globalización: introducción y recepción de productos externos. Workshop held in Seville,* October 6–7 (Unpublished paper).

Thirsk, Th. 1978. *Economic Policy and Projects. The Development of a Consumer Society in Early Modern England.* Oxford: Clarendom Press.

Van der Wee, H. 1967. 'Anvers et les innovations de la technique financière aux XVIe et XVIIe siècles'. *Annales ESC,* 22: 94–101.

Yun-Casalilla B. 2012. "Las instituciones y la economía política dela Monarquía Hispánica (1492–1714), Una perspectiva trans-nacional." In *Economía política desde Estambul a Potosí. Ciudades estado, imperios y mercados en el Mediterráneo y en el Atlántico ibérico, c. 1200–1800,* eds. B. Yun Casalilla y F. Ramos, 11–38. Valencia: Universidad de Valencia.

Yun Casalilla, B. 2014. "The Spanish Empire, Globalization, and Cross-Cultural Consumption in a World Context, c. 1400–c. 1750." In *Global Goods and The Spanish Empire, 1492–1824,* eds. B. Aram and B. Yun Casalilla, 277–308. New York: Palgrave-Macmillan.

Yun-Casalilla, B. 2016. 'Arbitristas, Projectors, Eccentrics and Political Thinkers. Contextualizing and "Translating" a European Phenomenon'. In *Reforming Early Modern Monarchies: The Castilian Arbitristas in Comparative European Prespectives,* eds. S. Rauschenbach and C. Windler, 101–122. Wiesbaden: Harrassowitz Verlag.

Zanetti, C. 2017. *JJanello Torriani and the Spanish Empire A Vitruvian Artisan at the Dawn of the Scientific Revolution.* Leiden: Brill.

Open Access This chapter is licensed under the terms of the Creative Commons Attribution 4.0 International License (http://creativecommons.org/licenses/by/4.0/), which permits use, sharing, adaptation, distribution and reproduction in any medium or format, as long as you give appropriate credit to the original author(s) and the source, provide a link to the Creative Commons license and indicate if changes were made.

The images or other third party material in this chapter are included in the chapter's Creative Commons license, unless indicated otherwise in a credit line to the material. If material is not included in the chapter's Creative Commons license and your intended use is not permitted by statutory regulation or exceeds the permitted use, you will need to obtain permission directly from the copyright holder.

Global Commodities in Early Modern Spain

Nadia Fernández-de-Pinedo

1 Introduction

The eighteenth century exemplifies the coexistence of continuity and change, both of which can be attributed to several centuries of maritime and colonial expansion. Trade during this era revolved around food (potatoes,[1] haricot beans, sweetcorn, tobacco, sugar, bananas, tomatoes and turkeys), stimulants (cocoa, coffee and tea),[2] dyes and fabrics (cotton, cochineal,[3] indigo and brazilwood), fauna (turkeys, horses and chickens) and timber (mahogany). Over time, this abundance of commodities reached societies all over the world, thus helping to cultivate varied tastes. American commodities (chili, pepper and peanuts) were quickly adopted by Chinese society (Baghdiantz 2015: 77–78), channelled through maritime and overland routes by Portuguese and Spanish trade, and then further traded by the East Indian Companies (the EIC and the VOC).[4] Because they provided more calories per unit of agricultural land, required less water to grow and could better survive bad

---

The author acknowledges financial support under grants HAR 2016-78026-PHs

---

N. Fernández-de-Pinedo (✉)
Universidad Autónoma de Madrid, Madrid, Spain

weather conditions than wheat or rice (Jia 2014: 93), sweet potatoes and maize were introduced rapidly in some areas of Asia. However, not all products followed the same rhythm or pace; maize and even potatoes were much slower to be adopted and consolidated as common staples in Africa (McCann 2001) and Europe (Nunn and Qian 2011; Fernández de Pinedo 1974).

Paintings reflect the social reshaping of this period. Oriental porcelain vessels, as well as the oriental folding screens that proliferated, show new beverages such as tea or chocolate being consumed (Dobado-González 2014)—a consequence of the material effects of colonialism (DuPlessis 2016). Fine, bright fabrics became desirable and were purchased not only in the cores of the empires, such as Madrid, Paris or London, but also in small towns, creating connections and new structures for shopping. As people sought to keep up appearances with these new products, luxuries (whether imports or home copies) and items that were simply new affected the demands of domestic settings not only in Europe but also all over the world.

Measuring this impact is not an easy task because there are many variables to consider. Mapping the diffusion of goods and trends is a complex challenge. We must remember that each country, and even each region, was a part of diverse, complex socioeconomic and cultural networks. A noble could take a cup of chocolate in a porcelain pot in Paris while a landowner in La Havana ate bread made from Castilian flour with cutlery from Sheffield and china from Mexico, but did these habits have the same connotations? Income availability, climate (the arrival of cold or heat), religion (holidays that affected working days, fasting and bans on food);[5] access to international networks (geographical proximity, merchants and peddlers);[6] periods of peace and war, drivers of changes in fashion (courts, ambassadors, nobility and traders), culture (shopping baskets that differed from region to region),[7] diasporas (Armenians, Jews)[8] all of these factors determined how gradually or rapidly products penetrated markets and fostered consumer habits. Whether intended or unintended, the cultural consequences of trade on consumption patterns are important.

Explaining the spread of consumption as part of the advent of industrialization in Europe is not the purpose of this chapter. In the last few decades, as mentioned by the editors of this book, we have seen the proliferation of numerous scholars and research groups seeking to measure, quantify and compare levels of income and consumption across countries, regions or societies to establish comparisons and long-term patterns. As Ogilvie has noted (2010), it does not appear that all of Europe followed the same rhythm during this process, and some economies, from East to West, could have experimented with earlier institutional, social and economic changes that allowed all social classes to foster demand (Pérez García 2017). However, this phenomenon did not necessarily occur in all countries, and neither did the so-called *Industrious revolution* advocated by Jan de Vries (De Vries 1994). A compelling debate is still in progress.[9] This is an ongoing field of research that requires reconstructing series of prices, nominal wages and real wages; scholars are still reporting on the evolution of these variables in different regions. Subsequently, in the near future we should have a clearer picture of this long and heterogeneous process of the globalization of consumption.

What seems beyond question is that no single pattern of consumption can be identified. In reality, the changes in each city were unique and the wealthier classes were—to a large extent—the forerunners in terms of access to new products (Fernandez-de-Pinedo and Thépaut-Cabasset 2017), at least until the mid-eighteenth century. It is precisely this last factor that we want to investigate—not so much the supply side, but rather we want to delve into the real demands of the urban classes. In this sense, Spain had the advantage of being the nexus of a broader network that had connected America, Asia and Europe since the end of the fifteenth century and had allowed the circulation of goods under an imperial structure. Its significance goes beyond the so-called Columbus exchange (Crosby 2003), the environmental impact (McNeill 1999) or the state-centred interpretations. Madrid, as the administrative centre of the kingdom, hosted a significant number of high-nobility members, top officers, and civil servants and merchants who were among the wealthiest inhabitants of the country and therefore were avid consumers of the latest fads and novelties.

As Belfanti (2008) has noted, the same desire for newness—and the penchant for challenging tradition through developing a taste for change—can also be found in Asia thanks to favourable economic conditions.[10] However, the process of globalization, in the sense of a gradual but permanent adoption of novelties, seems to be more evident in some regions of Europe than in Asia. Therefore, we attempt to offer a small picture of one European city, Madrid, which was characterized by high average incomes and contact with the court and new trends. With the highest per capita income among contemporary Spanish urban areas and also the most extreme differences among social groups, Madrid also helps to illuminate the preferences of the upper classes, providing the information we need to study the effects of income distribution on consumption and demand.

The source that allows us to obtain a real picture of the shopping baskets of Madrid's wealthy is a tax that recorded a series of products that—when introduced into the city of Madrid by consumers—were duty-free. These products did not require the payment of the taxes usually levied on their consumption, the extent of which is certainly underestimated. In this sense, our fiscal source offers a new window onto the ways in which new products and fashionable goods interfered in luxury networks throughout eighteenth-century Spain. Additionally, we can explore consumers' preferences for particular commodities linked with long-distance colonial-trade, such as sugar, luxury items such as porcelain china, or expensive and lavish commodities.

This chapter is part of a broader study on consumption in Madrid, a large city in the south of Europe. Therefore, we only can provide a brief discussion in these pages.

2   Source, Commodities and Consumers

Studies of material culture have traditionally depended on the evidence contained in probate inventories (van der Woude and Schuurman 1980), partitions of goods and a wide variety of tax documents.[11] 'Post-mortem' criticisms of inventories have already been described on numerous occasions (Yun-Casalilla 1999; Riello 2006). In particular, the representativeness of samples, both socially and geographically, has been discussed, as they only provide an approximation of consumption (Spufford 1999) and suffer from certain omissions, especially regarding property. They also lack detail in their descriptions of some commodities. While recognizing the relevance of inventories, in this study we have used a fiscal source that has the advantage of containing reliable data on actual purchases over a period of three years. The document is a tax called the *décima* (the tenth) (Fernández-de-Pinedo 2009), which was levied exceptionally[12] to finance the War of Jenkins' Ear against England. The tax, which would end once the specified amount was fully settled, was collected in different ways according to the agreements reached in each location.[13] In the particular case of Madrid, because the Big Five

GLOBAL COMMODITIES IN EARLY MODERN SPAIN 297

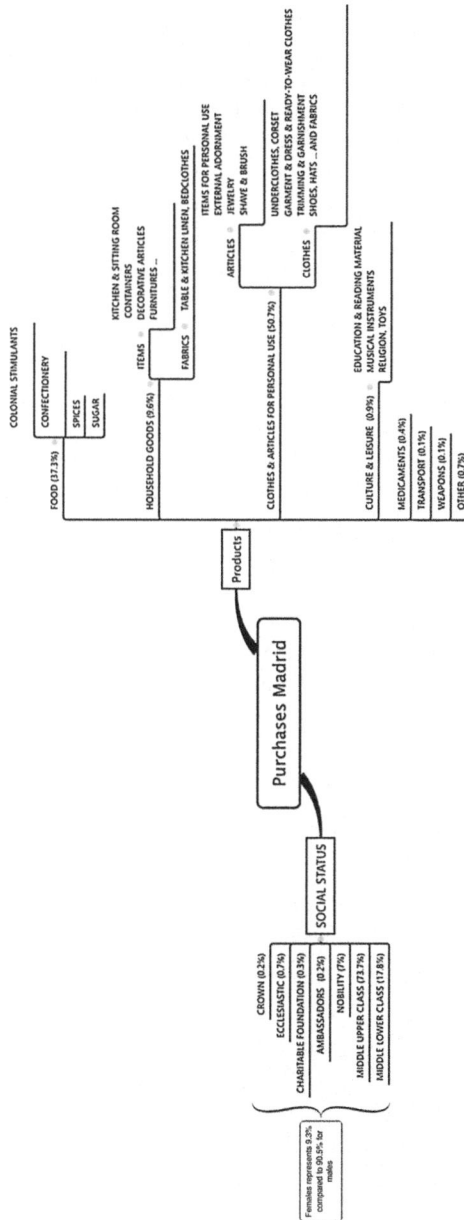

Fig. 1 Classification by record registered and social status

Guilds advanced the king the amount expected to be collected in each town, they were in charge of collections through the entrance gates of the city. A series of items or products that were introduced for personal consumption were taxed at approximately 10% of their value. Therefore, this was an indirect tax on personal consumption and serves as a reliable and accessible source for the study of consumption and distribution.

The 3,819 persons noted on the records from 1741 to 1743 have been classified according to their status and category (Fig. 1). What percentage of the population is represented in this sample? Madrid, according to the census of outsiders, had 111,268 inhabitants in 1742, while Estrada calculated the population at 109,550 for the year 1748, which was then criticized by Velarde (1752: 272) as being inaccurate. However, Isla (1987: 169) estimated 133,677 inhabitants for the period 1740–1744, a similar figure to that given by Carbajo, who estimated 130,000 for 1740 (Nieto Sánchez 2006: 86). In view of these data, our sample covers between 2.9 and 3.5% of Madrid's population, a considerable sample in any case. As each person was introducing not only products for himself or herself, but also goods for the whole household (wife, husband, children and servants), from textiles to furniture, the sample actually includes more people than the 3819 persons noted. If we think in terms of households instead of individuals, the sample is significant.

Bearing in mind the types of products that were recorded, it is doubtful that the disadvantaged classes could afford to buy many of these goods, especially the so-called colonials, furniture and silk products; therefore, it can be deduced that those who were introducing these goods were the wealthier classes and thus that this sample reflects the consumption habits of the well-to-do and middle classes of Madrid. The wealthiest are probably the best represented, as not everyone owned estates around Madrid or had the resources to go to fairs to purchase these goods. This 'large middle class' introduced 450 different products to the capital, including clothing, food and beverages, as well as housing.

3   Colonial Household Purchases in Madrid: From America to Asia

As households in urban areas are not self-sufficient (Overton et al. 2004), the needs of family members must be met through purchases from the market. Compared to households in rural areas, the demands of urban households are much more varied and expensive in terms of income availability. How varied and cosmopolitan were these Madrid households in the mid-eighteenth century? Thanks to this fiscal source, we can take a closer look at real demand over a three-year period and create a partial snapshot of the shopping basket of durable and semi-durable goods. If we leave out ambassadors, charitable foundations, the church and the crown, which together represent 1.4% of all persons recorded, we have three household profiles: nobility, middle upper class and middle lower class.

At a glance, two significant facts stand out (see Table 1). First, a higher percentage of members of the middle upper class[14] were avoiding shops or merchants within town, as they are highly represented in the sample. Second, 'luxury food' and textiles were the two most-introduced items. Although many products were of national origin, Madrid, due to its colonial history, had close ties with America and Asia, and tastes were therefore shaped by these connections.

In the foodstuffs category, which accounts for 37.3% of all records, the dominant sub-category is confectionary, which includes all types of related foods such as honey, jellies, syrups, orange blossoms and pastries; there is an emphasis on sweets (crystallised fruit made with sugar), colonial stimulants (coffee, tea and especially chocolate), sugar in all its forms, and spices or condiments. Spain's status as an empire and a colonial power had a clear influence on dietary changes and the standardization of the intake of certain products. In general, ambassadors ordered a variety of goods ranging from fabrics in silk, wool and linen (shirts, taffeta, velvet scarves, ready-made clothing and canvas), spices (nutmeg, cinnamon, clove, tea, pepper and chocolate) and miscellaneous objects (glasses, glass, straps for horses and blue powder). Their shopping basket indicates nobility and probably reflects new trends in fashion and tastes,

Table 1 Per Capita/Per Year purchases by social groups in pounds (weight)

Social status	Cocoa	Chocolate	Coffee	Tea	Sugar	Sweets	Spices[a]
Ambassadors		2.77		1.15		0.93	0.97
Ecclesiastics	4.93	6.73	–		13.99	1.23	0.03
Nobility	6.50	2.37		0.01	6.81	13.00	0.27
Middle upper class	3.13	5.13	0.06	0.01	4.22	7.53	0.07
Middle lower class	2.20	0.63		–	0.81	24.00	0.07

Source author's own elaboration based on AGS, Tribunal Mayor de Cuentas, leg. 1862
[a]Spices include saffron, pepper, cinnamon, ginger, anise, clove, nutmeg or Indian rosewood oil

as this group undoubtedly comprised fashion leaders who were also representatives of their own domestic industry. If we look specifically at the Dutch ambassador, he bought a large volume of spices: 112 kilos (or 247 lb) of spices and beverages, which is 37.3 kilos per year. The Dutch still controlled the international spice trade, so they indirectly promoted spices through their meals, aside from the fact that using spices was one of their habits. Even if French cuisine was influencing cooking at the time, spices such as cinnamon, nutmeg, cloves and pepper—which were typical of medieval cuisine—were still in use. The Comtesse d'Aulnoy (Aulnoy 1874, 1: 475) noted that the meats served in the Spanish court were flavoured or filled with peppers and spices. What is striking is that the Dutch ambassador, who was the only person buying tea (14 kilos in three years), purchased an even higher quantity of chocolate (34 kilos). It seems that the diplomat had acquired the Spanish habit of accompanying breakfast and afternoon gatherings with chocolate, which was essential in any wealthy dwelling in Madrid. As a general trend, it is noticeable that even if the sample is small in number—nine representatives from France, Netherlands, Denmark, Sweden, Sardinia, Venice and Malta—it reflects a different pattern of consumption (Table 1). There is a clear preference for sweet things over savoury ones among the Spanish population, whereas the diplomats from abroad expressed a taste for savoury and spicy things. In this sense, culture also matters. If there was a previous preference for or familiarity with sweet things, as was the case in the Iberian Peninsula (see Table 1), it would be easier to include new sweetened foodstuffs such as chocolate than sharp or savoury products such as tea, coffee or spices. Northern European countries, in this sense, had a distinct taste for spices. The recipe for chocolate reflects this tendency: no pepper (Stobart 2013: 35) or ginger was added in Spain, but cinnamon and vanilla were gladly used to season cocoa.

Tea, coffee and cocoa (Dobado-Gonzalez 2015: 39), each originating from a different continent, were soon introduced to European diets. However, in Spain until the late eighteenth century, chocolate was the leading product. For Sophie and Michael Coe, Spain was a nation of chocolate drinkers (Coe and Coe 2007: 203), just as England was a nation of tea drinkers.[15] Some authors suggest that chocolate became popular in the seventeenth century because women and clergy in America were fond of it and quickly spread the habit to cities (Martínez Llopis 1995: 199). Chocolate spread from the Aztecs and Mayas to the elites of Europe.

According to statistical data provided by Ronald R. Hussey (1962) on ships that arrived in Spain with cocoa, it seems that there is no positive correlation between the dates of consumption of certain colonial products and the arrival of these goods in America. Few ships delivered cocoa in November or December. However, a considerable portion of colonial products was consumed around Christmas and remained stored for a long time, despite the costs of storage, the immobilization of capital and the risks of deterioration. There were multiple causes of spoilage and loss. Hence, the aforementioned reasons for the rebound in the prices of these goods were still dominant at this time.

The leading purchasers of cocoa were the nobility (6.5 lb/3 kilos), and especially noble women, who purchased 8.9 lb (or 4 kilos) of cocoa per capita per year, followed of course by the clergy[16] (4.94 lb/2.3 kilos) and the middle upper class (3.19 lb/1.5 kilos). The combination of cocoa's psychoactive qualities, its status as a great source of energy and heat, and its close relationship with leisure[17] undoubtedly had much to do with its spread compared to coffee or tea. Although compared to coffee or tea, chocolate[18] has fewer stimulating effects, it also has a strong nutritional profile, which made it very appealing to the whole Catholic world. As liquids did not break the fast, chocolate substituted for food during Lent. In this way, it became the indispensable drink in Catholic countries such as Spain and Italy (Schivelbusch 1995: 110–111), just as coffee was for the Islamic world.[19] Banning certain aliments in the Catholic (meat during Lent) or Muslim (alcohol and pork) worlds had important consequences for the shopping basket and promoted substitutions and mixed menus. In any case, our data highlight that the clergy took the lead in chocolate purchases, followed by the middle upper class.

Kinship and gift[20] exchanges jointly played an important role. Giving gifts of food was standard practice, such as delivering food to a monastery, to congregations or even to individuals during certain festivities—these practices were not unusual among royalty. Giving food was also common at weddings or religious professions. According to our source, Don Francisco Gonzalez gave 1,453 lb of cocoa as gifts[21] and Don Joseph Larrategui gave 9,000 lb of chocolate, one-third being a gift from the Consulate.

According to the recipes of Didier (Coe and Coe 2007: 163), preparing chocolate in Spain required one pound of fine sugar for every two pounds of cocoa. In the Seminario de Nobles of Madrid,[22] similar proportions of cocoa and sugar were used: for each pound of cocoa, 0.477 lb of sugar were added. At the end of the eighteenth century,

Antonio Lavedan (1796: 217 and 219) noted that one-third or half a pound of sugar must be added.

On the streets of Madrid, a wide variety of stalls proliferated that sold chocolate in bowls. This was particularly true after 1730, when the *Real Compañía Guipuzcoana de Caracas* began to ship cocoa from the port of La Guaira to Spain. Philip V argued that one reason to grant the monopoly to this company was to crack down on smuggling and to remedy the shortage of cocoa the metropole was suffering, as it had become very fond of chocolate.[23] At that time in Spain, Madrid had more chocolate grinders[24] than any other city in the country; in 1772 there were approximately 150. As Norton notes, 'the migration of the habit of consuming chocolate led to the transmission of intercultural tastes'.[25] Some spices, such as vanilla, cinnamon and pepper, also spread rapidly, as they were linked with chocolate consumption and its varied recipes. Chocolate was not only consumed as a drink but also as a condiment in dishes, as seen in Brian's *Dictionnaire*.[26]

Estimating sugar consumption[27] is difficult because we must take into account not only imports of sugar in all its forms but also the amount of sugar added to chocolate and other products. Sugar had long been used as a condiment in the kitchen: in beverages, in confectionery industries, in pastry, in distilleries, in the manufacture of rum and beer, and as an adulterant of snuff. Although Spain grew sugar cane in the metropolis, Spanish tariff policy favoured sugar production in the colonies over national production until 1862. Our source helps us appreciate the range of types of sugar used in the early eighteenth century, as it specifically lists ten different forms, including sugar candy, sugar crust, pink sugar, rock sugar, sugar foam, sugar loaf and sugar foil. As in the case of cocoa, sugar was in demand, especially among ecclesiastics, nobles and the middle class, and was imported mainly from Cuba. Only small amounts were recorded from southern Spain and from France.

Because Spain lacked refineries, once sugar as a commodity was developed in Cuba, there was no choice but to install refineries soon afterwards. This lack of interest on the part of the metropolis in imitating its direct competitors (Britain and France) and the lack of initiative to promote the cultivation of sugar cane in Spain are both surprising for two reasons.[28] First, of all European countries, only Spain, along with neighbouring Portugal, had an adequate climate for cultivating sugar cane in the metropolis itself (Hugill 1993: 59). Second, fiscal policy governed metropolitan agriculture. Since 1719 (Canga Argüelles 1826: 144–145), the tax affecting sugar from southern Spain had increased, making the crop unprofitable, while imports of West Indian sugar were favoured. The Spanish tariff policy was designed to promote domestic agriculture for exportation to the colonies, and perhaps for that reason it did not sufficiently support the development of a domestic sugar industry until the 1862 tariff, by which point a barrier had been established against colonial sugar in favour of peninsular sugar. Another important fact to consider when studying sugar consumption is the presence of competitors such as honey.[29] In Catholic countries, where the amount of wax required to illuminate churches, in addition to homes, was significant, honeycomb proliferated. Consequently, honey abounded and the lower classes probably took longer to include sugar in their habits; at least until the price decreased enough for the lower classes to purchase it, sugar was not a basic food.[30] Table 1 shows the differences among social classes, from the 14 lb/6.3 kilos per year of the clergy to the 6.8 lb/3 kilos of the nobles or even the 4.2 lb/1.9 kilos of the middle upper class to the barely 0.8 lb/0.4 kilos of the middle lower class.

What is striking is that there is a market seasonality in the purchase of foodstuffs, especially in November and December. Of all annual holidays, Christmas is the most important (from 24 December), and the various social classes made great efforts to purchase the typical foodstuffs, especially sweets, available at that time of year. If we include consumption during January (Epiphany is 6 January), which represents 7.6% of purchases, three months accounted for more than half of the purchases of colonial products during the entire year.

4 Content and Containers

The high degree of social contact between the Spanish peninsula and the Spanish colonies favoured not only the transmission of new staples but also new forms of crockery and table manners. Each beverage is associated with its own material culture (Sherratt 2007a: 13). For example, accompanying imported cocoa we find lacquered gourds or pumpkins that were customarily used to drink it. Gradually, Europeans substituted American gourds for Spanish ceramics and Chinese porcelain (Table 2). Imitations spread, as Mexican porcelain imitated 'China' teacups, although with limited success.

The demand for stimulant beverages was also accompanied by the purchase of at least 252 bowls and dishes for drinking hot chocolate, as

Table 2 Items from China introduced in Madrid for personal consumption, 1741–1743

Items	Unit	Box	Pieces	Set	Unknown
Bedspread	1				
Crockery/loza		47	399	2 (ª)	
Ebony small box	1				
Fan	2				
Gourd/jícara	60				
Gourd with plates	192	1			
Knives	12				
Large bowl/taza grande	1				
Large earthenware jar with top/tíbor con tapas	2				
Monicongos de China^c					X
Saucer (common, small)/platillos	54				
Saucer and gourd		1			
Several items/piezas	72 (ᵇ)				
Small earthenware jar/orzas	2				
Small bowl/pocillos	42				
Sugar bowl	1				
Teapot	1				
Toys		3			
Vase/búcaros	80				

Source author's own elaboration based on AGS, Tribunal Mayor de Cuentas, leg. 1862
Note (ª) 1 set was introduced by the Marquis of Ensenada, 1 set was a coffee set bought by Francisco Barquinero; (ᵇ) two entries did not mention the amount or quantity
^cWe cannot be certain what items are referred to here. Some definitions in Pariente (1973: 93–94) and even Cervantes in his masterpiece *Don Quixote* mentioned monicongo as: 'Nombre del soberano y los súbditos del Reino Congo, en las orillas del Zaire; frente a los otros negros africanos, se decía que eran muy agudos y hablaban "por metáforas y circunloquios exquisito". Sin embargo no se deben descuidar las resonancias del moni- inicial.'

well as 24 crystal glasses. The purchase of chocolate pots and utensils, such as bowls (*jícaras*), was dominant in Spain compared to tea and coffee pots due to the non-existent, or at least limited, culture of tea-drinking during this period.

Changes in diet implied changes in social customs and tastes (Overton et al. 2004: 120). Decorative elements used to serve new beverages began to proliferate among the upper classes, including linen tablecloths (Weatherill 1796: 159) and table napkins.[31] In Madrid, we can find, above all, tablecloths from *La Maestranza* and also from France. These were required only by the nobility and middle upper class, as no member of the middle lower class introduced any of these goods. Therefore, we can appreciate that the two middle classes had different shopping baskets. Also striking is the role of gender in these types of purchases. As a general trend, women tend to concentrate their purchases a bit more than men, especially in category of 'Clothes and Articles for personal use'. Looking at the nobility, only noble women introduced tablecloths or table napkins because no men demanded them, in contrast to the middle upper class, whose men introduced the greater proportion of table linens. Moreover, women from the middle lower class only introduced items from three categories—'Food', 'Clothes and Articles for personal use' and 'Household goods'—while among the nobility there seems to be a certain equality in the products that both sexes introduced. Depending on their social class, women seem to exercise a greater or lesser influence on shopping, which is probably linked to income availability or access to their dowries, particularly among the nobility.

America provided sugar and chocolate and Asia provided a complete set of dishes (see Table 2). The attraction of Asian porcelain not only gave a boost to imports but, as Dobado-Gonzalez notes, also fuelled imitation—from the lowest to the highest quality—under the auspices of almost every European state (Dobado-González 2014: 19–20) until the eighteenth century.

In general, the products of Chinese origin in our source that were demanded by the nobility and middle upper class seem to be utilitarian items for domestic use (crockery, bowls, plates and even cutlery), for the consumption of chocolate (gourds) or for storage, display or drinking from jars and vases (*búcaros* and *tibores*). The latter were highly appreciated in Spain for their technical and decorative qualities.[32]

The large earthenware items with tops (*tíbor*)[33] were made of high-quality porcelain and came in sets. They were widely used to decorate rooms, corridors and chapels, and ranged in size between 12 cm and 1.2 m high (Obregon 1964: 294). Those entering Madrid might be from the K'ien Lug period (1735–1795). The (*búcaros*) ceramic ware or so-called Indian earthenware 'of an extremely fine and light paste, brown, red or chocolate colour' (Burty 1869: 132) was highly appreciated by the elites in Spain. A display of elite through Chinese porcelain (Burty 1869, 131–173) was used not only as mere decoration but also in daily life, in gathering afternoons or dinners (Riello and Gerritsen 2015: 112). Inviting guests to one's home allowed the owner to show off not only the quality of one's food but also how it was served and where; all of this revealed the status and educational level of the host.

The majority of the products noted as coming from the East were linked to the kitchen-household. Only toys, an ebony box, and fans are not enshrined in the crockery framework. Only two fans from Asia are recorded, even though these accessories were in ever-increasing demand for everyday use. Although in Chinese culture both sexes used fans, in Europe only women utilized these precious accessories, especially up to 1660, due to their rich decoration and materials. Print culture in fan decoration was in vogue, and artists signed their paintings. In Spain, fan iconography used decorative motifs inspired by the Bible or mythology, although rustic scenes and exotic designs were also gaining ground (Restauración 2015: 112 and 115).

Therefore, fans were very popular gifts (Avery, Calaresu and Laven 2015: 135). Until the eighteenth century, fans[34] were more of an upper-class item, essential at any social event. As demand rose in Europe and America, China started to produce fans specifically for exportation, thus competing with the European fan-making industry (Werlin 2016: 98). Chinese common fans had leaves made of paper or fabric and sticks of bamboo or other fragrant woods, while the most luxurious fans were made of ivory, nacre or whalebone sticks. Fans are a traditional cross-cultural and global item; they could combine East and West when the ivory of the sticks came from Asia and the leaves from European textiles or paper. Fans could have several lives due to their construction, as the paper, silk and taffeta could be replaced when the sticks were made of high-quality materials such as ivory or bone (one exception was a type of folding fan, the folding *brisé* fan, in fashion in the early eighteenth century—Blanco and Doering 2016: 1:8). Consequently, as Maxine Berg (2004: 126) pointed out, 'Asian commodities were especially admired as luxuries', the craftsmanship being skilfully appealed and imitated profusely.

5 Concluding Remarks: Global Products

Trading networks among Europe, Asia and America modified the habits of Europeans. Exotic luxuries were selectively adopted, and they spread with varying degrees of intensity depending on a series of factors, as discussed above. In this sense, the colonizers of territories determined the distribution of certain products. In the words of Bartolomé Yun-Casalilla (1999), this cross-cultural exchange was not always peaceful;

it could be violent, sometimes leading to the imposition of hybrid habits and societies (Gruzinski 2001: 113). Most of the so-called colonial products were promoted by their respective governments in the form of monopolies and later by fiscal[35] incentives or disincentives, not only in the metropole or the empire itself, but also outside the former home network. Psychoactive substances in general—wine, tobacco, opium, tea, coffee and cocoa—were socially and economically important, from their indigenous origins to their worldwide consumption. Early on, states discovered the significant value of these products in terms of fiscal revenue and establishing monopolies (Sherratt 2007b: 8). Such products were first received with hostility and suspicion, as they were associated with vices and bad habits. Therefore, taxing these goods was—up to a certain point—seen as natural and understandable.

The diffusion of new commodities in Europe followed two distinctive routes. The first was related to half-finished products such as silk, cotton, cocoa and sugar—that is, products that required a second transformation in order to be consumed (refining, grinding or stamping) and for which the cost of transport affected final prices. The diffusion of these commodities was generally linked to a trickle-down effect, taking into account that their spread was more correlated with price than with need. The second group included products such as seeds (maize, potato, tomato, wheat and pepper) and animals (horses, chickens and turkeys), which were linked to the diets of the lower strata of society and were easily adapted to the climate and soils of Europe. Here, the freightage and cost of transport had a limited impact, but the products had a wide impact from an economic point of view.

Throughout the eighteenth century, many of these overseas products played a central role as social markers, especially in urban populations (Thépaut-Cabasset 2010). Madrid offers a good example of changes in material practice and cultural dynamics. Looking at tastes, clothing and household goods, we can map the origins of products that were in demand in Madrid. Cocoa was imported specifically from Caracas[36] and sugar from Cuba, while chocolate quickly became fashionable in the high society of the Iberian Peninsula. Coffee and tea took much longer to become popular in comparison to Northern Europe. From China especially, crockery such as teapots, vases, plates, cups and drinking bowls, as well as fans and bedspreads, were integrated into sociability and fashionable displays. Domestic rituals of drinking chocolate, dressing fashionably and showing off particular objects such as table clocks or porcelain and gourds framed social life and hierarchies, and were symbols of respectability.

Many patterns of consumption in the first half of the eighteenth century were the result of centuries of relations between East and West. In the words of Gruzinski, they were a result of 'les mondes mêlés de la monarchie' in the case of the Iberian World (Gruzinski 2001: 113). European cultural patterns were no longer exclusively European, but rather global, as nations were part of international networks and were agents and representatives not only of their domestic industries but also of colonial industries, reflecting national consumption. However, the consumption of certain commodities[37] was higher in urban areas due to contact with other influences and the cultural habits of travellers, merchants and foreigners (Pérez-García 2013). According to our source, in early eighteenth-century Madrid, each social class highlights a particular pattern of consumption. Even within the upper class, some purchasing differences can be noted according to income levels, as shown in our comparison of the middle upper class and middle lower class. Therefore, we cannot confirm that colonial products such as chocolate, sugar or porcelain were consumed at a global scale in Madrid in the first half of the eighteenth century. Even if cultural models of consumption privileged some exotic commodities over others, Madrid exhibits the dynamics of consumption of an imperial capital served by products from every corner of the world (Fernández de Pinedo and Fernández de Pinedo 2013).

Notes

1. The potato was not widely traded until the end of the eighteenth century.
2. Tea was imported to Europe from China and the most reputed and expensive cochinchin was imported from Japan Savary Des Bruslons, Dictionnaire universel de commerce, contenant tout ce qui concerne le commerce qui se fait dans les quatre parties du monde. (A–E), 1: 1118.
3. See Marichal Salinas' chapter in this book.
4. Berg 2004; Parthasarathi 2001; Prakash 1998; Riello and Parthasarthi 2009; Riello and Gerristsen 2015; Souza 2005.
5. García-Zuñiga, 'Fêtes Chômées et Temps de Travail En Espagne (1250–1900)'
6. Pérez-García, 'Vicarious Consumers'. Trans-National Meetings between the West and East in the Mediterranean World (1730–1808), 196.
7. Robert C. Allen has reopened a line of investigation by constructing several standardized consumption baskets, taking into account daily caloric

and protein intake that can facilitate international comparisons (Allen, Bengtsson, and Dribe 2005). In Spain, numerous studies have revealed patterns of consumption, life styles and standards of living that are allowing precise comparisons within the European framework. These studies fall along a broad spectrum and analyse many different themes. We can only point out a small sample of all the works and topics being done in recent years such as the influence of taxation on consumption and prices, standards of living as reflected in shopping baskets and wages (Calderón et al. 2017; Llopis and García 2011; Llopis Agelán et al. 2009; Dobado-González 2015; López Losa 2013; Feliu 2014), consumption of textiles (Yun-Casalilla and Torras Elias, 1999), tobacco (Meléndez, Ferri, and Laforet, 2000), fish (López Losa and Piquero 2006), wheat (Bernardos 2003), distribution and commercial networks (Pérez-García 2013; Fernandez-de-Pinedo and Fernández de Pinedo 2013), meat (Bernardos 1997; Hernández Franco 1981), bread (Caro López 1987) or the second hand markets (López Barahona and Nieto Sanchez 2012) and much more.

8. Baghdiantz McCabe, Harlaftis, and Minoglou, Diaspora Entrepreneurial Networks; Baghdiantz McCabe, A History of Global Consumption, 129; Ogilvie and Carus, 'Institutions and Economic Growth in Historical Perspective'; Baena Zapatero and Lamikiz, 'Presencia de Una Diáspora Global'.

9. For example, the volume 33(1) of the *Revista de Historia Económica/Journal of Iberian and Latin American Economic History*, March 2015.

10. This holds true even though differences between East and West can be found, such as changes in style of clothing or a broader diffusion trickle-down and even trickle-up effects in the case of Europe. (Belfanti 2008: 442).

11. The interpretation of that data is another matter altogether (Riello 2006: 16, note 10).

12. For more detail, see Fernández-de-Pinedo 2012; AGS, Tribunal Mayor de Cuentas, leg. 1862.

13. Copia de la instrucción dada, en consecuencia de lo que mandó S. M. por el Ilustrísimo Señor Don Joseph del Campillo, a todos los Superintendentes del Reyno, para la cobranza del Diez por Ciento, BNE, Mss. 11.259 (39) Aranjuez, May 31st of 1741.

14. All persons included in these social strata had the 'Don/Doña' distinction, which, although open to interpretation, denotes certain social and economic characteristics; we believe that certain noblemen, as well as traders, merchant bourgeoisie, officials of the administration, senior

officials or property owners might belong to this category. Although members of this category would not have had a homogeneous level of income, they could all be considered as middle upper class. The middle lower class group encompassed those people who did not have any distinctive title, which does not necessarily mean that they were poor.
15. Shammas and McCants point to the decades of the 1730s and 1740s as the beginning of mass consumption of tea in England and the Netherlands, respectively (Shammas 1990; McCants 2007).
16. 'As usual the Jesuits in Spain were great imbibers (and importers) of chocolate' (Martínez 1995: 210–211). It should not be forgotten that chocolate was also the ideal drink to mask poison.
17. 'Urban life and culture focused on display and on the concentration of leisure and other facilities for people to meet each other' (Weatherill 1988: 81).
18. Among other references, see Foster 1992; Coady and Wright 1993; Markle and Harper 2004; McNeil 2006; Coe and Coe 2007; Norton 2008; Hackenesch 2011; Fattacciu 2012; McCabe 2015.
19. Coffee was, for example, very important during Ramadan, according to Ina Baghdiantz McCabe (2015: 125).
20. Let us not forget that a gift was always something expensive and/or exotic. It was frequent to give exotic animals, jewellery, tapestries, etc.
21. 'Razón por la cual solo pago los 2/3 y no el 100%'.
22. Archivo Histórico Nacional, Universidades, 1797, legajo 641. Documento facilitado por Santiago Piquero.
23. Real Cedula de S.M. para el establecimiento de la Real Compañía Guipuzcoana de Caracas; Imprenta Real, Madrid, 1765.
24. On problems of creating a Chocolate Guild, see Fattacciu's account in Madrid 6 mills in 1772: Fattacciu 2011.
25. (Norton 2008: 43)
26. For example, chocolate was used to cook the 'crème de chocolat au bain-marie' or the 'crème veloutée au chocolat' by adding lemon, cinnamon, coriander, milk and six chocolate bars (Briand 1750: 1:369).
27. Spain did not reach a consumption level of two kilos per person per year until the mid-nineteenth century (Fernandez-de-Pinedo 2003: 79).
28. Martín et al. 1992. See especially Chap. 6 regarding the cultivation of sugar on the Andalusian coast.
29. Medieval cuisine was influenced by the Muslims, who incorporated sweets made with a mixture of honey, nuts and dried fruit (Prats and Martín 2003: 54).

30. Sugar was not only a commodity, as noted by Sidney Mintz (1986). A whole 'sugar-world system' emerged in which transfers of forced migration from Africa and Asia, financial systems, taxes, agricultural plantation systems, state monopolies and technology were entangled in a complex worldwide network with significant long-term consequences. This was far more important than the consumption of sugar.
31. This is also associated with the fact that 'simple-knives, forks, and napkins had begun to appear in the homes of the more wealthy by 1725' (Martin 1993: 153).
32. Fournier and Moynahan (2014) notes 2 and 3.
33. To see some samples, visit the Museo Nacional de Artes Decorativas de Madrid Tabar de Anitua, Cerámicas de China y Japón en el Museo Nacional de Artes Decorativas, 156/XXXII.
34. For more details, see, among others, Ribeiro 1985; Cumming, Cunnington and Cunnington 2010; Ribeiro and Cumming 2014.
35. Spain was one of the nations able to reconcile its colonial and fiscal objectives, e.g. Cuba. See Pretel and Fernandez-de-Pinedo 2015; Fernández-de-Pinedo, Saiz and Pretel 2011.
36. Cocoa from Caracas was preferred to that from the British islands, such as Barbiche Island, due to its less bitter flavour: Buc'hoz 1812: 29. 'Cocoa of Caracas' commonly referred to all cocoa grown in Venezuela because the main shipping port to Europe was the port of Caracas. The Spanish crown gave the monopoly to the Real Compañía Guipuzcaona de Caracas on 17 November 1728. A total of 80.25% of Spanish imports of cocoa in 1792 were Caracas cocoa, Guayaquil followed with 14%, while cocoa from Soconusco represented only 0.03 per cenrt. In 1827, these proportions persist: 79.53% came from Caracas, followed by Guayaquil with 17%. Balanza del comercio de España con los dominios de S.M. en America y en la India en el año de 1792 y 1827.
37. Initially, novelties could only be obtained through traders or diplomats who had easy access through their professions. In the medium term, the rest of the population would benefit from a greater variety of products, even if some commodities would never be accessible to the overall population, and a trickle-down effect would always be a reality in this sense.

References

Allen, Robert C. 2001. The Great Divergence in European Wages and Prices from the Middle Ages to the First World War. *Explorations in Economic History* 38 (4): 411–447.
Allen, Robert C., Tommy Bengtsson, and Martin Dribe (eds.). 2005. *Living Standards in the Past: New Perspectives on Well-Being in Asia and Europe*. Oxford: Oxford University Press.
Aulnoy, Marie-Catherine Le Jumel de Barneville. 1874. La cour et la ville de Madrid vers la fin du XVIIe siècle. Relation du voyage d'Espagne par la comtesse d'Aulnoy. Èdition annotée par Mme B. Carey. Vol. 1. Paris: E. Plon et Cie Imprimeurs Éditeurs.
Avery, Victoria, Melissa Calaresu, and Mary Laven. 2015. *Treasured Possessions: From the Renaissance to the Enlightenment*. Cambridge: Philip Wilson Publishers.
Baena Zapatero, Alberto, and Xabier Lamikiz. 2014. Presencia de una diáspora global: comerciantes armenios y comercio intercultural en Manila, c. 1660–1800. *Revista de Indias* 74 (262): 693–722.
Baghdiantz McCabe, Ina. 2015. *A History of Global Consumption : 1500–1800*. New York: Routledge.
Baghdiantz McCabe, Ina, Gelina Harlaftis, and Ioanna Pepelasis Minoglou. 2005. *Diaspora Entrepreneurial Networks: Four Centuries of History*. London: Bloomsbury Academic.
Belfanti, Carlo Marco. 2008. Was Fashion a European Invention? *Journal of Global History* 3 (3): 419–443.
Berg, Maxine. 2004. In Pursuit of Luxury: Global History and British Consumer Goods in the Eighteenth Century. *Past & Present* 182 (1): 85–142.
Bernardos, José Ubaldo. 1997. *No Sólo de Pan Ganadería, Abastecimiento Y Consumo de Carne En Madrid (1450–1805)*. Madrid: Universidad Autónoma de Madrid.
Bernardos, José Ubaldo. 2003. Trigo castellano y abasto madrileño: los arrieros y comerciantes segovianos en la Edad Moderna. Madrid, Junta de León y Castilla. Consejería de Educación y Cultura.
Blanco, José, and Mary Doering (eds.). 2016. *Clothing and Fashion: American Fashion from Head to Toe*, vol. 1. Santa Barbara, California- Denver, Colorado: ABC-CLIO.
Briand. 1750. *Dictionnaire des aliments, vins et liqueurs : leurs qualités, leurs effets, relativement aux différents âges, & aux différents tempéraments : avec la manière de les apprêter, ancienne et moderne, suivant la méthode des plus habiles chefs-d'office & chefs de cuisine, de la cour, & de la ville. Ouvrage très-utile dans toutes les familles*. Vol. 1. Paris: Gissey et Bordelet.
Buc'hoz, Pierre-Joseph. 1812. *Traité Usuel du Chocolat*. Paris: Chez Chambon.

Burty, Philippe. 1869. *Chefs-D'œuvre of the Industrial Arts*. London: Chapman and Hall.
Canga Argüelles, José. 1826. *Diccionario de hacienda*. Madrid: Impr. española de M. Calero.
Calderón-Fernández, Andrés, Héctor García-Montero & Enrique Llopis-Agelán. 2017. New research guidelines for living standards, consumer baskets, and prices in Madrid and Mexico, Working Papers 097, "Carlo F. Dondena" Centre for Research on Social Dynamics (DONDENA), Universitá Commerciale Luigi Bocconi.
Caro López, Ceferino. 1987. Los precios del pan en Murcia en el siglo XVIII. *Revista de Historia Económica - Journal of Iberian and Latin American Economic History* 5 (1): 31–48.
Coady, Chantal, and Liz Wright. 1993. *Chocolate: The Food of the Gods*. San Francisco: Chronicle Books.
Coe, Sophie D., and Michael D. Coe. 2007. *The True History of Chocolate*. New York: Thames and Hudson.
Crosby, Alfred W. 2003. *The Columbian Exchange: Biological and Cultural Consequences of 1492*, 30th Anniversary Edition. Westport: Greenwood Publishing Group.
Cumming, Valerie, C.W. Cunnington, and Cunnington P.E. 2010. *The Dictionary of Fashion History*. Oxford: Berg Publisher.
De Vries, Jan. 1994. The Industrial Revolution and the Industrious Revolution. *The Journal of Economic History* 54 (2): 249–270.
Dobado-González, Rafael. 2014. La globalización hispana del comercio y el arte en la Edad Moderna. *Estudios de Economía Aplicada* 32 (1): 13–42.
Dobado-González, Rafael. 2015. Pre-Independence Spanish Americans: Poor, Short and Unequal… or the Opposite? *Revista de Historia Económica* (New Series) 33 (1): 15–59.
DuPlessis, Robert S. 2016. *The Material Atlantic Clothing: Commerce and Colonization in the Atlantic World, 1650–1800*. Cambridge: Cambridge University Press.
Fattacciu, Irene. 2011. Gremios y evolución de las pautas del consumo en el silgo XVIII: la industria artesanal del chocolate. In *Comprar, vender y consumir: Nuevas aportaciones a la historia del consumo en la España moderna*, ed. Daniel Muñoz Navarro, 153–172. Valencia: Universitat de València.
Fattacciu, Irene. 2012. Atlantic History and Spanish Consumer Goods in the 18th Century: The Assimilation of Exotic Drinks and the Fragmentation of European Identities. Nuevo Mundo Mundos Nuevos [En línea], Coloquios, on-line 27th June 2012: http://nuevomundo.revues.org/63480.
Feliu, Gaspar. 2004. Aproximació a un índex del cost de la vida a Barcelona, 1501–1807. In *Josep Fontana: història i projecte social : reconeixement a una trajectòria*, ed. Josep Fontana, 151–170. Barcelona: Crítica.

Fernández de Pinedo Fernández, Emiliano. 1974. *Crecimiento económico y transformaciones sociales del país vasco (1100–1850)*. Madrid: Siglo XXI de España Editores, S.A.

Fernández-de-Pinedo, Nadia. 2003. Un primer avance de investigación: el azúcar ultramarino y su consumo en España en la primera mitad del siglo XIX. *Ibero-Americana Pragensia Supplementum* 11: 77–90.

Fernández-de-Pinedo, Nadia. 2012. Tax Collection in Spain in the 18th Century: The Case of The "décima". In *Taxation and Debt in the Early Modern City*, ed. Jose Ignacio Andrés, and Michael Limberger, 153–172. London: Pickering & Chatto Publishers.

Fernández-de-Pinedo, Nadia, and Corinne Thépaut-Cabasset. 2017. *A Taste for French Style in Bourbon Spain: Food, Drink and Clothing in 1740s Madrid*. London: Bloomsbury Academic, 219–241.

Fernández-de-Pinedo, Nadia, and Emiliano Fernández de Pinedo. 2013. Distribution of English Textiles in the Spanish Market at the Beginning of 18th Century. *Journal of Iberian and Latin American Economic History* 31 (2): 253–284.

Fernández-de-Pinedo, Nadia, Patricio Saiz, and David Pretel. 2011. Patent, Sugar Technology and Sub-Imperial Institutions in Nineteenth Century Cuba. *History of Technology Volume 30: European Technologies in Spanish History* 30: 46–62.

Foster, Nelson. 1992. *Chilies to Chocolate: Food the Americas Gave the World*. Tucson: The University of Arizona Press.

Fournier, Patricia, and Bridget M. Zavala Moynahan. 2014. Bienes de consumo cotidiano, cultura material e identidad a lo largo del Camino Real en el norte de México. *Xihmai* 9 (18): 2 On-line.

García-Zuñiga, Mario. 2014. Fêtes chômées et temps de travail en Espagne (1250–1900). In *Les Temps Du Travail. Normes, Pratiques, Évolutions*, eds. Corine Maitte, and Didier Terrier, 63–80. Rennes: Presses Universitaires de Rennes.

Gruzinski, Serge. 2001. Les mondes mêlés de la Monarchie Catholique et autres «Connected Histories». Annales. *Histoire, Sciences Sociales* 56 (1): 85–117.

Hackenesch, Silke. 2011. Chocolate, Race, and the Atlantic World: A Bittersweet History. *Comparativ: Zeitschrift Für Globalgeschichte Und Vergleichende Gesellschaftsforschung* 21 (5): 31–49.

Hernández Franco, J. 1981. El precio del trigo y la carne en Lorca durante el siglo XVIII. *Revista Murgetana* 61: 81–97.

Hugill, Peter J. 1993. *World Trade Since 1431. Geography, Technology and Capitalism*. Baltimore: The John Hopkins University Press.

Hussey, Roland Dennis. 1962. *La Compañia de Caracas, 1728–1784*. Caracas: Banco Central de Venezuela.

Isla, María F. Carbajo. 1987. La Población de la Villa de Madrid: Desde finales del siglo XVI hasta mediados del siglo XIX. Madrid: Siglo XXI de España Editores.
Jia, Ruixue. 2014. Weather Shocks, Sweet Potatoes and Peasant Revolts in Historical China. *The Economic Journal* 124 (575): 92–118.
Lavedan, Antonio. 1796. *Tratado de los usos, abusos, propiedades y virtudes del tabaco, café, té y chocolate*. Madrid: Imprenta Real.
Llopis Agelán, Enrique, Alfredo García-Hiernaux, Héctor García Montero, Manuel González Mariscal, and Ricardo Hernández García. 2009. Índices de Precios de Tres Ciudades Españolas, 1680–1800: Palencia, Madrid y Sevilla. *América Latina en la Historia Económica, no.* 32: 29–80.
Llopis Agelán, Enrique and Héctor García Montero 2011. Precios y salarios en Madrid, 1680–1800. *Investigaciones de Historia Económica-Economic History Research* 7 (2): 295–309.
López Barahona, Victoria, and José Nieto Sánchez. 2012. Dressing the Poor: The Provision of Clothing among the Lower Classes in Eighteenth-Century Madrid. *Textile History* 43 (1): 23–42.
López Losa, Ernesto. 2013. The Legacy of Earl J. Hamilton. New Data for the Study of Prices in Spain, 1650–1800. *Investigaciones de Historia Económica - Economic History Research* 9 (2): 75–87.
López Losa, Ernesto, and Santiago Piquero. 2006. New Evidence for the Price of Cod in Spain: The Basque Country, 1560–1900. In *The North Atlantic Fisheries: Supply, Marketing and Consumption, 1560–1990*, eds. David J. Starkey and James E. Candow, 195–211. Studia Atlantica 8. University of Hull, Maritime Historical Studies Centre, NAFHA.
Markle, Sandra, and Charise Mericle Harper. 2004. *Chocolate: A Sweet History*. Grosset & Dunlap.
Martin, Ann Smart. 1993. Makers, Buyers, and Users: Consumerism as a Material Culture Framework. *Winterthur Portfolio* 28 (2/3): 141–157.
Martín, Manuel, Manuel Martín Rodríguez, Antonio Malpica, and Antonio Malpica Cuello. 1992. *El azúcar en el encuentro entre dos mundos*. Madrid: Asociación General de Fabricantes de Azúcar de España.
Martínez Llopis, Manuel. 1995. *Historia de la gastronomía española*. Huesavca: Ediciones Val de Onsera y Ministerio de Agricultura, Pesca y Alimentación.
McCann, James. 2001. Maize and Grace: History, Corn, and Africa's New Landscapes, 1500–1999. *Comparative Studies in Society and History* 43 (2): 246–272.
McCants, Anne E.C. 2007. Exotic Goods, Popular Consumption, Andthe Standard of Living: Thinking about Globalization in the Early Modern World. *Journal of World History* 18 (4): 433–62.
McNeil, Cameron L. 2006. *Chocolate in Mesoamerica: A Cultural History of Cacao*. Gainesville: University Press of Florida.

McNeill, John R. 1999. Islands in the Rim: Ecology and History in and around the Pacific, 1521–1996. In *Pacific Centuries: Pacific and Pacific Rim Economic History Since the Sixteenth Century*, ed. Dennis O. Flynn, Lionel Frost, and A.J.H. Latham, 70–84. New York: Routledge.

Meléndez, Santiago de Luxán, Sergio Solbes Ferri, and Juan José Laforet. 2000. *El mercado del tabaco en España durante el siglo XVIII: fiscalidad y consumo*. Las Palmas: Fundación Altadis, Universidad de Las Palmas de Gran Canaria y Real Sociedad Económica de Amigos del País de Gran Canaria.

Mintz, Sidney Wilfred. 1986. *Sweetness and Power: The Place of Sugar in Modern History*. London: Penguin Books.

Nieto Sánchez, José A. 2006. *Artesanos y Mercaderes: Una historia social y económica de Madrid (1450–1850)*. Madrid: Editorial Fundamentos.

Norton, Marcy. 2008. Chocolate para el Imperio: La Interiorización Europea de la estética Mesoamericana. *Revista de Estudios Sociales* 29: 42–69.

Nunn, Nathan, and Nancy Qian. 2011. The Potato's Contribution to Population and Urbanization: Evidence From A Historical Experiment. *The Quarterly Journal of Economics* 126 (2): 593–650.

Obregon, Gonzalo. 1964. Influencia y contrainfluencia del Arte Oriental en Nueva España. *Historia Mexicana* 14 (2): 292–302.

Ogilvie, Sheilagh. 2010. Consumption, Social Capital, and the "Industrious Revolution" in Early Modern Germany. *The Journal of Economic History* 70 (2): 287–325.

Ogilvie, Sheilagh, and André W. Carus. 2014. Institutions and Economic Growth in Historical Perspective: Part 1 and 2. SSRN Scholarly Paper ID 2463598. Rochester, NY: Social Science Research Network.

Overton, Mark, Jane Whittle, Darron Dean, and Andrew Hann. 2004. *Production and Consumption in English Households, 1600–1750*. (*Routledge Explorations in Economic History*, 19). London [etc.]: Routledge.

Pariente, Ángel. 1973. El elemento presufijal cachi. Archivum. *Revista de la Facultad de Filosofía y Letras* 23: 73–103.

Parthasarathi, Prasannan. 2001. *The Transition to a Colonial Economy: Weavers, Merchants and Kings in South India, 1720–1800*. Cambridge University Press: Cambridge Studies in Indian History and Society.

Pérez-García, Manuel. 2013. *Vicarious Consumers. Trans-National Meetings between the West and East in the Mediterranean World (1730–1808)*. London: Ashgate.

Pérez-García, Manuel. 2017. Historia Global vs. Eurocentrismo: Revisión Historiográfica. Análisis de consumo y un caso de estudio comparativo entre China y Europa (1730-1808). *Investigaciones de Historia Económica – Economic History* 13 (1):1–13.

Prakash, Om. 1998. Financing the European Trade with Asia in the Early Modern Period: Dutch Initiatives and Innovations. *Journal of European Economic History* 27 (2): 331–356.

Prats, Joaquim, and Carina Rey Martín. 2003. Las bases modernas de la alimentación tradicional. In *Historia de la alimentación rural y tradicional : recetario de Almería*, coord. José Miguel Martínez López. Almería. Instituto de Estudios Almerienses. Diputación de Almería, 53–61.

Pretel, David, and Nadia Fernandez-de-Pinedo. 2015. Circuits of Knowledge: Foreign Technology and Transnational Expertise in Nineteenth-Century Cuba. In *The Caribbean and the Atlantic World Economy Circuits of Trade, Money and Knowledge, 1650–1914*, eds. David Pretel and Adrian Leonard, 1st ed, 263–289. (Cambridge Imperial and Post-Colonial Studies Series). New York [etc.]: Palgrave Macmillan.

Restauración, Alet. 2015. Los Abanicos de Colección: sus Patologías y su Conservación. *Ge-Conservación / Conservação* 8: 107–121.

Ribeiro, Aileen. 1985. *Dress in Eighteenth-Century Europe, 1715–1789*. New York: Holmes & Meier.

Ribeiro, Aileen, and Valerie Cumming. 2014. *Visual History of Costume: Seven Centuries of Costume History in One Volume*. London: Pavilion Books.

Riello, Giorgio. 2006. *A Foot in the Past: Consumers, Producers and Footwear in the Long Eighteenth Century*. Oxford University Press.

Riello, Giorgio, and Anne Gerritsen. 2015. Spaces of Global Interactions: The Material Landscapes of Global History. In *Writing Material Culture History*, ed. Giorgio Riello, and Anne Gerritsen, 111–133. London: Bloomsbury.

Riello, Giorgio, and Prasannan Parthasarathi. 2009. *The Spinning World: A Global History of Cotton Textiles, 1200–1850*. Oxford; New York: Oxford University Press : Pasold Research Fund.

Savary Des Bruslons, Jacques. 1726. *Dictionnaire universel de commerce, contenant tout ce qui concerne le commerce qui se fait dans les quatre parties du monde*. (A-E). Vol. 1. Waesberge (Amsterdam): chez les Jansons.

Schivelbusch, Wolfgang. 1995. *Historia de los estimulantes: el paraíso, el sentido del gusto y la razón*. Barcelona: Anagrama.

Shammas, Carole. 1990. *The Pre-Industrial Consumer in England and America*. Oxford: Oxford University Press.

Shammas, Carole. 1993. Changes in English and Anglo-American Consumption from 1550 to 1880. In *Consumption and the World of Goods*, ed. John Brewer, and Roy Porter, 177–205. London: Routledge.

Sherratt, Andrew. 2007a. Alcohol and its Alternatives. Symbol and Substances in Pre-Industrial Cultures. In *Consuming Habits: Global and Historical Perspectives on How Cultures Define Drugs*, 2nd ed, 11–45. London: Routledge.

Sherratt, Andrew. 2007b. Introduction. Peculiar Substances. In *Consuming Habits: Global and Historical Perspectives on How Cultures Define Drugs*, 2nd ed, 1–10. London: Routledge.
Souza, George Brian. 2005. Convergence before Divergence: Global Maritime Economic History and Material Culture. *International Journal of Maritime History* 17 (1): 17–28.
Spufford, Margaret. 1999. *Figures in the Landscape: Rural Society in England 1500–1700*. Aldershot: Ashgate.
Stobart, John. 2013. *Sugar and Spice. Grocers and Groceries in Provincial England, 1650–1830*. Oxford: Oxford University Press.
Tabar de Anitua, Fernando. 1983. *Cerámicas de China y Japón en el Museo Nacional de Artes Decorativas*. Madrid: Ministerio de Cultura.
Thépaut-Cabasset, Corinne. 2010. *L'Esprit des Modes au Grand Siècle*. 66. Paris: Éditions du CTHS.
Velarde, Pedro Murillo. 1752. *Geographia historica: donde se describen los reynos, provincias, ciudades, fortalezas, mares, montes, ensenadas, cabos, rios, y puertos, con la mayor individualidad, y exactitud, y se refieren las guerras y sucessos memorablesy se hace una compendiosa memoria de los varones insignes de cada reyno. En la oficina de Gabriel Ramírez*.
Weatherill, Lorna. 1988. *Consumer Behaviour and Material Culture in Britain 1660–1760*. London-New York: Routledge.
Werlin, Kate. 2016. Fans. In *Clothing and Fashion: American Fashion from Head to Toe*, eds. José Blanco and Mary Doering, Vol. 1. Santa Barbara, California & Denver, Colorado: ABC-CLIO.
Woude, A.M. van der, and Anton Schuurman. 1980. Probate Inventories: A New Source for the Historical Study of Wealth, Material Culture, and Agricultural Development: Papers Presented at the Leeuwenborch Conference (Wageningen, 5–7 May 1980).
Yun-Casalilla, Bartolomé. 1999. Inventarios "post-Mortem", consumo y niveles de vida del campesinado del Antiguo Régimen: problemas metodológicos a la luz de la investigación internacional. In *Consumo, Condiciones de Vida Y Comercialización: Cataluña, Castilla, Siglos XVII-XIX*, eds. Bartolomé Yun-Casalilla and Jaume Torras Elias, 27–40. Ávila: Junta de Castilla y León.
Yun-Casalilla, Bartolomé. 2014. The Spanish Empire, Globalization, and Cross-Cultural Consumption in a World Context, C. 1400–C. 1750. In *Global Goods and the Spanish Empire*, 1492–1824, eds. Bartolomé Yun-Casalilla and Bethany Aram, 277–306. London: Palgrave McMillan.
Yun-Casalilla, Bartolomé, and Jaume Torras Elias, eds. 1999. *Consumo, condiciones de vida y comercialización: Cataluña, Castilla, siglos XVII-XIX*. Valladolid: Consejería de Educación y Cultura, Junta de Castilla y León.

Open Access This chapter is licensed under the terms of the Creative Commons Attribution 4.0 International License (http://creativecommons.org/licenses/by/4.0/), which permits use, sharing, adaptation, distribution and reproduction in any medium or format, as long as you give appropriate credit to the original author(s) and the source, provide a link to the Creative Commons license and indicate if changes were made.

The images or other third party material in this chapter are included in the chapter's Creative Commons license, unless indicated otherwise in a credit line to the material. If material is not included in the chapter's Creative Commons license and your intended use is not permitted by statutory regulation or exceeds the permitted use, you will need to obtain permission directly from the copyright holder.

Big History as a Commodity at Chinese Universities: A Study in Circulation

David Pickus

There is no way to date when histories first became interested in the history of commodities. From the start of history writing in antiquity, one can find some notice taken of what people purchased and consumed, and conditions under which they did so (Breisach 2007; Burrow 2008). The more social life is studied, the more information is collected about commodities in particular and in general. In the second decade of the twenty-first century, it is heartening to think that the history of commodities must no longer be folded into narratives that treat them only tangentially. The number of historical studies devoted to specific commodities, as well as the nature of general commodification, grows at a prodigious rate (Warman 2003; Abbot 2008; Riello and Parthasarathi 2011; Marton 2014; Bray et al. 2015, etc.). Certainly, no one can keep abreast of literature rapidly expanding in so many directions. However, we can and should step back and reflect on what this increase in knowledge means. This wider reflection, I believe, is also an educational issue. The more scholars know about the importance of commodification in historical development, the more urgent becomes the question of how

D. Pickus (✉)
Zhejiang University, Hangzhou, China

© The Author(s) 2018
M. Perez Garcia and L. de Sousa (eds.), *Global History and New Polycentric Approaches*, Palgrave Studies in Comparative Global History,
https://doi.org/10.1007/978-981-10-4053-5_15

to impart this history to students. And, from the converse angle, once we reflect on commodity history as an educational issue, it colours our historical understanding of commodity production and exchange (Brooks and Normore 2010). Thus, this pedagogical challenge, and its implications for economic history, is what this chapter is about. I will use examples from China and Chinese universities to make a case about the opportunities and pitfalls contained in asking students, especially those new to the study of economic history, to think about the history of commodities as a distinct and valuable intellectual realm.

Some words of context not only set the stage for this discussion, but also give some clue as to what is at stake in the effort as a whole. At the time of this writing, a momentous transformation is taking place in the nature of global education. This is an announcement by China's Ministry of Education that, as the *China Daily* headline on 8 April 2016 runs: 'One in Five of the World's College Students are in China'. To make sense of this, we must register the magnitude of this growth in student numbers in China. Indeed, from an—even for the times—insignificant figure of 117,000 at the founding of the People's Republic of China in 1949, reports for 2015 like that appearing in the *Asian Correspondent* on 8 April 2016 put the number at some 37 million. This means that in 1949, about one in 400 Chinese 18–22-year-olds attended institutions of higher education, while, by the close of the 2010s, the number will likely be one in two. If we look to the future in general, it is easy to find projections that the worldwide higher education student population will reach 262 million, with 'more than half in India and China alone' according to *University World News* on 19 February 2012. Whatever the exact number, the significance of these figures is their likely impact. This ever-growing cohort will undoubtedly be distributed around the globe, but how? What will happen to both China and the world when the (baseline figure) of one in five of the world's college students graduate and go on to make their way, particularly given the difficulties of providing these students with a thorough and rigorous education (Sheng 2016)?

These questions may sound too wide-ranging to link to the hardheaded analysis of the impact and significance of commodity exchange (Van der Spek et al. 2014). Yet, I argue that as we investigate market integration and the circulation of commodities, we should also pay attention to the consequences of the knowledge of global economic history on this rising cohort of Chinese students in particular and on the next generation of students as a whole. After all, the 'massification' of Chinese universities is deeply linked to the development of the global economy and all its attendant commodification (Hayhoe et al. 2012). In other words, the processes that are creating integrated global markets are also driving the growth of higher education in places like China. Here we come to specifics: as economies integrate and educational institutions grow, the question of what students learn about world economic history rises to a level of critical importance. To a great extent, these are the decision-makers of the future. Their subsequent behaviour will be shaped by the information they absorb and the ideas they endorse about the creation and present-day nature of global economic integration. To that end, we should pay closer attention to what Chinese students are learning and what might strengthen their understanding as they grow to become active participants in the world's next round of globalization.

I will further argue that the historiographical development called 'big history' offers a valuable opportunity to assess Chinese university students' understanding of economic integration and global commodification. To make this case, I will argue that big history itself should be treated as a commodity that packages for intellectual consumption a story of global marketization, embedding it in a context that places economic activity within an account of nature and humanity's engagement with it. This mode of grasping history is particularly useful for students in expanding educational systems like the Chinese. To understand why, we should consider a perceptive comment on how these students learn originally published in Chinese in 2004, but still valid over ten years later. The scholar Yang Dong Ping addressed the issue of the commodification of education and argued that, given the fact that 'higher education and professional education beyond compulsory education offers a kind of quasi-public product', current circumstances in China require a critical, yet open embrace of commodification in education. This process is not, as Yang puts it, 'evil' (2004: 55), but necessary for the establishment of a pedagogical system suited to twenty-first-century realities. As such, it should not be wholly directed by governmental institutions. Simultaneously, however, 'The enormous market created by the shortage of educational resources in an obsolete system has brought about rent-seeking activities, deviant behavior and corruption in education' (Yang 2004: 59). For this reason, the embrace of commodification cannot lose sight of the overarching goal of cultivating the student and 'upholding the value of education' (Yang 2004: 60). Thus, this rising cohort of students will be educated in a world where they have a growing number of ways to place commodification in a global context. Some of these ways will be more responsible than others, and none of them guarantees the insights and mastery they need. However, the confluence of new syntheses of global and big history, along with expanding markets for it in places like Chinese universities, presents valuable opportunities for all involved. We should attend to the general situation.

The intervening years since Yang was writing in 2004 have sharpened the urgency of these concerns. In addition, the ongoing professionalization and globalization of higher education has heightened sensitivity to lapses in standards and has dampened the frequency of mismanagement and malfeasance. At the same time, the complexity of educational commodification has magnified significantly. Presently, Chinese universities, particularly central research institutions, host a wide and complicated array of public-private partnerships. Beyond this, and in some ways even more wide-ranging in its implications, Chinese students today are likely to be more than consumers of official, degree-granting education. A myriad array of educational services, combined with skill and career-enhancing opportunities at home and abroad (often at considerable expense) combines to overlay and honeycomb participation in official education with the consumption of supplementary and intensifying educational products. To the extent that personal experience sheds light on the matter, in working with Chinese students, I have found that a majority continue to purchase pedagogical commodities beyond tuition and expenses for a degree. Those who do not are likely motivated by a lack of financial resources as much as absence of interest. More empirical research will document patterns and trends, but the undoubted growth in China's higher education system continues to be intertwined with an intensification of educational market activity and commodification.

This leads to the main point. The ways in which Chinese graduates understand the global spread of marketization and commodification makes a difference. Commonplace sentiments about students representing the future need to be specified in relation to the knowledge that this rising generation has. From the standpoint of the sociology of knowledge (Collins 1998), it becomes more plausible to maintain that ideas do not merely circulate. Specifically, ideas about markets and commodities are bound up with the allegiances held by this growing cohort, along with the conflicts these allegiances engender. Hence, I will make a case as to how and why big history can be presented to Chinese students as a commodity that explains commodification. In doing this, I argue that instruction in big history can be tailored to address meaningful concerns about the creation and nature of global markets. In the conclusion, I will suggest paths for future collaborative work between scholars concerned with economic history and contemporary market integration, and pedagogical specialists seeking more effective ways to ensure the validity and relevance of the higher education given to Chinese students and their counterparts. I will start with the question of what a field with an expansive name like 'big history' has to offer a very big cohort of students facing an uncertain future.

1   Consuming Commodification

In the simplest sense, 'commodification' refers to the emergence of new goods and services to purchase, and in practice is linked to processes of 'monetization', a term that not only connotes the fixing of a currency value to a commodity, but also the creation of economic networks whereby the value of commodities can be apprehended and calculated abstractly. From a teaching standpoint, the question is what basic knowledge do students need of commodification and monetization? And once they acquire this basic knowledge, how can advanced students continue to obtain the mastery they need? Before answering these questions, it is necessary to grasp that they are not only academic one, for experiences of the commodification and monetization of regional and national economies are not new phenomena in China, and opportunities for the public to learn more about the nature of these economic transformations are available and intelligible to a wider public. For instance, southwest of the provincial capital of Taiyuan lies the sleepy (by Chinese standards) town of Pingyao, itself in the relatively less developed province of Shanxi. Yet, throughout the year, masses of tourists, mostly Chinese, visit Pingyao in order to see something that is not easy to find in twenty-first-century China, namely a well-preserved town conveying the atmosphere of the late Qing dynasty (1644–1911), the period of China's last experience of imperial rule. The crowds wandering the streets are likely not thinking of economic rationalization and commodity networks, but Shanxi has a widespread reputation for producing clever merchants, and the bulk of sites open to tourists are, in fact, the physical remains of trade networks and a Qing version of counting houses (Wilson and Yang 2016). This is clearly visible in what the city's tourist board lists as a central attraction:

the headquarters and attendant social institutions of the *rishengcheng* banking and commercial exchange network. These were clan-run enterprises which served to move both goods and treasure at a time when imperial China had difficulty sustaining standardized currency, communication and distribution systems (Yang 1952). In short, in front of tens of thousands of people is a lesson on a commodification and distribution system from the early modern era to the nineteenth century that might, under other circumstances, have developed into the dominant one in China and regionally. Why it developed the way it did—as well as the way it did not—is a valuable story, one that if transformed into a more rigorous and analytical narrative could helpfully be disseminated to the rising generation of students. Indeed, this is the kind of exercise students need in order to grasp the larger picture. And the story of Pingyao is one of many. Other examples could be found in the history of China's adoption of silver coinage or in the dramatic rise and fall of Qing dynasty financiers like Hu Xueyuan.

Thus, the point is not to elevate a single site or episode above all other matters of relevance and interest; it is to emphasize that one does not need to begin with abstract and unfamiliar matters to focus attention on the origin, extent and dissolution of economic networks and commodity chains. Visible reminders are all around students, and comparisons between Chinese and international histories are easily broached for discussion. For instance, once students are asked to consider the history of river guilds along the Grand Canal, they could also be asked to compare them to syndicates and merchants' leagues in other parts of the world. These efforts are needed, for while there is indeed some specialization in global economic history at Chinese universities, along with some understanding of the subject that has percolated into general academic consciousness, there is, as yet, little agreement or even much collective discussion on what basic knowledge students ought to obtain, and how an engagement with East Asian economic and social history fits into their education as a whole. To be sure, a discussion might not yield a consensus or even a shared pedagogical plan. But it will crystalize what is at stake in reaching out to this cohort of students. This is where big history meets an emerging need.

Why? For what reason do we need a vast, new field like big history rather than something more circumscribed? To take up this question, it is best to define the term 'big history' itself. Consider one effective summing up:

Big History is a young, transdisciplinary field, in which scholars from diverse academic disciplines seek to make sense of the story told by the entirety of human knowledge. Big History bends what is considered 'history' back to the beginning of the universe. It begins with cosmology and physics and moves on through astronomy, chemistry, geology, paleontology, evolutionary biology, archaeology, and anthropology. Ultimately, it recontextualizes traditional 'recorded' human history as inseparable from natural history, environmental geography, and the story of the cosmos. And it is bound together with the art of storytelling that is the province of the humanities. (Simon 2015: 11–12)

Except for the now, slightly strained 'young', Richard B. Simon's definition combines the two parts that should form the warp and woof of every functioning definition of big history: first, an integration of what is called 'history' within the larger story of 'natural history', stretching into an account of the universe as a whole; and, second, an effort to narrate both sides of the story in a way that lends it substance and meaning.

Obvious objections arise in relation to the ambition of pursuing big history. On the one hand, the task seems impossibly large. It is daunting enough to practise global history, let alone a global history that incorporates an incomparably larger history of the planet and the cosmos. On the other hand, the question of discovering an underlying meaning to history is fraught with peril even when the scope of the subject studied is a single village in a circumscribed period. How can the expansion of subject matter to great proportions make the challenge any easier? Yet, the point of referring to big history in this context is not to find a single meaning to history, but to address a specific need in the education of these students, namely an apprehension of how (and what kind) of global nexuses of exchange come into being and why they do so. This task is inseparable from the corollary question of why other nexuses fall apart or never come to be. Big history can aptly help us do that and we should keep in mind that it is not an artifice forced upon the data; rather, it stems from a recognition that current disciplinary knowledge areas flow into each other, and that traditional intellectual boundaries, if not reflected upon, impede the pursuit of understanding.

To provide one example of a place where considerations of the origins of our contemporary global economy also evoke a need for the wider context of big history, consider this passage from William J. Bernstein's *A Splendid Exchange: How Trade Shaped the World*. Bernstein noted that the Western-led global nexus established in c. 1500 came in the wake of vast epidemics that laid low expansive empires and economic networks in eastern and western Asia. After quoting the fourteenth-century historian Ibn Khaldun on plague obliterating whole cities, Bernstein writes:

> In the fourteenth through the sixteenth centuries, the furies reached out and with a perverse will savaged the planet's long-distance trading apparatus, and along with it the most advanced commercial societies: the great Muslim civilizations of the Middle East and the entrepôts of India and China that so dazzled Marco Polo and Ibn Battuta. Europe too had been devastated, but within a few centuries its survivors, wielding a fearsome combination of religiously inspired brutality and quantitative genius, would wade into the wreckage and establish the modern Western domination of trade. (Bernstein 2008: 151)

It is hard to agree unreservedly that microbes set upon a trade network with a 'perverse will', but Bernstein is right to draw attention to the link between 'plagues and people' and a world economy. And this turn requires some knowledge of how civilization clusters formed in different geographical regions, with their ecological and technological adaptations and value systems (McNeill and McNeill 2003). This, for its part, requires some sense of human origins, which blends into the larger story of evolution and so forth. In short, an idea of big history is already implicit in the study of trade links and commodification.

It may be protested that these wider chains of connections are already part of existing sciences. This is true in the sense that big history does not present itself as an antagonist to existing knowledge. However, the point of such analyses is not to invent something that rejects existing scholarship or cultivate quarrels with individual authors. Instead, it is to ask observers to reflect on the connections that are, in fact, before them. This returns us to the crowds of visitors at Pingyao, and the future of the students who gain some cognizance of China's financial history. The connections between what was once China's economy and what it became are literally before the eyes of those who walk its streets. Likewise, the thought of what might have happened to the global trade network had the history of China taken another path accompanies all reflection on China's economic history. Yet, we still must know how to take disparate and often inchoate recognition and weld it together so that it is grasped by those on their way to becoming the world's majority student cohort. To go forward, it is necessary to shift perspective back to the viewpoint of a student and to look more closely at how those at Chinese universities experience the intellectual challenge of making meaning out of the data before them.

2   Student Response

In the spring of 2016, collaborating with local colleagues, I surveyed students about their knowledge of world commodity history at two Chinese universities: the Beijing Technology and Business University (北京工商大学) and the RenMin University of China (中国人民大学). Each institution attracts students interested in international business and seeks to offer a globally competitive education. The Beijing Technology and Business University currently has about 20,000 full-time and part-time attendees in undergraduate and postgraduate programmes. As befits its name, the school attracts the career-minded, and undergraduates are required to take a course in 'business essentials'. Students in this class of forty were surveyed about their knowledge of global economic and commodity history, as well as their opinions as to why it would (or would not) be worth their while to know about the subject. While single surveys produce inconclusive data, they do generate evocative material, especially in areas that are little investigated.

From this perspective, one result of the survey is particularly noteworthy, even by relaxed standards: students were not able to give details about the history of individual commodities. This included traditional products like silk—whose history and development is commonly found in Chinese school curricula, as well as products like PCs, as students often mentioned names like Steve Jobs without providing any concrete detail of his accomplishments. Beyond this, although students generally acknowledged the value of studying this subject, the reasons they supplied were themselves highly abstract, and they did not show much evidence of having been exposed to commodity history. To illustrate by example, one of the best and most-informed answers was provided by a student who chose to express herself in English:

> All I know about individual commodities are three people. The first is Zheng Ho, who sailed to the Western world in the Ming Dynasty. He brought gunpowder to other countries. The second person is Xuan Zang, who was famous of the Silk Roads. He brought silk, silkworm tea to Europe. This is why British people drink afternoon tea. The last one is

the Italian sailor Columbus. He found the new world and brought Indian spice back to Italy. (Response I, March 2016)

Factually, there is something wrong about everything the student wrote. Columbus returned to Spain, Xuan Zang went to India, and the Byzantines had knowledge of Chinese sericulture over a hundred years before he travelled. Likewise, Zheng Ho sailed west of China, but never left the Indian Ocean, and in any event, knowledge of gunpowder was diffused by the Mongols along the Silk Road, and was used in the Mediterranean and Europe at least a century before he sailed. Yet, the point is not to ridicule an answer that, in its own way, demonstrated an awareness of the underlying issues at stake. Thus, the story of gunpowder indeed encompasses the important movement of technology and goods from China, as well as back to it. Likewise, while the process whereby the British became a nation of tea drinkers did not depend on a Tang dynasty monk, the student was right to intuit a global nexus of exploration, trade and (presumably) conflict. In fact, this answer suggests an implicit desire to grasp the underlying links in the development of the world economy more thoroughly.

This is where big history can help the current cohort in their understanding of global economies and networks of exchange. RenMin University has some 12,000 students and specializes in the social sciences, attracting students who seek careers in upper-level management and knowledge industries. Unlike the college students surveyed earlier, graduate students at RenMin often have some idea of big history, and more readily agree that the history of commodities must be woven into it. However, they agree that the large questions require much study to answer. For instance, one student wrote:

I have learnt about some history of porcelains in another course. I think maybe as a traditional way, we learn the history of porcelain to know how it affected the economy, politics or something else of one or more countries. But from the angle of big history, I think there can be more things to research, such as how ancient people found the way to product porcelains, why porcelains are invented by the specific people, and as we have produced a lot of porcelains, how the castoff porcelains will affect the environment. All in all, studying the history of commodities can help us to learn how did those who lived in different places know and use some kinds of resources and whether the trade influence the usage of resources in the perspective of all humankind. (Response II, March 2016)

Yet, what most differentiates this student from others less versed in the subject is not the account of porcelain. Some awareness of traditional products and goods is common in this cohort. Rather, what stands out

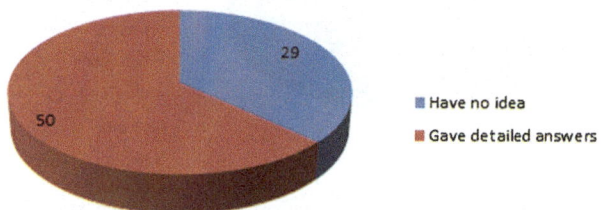

Fig. 1 Student responses to the question: 'What qualities do nations need to engage successfully in international trade?' *Source* Author's survey at Beijing Technology and Business University (2016)

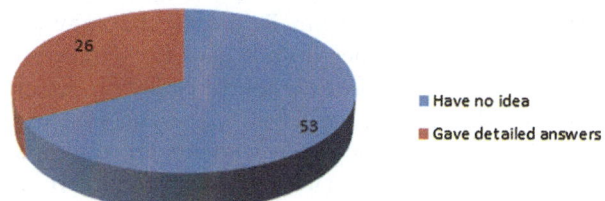

Fig. 2 Student responses to the question: 'Do you know the history of any individual commodities? How did you learn about it?' *Source* Author's survey at Beijing Technology and Business University (2016)

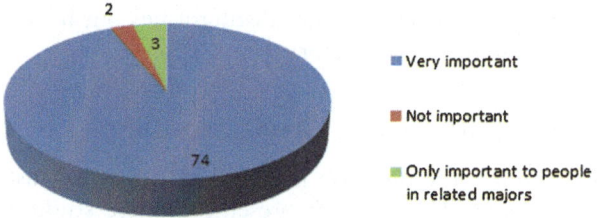

Fig. 3 Student responses to the question: 'How important is it to know world economic history and why?' *Source* Author's survey at Beijing Technology and Business University (2016)

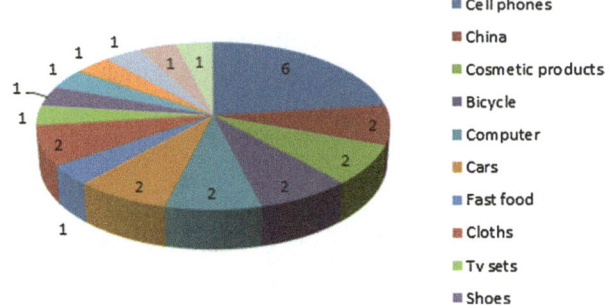

Fig. 4 Students' responses to the question 'Do you have specific knowledge of the history of any commodity?' *Source* Author's survey at Beijing Technology and Business University (2016)

is the awareness of benefits of raising questions about the commodity's larger context. The majority of students do not have this. A glance at the four pie charts for the students from Beijing Technology and Business University makes evident that they do not have the detailed information required to answer questions about the global economic system that they themselves acknowledge as essential (Figs. 1, 2, 3 and 4).

To be sure, these seventy-five or so students are only a small number of the total, and more systematic studies would be revealing. Still, in the process of soliciting student views, I found little to suggest that their sensibilities are atypical. Until now, big history is not a commonly taught subject at Chinese universities. Nevertheless, I believe that it is currently the best pedagogical commodity available to them to better grasp the connecting links in understanding the emergence of a global economy and transnational civilizations. To spell out why this is so, we must go into more detail about what distinguishes big history from the more commonly taught global history.

3 From Global to Big

In pedagogical terms, the question is what kind of global historical consciousness a student will obtain. At present, Chinese students are commonly exposed to a version of global transformation that ascribes great importance to market forces. Such curricula typically aim to inculcate awareness of the role Marx and Engels ascribed to the bourgeois. Leaving aside political differences and polemical conflicts, there are aspects of this historical understanding that also lead to an appreciation of big history. Thus, passages like this one from *The Communist Manifesto* provide some notion of the kind of impact ascribed to marketization:

> The bourgeoisie, by the rapid improvement of all instruments of production, by the immensely facilitated means of communication, draws all, even the most barbarian, nations into civilization. The cheap prices of commodities are the heavy artillery with which it batters down all Chinese walls, with which it forces the barbarians' intensely obstinate hatred of foreigners to capitulate. It compels all nations, on pain of extinction, to adopt the bourgeois mode of production; it compels them to introduce what it calls civilization into their midst, i.e., to become bourgeois themselves. In one word, it creates a world after its own image. (Marx 1848)

Despite the unresolved ideological questions of how to define the bourgeois, this notion of battering down Chinese walls is a helpful reminder that commodification is inseparable from a wider story of human disequilibrium. And this story is put into full focus with an account of humanity's place in nature. Consider the larger significance of this comment from the science journalist and historian Charles C. Mann:

> It is strange, too, to realize that globalization has been enriching the world for nigh on five centuries. And it is unsettling to think of globalization's equally long record of ecological convulsion, and the suffering and political mayhem caused by that convulsion. But there is grandeur, too, in this view of our past; it reminds us that every place has played a part in the human story, and that all are embedded in the larger, inconceivably complex progress of life on this planet. (Mann 2011: xxviii)

This conscious evocation of Darwin's 'there is grandeur in this view of life' is designed to alert readers to the fact that he is quite aware of the widest consequences of this 'beating down of walls' and that he wishes all aspects of it be seen with open eyes. This requires a broader view towards life on the planet as a whole, one focusing on ecology in its broadest sense. Simultaneously, it requires a more detailed picture of the everyday movement of life, which in practice means an appreciation of global economic history. Otherwise, passed-on sentiments about globalization and the bourgeois creating a 'world after its own image' remain abstractions, and student knowledge will concomitantly remain abstract and haphazard. Here is the challenge for educators and why the relatively smaller topics of marketization and commodification are best placed in the wider context of big history. We must ask ourselves what can be done to anchor student knowledge of the complexity of life on the planet within an accurate perception of the place of exchange—particularly commodity exchange—in creating our current form of inter-linked globalization.

To answer this question, we must examine the ways in which big history developed in the past, going on to consider the directions it might take in the future. According to Cynthia Stokes-Brown in her essay 'A Little History of Big History', although the 1970s saw renewed efforts by scientists to popularize knowledge of the larger story of the cosmos, it was only the 1990s that saw the crystallization of big history as both a coherent intellectual programme and a discrete offering in the university curriculum (Stokes-Brown 2015: 301–303). As she tells it, there was a close connection between intellectual aspiration and pedagogical need. Students were arriving at universities with a need to establish a mental framework or explanatory paradigm that would allow them to make sense of the wide range of information they were being asked to learn, as well as to find a scientifically responsible sense of meaning within this (for them) new and potentially exciting world of information. Simultaneously, within academia, emerging with some poignancy within the historical profession, hyperspecialization was provoking its own counter-reaction. An older, and often derided, historiographical tradition of telling the largest possible story of humanity's place in the universe returned and began to challenge the widespread view that these vast narratives are too speculative and unrigorous to belong in the scholarly mainstream.

A central figure in this transformation is David Christian (b. 1946). A British-American historian of Russia, while teaching at Macquarie University in Australia in the 1980s, he began offering an introductory course that explicitly sought to place the human experience of the last three to five-thousand years within the much larger contexts of the development of terrestrial life and the cosmos itself. Out of this course, he produced in 2005 the fully-elaborated study *Maps of Time: An Introduction to Big History*, the book that most anchored big history's wider reputation in a wider reading public. For our purposes, what is most important is that Christian not only practised big history, but also put forward theoretical pieces explaining the underlying purposes in the project. Most helpful are his 'The Case for Big History' (Christian 1991) and 'The Return of Universal History' (Christian 2011). These essays together enable us to summarize what big history can offer Chinese students about the place of marketization and commodification within a global context.

The foundation of Christian's case is that while big history is difficult in practice, advances in all historically-minded scholarship—biology and geology, for instance—as much as history itself allow different scales of time to be linked together in an overarching narrative of increasing thresholds of complexity. This includes advances in the popularization of technical fields to non-specialists. Once it is grasped that these scholarly tools are available, larger questions can be asked and answered in sufficient detail to shape our understanding of history's meaning. What relationship does this have with the main question of the meaning of economic activity and commodity exchange? Christian provides an illuminating answer. Responding to a view of human nature widely associated with Adam Smith that human beings have a natural tendency to 'truck and barter', he responds that such a view of 'economic man' does not take into account the much longer pre-history of humanity's time as hunter-gatherers, for:

> There is nothing 'natural' about the state, or civilization, or economic growth. The entire history of agrarian and now industrial civilizations is from this point of view a curious and rather surprising coda tacked onto the end of human history. (Christian 1991: 10)

Putting the matter this way enables Christian to raise the most telling pedagogical questions of his own:

> Should we admire the explosive growth of the past few millennia? Is it, perhaps, what distinguishes us from other living species? Or can we identify similar turning points in the history of other living species? Is human history governed, ultimately, by the rhythms of natural history as a whole? What is the likely impact of our own history on the history of the planet as a whole? Is the rapid growth of human society proof of a fertility in invention so astonishing (and so untypical of animal species as a whole) that it will continually outstrip the dangers it creates? (Christian 1991: 10)

These questions are not rhetorical; rather, they are challenges that arise from the ongoing integration of big history into our intellectual awareness. Writing almost two decades later, after the idea of big history gained wider acceptance, an even more forthright Christian specified the change in thinking he sought:

> I predict that in fifty years' time, all historians will understand that it is possible and fruitful to explore the past on multiple scales, many extending far beyond Braudel's *longue durée*, by reaching back to the origins of our species, the origins of the earth, and even the origins of the cosmos. The new universal history will transcend existing disciplinary boundaries, exploiting the powerful intellectual synergies available to those willing to deploy the methods and insights of multiple disciplines. (Christian 2011: 7)

The transformation ensures that 'history rediscovers an interest in deep, even law-like patterns of change' as opposed to breaking into 'many isolated islands of knowledge'. In the end, Christian envisions a change in sensibilities, even if most historians stick to their specialties, since 'the context of historical research will be transformed. Seeing human history as part of a much larger story will affect how historians think about research, the questions they ask, the ways they collaborate, and the way they judge the significance of scholarship'. In particular: 'At large scales, the pixels of human action generate clear patterns, and awareness of these patterns will inevitably change how we think about history at smaller scales' (Christian 2011: 21).

Another way to put this is that the smaller questions we ask about the history of commodity exchange will acquire more meaning when we recognize fully both the vast difference (and some underlying continuities) between a world of economic exchange and the 'pre-historic' and natural worlds that came before it. This also has significant pedagogical implications, particularly in giving students a sense of overarching human concern throughout the various subjects of their studies. Here is what is at stake in students' accounts of commodification: it is helping them grasp that learning more about the history of commodification can help them to understand the important debate about universal history as a whole. This challenge returns us to the world of Chinese students and their global counterparts.

4 Conclusion: Tying the Threads Together

A central thrust of the argument presented here is that big history be presented to the current cohort of university students as a commodity that helps them to make sense of their own world of commodities and to interpret it within the wider world of nature. Such a product could take the form of elective courses offered to a broad range of students, as well as study aides and popularizations that provide intellectual and narrative coherence to the complex of themes that big history treats. That some courses in big history are beginning to be offered and some of the literature treating big history is spreading in China only underscore the need to make the case for it more energetically and directly. This is a pedagogical project that can invigorate student comprehension of, and participation in, some of the most vital debates of the day about the intersection of humanity's economies, resources, and dreams and aspirations. Moreover, that students in China are not the only ones who would gain from this immersion follows from the argument. Chinese students currently represent an enormous percentage of the number of the world's students overall, and their needs reveal much about the needs and circumstances of world students altogether.

Yet, the conclusion should not stop with students and their situation. Engaging this topic is not a deviation for scholars working in the field of global commodity exchange, both past and present. Specialists in commodity sub-fields would profit from asking how their own sphere of activity could be presented to the students consuming big history. The questions of overall meaning that are inherent in such a large perspective would come to the fore in a salutary way and David Christian's call for a return to a universal history could be channelled into needed debates about what he called the 'pixels' of meaning in this cosmic story. In short, though this essay may have begun with the flow of Chinese students into the world's higher education system, its current of thought circles back into the scholarly mainstream. These are the people who, if given the full opportunity to do so, will consume the narratives of meaning provided by their teachers and guides. It can only help to address them directly, and presenting them with a version of big history that addresses fundamental economic questions is an effective and compelling means to do so.

References

Abbot, Elizabeth. 2008. *Sugar: A Bittersweet History.* Toronto: Penguin Books.
Bernstein, William J. 2008. *A Splendid Exchange: How Trade Shaped the World.* New York: Atlantic Monthly Press.
Bray, Francesca, Peter A. Coclanis, Edda A. Fields-Black, and Dagmar Schäfer (eds.). 2015. *Rice: Global Networks and New Histories.* Cambridge, UK: Cambridge University Press.

Breisach, Ernst. 2007. *Historiography: Ancient, Medieval and Modern*, 3rd ed. Chicago: University of Chicago Press.

Brooks, Jeffery, and Anthony Normore. 2010. Educational Leadership and Globalization: Literacy for a Global Perspective. *Educational Policy* 24: 52–82.

Burrow, J.W. 2008. *A History of Histories: Epics, Chronicles, Romances, and Inquiries from Herodotus and Thucydides to the Twentieth Century*. New York: Knopf.

Christian, David. 1991. The Case for Big History. *Journal of World History* 2: 223–238.

———. 2006. *Maps of Time: An Introduction to Big History*. 2nd ed. Berkeley: University of California Press.

———. 2011. The Return of Universal History. *History and Theory* 49: 6–27.

Collins, Randall. 1998. *The Sociology of Philosophies: A Global Theory of Intellectual Change*. Cambridge, MA: Harvard University Press.

Hayhoe, Ruth, Jun Li, Jing Lin and Qiang Zha. 2011/2012. *Portraits of 21st Century Universities: In the Move to Mass Higher Education*. Dordrecht: Springer.

Mann, Charles C. 2011. *1493: Uncovering the New World Columbus Created*. New York: Knopf.

Marton, Renee. 2014. *Rice: A Global History*. London: Reaktion Books.

Marx, Karl. 1848. They year is correct. "*The Manifesto of the Communist Party*," www.marxists.org/archive/Marx/works/1848/communistmanifesto.

McNeill, J.R., and William H. McNeill. 2003. *The Human Web: A Bird's-Eye View of World History*, 1st ed. New York: W.W. Norton.

Riello, Giorgio, and Prasannan Parthasarathi. 2011. *The Spinning World: A Global History of Cotton Textiles, 1200–1850*. Oxford, UK: Oxford University Press.

Sheng, Anfeng. 2016. On the 'Intrinsic Development' of Higher Education in China. *European Review* 24: 347–357.

Simon, Richard B. 2015. What is Big History? In *Teaching Big History*, ed. Richard B. Simon, Mojgan Behmand, and Thomas Burke, 11–20. Oakland, CA: University of California Press.

Stokes-Brown, Cynthia. 2015. A Little History of Big History. In *Teaching Big History*, ed. Richard B. Simon, Mojgan Behmand, and Thomas Burke, 296–308. Oakland, CA: University of California Press.

Van der Spek, R.J., Bas van Leeuwen, and Jan van Zanden (eds.). 2014. *A History of Market Performance: From Ancient Babylonia to the Modern World*. London: Routledge.

Warman, Arturo. 2003. *Corn & Capitalism: How a Botanical Bastard Grew to Global Dominance*. Chapel Hill, NC: University of North Carolina Press.

Wilson, Craig, and Fan Yang. 2016. Shanxi Piaohao and Shanghai Qianzhuang: A Comparison of the Two Main Banking Systems of Nineteenth-Century China. *Business History* 58: 433–452.

Yang, Dong Ping. 2004. An Analysis of Commodification of Education. *Chinese Education and Society* 39: 55–62.

Yang, Liangcheng. 1952. *Money and Credit in China: A Short History*. Cambridge, MA: Harvard University Press.

Open Access This chapter is licensed under the terms of the Creative Commons Attribution 4.0 International License (http://creativecommons.org/licenses/by/4.0/), which permits use, sharing, adaptation, distribution and reproduction in any medium or format, as long as you give appropriate credit to the original author(s) and the source, provide a link to the Creative Commons license and indicate if changes were made.

The images or other third party material in this chapter are included in the chapter's Creative Commons license, unless indicated otherwise in a credit line to the material. If material is not included in the chapter's Creative Commons license and your intended use is not permitted by statutory regulation or exceeds the permitted use, you will need to obtain permission directly from the copyright holder.

Index

A

Acemoglu, Daron, 276, 286
Adrião Almada, 188
Afonso d'Albuquerque, 40
Age of Parity, 42
Ahmad, 148, 149
Aires Gonçalves de Miranda, 187, 192, 207
Akizuki Tanezane 秋月種実, 168
Alentejo, 198
Allen, Robert, 89, 90, 95
Almaden, 278
Amdo, 145, 153
America, 3, 37, 60, 244, 278–282, 284, 295, 299, 300, 301, 305, 306
American Historical Association, 242
Andrade, Tonio, 42
Angra, 198
Antequera, 198
Antilles, 282
Anti-Semitic policy, 196, 197
António Nóbrega, 188
Aomen 澳門 (Macau/Macao), 44
Arakan, 164
Aristocrats, 26, 255, 277–279
Arughtai, 145
Asian Correspondent, 322
Asiatic Mode of Production Theory, 26
Atarashii Sekaishi 新しい世界史, 5
Atwell, William, 83
Authorized tribute missions, 41
Ayutthaya, 165, 166, 171, 177
Azores Islands, 198, 282
Aztec Empire, 256

B

Bacon, Francis, 230
Banno, Masataka 坂野正高, 138, 156n2
Barbarian language, 26
Baring Brothers of London, 269
Baskes, Jeremy, 261–263
Batavia, 164
Bay of Bengal, 164, 185
Becher, Admiral Alexander, 220
Beijing, 4, 14, 41, 44, 47, 90, 95, 96, 150, 151
Bengal, 84, 223
Bernoulli, 231
Bernstein, William J., 327, 328

Big Five Guilds, 296–298
Bishbalik, 141, 145
Bishop Leonardo de Sá O.C., 191
Bodde, Derk, 30
Borao, J. E., 175
Borneo, 39
Boyajian, James, 193
Braudel, Fernand, 3, 38, 124, 132n25
Bribery, 44
Brihuega, 279, 282
Broadberry, Stephen, 86, 87, 89, 113
Bronze coin-denominated paper notes (*qianpiao*), 103
Buddhism, 25, 29, 145, 147, 169, 170
Bungo, 165, 166, 198
Burgerweeshuis, Regents of the Amsterdam Municipal Orphanage(BWH), 248–250
Burgos, 267

C

Cadiz, 266, 267, 269, 270
Cai Ruxian 蔡汝賢, 45
California School, 3, 7, 58, 84, 85, 110
Campeche, 265, 279
Canary Islands, 264, 270, 271, 282
Cannibalism, 41
Cao Shuji 曹树基, 57
Capponi family, 267
Caravan, 145, 146, 148, 151, 157n8
Cartography, 38, 223, 229, 277, 284
Carvalho, 172, 199
Castile, 185, 194, 278, 279, 286
Catholic Church, 199, 209, 255
Central Europe, 278, 280
Central Oaxaca Valley, 256
Central Plain 中原区域, 67
Centripetal trade system, 142
Ceylon, 144, 146

Chamasi, 142
Champa, 39, 40, 141, 143, 146, 147, 149
Changzhou 常州, 63, 64
Charles V, 256, 277
Charnock, 226
Chen Shuping 陈树平, 57, 66, 71
Chieftains, 144, 154, 155
Chili (làjiāo 辣椒), 54, 55, 293
China's Ministry of Education, 322
Chinese characteristics 中国特色 zhōngguó tèsè, 5, 6, 60
Chinese Communist Party, 23
Chinese Dream 中国梦 zhōngguó mèng, 59
Chinese economy, 7, 19, 54, 55, 58, 59, 82, 83, 88, 90, 99, 107–110
Chinese historiography, 4–7, 54, 55, 58
Chōshō-ji 長生寺, 168
Chosŏn 朝鮮Kingdom, 143
Cirurgião-Mor, 199
Civilisation, 22–26, 31
Cliometric history, 243
Clothing, 93, 177, 249, 298, 299, 307
Cochinchina, 170, 175, 176, 207
Coe, Michael, 300
Coe, Sophie, 300
Cohen, Hendrik Floris, 24
Columbus, Chirstopher, 62, 295, 330
Commodification, 321, 323–326, 328, 333–336
Commodities, 8, 12, 13, 19, 26, 40, 55, 60, 62, 73, 154, 203, 205, 244, 249, 252n5, 257, 258, 261, 266, 268, 272n3, 293, 296, 306–308, 311n37, 321, 322, 324, 325, 329, 330, 333, 336
Commodity chains, 13, 257, 326
Compensation, 142

Confrontation, 14, 56, 143, 145, 149, 190
Confucianism, 27, 28, 76, 78
Congregação Provincial Portuguesa, 197
Congruent, 233
Cóngshū 丛书, 4
Constantinople, 266
Consumer revolution, 12, 244–248, 250, 252n9
Consumer society, 244, 246, 247
Consumption, 3, 12, 54, 55, 60, 68, 88, 89, 244–250, 251, 259, 294–296, 298, 300–303, 305, 307, 308, 323, 324
Contradiction, 149
Corn (yùmǐ 玉米), 54, 57, 70, 71, 279
Cornwall, 219
Cosmological, 45, 228
Cruzados, 193–195
Cultivation techniques, 54, 56, 69, 279, 281, 282
Cultural Revolution, 57–59, 61
Curtail, 146, 148
Curt Ebbesmeyer, 220

D

Dainichi 大日, 169
Damião Gonçalves, 191
Da Ming huitian, 138, 139, 157n3
Daoguang Depression, 82, 84, 85, 96, 108, 110
Daoism, 25, 27–29
Deacon, 226, 227, 230
Dead-reckoning, 231
De Cárdenas, Juan, 280
De Menonville, Thierry, 270
De Sahagún, Bernardino, 259
Descendant, 64, 183–185, 194–197
De Sousa, Lucio, 1, 11, 12, 184
Detachment, 234

De Tocqueville, Alexis, 29
Diáspora, 47n4, 128n2, 164, 165, 178, 184, 185, 190, 196, 212, 252n5, 294, 309n8
Díaz de Cáceres, 191, 192, 204
Diogo de Vasconcelos, 195
Dioscorea fordii Prain et Burk (mountain potato), 61
Discriminatory, 197
Disembark, 186
Dispatch, 141, 143, 145, 147, 149, 151, 152, 165
Diversity, 6, 14, 32, 45, 56, 249
Dongguan 东莞, 64, 66
Dongyi tushuo 東夷圖說, 45
Donkin, Richard, 258
Dragon fruit or pitalla (huǒlóng guǒ 火龙果), 54
Duarte de Sande, 198
Duke of Lerma, 194
Dusi 都司, 144
Dystopias, 234

E

Eamon, W., 276
Eastern Zone, 138, 143, 147, 149, 150, 153, 155, 157n3
East Indian Companies, 293
Ecological environment, 32, 70
Economic exploitation, 38
Economic History Association, 242
Edo period, 166, 167, 171, 172
Ejima, 144, 151, 154, 155
Elman, Benjamin, 22, 23
English crown, 281
Environmental studies, 125
Envoy, 142, 143, 146, 156, 157n7, 166, 177
Epstein, Leonard, 277
Equilibrium, 84, 86, 110, 231

Esen, 146, 147
Estêvão Gomez, 188
Ethnographical, 45
Évora, 193, 198
Exclusión, 29, 128, 142, 144, 147, 156
Expedition, 39, 42, 43, 143–145, 220, 222, 224, 227, 231
Extremadura, 198

F
Fairbank, 59, 137–139, 156n2
Fawang 法王, 145
Fernandez Pinedo, Nadia, 12, 13
Financial, 145, 170, 180n19, 200, 267, 269, 270, 281, 284, 286, 293, 311n30, 324, 328
Finta, 195, 211
Fisheries, 125
Fluid, 129, 138, 151, 156
Fo-lang-chi/Feringhi, 41
Foreign trade, 38, 105, 137, 138, 142, 143, 149–151, 155, 156, 167
Formation, 94, 126, 138, 151, 156, 184, 248
Francisco de Azurara Father, 188
Francisco de Sandoval y Rojas, 194
Frois, 167, 168, 179
Fugger familiy, 278, 281
Fujian 福建, 19, 40, 42, 43, 61–69, 147, 154
Fujianese, 40, 43, 46–48
Fung Yu-lan (Feng Youlan 馮友蘭), 25

G
Gakusho, Nakajima, 11, 137
Gansu 甘肅, 148, 153
Gaspar Coelho, 198
Gateway, 106, 145, 148
GECEM project (Global Encounters between China and Europe), 2

General Pardon, 193–195
Genna kōkai ki 元和航海記, 175
Genoa, 267, 269
Ginsburg, Carlo, 283
Ginseng, 144
Global Economic History, 322, 326, 333
Global history, 1–15, 21–22, 25, 31, 39, 55, 56, 60, 73, 120, 126, 128–130, 132n27, 178, 241, 244–245, 247–248, 250, 327, 332
Global History Network (GHN) in China, 1
Global political economy, 243
Global system, 243
Global trade, 12, 13, 82, 83, 244, 245, 257, 263, 328
Goa, 38, 44, 184, 185, 187–193, 195, 196, 198, 202, 206, 207, 209, 212, 213n13
Goodman, David, 276, 283, 286, 289
Google books database, 245
Google Ngram Viewer, 244
Gorelik, Gennady, 31
Goshi taise, 137
Grain prices, 93, 94, 106
Grain production, 70–72
Granados, 226, 230
Grand Canal, 106, 326
Great Depression, 244
Great Divergence, 3, 4, 7, 54, 73, 84, 242
Greater East Asia Co-Prosperity Sphere, 121
Great Leap Forward, 59, 84
Gresik, 39
Griffiths, Gwyn, 222, 232
Groslier, Bernard P., 165
Gross Domestic Product (GDP), 7, 85
Guangdong 广东, 64
Guangzhou 广州, 37, 39, 41–43, 47, 67, 95, 106–108, 143, 150

Guanning 廣寧, 144
Gujaratis, 40
Guo Liuguan 郭六官, 166
Guo Songyi 郭松义, 57, 66
'gurobaru hisutori' グローバル・ヒストリー, 5

H
Habsbourg monarchy, 267, 280
Hagiwara, 146, 148, 149
Hǎiwài rén海外人, 6
Haixi 海西, 144
Hakata 博多, 165, 167, 168
Hamashita Takesi, 6, 102, 123, 137
Hami, 145, 146, 148, 149, 150, 151, 153
Hamnett, Brian, 261
Han dynasty, 25, 61, 226
He Bingdi 何炳棣, 54, 57, 65–66, 69, 70, 72, 74
Hernández, Francisco, 279
Hernando de la Vega, 192
Heunemann, 226, 227
Hexi 河西 corridor, 145, 146, 148, 149, 153
Heyday, 144
Hibiya Ryōkei日比屋了珪, 168
Hideaki, Suzuki, 5, 10, 11
Hideyoshi 豊臣秀吉, 167, 169, 171, 203
Hierarchy, 27, 29, 189, 198, 205, 255
Hieronymites, 282
Hikoichi Yajima, 122, 132n14, 133n28
Hirado, 166, 175, 192, 202, 205
Histoire du Monde, 12, 245
Histoire mondiale, 12, 245
Historical system, 137
Ho, Peng Yoke, 29
Hoberman, Louisa, 267, 268
Hoffman, Phillip, 242
Hokiichi Hanawa, 121
Hokkien merchants, 40

Holy Inquisition, 188, 202
Holy Office, 189, 283
Hongwu, 141–143
Hope and Company of Amsterdam, 269
Horizon, 139
Hormuz, 144, 185
Horse market, 144, 150, 151, 154
Horse-tea, 145
Hosokawa 細川, 147, 149
Human affairs, 28
Humanities, 3, 23, 55, 58, 125, 200, 327
Hushi tizhi, 137
Hussey, Ronald, 301
Hu Xueyuan, 326

I
Iberian Peninsula, 163, 164, 184, 185, 196, 197, 199, 276, 277, 280, 286, 300, 307
Ibero-America, 279
Ibn Khaldun, 328
Ignatius of Loyola, 196, 197
Ikeda Yoemon 池田与右衛門, 175
Ilibalik, 145, 146, 148
Imperialism, 38, 82
Imprisonment, 188, 192
Indispensable, 145, 301
Indochina, 163, 164
Indonesian vessels, 39
Indo-yō kaiiki-sekai (Indian Ocean Kaiiki World), 122
Industrial Revolution, 2, 3, 12, 21, 73, 82, 84, 264, 271
Inner Asia, 138, 139, 143, 144, 146–149, 156
Inquisition, 164, 178, 185, 187–194, 202, 204–207, 208, 209, 212, 277, 283
Inroad, 148–150
Internationalization, 6, 14, 56, 60

346 INDEX

International political economy, 7, 243
International Science Commission, 23
International trade network, 137
Ipomoea batatas (sweet potato), 54, 61
Iraeta merchant family, 270
Island of Terceira, 198
Iwai Shigeki, 137

J
Japanese Mission, 172, 198
Java, 39, 40, 143, 146, 147, 149
Javanese Muslims, 40
Jesuits, 45, 168–173, 175, 176, 197, 199–203, 205, 281, 282
Jesuits Luís de Almeida e Aires Sanches, 198
Jewish, 27, 48, 184, 185, 186–188, 190, 192, 196, 199, 200, 202, 205, 207, 208, 209–211
Jiangnan region of China, 84, 85, 88, 89, 90, 91, 97, 103, 107, 109
Jiangsu 江苏, 42, 63, 67
Jiangxi 江西, 67, 68
Jianzhou 建州, 144
Jiaowang 教王, 145
Jiaqing 嘉庆, 69, 70
Jin dynasty, 61
Jitsuzō Kuwabara, 120, 131
João Gomes Fayo, 189, 190, 191, 192, 213
Judaizing, 188, 193
Judeo-conversos, 11, 184–197, 199, 201, 202, 203, 204, 206, 208–211, 213
Jurchen, 144, 151, 155, 157

K
Kageyama Kyūdayū 陰山九太夫, 177
Kaiiki-shi 海域史, 5, 11, 12, 119–130

Kaiyuan 開原, 144
Kantō Plain in Japan, 84, 88
Keightley, David N., 24
Kenji Yanai, 121
Kermes, 255, 265, 266
Kham, 145
K′ien Lug period, 305
King Sathta, 165
King Sebastian of Portugal, 186, 198
Kneitz, Agnes, 12
Kobata, 147
Korean War, 23
Koryŏ 高麗, 143
Kōzen-machi 興膳町, 168–170
Kuroda Akinobu, 103
Kuten Zenryō 玖天全良, 168
Kwass, Michael, 244
Kyushu, 43, 125, 165, 166

L
Lacquer, 26, 303
La Guaira, 302
La Havana, 13, 294
Lampacau (Langbaigang 浪白窰), 43
Lavedan, Antonio, 302
Le Blanc, Charles, 30
Lê 黎Kingdom, 146
Liampó (Liuhengdao 六橫島), 42
Liaodong 遼東, 144, 153–155
Li Bozhong, 6, 59, 88, 89, 108, 112
Library of the Escorial, 284
Li Donghua, 121, 131
Liebman, 191, 213n3
Limpieza de sangre, 196, 197
Lin Fu 林富, 43
Lin Xiyuan 林希元, 42
Lisbon, 46, 47, 183, 185, 187, 190, 193, 194, 196, 199, 200, 207, 213n17
Liu Beicheng, xv, 7, 56
Liu Ti, 86–88, 90

Liu, William, 86
Livorno, 266, 267
Li Yingfa 李映发, 58
Longvek Era, 165
Lord Maccartney, 54
Loureiro, 186
Low Countries, 84, 277
Lu Gwei-djen 鲁桂珍, 23
Luís de Almeida, 168, 198–200
Luís Fróis, 168
Luochong lu 贏蟲録 (The record of naked creatures), 45
Lyon, 266

M
Ma, Debin, 58
Macau (Macao) 澳门, 6, 11, 19, 38, 43–47, 68, 184–193, 195, 196, 198–202, 204–213
Machida Sōka 町田宗加, 171–172
Mackerras, Colin, xvi, 10–11, 21
Maddison, Angus, 85
Madeira, 282
Madrid, 13, 287, 294–296, 298–310, 311
Magalhães Godinho, Vitorino, 38
Magdalena Valley, 280
Malacca, 37, 39–43, 47, 185, 189, 190
Malay Peninsula, 39, 149
Maldonado, 198
Malta, 300
Malthusian, 54, 90, 93, 108, 109
Malthusian demographic crisis, 93
Maluenda merchant bankers, 267
Mancall, 139, 157
Manchuria, 93, 144, 151, 157
Manila galleons, 257
Marichal Salinas, Carlos, 255, 308
Marine engineering, 125
Maritime commerce, xii, xiii, 26

Maritime history, 5–7, 12, 39, 119, 120, 130
Maritime prohibitions (haijin 海禁), 40
Marxist School, 6, 7, 55, 60
Mascarenhas, Ana, 188
Mashi 馬市, 144
Matsura 松浦, 166
McCants, Anne EC, xv, 3, 12, 310
McCloskey, Deirdee, 242
Mécia Leitoa, 188
Meiji Government, 121
Meiji Restoration, 59
Mekrid, 148
Melaka, 141, 143, 147, 149
Méndez Nieto, Juan, 280
Military guards, 145
Miller, 225, 227, 231
Ming dynasty, 4, 39, 54, 60–62, 66, 67, 69, 138, 154, 157n2, 329
Ming-Qing Empire, 137
Miño, Manuel, 258
Min Zongdian 闵宗殿, 57
Missionary, 167, 169, 170, 172, 174–177, 180
Mission Statement of the North American based World History Association (WHA), 241, 251
Moctecuhzoma II, 256
Modern science, 10, 22, 27, 29, 31, 32, 38, 61, 231
Moghulistan Khanate, 145, 148
Mokyr, Joel, 242
Monarch, 194, 195
Monardes, Nicolás, 279, 281
Monetization, 325
Mongol invasion, 22
Mongols, 138, 144, 145, 147, 148, 150, 153–155, 157, 330
Morris, Ian, 242
Moulder, Frances, 83
Moyle, Dorothy, 23

Munro, John, 265
Murayama Antonio Tōan 村山等安, 169
Muromachi 室町, 147, 167
Muslim sultanate, 40
Mutual trade system, 11, 137, 138, 151, 155

N
Nação Portuguesa, 184
Nagamoto, 145
Nanban-jin, 163
Nanchang upland 南昌高地, 67
Naojirō Murakami, 121
Napoleonic Wars, 106, 221, 262
Nationalization, 54, 55
National Knowledge Infrastructure (CNKI), 55
National narratives, 2, 5, 8, 10, 11, 19, 53
Natural geography, 125
Navigation, 12, 38, 211, 219, 226, 229, 230–233, 264, 276, 277, 284
Needham, Joseph, 23–33, 220–228, 232–233
Needham Question, 3, 11, 21, 22, 24, 31, 32
Neo-colonialist strategy, 6
Neo-Confucianism, 28, 29
Neo-Confucian policies, 6, 55
Neo-Malthusian, 82, 84
Netherlands, 2, 10, 12, 85, 88, 89, 90, 251, 287, 310
New-Christian, 196
Newcomer, 190–192
New global history, 19
New Spain, 8, 62, 194, 204, 256, 260, 264, 265, 267, 270, 271
Ningbo 寧波, 42
Ningbo Incident 寧波の乱, 165

North Korea, 23
North, Michael, 248
Northern Song, 86, 103
Nuestra Señora de la Concepción, 191
Nuno de Soto Maior, 195
Nuzhen 女真, 144

O
O'Brien, Patrick, xiii, 7, 15n1, 38
Oceanography, 223, 227–229
Oceanology, 125
Oirads, 144, 146, 147
Oka, Mihoko, xiii, 11, 152, 168, 169, 173
Okamoto, 138, 147, 179
Okufune 奥船, 176
Olive, 192
One Belt, One Road 一带一路 yīdài yīlù, 4, 59
Opium War, 9, 59, 82, 83, 107, 137, 226
Oriental Despotism, 26
Ōsumi, 142, 143, 146
Ottoman Empire, 109, 185, 256
Ōuchi 大内, 147, 149, 165
Overseas voyage, 142

P
Pardaos, 188
Patriotic myopias, 56
Pearl River, 37
Pedro Álvares Pereira, 193
Pegu, 164
Pereira, 191
Pereira, Jerónimo, 191
Perez Garcia, Manuel, 1, 10, 11, 15n1, 53, 75, 184, 275
Peripheries, 38, 142, 149–151
Pêro Fernandes d'Arias, 188
Persecution, 186, 205, 206, 208, 209, 211, 212

INDEX 349

Petterson, 220
Philip II, 175, 193, 203, 265, 276, 279, 283–287
Philip V, 302
Physical environment, 25–27, 29–31
Pickus, David, 13
Piketty, Thomas, 242
Pirate, 42–44, 74
Pires, Tomé, 41, 147
Plateau, 90, 144–146, 149
Polycentric world, 10
Pomeranz, Kenneth, 3, 7, 22, 42, 54, 58, 74n4, 84, 85, 88–90, 107, 112, 242
Pragmatist, 45
Precious metals, 26, 99, 266
Prevailing discourse, 138
Protoglobalization, 264
Protoindustrialization, 257
Ptak, Roderich, 43, 45–48, 141, 144, 146–147, 149–150, 157, 222, 228–230
Puebla, 279, 282

Q
Qianglong (emperor Qianlong), 54
Qing (Qing Dynasty), 47, 54, 56, 67, 69, 70–72, 81, 82, 86, 88–91, 97–100, 103, 112, 138, 151, 156, 325, 326
Quánqiú shǐ 全球史, 4, 5
Quanzhou 泉州, 39, 64, 67, 143

R
Rastoin, 197
Rationalist, 28
Real Compañía Guipuzcoana de Caracas, 302, 310
Reductionism, 26
Regionalization, 107
Reidy, Michael, 220, 223, 225, 231

Reinhard, Wolfgang, 222
Religious patrons, 145
Rennell, James, 220–228, 231–234
Repartimiento, 261, 262
Revival, x, 99, 144, 151
Roman Empire, 164, 255
Ronan, Colin A., 28, 29
Roshental, Jean-Laurent, 242
Rossabi, Morris, 143, 145, 148, 150, 151, 155, 157
Rouen, 266, 269
Rozwadowski, Helen, 233
Rui Boto, 188
Ruiz-de-Medina, Juan, 198
Ruiz Martín, Felipe, 266, 267
Rupke, Nicholas, 221, 223, 232
Rustification, 107, 109
Ryukyu (Zhongshan 中山), 138, 143, 146, 147, 152–157
Ryukyuans, 40
Ryūkyū Islands, 39

S
Saint Domingue (Haiti), 270
Sakai 堺, 165
Sakuma, Shigeo 佐久間重男, 142, 143, 147, 149, 150, 152
Salomon, Claudine, 223, 230
Samarkand, 141, 143, 145, 146, 157
Sánchez Gómez, Julio, 280
Sánchez Silva, Carlos, 261
San Pedro, 191
Sappanwood, 144
Sardinia, 300
Satō, Hishashi, 145
Sattelzeit, 224, 225, 228, 233, 234
School of Annales, 3, 303
Schottenhammer, Angela, 2, 26, 221, 230, 231
Scientific discovery, 21
Scientific spirit, 21, 30
Seiichi Iwao, 121, 122, 131

Sephardic Jews, 45, 183, 185
Sephardim, 164
Serruys, Henry, 142, 144–146, 148, 149, 151, 154, 155
Shanxi 山西, 153, 325
Sheffield, 294
Shìjiè lìshǐ 世界历史, 4, 5
Shimazu 島津, 166
Shimoda Yasōemon 下田弥惣右衛門, 177
Shingon Buddhism 真言宗, 169
Shogunate, 121, 147
Shuangyu 雙嶼, 42, 150
Shuinsen 朱印船, 11, 163, 166, 167, 171, 174–179
Siam, 40, 141, 143, 147, 149, 152–155, 164–167, 170, 171, 175, 201, 207, 208
Simancas Archive, 284
Sivin, Nathan, 23
Siyi 四夷 (non-Chinese peoples), 45
Small-farm peasant economy, 82
Smithian dynamics, 84
Smuggling, 44, 99, 146, 148, 150, 153–155, 157, 175, 177, 192, 302
Social networks, 8, 13, 276
Social sciences, ix, xiv, 3, 8, 32, 55, 125
Société de consommation, 12, 245
Society of Jesus, 179, 180, 184, 190, 192, 196–200, 203, 206–209, 213
Soft power, 19, 58, 59
Song dynasty, 28, 83, 86, 103, 120
Songjiang prefecture, 88
Spanish crown, 12, 26, 70, 211, 264, 283, 311
Spanish-Portuguese dual monarchy, 47
Spice Islands, 40, 256
Stommel, Henry, 227
Subgroup, 197
Suchou 肅州, 148

Suetsugu Kōzen 末次興膳, 168
Suffolk, 266
Sulu, 39, 157
Supervisorates, 142, 143
Supreme Council of the Indies, 282, 284
Surabya, 39
Suzerainty, 142
Suzhou, 90, 95, 106, 107, 148, 151

T
Tadatsugu 忠次, 171
Taihoku Imperial University, 121–123, 131
Taiping Rebellion, 82, 109
Taiyuan, 325
Takagi Ryōka 高木了可, 171
Takeo Tanaka, 122, 123, 131
Takio Izawa, 121
Tamils, 40
Tanegashima 種子島, 43, 165, 178
Tani, 143, 145
Tarim basin, 145, 148
Teixeira, Manuel, 175, 188, 212
The Nanfang Caomu Zhuang (南方草木状 Plants of the Southern Regions), 61
The Sengoku period 戦国時代, 43
The White Lotus Rebellion, 81, 91, 106
The Yiwu Zhi (异物志 Record of Foreign Matters), 61
Tibetan Buddhism, 145, 147
Timurid Empire, 145
Tlaxcala, 256, 260
Tokugawa period, 122
Tongtaisheng, 94
Tonlé Sap, 165
Toungoo Dynasty, 165
Tōzai kōshō-shi (東西交渉史) history of East-West, 120, 122
Transaction, 42, 45, 109, 142, 168, 193, 270, 286

Transformation, 54, 129, 136–139, 251, 307, 322, 325, 332, 334, 336
Transitional state, 138, 156
Treasury Council, trustworthiness, 193
Treaty system, 137
Tributaries, 138, 139, 142, 143, 157
Tribute trade, 132n23, 137–139, 142–157
Tuban, 39
Tumu 土木, 146
Tunmen 屯門, 37
Turfan, 141, 145, 146, 148–151

U
Ueda Makoto, 137
Unitary, 138, 156
Uriyanghad, 144, 154

V
Van der Wee, Herman, 286
Vasco da Gama, 185
Venice, 151, 266, 300
Veracity, 211
Veracruz, 266, 268, 270
Von Glahn, Richard, xv, 10, 58, 74n4, 81, 103, 111, 112, 156

W
Wada, 144
Wagaku kōdanjyo (Institute of Japanese Studies), 121
Wallerstein, Immanuel, 3, 8, 12, 38, 83
Wang 王, 144
Wang Bo 王柏, 43
Wang Hong 汪鋐, 42
Wang Jiaqi 王家琦, 57, 60, 61
Wang Zhi 王直, 165
Wanli (万历) emperor, 69

War of Jenkins' Ear, 296
Wei 衛, 144
Welfare ratio, 95
Welser, 278, 281
Wine, 192, 307
Wittfogel, Karl August, 26, 27
Wokou 倭寇 (dwarf pirates), 43, 143, 150, 165, 178
Wong, Bin, 54, 58, 72, 74n4, 242
Wrigley, Anthony, 242
Wu Deduo 吴德铎, 57
Wu Lao 吳老, 166
Wulianghа sanwei 兀良哈三衛, 144

X
Xavier, Francis, 169, 197
Xia Nai 夏鼐, 57
Xu Guangqi 徐光启, 61

Y
Yajima, 122, 123, 132, 133, 144
Yang Dong Ping, 323
Yang Shen 楊愼, 45
Yaxiya 亞細亞 (Asia), 45
Yellow River, 26, 67, 69, 81
Yeren 野人, 144
Yongle 永樂 emperor, 39, 143–145
Yoshishige 大友義鎮, 165–167
Yun-Casalilla, Bartolome, 275, 278, 279, 284–286, 296, 306, 309
Yunnan 云南, 45, 62, 65, 67, 71, 97, 98, 107, 111, 153, 309

Z
Zennyū 善入, 169
Zhangjian 张箭, 57
Zhangzhou 漳州, 43
Zhengde 正德 emperor, 41
Zheng He 鄭和, 39, 143, 144, 230, 231

Zhongshun wang 忠順王, 145
Zhoushan 舟山, 42, 67, 150
Zhujiang River Basin 珠江流域, 67
Zilsel, Edgar, 22, 27

Zurndorfer, Harriet, xv, 10, 37, 42, 43, 47, 53, 74, 75, 226

The manufacturer's authorised representative in the EU is Springer Nature Customer Service Centre GmbH, Europaplatz 3, 69115 Heidelberg, Germany. If you have any concerns regarding our products, please contact ProductSafety@springernature.com

Printed and bound by CPI Group (UK) Ltd, Croydon, CR0 4YY

23/03/2026

02076667-0010